The Stuff of Which Hospitality Marketing is Made: A Guided Tour

© Hospitality Resources Ink, 1989.
ISBN 0-924034-03-3.

<u>edited by</u>:

Dr. Bonnie Knutson, Michigan State University
Dr. Ken McCleary, Virginia Polytechnic and State University
Dr. Pete Stevens, Michigan State University

Hospitality Resources Ink, P.O. Box 6732, East Lansing, Michigan 48826-6732

Table of Contents

Introduction

by Pete Stevens

A "guided tour"? Well, in the sense that the editors have selected what to include and exclude, have put readings in some order, and have included their biases by way of "introductions" to each of the sections. Yes, this *is* a "*book of readings*".

Most of the readings are published articles from journals and magazines and most are quite recent. A few aren't recent, but they could be. We think they're *classics*, that they stand the test of time. We've learned something and gained some insight from each of the included pieces, and so we hope that you do too.

The subject is *marketing*. There'll be lots of perspectives of just what that is in the book, but generally, we're talking about the art/science of getting customers, keeping customers and making money. Actually, the subject is *hospitality marketing*. Lodging, food service, travel, clubs, *et cetera*. Not automobiles or toothpaste.

"*Stuff*"? We could have titled the book something like "Selected Readings ..." We could have. We really struggled trying to figure out what to call this stuff. And we didn't want to be *stuffy*.

The book is divided into sections, eight of them. Each has an intro to tell you what it's about from our perspective. We start with some fundamentals, then get more specific. Marketing research, segmentation, positioning, products, pricing, promotion, menuing, and service. This, then, is the guided tour.

We hope that you not only learn some things and gain some insights, but enjoy the process as well.

Sine Qua Non: Without these, you're nowhere.

Introduction by Pete Stevens

This first section of the book presents some fundamental basics, *without which there is nothing*. I see three articles as "classics" and two as important, timely and topical.

Freed's *"Why can't customers complain better?"*, though hot off the presses, is our lead-off *classic*. I hope that both you and we follow Freed's *gospel*. We got off to a good start, I think, by using the word "stuff" in the title.

Anyone choosing to play in the hospitality game should understand why it's much harder to manage Geno's than Geritol, Domino's than Dodge, Hilton than Lincoln. KFC *versus* P&G. Ted Levitt's HBR piece on *Intangibles* should help a lot.

The *classic classic*, the platinum piece of business genius herein, is Levitt's "Marketing Myopia". It is just as current and vital today as thirty-some years ago when first published in *Harvard Business Review*. A "need" is a problem, maybe physiological, maybe psychological, maybe both. A "want" is a *perceived solution*. In defining the business you're in, I think Levitt would tell us that people **don't need** a better mouse trap and they also don't need drills. They **do need** an absence of mice and they do need holes. Companies like New York Central, Pennsylvania & Ohio, and Santa Fe thought people needed railroads.

Scott Matulis echoes a bias long-held by the editors, so gains inclusion here. Huffman's "Service Boom -- No End in Sight" might possibly be read while "Marketing Myopia" is still fresh in your mind. The "railroad" companies saw no end in sight either.

Why can't customers complain better?

David H. Freed

The Mount Sinai Hospital, New York City, , New York, U.S.A.

I'm getting awfully tired of customers who don't complain well. Not customers who complain, mind you, but those who do it with all the finesse of King Kong performing microsurgery. Meat which tastes like 'shoe leather', for example, is wearing thinner after fifteen years of operating food services than the soles on my oldest pair of loafers. And I'm getting ready to feed them to the next misguided person who analogizes shoe bottoms and bottom rounds! Why can't customers learn to complain better?

Don't get me wrong: It's perfectly acceptable to register dissatisfaction when products or services aren't up to snuff. But snuffing out the person taking the complaint is another story altogether. What exactly is a waiter supposed to do about food which tastes like 'shirt cardboard'? Taken at face value, this complaint suggests that the guest dines at laundries often enough to recognize the taste of cardboard when he comes across it. If that is the case, then a larger problem than the meal at hand suggests itself.

And why do the hospitality service industries seem to take a disproportionate amount of abuse relative to other businesses? Imagine, for example, that the same customer who just accused a restaurant of serving shirt cardboard has his shirts mangled at the laundry. Would he be so quick to say that his shirts look like chopped steak? I doubt it. And I'll bet he wouldn't drag shoe leather into the conversation, either!

Another common complaint—food that a guest 'wouldn't feed to my dog'—seems more directed at getting attention than substantive action and resolution. If there's any doubt, consider the fact that the expression is used only in a negative and inflammatory context, never a complimentary one. ('Waiter, the lobster was excellent—I would feed it to my dog.') That is the same reason a waiter would not appear responsive if he addressed the complaint objectively, for example, 'The chef will be pleased to prepare another lobster at no charge. How would your dog like it cooked this time?'

Pig slop, styrofoam, and ten-foot poles: a visitor to this country would think that these are legitimate menu terms judging by the frequency with which they are used. The more I hear them, the more I want to respond in kind. At a minimum, anyone complaining in these terms ought to be reported to their mother for a reprimand about whether they would

Reprinted by permission from *International Journal of Hospitality Management* vol. 7 no. 2 1988. ©1988 Pergamon Press Ltd.

use that kind of language at home. At a maximum, the guest's words could be delivered upon literally, for example, a bale of styrofoam brought to his table so he can make an accurate and objective taste comparison. Many midpoints can also be imagined in order to effectively fight anecdotes with anecdotes.

A serious and well intended program of customer education would fare no better. Can you imagine the look on a guest's face as his colorful complaint is greeted with a polite and informative explanation of the reasons why the complaint may be misinterpreted as potentially inappropriate or even inflammatory to those who are trying sincerely to provide an acceptable level of service? Consider also that 'the customer is always right' in the hospitality service industries and cannot be taught a lesson as a practical matter. Teaching a customer to complain better only teaches him not to come back, and that is an education few establishments can afford to provide. The search for acceptable alternatives must extend well beyond behavior modification for customers as a result.

Stipulating that customers simply don't behave the way they ought to can be quite liberating. It dismisses the theoretical pretense of the 'prudent man' and enables reasons why people don't complain objectively to be considered from other perspectives. So let's shift the emphasis for a few paragraphs from how customers talk to hospitality service businesses to how these same businesses communicate with their customers:

- A flight attendant who puts out her own cigarette on the way to the airport instructs passengers to 'extinguish all smoking materials' once aloft.
- A waiter who orders tuna with lettuce for his own lunch recites that today's fruit salad platter is 'served on a bed of lettuce'.
- A hotel credit manager writes 'I want you to know' to his friends but 'Please be advised' to hotel guests.

Why do people in the hospitality service industries start speaking so unusually when they go to work? Verbiage like the aforementioned, I mean, like that you just read, is at once both so generic and contrived that it has to make customers uncomfortable. 'Smoking materials?' Just try going to a convenience store and asking for some. You're likely to get either a bag of charcoal or directions to the nearest fire station. A 'bed of lettuce' violates in a single image the time honoured proscription against eating in bed. Would a cracker on the platter qualify as a headboard? And who's kidding whom by burying a no-nonsense legal dessert ('be advised') under some precatory icing? ('Please'.) Subpoenas instruct people to 'be advised'; I've never heard someone serving one say 'please' nor someone being served say 'thank you'.

Have you travelled lately? Think for a moment about the disclaimers directed at you at every stage of the trip. In the parking garage: 'Management cannot be responsible for personal possessions left in cars'. At the airline ticket counter: 'Flight schedules are subject to revision'. While renting a car: 'Subject to availability . . . other charges may apply'. At the hotel front desk: 'Personal checks not accepted without identification.' In the finest restaurants: 'Minimum charge per person at tables $X'. Can you help but feel defensive or that you've done something wrong?

How the customer himself gets addressed at different points on his trip is equally noteworthy. He leaves home with a goodbye directed to a person, for example, 'Charles', 'Dad', or 'Dear'. But as soon as he reaches the parking garage, signage addresses him by how long he parks (e.g. 'Daily parkers only') or what he drives ('Reserved for compact cars'). At the airline terminal he becomes a 'departure', and to his airline he is successively 'business class', 'no-smoking', and one of a class of 'passengers in rows 10–29' who may board the aircraft at a certain time. At his destination the traveller changes from a 'passenger' to an 'arriving passenger', and again when a driver radios that he's just picked up a 'fare' at the airport. The metamorphosis continues when his hotel greets this 'guest' but qualifies the greeting by addressing him as a 'party of one' in the hotel restaurant and as a 'checkout' the next morning. A potential identity crisis becomes clear as the traveller must keep reclassifying himself for the convenience of the 'service' businesses he patronizes.

Why can't customers complain better? Some introspection suggests that the cause may be businesses which can't communicate better with their customers. It is axiomatic that the most effective educators teach students, not subjects. The best physicians treat patients rather than illnesses. Similarly, hospitality service businesses which expect better (i.e. more moderate and objective) complaints will have to begin serving people rather than food, for example, and doing so in familiar rather than efficient language. Otherwise, customers will continue seeking to maintain some individuality by complaining in colorful terms which demand an immediate and personalized response. Nor will defensiveness and the perceived need to create a 'scene' in order to get results diminish.

Overhauling communications in this manner represents an ambitious agenda for the hospitality service industries. At the same time, it is worthwhile and quite simple in principle.

- Communications with customers must be directed to people rather than classes of people. 'Passengers departing for Saint Louis . . .' is just as easily expressed as 'If you're going to Saint Louis . . .' It transmits the same information, but in language which parallels the way people think about themselves, i.e. as people going somewhere, instead of as 'passengers'. Similarly, people leaving hotels do think of themselves as checking out—an action they are taking—but don't think of themselves as checkouts—a collective term which aggregates strangers on the basis of a characteristic which is not meaningful to them. Artificial aggregation in this manner makes people defensive in a subtle but certain way. Addressing them individually is preferable to grouping them for the convenience of the business.

- Cliches must be replaced with familiar words. Two simple rules are remarkably effective here: don't write words you wouldn't say, and don't say words you wouldn't use outside of work! The first rule is protection against overworking worn phrases like 'tangy' and 'zesty' on the menu or 'enclosed please find' on a reservations confirmation. No one in real life says those words in conversation! The second rule discourages calling two people a 'party of two', instructing those on a jet to 'deplane', or serving a 'medley' of anything on a 'bed' of anything else. No one in real life says those words at home!

- Restrictive language should be used sparingly and expressed positively. When 'management cannot be responsible', that management should either resign or explain why it appears so irresponsible. The declaration could be made just as effectively by a positive message which asks people to take their valuables with them. Otherwise customers will interpret 'cannot' as 'does not want to' and become resentful.

In the final analysis, every complaint does two things: it cries out for attention and asks for a resolution. Imploring customers to complain better is not the same as denying their perfect right to a valid resolution. Rather, it is asking them not to cry so loudly for attention! This objective will be met once meaningful communications and interactions are substituted for the attention-denying jargon which now provokes people. I am confident that customers and operators alike will find complaining much more palatable and matter-of-fact at that point.

Which will raise another difficult question: Why can't customers compliment better?

Marketing Intangible Products and Product Intangibles

Theodore Levitt

Distinguishing between companies according to whether they market services or goods has only limited utility. A more useful way to make the same distinction is to change the words we use. Instead of speaking of *services* and *goods*, we should speak of *intangibles* and *tangibles*. Everybody sells intangibles in the marketplace, no matter what is produced in the factory.

The usefulness of the distinction becomes apparent when we consider the question of how the marketing of intangibles differs from the marketing of tangibles. While some of the differences might seem obvious, it is apparent that, along with their differences, there are important commonalities between the marketing of intangibles and tangibles.

Put in terms of our new vocabulary, a key area of similarity in the marketing of intangibles and tangibles revolves around the degree of intangibility inherent in both. Marketing is concerned with getting and keeping customers. The degree of product intangibility has its greatest effect in the process of trying to get customers. When it comes to holding on to customers—to keeping them—highly intangible products run into very special problems.

First, this article identifies aspects of intangibility that affect sales appeal of both intangible and tangible products. And, next, it considers the special difficulties sellers of intangibles face in retaining customers.

Intangibility of all products

Intangible products—travel, freight forwarding, insurance, repair, consulting, computer software, investment banking, brokerage, education, health care, accounting—can seldom be tried out, inspected, or tested in advance. Prospective buyers are generally forced to depend on surrogates to assess what they're likely to get.

They can look at gloriously glossy pictures of elegant rooms in distant resort hotels set exotically by the shimmering sea. They can consult current users to see how well a software program performs and how well the investment banker or the oil well drilling contractor performs. Or they can ask experienced customers regarding engineering firms, trust companies, lobbyists, professors, surgeons, prep schools, hair stylists, consultants, repair shops, industrial maintenance firms, shippers, franchisers, general contractors, funeral directors, caterers, environmental management firms, construction companies, and on and on.

Tangible products differ in that they can usually, or to some degree, be directly experienced—seen, touched, smelled, or tasted, as well as tested. Often this can be done in advance of buying. You can test-drive a car, smell the perfume, work the numerical controls of a milling machine, inspect the seller's steam-generating installation, pretest an extruding machine.

In practice, though, even the most tangible of products can't be *reliably* tested or experienced in advance. To inspect a vendor's steam-generating plant or computer installation in advance at another location and to have thoroughly studied detailed proposals and designs are not enough. A great deal more is involved than product features and physical installation alone.

Though a customer may buy a product whose generic tangibility (like the computer or the steam plant) is as palpable as primeval rock—and though that customer may have agreed after great study and extensive negotiation to a cost that runs into millions of dollars—the process of getting it built on time, installed, and then running smoothly in-

Author's note: The current article expands on and further develops some of the concepts I introduced in my last article for HBR, "Marketing Success Through Differentiation—Of Anything," which appeared in the January-February 1980 issue. Other articles I have written for HBR treat this general subject in yet other ways. These include "The Industrialization of Service" (September-October 1976) and "Production-Line Approach to Service" (September-October 1972). To drive home what I believe is a badly neglected distinction, the present article refers to the role of management in the industrial revolution, a subject more fully developed in my article, "Management and Post Industrial Society," *The Public Interest*, Summer 1976.

volves an awful lot more than the generic tangible product itself. Such intangibles can make or break the product's success, even with mature consumer goods like dishwashers, shampoos, and frozen pizza. If a shampoo is not used as prescribed, or a pizza not heated as intended, the results can be terrible.

Similarly, you commonly can't experience in advance moderate-to-low-priced consumer goods such as canned sardines or purchased detergents. To make buyers more comfortable and confident about tangibles that can't be pretested, companies go beyond the literal promises of specifications, advertisements, and labels to provide reassurance.

Packaging is one common tool. Pickles get put into reassuring see-through glass jars, cookies into cellophane-windowed boxes, canned goods get strong appetite-appealing pictures on the labels, architects make elaborately enticing renderings, and proposals to NASA get packaged in binders that match the craftsmanship of Tyrolean leatherworkers. In all cases, the idea is to provide reassuring tangible (in these examples, visual) surrogates for what's promised but can't be more directly experienced before the sale.

Hence, it's sensible to say that all products are in some important respects intangible, even giant turbine engines that weigh tons. No matter how diligently designed in advance and carefully constructed, they'll fail or disappoint if installed or used incorrectly. The significance of all this for marketing can be profound.

When prospective customers can't experience the product in advance, they are asked to buy what are essentially promises—promises of satisfaction. Even tangible, testable, feelable, smellable products are, before they're bought, largely just promises.

Buying promises

Satisfaction in consumption or use can seldom be quite the same as earlier in trial or promise. Some promises promise more than others, depending on product features, design, degree of tangibility, type of promotion, price, and differences in what customers hope to accomplish with what they buy.

Of some products less is expected than what is actually or symbolically promised. The right kind of eye shadow properly applied may promise to transform a woman into an irresistible tigress in the night. Not even the most eager buyer literally believes the metaphor. Yet the metaphor helps make the sale. Neither do you really expect the proposed new corporate headquarters, so artfully

rendered by the winning architect, automatically to produce all those cheerfully productive employees lounging with casual elegance at lunch in the verdant courtyard. But the metaphor helps win the assignment.

Thus, when prospective customers can't properly try the promised product in advance, metaphorical reassurances become the amplified necessity of the marketing effort. Promises, being intangible, have to be "tangibilized" in their presentation—hence the tigress and the contented employees. Metaphors and similes become surrogates for the tangibility that cannot be provided or experienced in advance.

This same thinking accounts for the solid, somber Edwardian decor of downtown law offices, the prudentially elegant and orderly public offices of investment banking houses, the confidently articulate consultants in dark vested suits, engineering and project proposals in "executive" typeset and leather bindings, and the elaborate pictorial documentation of the performance virtuosity of newly offered machine controls. It explains why insurance companies pictorially offer "a piece of the rock," put you under a "blanket of protection" or an "umbrella," or place you in "good hands."

Not even tangible products are exempt from the necessity of using symbol and metaphor. A computer terminal has to look right. It has to be packaged to convey an impression of reliable modernity—based on the assumption that prospective buyers will translate appearance into confidence about performance. In that respect, the marketing ideas behind the packaging of a $1 million computer, a $2 million jet engine, and a $.5 million numerically controlled milling machine are scarcely different from the marketing ideas behind the packaging of a $50 electric shaver or a $2.50 tube of lipstick.

Importance of impressions

Common sense tells us, and research confirms, that people use appearances to make judgments about realities. It matters little whether the products are high priced or low priced, whether they are technically complex or simple, whether the buyers are supremely sophisticated in the technology of what's being considered or just plain ignorant, or whether they buy for themselves or for their employers. Everybody always depends to some extent on both appearances and external impressions.

Nor do impressions affect only the generic product itself—that is, the technical offering, such as the speed, versatility, and precision of the lathe; the color and creaminess of the lipstick; or the appearance and dimensions of the lobster thermidor. Consider, for example, investment banking. No matter how thorough and persuasive a firm's recommendations and assurances about a proposed underwriting and no matter how pristine its reputation for integrity and performance, somehow the financial vice president of the billion-dollar client corporation would feel better had the bank's representative not been quite so youthfully apple-cheeked.

The product will be judged in part by who offers it—not just who the vendor corporation is but also who the corporation's representative is. The vendor and the vendor's representative are both inextricably and inevitably part of the "product" that prospects must judge before they buy. The less tangible the generic product, the more powerfully and persistently the judgment about it gets shaped by the packaging—how it's presented, who presents it, and what's implied by metaphor, simile, symbol, and other surrogates for reality.

So, too, with tangible products. The sales engineers assigned to work with an electric utility company asking for competitive bids on a $100 million steam boiler system for its new plant are as powerfully a part of the offered product (the promise) as is the investment banking firm's partner.

The reason is easy to see. In neither case is there a product until it's delivered. And you won't know how well it performs until it's put to work.

The ties that bind

In both investment banking and big boilers, becoming the designated vendor requires successful passage through several consecutive gates, or stages, in the sales process. It is not unlike courtship. Both "customers" know that a rocky courtship spells trouble ahead. If the groom is not sufficiently solicitous during the courtship—if he's insensitive to moods and needs, unresponsive or wavering during stress or adversity—there will be problems in the marriage.

But unlike a real marriage, investment banking and installed boiler systems allow no room for divorce. Once the deal is made, marriage and gestation have simultaneously begun. After that, things are often irreversible. Investment banking may require months of close work with the client organization before the underwriting can be launched—that is, before the baby is born. And the construction of an electric power plant takes years, through sickness and in health. As with babies, birth of any kind presents new problems. Babies have to be coddled to see them through early life. Illness or relapse has to be conscientiously avoided or quickly corrected. Similarly, stocks or bonds should not go quickly to deep discounts. The boiler should not suddenly mal-

function after several weeks or months. If it does, it should be rapidly restored to full use. Understandably, the prospective customer will, in courtship, note every nuance carefully, judging always what kind of a husband and father the eager groom is likely to make.

The way the product is packaged (how the promise is presented in brochure, letter, design appearance), how it is personally presented, and by whom—all these become central to the product itself because they are elements of what the customer finally decides to buy or reject.

A product is more than a tangible thing, even a $100 million boiler system. From a buyer's viewpoint, the product is a promise, a cluster of value expectations of which its nontangible qualities are as integral as its tangible parts. Certain conditions must be satisfied before the prospect buys. If they are not satisfied, there is no sale. There would have been no sale in the cases of the investment banker and the boiler manufacturer if, during the prebidding (or courtship) stages of the relationship, their representatives had been improperly responsive to or insufficiently informed about the customers' special situations and problems.

In each case, the promised product—the whole product—would have been unsatisfactory. It is not that it would have been incomplete; it just would not have been right. Changing the salespeople in midstream probably would not have helped, since the selling organization would by then have already "said" the wrong thing about its "product." If, during the courtship, the prospective customer got the impression that there might be aftermarket problems—problems in execution, in timeliness, in the postsale support necessary for smooth and congenial relations—then the customer would have received a clear message that the delivered product would be faulty.

Special problems for intangibles

So much, briefly, for making a sale—for getting a customer. *Keeping* a customer is quite another thing, and on that score more pervasively intangible products encounter some distinct difficulties.

These difficulties stem largely from the fact that intangible products are highly people-intensive in their production and delivery methods. Corporate financial services of banks are, in this respect, not so different from hairdressing or consulting. The more people-intensive a product, the more room there is for personal discretion, idiosyncracy, error, and delay. Once a customer for an intangible product is sold, the customer can easily be unsold as a consequence of the underfulfillment of his expectations. Repeat buying suffers. Conversely, a tangible product, manufactured under close supervision in a factory and delivered through a planned and orderly network, is much more likely than an intangible product to fulfill the promised expectation. Repeat buying is therefore less easily jeopardized.

A tangible product is usually developed by design professionals working under conditions of benign isolation after receiving guidance from market intelligence experts, scientists, and others. The product will be manufactured by another group of specialists under conditions of close supervision that facilitate reliable quality control. Even installation and use by the customer are determined by a relatively narrow range of possibilities dictated by the product itself.

Intangible products present an entirely different picture. Consider a computer software program. The programmer does the required research directly and generally on the customer's premises, trying to understand complex networks of interconnecting operations. Then that same person designs the system and the software, usually alone. The process of designing is, simultaneously, also the process of manufacturing. Design and manufacturing of intangible products are generally done by the same people— or by one person alone, like a craftsman at a bench.

Moreover, manufacturing an intangible product is generally indistinguishable from its actual delivery. In situations such as consulting, the delivery *is* the manufacturing from the client's viewpoint. Though the consulting study may have been excellent, if the delivery is poor, the study will be viewed as having been badly manufactured. It's a faulty product. So too with the work of all types of brokers, educators and trainers, accounting firms, engineering firms, architects, lawyers, transportation companies, hospitals and clinics, government agencies, banks, trust companies, mutual funds, car rental companies, insurance companies, repair and maintenance operations, and on and on. For each, delivery and production are virtually indistinguishable. The whole difference is nicely summarized by Professor John M. Rathwell of Cornell University: "Goods are produced, services are performed." [1]

Minimizing the human factor

Because companies making intangible products are highly people-intensive operations, they have an enormous quality control problem. Quality control on an automobile assembly line is built into the system. If a yellow door is hung on a red car, somebody on the line will quickly ask if that's what was in-

tended. If the left front wheel is missing, the person next in line, whose task is to fasten the lug bolts, will stop the line. But if a commercial banker misses an important feature of a financing package or if he doesn't do it well, it may never be found—or found too late. If the ashtrays aren't cleaned on a rented car, that discovery will annoy or irritate the already committed customer. Repeat business gets jeopardized.

No matter how well trained or motivated they might be, people make mistakes, forget, commit indiscretions, and at times are uncongenial—hence the search for alternatives to dependence on people. Previously in HBR, I have suggested a variety of ways to reduce people dependence in the so-called service industries. I called it the *industrialization of service*, which means substituting hard, soft, or hybrid technologies for totally people-intensive activities:

☐ *Hard* technologies include automatic telephone dialing for operator-assisted dialing, credit cards for repetitive credit checking, and computerized monitoring of industrial processes. And the benefits are considerable. Automatic telephone switching is, for example, not only cheaper than manual switching but far more reliable.

☐ *Soft* technologies are the substitution of division of labor for one-person craftsmanship in production—as, for example, organizing the work force that cleans an office building so that each worker specializes in one or several limited tasks (dusting, waxing, vacuuming, window cleaning) rather than each person doing all these jobs alone. Insurance companies long ago went to extensive division of labor in their applications processing—registering, underwriting, performing actuarial functions, issuing policies.

☐ *Hybrid* technologies combine the soft and the hard. The floor is waxed by a machine rather than by hand. French fries are precut and portion packed in a factory for finishing in a fast-food restaurant in specially designed deep fryers that signal when the food is ready. A computer automatically calculates and makes all entries in an Internal Revenue Service form 1040 after a moderately trained clerk has entered the raw data on a console.

The managerial revolution

Industrializing helps control quality and cut costs. Instead of depending on people to work *better*, industrialization redesigns the work so that people work *differently*. Thus, the same modes of managerial rationality are applied to service—the production, creation, and delivery of largely intangible products—that were first applied to production of goods in the nineteenth century. The real signifi-

11

cance of the nineteenth century is not the industrial revolution, with its shift from animal to machine power, but rather the managerial revolution, with its shift from the craftsman's functional independence to the manager's rational routines.

In successive waves, the mechanical harvester, the sewing machine, and then the automobile epitomized the genius of that century. Each was rationally designed to become an assembled rather than a constructed machine, a machine that depended not on the idiosyncratic artistry of a single craftsman but on simple, standardized tasks performed on routine specifications by unskilled workers. This required detailed managerial planning to ensure proper design, manufacture, and assembly of interchangeable parts so that the right number of people would be at the right places at the right times to do the right simple jobs in the right ways. Then, with massive output, distribution, and aftermarket training and service, managers had to create and maintain systems to justify the massive output.

On being appreciated

What's been largely missing in intangible goods production is the kind of managerial rationality that produced the industrial revolution. That is why the quality of intangibles tends to be less reliable than it might be, costs higher than they should be, and customer satisfaction lower than it need be.

While I have referred to the enormous progress that has in recent years been made on these matters, there is one characteristic of intangible products that requires special attention for holding customers. Unique to intangible products is the fact that the customer is seldom aware of being served well. This is especially so in the case of intangible products that have, for the duration of the contract, constant continuity—that is, you're buying or using or consuming them almost constantly. Such products include certain banking services, cleaning services, freight hauling, energy management, maintenance services, telephones, and the like.

Consider an international banking relationship, an insurance relationship, an industrial cleaning relationship. If all goes well, the customer is virtually oblivious to what he's getting. Only when things don't go well (or a competitor says they don't) does the customer become aware of the product's existence or nonexistence—when a letter of credit is incorrectly drawn, when a competitive bank proposes better arrangements, when the annual insurance premium notice arrives or when a claim is disputed,

when the ashtrays aren't cleaned, or when a favorite penholder is missing.

The most important thing to know about intangible products is that the *customers usually don't know what they're getting until they don't get it.* Only then do they become aware of what they bargained for; only on dissatisfaction do they dwell. Satisfaction is, as it should be, mute. Its existence is affirmed only by its absence.

And that's dangerous—because the customers will be aware only of failure and of dissatisfaction, not of success or satisfaction. That makes them terribly vulnerable to the blandishments of competitive sellers. A competitor can always structure a more interesting corporate financing deal, always propose a more imaginative insurance program, always find dust on top of the framed picture in the office, always cite small visible failures that imply big hidden ones.

In getting customers for intangibles it is important to create surrogates, or metaphors, for tangibility—how we dress; how we articulate, write, design, and present proposals; how we work with prospects, respond to inquiries, and initiate ideas; and how well we show we understand the prospect's business. But in keeping customers for intangibles, it becomes important regularly to remind and show them what they're getting so that occasional failures fade in relative importance. If that's not done, the customers will not know. They'll only know when they're *not* getting what they bought, and that's all that's likely to count.

To keep customers for regularly delivered and consumed intangible products, again, they have to be reminded of what they're getting. Vendors must regularly reinstate the promises that were made to land the customer. Thus, when an insurance prospect finally gets "married," the subsequent silence and inattention can be deafening. Most customers seldom recall for long what kind of life insurance package they bought, often forgetting as well the name of both underwriter and agent. To be reminded a year later via a premium notice often brings to mind the contrast between the loving attention of courtship and the cold reality of marriage. No wonder the lapse rate in personal life insurance is so high!

Once a relationship is cemented, the seller has created equity. He has a customer. To help keep the customer, the seller must regularly enhance the equity in that relationship lest it decline and become jeopardized by competitors.

There are innumerable ways to do that strengthening, and some of these can be systematized, or industrialized. Periodic letters or phone calls that remind the customer of how well things are going cost little and are surprisingly powerful equity maintainers. Newsletters or regular visits suggesting new, better, or augmented product features are useful. Even nonbusiness socializing has its value—as is affirmed by corporations struggling in recent years with the IRS about the deductibility of hunting lodges, yachts, clubs, and spouses attending conferences and customer meetings.

Here are some examples of how companies have strengthened their relationships with customers:

☐ An energy management company sends out a periodic "Update Report" on conspicuous yellow paper, advising clients how to discover and correct energy leaks, install improved monitors, and accomplish cost savings.

☐ A computer service bureau organizes its account managers for a two-week series of blitz customer callbacks to "explain casually" the installation of new central processing equipment that is expected to prevent cost increases next year while expanding the customers' interactive options.

☐ A long-distance hauler of high-value electronic equipment (computers, terminals, mail sorters, word processors, medical diagnostic instruments) has instituted quarterly performance reviews with its shippers, some of which include customers who are encouraged to talk about their experiences and expectations.

☐ An insurance company sends periodic one-page notices to policyholders *and* policy beneficiaries. These generally begin with a single-sentence congratulation that policy and coverage remain nicely intact and follow with brief views on recent tax rulings affecting insurance, new notions about personal financial planning, and special protection packages available with other types of insurance.

In all these ways, sellers of intangible products reinstate their presence and performance in the customers' minds, reminding them of their continuing presence and the value of what is constantly, and silently, being delivered.

Making tangible the intangible

It bears repeating that all products have elements of tangibility and intangibility. Companies that sell tangible products invariably promise more than the tangible products themselves. Indeed, enormous efforts often focus on the enhancement of the intangibles—promises of bountiful benefits conferred rather than on features offered. To the buyer of photographic film, Kodak promises with unremitting emphasis the satisfactions of enduring remembrance, of memories clearly preserved. Kodak says almost nothing about the superior luminescence of its pictures. The product is thus remembrance, not film or pictures.

The promoted products of the automobile, as everyone knows, are largely status, comfort, and power—intangible things of the mind, rather than tangible things from the factory. Auto dealers, on the other hand, assuming correctly that people's minds have already been reached by the manufacturers' ads, focus on other considerations: deals, availability, and postpurchase servicing. Neither the dealers nor the manufacturers sell the tangible cars themselves. Rather, they sell the intangible benefits that are bundled into the entire package.

If tangible products must be intangibilized to add customer-getting appeal, then intangible products must be tangibilized—what Professor Leonard L. Berry calls "managing the evidence." [2] Ideally, this should be done as a matter of routine on a systematic basis—that is, industrialized. For instance, hotels wrap their drinking glasses in fresh bags or film, put on the toilet seat a "sanitized" paper band, and neatly shape the end piece of the toilet tissue into a fresh-looking arrowhead. All these actions say with silent affirmative clarity that "the room has been specially cleaned for your use and comfort"—yet no words are spoken to say it. Words, in any case, would be less convincing, nor could employees be reliably depended on to say them each time or to say them convincingly. Hotels have thus not only tangibilized their promise, they've also industrialized its delivery.

Or take the instructive case of purchasing house insulation, which most home owners approach with understandable apprehension. Suppose you call two companies to bid on installing insulation in your house. The first insulation installer arrives in a car. After pacing once around the house with measured self-assurance and after quick calculations on the back of an envelope, there comes a confident quote of $2,400 for six-inch fiberglass—total satisfaction guaranteed.

Another drives up in a clean white truck with clipboard in hand and proceeds to scrupulously measure the house dimensions, count the windows, crawl the attic, and consult records from a source book on the area's seasonal temperature ranges and wind velocities. The installer then asks a host of questions, meanwhile recording everything with obvious diligence. There follows a promise to return in three days, which happens at the appointed hour, with a typed proposal for six-inch fiberglass insulation at $2,800—total satisfaction guaranteed. From which company will you buy?

The latter has tangibilized the intangible, made a promise into a credible expectation. Even more persuasive tangible evidence is provided by an insulation supplier whose representative types the relevant information into a portable intelligent printing terminal. The analysis and response are almost instant, causing one user to call it "the most powerful tool ever developed in the insulation industry." If the house owner is head of a project buying team of an electric utility company, the treasurer of a mighty corporation, the materials purchasing agent of a ready-mixed cement company, the transportation manager of a fertilizer manufacturer, or the data processing director of an insurance company, it's almost certain this person will make vendor decisions at work in the same way as around the house. Everybody requires the risk-reducing reassurances of tangibilized intangibles.

Managers can use the practice of providing reassuring ways to render tangible the intangible's promises—even when the generic product is itself tangible. Laundry detergents that claim special whitening capabilities lend credibility to the promise by using "blue whitener beads" that are clearly visible to the user. Procter & Gamble's new decaffeinated instant coffee, "High Point," reinforces the notion of real coffee with luminescent "milled flakes for hearty, robust flavor." You can *see* what the claims promise.

Keeping customers for an intangible product requires constant reselling efforts while things go well lest the customer get lost when things go badly. The reselling requires that tasks be industrialized. The relationship with the customer must be managed much more carefully and continuously in the case of intangibles than of tangible products, though it is vital in both. And it gets progressively more vital for tangible products that are new and especially complex. In such cases, "relationship management" becomes a special art—another topic all its own.

Meanwhile, the importance of what I've tried to say here is emphasized by one overriding fact: a customer is an asset usually more precious than the tangible assets on the balance sheet. Balance sheet assets can generally be bought. There are lots of willing sellers. Customers cannot so easily be bought. Lots of eager sellers are offering them many choices. Moreover, a customer is a double asset. First, the customer is the direct source of cash from the sale and, second, the existence of a solid customer can be used to raise cash from bankers and investors—cash that can be converted into tangible assets.

The old chestnut "nothing happens till you make a sale" is awfully close to an important truth. What it increasingly takes to make and keep that sale is to tangibilize the intangible, restate the benefit and source to the customer, and industrialize the processes.

1. John M. Rathwell, *Marketing in the Service Sector* (Cambridge, Mass.: Winthrop Publishers, 1974), p. 58.
2. Leonard L. Berry, "Service Marketing Is Different," *Business*, May-June 1980, p. 24. He is with the University of Virginia, Charlottesville.

Mr. Levitt is the Edward W. Carter Professor of Business Administration and head of the marketing area at the Harvard Business School. He has written nearly two dozen articles for HBR, including the well-known "Marketing Myopia" (published in 1960 and reprinted as an HBR Classic in September-October 1975) and "Marketing When Things Change" (November-December 1977).

The Customer Is King

Keeping customers happy can give your business the competitive edge

by Scott Matulis

Economist Adam Smith once said, "Consumption is the sole purpose of all production; and the interest of the producer should be attended to only so far as it may be necessary for promoting that of the consumer." Translated into a modern-day corporate slogan, this would read, "The customer is king," or "Our customers are our most valuable asset," or any of a number of similar sentiments that businesses claim to live by.

Smith, however, might have trouble deciding whether or not American companies are following his advice. Even though experts such as futurist John Naisbitt and the U.S. Department of Commerce have been telling us for some time that America is moving briskly towards becoming a service economy, the quality of service in this country is still far from what it could be.

The U.S. Office of Consumer Affairs sponsored two National Consumer Surveys conducted by the Technical Assistance Research Programs Institute (TARP), one survey between 1974 and 1979 and another one between 1985 and 1986. According to Bonnie Jansen, associate director of the division of information at the U.S. Office of Consumer Affairs, the surveys found that the level of service in this country is "not very good." One-third of the households interviewed had experienced at least one significant consumer problem during the preceding year. More than 60 percent of these households reported financial losses averaging $142. For service companies, in particular, these results should be a little frightening.

During the recession of the early '80s, consumers blithely traded away high-quality service in exchange for price reductions or convenience. Now, those customers are demanding service again, and companies that have made a commitment to customer service have a competitive advantage over companies that haven't. "Consumers are beginning to feel that their needs haven't been met," explains Jansen. "They're sick and tired of being batted around; they're sick of getting poor service all the time."

Adds John Goodman, president of TARP, "In the mid-1970s, businesses—auto manufacturers, for instance—would try to handle customer complaints only because if they didn't somebody would come and picket them, or the government would come down on them. But in the past few years, companies began to realize that service was really a competitive factor, and they began to view service as an integral part of their product."

TARP's National Consumer Surveys have found that many of the respondents who did have service problems didn't even complain to the company about them. The reasons they gave for not doing so show that consumers don't think much of the way companies handle complaints. According to the study, the three major reasons why consumers don't file complaints are:

1. Complaining wasn't worth their time and effort;
2. They believed that complaining wouldn't do any good and that no one wanted to hear about their problems;
3. They didn't know where or how to complain.

The study also found that 40 percent of the households that *did* complain were unhappy with the action the company took to resolve their complaints.

Luckily, due to a growing economy and increased customer expectations, things are changing. A number of large companies have instituted highly effective customer service policies. Small business owners hoping to improve the quality of their service would do well to study these policies.

By far the most commonly cited example of improved customer service is the story of Scandinavian Airline Systems (SAS). When Jan Carlzon took over as president in 1981, the company was sliding downhill. But by instituting an aggressive service policy, Carlzon took SAS from an $8 million loss to a gross profit of $71 million in a little over one year. Carlzon's success was so spectacular that his style of management, christened "service management," became a buzzword in businesses throughout the world.

Better Service Means Better Business

A quick look at statistics should prove to even the most skeptical that keeping customers happy can do great things for a company's bottom line. Experts now use sophisticated measurement systems to show companies just what kind of a return they will see for each dollar they spend on service.

John Goodman explains, "The traditional problem with customer service and quality has been that you know how much money you have to spend to achieve it, but you don't really know what the company is getting back. But using these measurement systems, we can actually establish a return on investment for every improvement in service. And the minute you can quantify [the results of better service], many more companies are going to buy into it."

Improved service led to dramatically higher profits for Grand Junction Hamburger Stations, based in Lexington, Kentucky. To compete with giants like McDonald's and Burger King, the 13-outlet franchise instituted its "Meal in a Minute" policy to capitalize on what it did best—serving customers faster than anybody else.

Company president Bert Spinks explains, " 'Meal in a Minute' is a guarantee to all of our customers that they will receive their order, whatever the time of day or the size of the order, within one minute after they reach our drive-through window, or they will get their next meal free."

As unbelievable as it may sound, it is possible to serve a hamburger in under a minute, and the concept has been hugely successful for Grand Junction. Since the policy was instituted in February, the company's sales have jumped 64 percent. What's more, Grand Junction has had to make good on its guarantee only a scant 5.8 percent of the time; the average meal is served in 53 seconds.

The National Consumer Survey offers some hard statistics to show why businesses should try to make customers happy—and why they should try harder to resolve customer complaints. Respondents were divided into two categories: those with minor complaints (losses of $1 to $5) and those with major complaints (losses of over $100). According to the survey, only 9 percent of those who suffered minor

---

"Handling complaints is not only a way for your company to be the good guy, it's a way to actually make a profit."

---

losses and *didn't* complain would maintain brand loyalty; however, 54 percent of those who did complain and whose complaints were satisfactorily resolved would maintain brand loyalty. For major losses, the numbers were 37 percent and 70 percent respectively.

"Generally speaking," says Bonnie Jansen of the U.S. Office of Consumer Affairs, "the TARP survey found that if you invest in an aggressive, active complaint-handling system and you do it right, you can see a return on your investment of between 15 and 400 percent. So not only is a complaint-handling center a place where you can be the good guy, it's another way for your company to actually make a profit."

What Causes the Complaints?

In response to customer demand, many major corporations are instituting aggressive new service systems. The first step in doing this is to find out what makes customers in your particular industry unhappy. TARP president John Goodman, whose company has done customer service surveys for several hundred American corporations, points to three major causes of customer dissatisfaction.

1. About 20 percent of dissatisfaction is caused by the attitude or performance of employees.
2. About 40 percent of dissatisfaction is caused by companies whose structure, rules, or operating procedures are not designed for customer satisfaction. If there is no department with ultimate responsibility for customer service, problems are sure to occur, as customers with complaints are sent from one department to another until they give up in frustration. "Companies have to remember that they are creating [rules and structures] for the customer, not just for their own organizational purposes," says Jansen. "The person who deals with the consumer must have the authority to help the consumer in almost any way possible, without always transferring him or her to someone else."
3. Interestingly, 40 percent of dissatisfaction is caused by customers who misuse products or don't read the directions. Goodman says Sharp Electronics once got so frustrated by this kind of complaint that the company began putting red labels on its products' boxes which read, "When all else fails, read the directions."

Another company that has gone to extreme lengths to protect customers

from themselves is Armstrong World Industries, which makes Solarium no-wax floor tiles. The problem: Many customers would ignore the directions that came with the tile, use the wrong cleansers on the floors, and ruin them.

In just one year, improved customer service took Scandinavian Airlines from an $8 million loss to a $71 million profit.

Then they'd call Armstrong and angrily demand a new floor. "So now Armstrong prints a toll-free [customer service] phone number on the new floors," says Goodman. "That means Armstrong gets thousands of phone calls asking, 'How can I get that 800 number off my floor?' Then, while they've got the customer on the phone, they tell them what they need to know about maintaining the floor. Armstrong basically views the cost of the phone call, which they try to force [customers] to make, as insurance against [losing the customer's future business]."

Courting Customers With Service

No longer is price the only mode of competition and differentiation within an industry; companies are wooing customers with the promise of good service. "For many companies, their whole pitch now is that they don't necessarily offer the lowest prices, but they offer the highest quality service," explains Liz Buyer, a senior analyst at Prudential Bache Securities. "For instance, a lot of the people selling computers try to distinguish themselves from other people selling the exact same machine by offering to provide service contracts or design systems for [customers'] offices."

A consistent winner in the customer satisfaction war is mail order giant L.L. Bean Inc. Since most of the company's business comes over the phone, L.L. Bean's toll-free lines (not to mention its retail store in Freeport, Maine) are open 24 hours a day, every day. Of the 28,000 orders placed each day, 99.8 percent are filled accurately, and L.L. Bean accepts returns at any time, for any reason. L.L. Bean's customers consistently list quality as the attribute they like most about the company.

"The [new emphasis on] customer service is all part of a general awareness of quality," contends Jerome Vallen, dean of the School of Hotel Management at the University of Nevada, Las Vegas. "When you talk about quality in automobiles, you talk about doors that close tightly and things of that nature. When you talk about the service industry, you're talking about a kind of commodity as well. And quality isn't necessarily things like the best-cooked food or the coldest drink as much as it is the personality and attitude of the service person."

Most experts agree with Vallen that training programs for the "front-line" service people who interact with customers are crucial. Knowing this, the Santa Monica Hospital Medical Center in California turned to Dr. Karl Albrecht, co-author of *Service Amer-ica: Doing Business in the New Economy*, to help design a service management program. Albrecht helped the medical center identify the areas it needed to work on, and in August of 1985, the Service Management

---

"Quality doesn't necessarily mean the best-cooked food or the coldest drink—it means the personality and attitude of the service person."

Project went into effect. Every one of the medical center's employees and volunteers, including managers, must complete a two-day training program designed to help them recognize and alleviate customer dissatisfaction. According to Angie Twarynski, who was the medical center's director of education at the time the program was insti-tuted, the program has been a success. "There's been a marked change in the perception customers have of the medical center's services," says Twarynski.

In short, the service sector of American business is beginning to realize that Adam Smith was right on target. Toll-free customer service numbers are gaining in popularity as a way to make it easier for customers to complain and to increase interaction between customers and businesses in general. Companies such as Polaroid, General Motors Corp., Digital Equipment Corp., Northern Telecom Inc., and Neiman-Marcus have been cited by the U.S. Office of Consumer Affairs for innovative responses to the customer service problem. Other companies would be wise to take the same kind of steps, because if all the statistics are correct, customers really are a company's greatest asset. ∎

Marketing Myopia

Theodore Levitt

Every major industry was once a growth industry. But some that are now riding a wave of growth enthusiasm are very much in the shadow of decline. Others which are thought of as seasoned growth industries have actually stopped growing. In every case the reason growth is threatened, slowed, or stopped is *not* because the market is saturated. It is because there has been a failure of management.

Fateful purposes: The failure is at the top. The executives responsible for it, in the last analysis, are those who deal with broad aims and policies. Thus:

☐

The railroads did not stop growing because the need for passenger and freight transportation declined. That grew. The railroads are in trouble today not because the need was filled by others (cars, trucks, airplanes, even telephones), but because it was *not* filled by the railroads themselves. They let others take customers away from them because they assumed themselves to be in the railroad business rather than in the transportation business. The reason they defined their industry wrong was because they were railroad-oriented instead of transportation-oriented; they were product-oriented instead of customer-oriented.

☐

Hollywood barely escaped being totally ravished by television. Actually, all the established film companies went through drastic reorganizations. Some simply disappeared. All of them got into trouble not because of TV's inroads but because of their own myopia. As with the railroads, Hollywood defined its business incorrectly. It thought it was in the movie business when it was actually in the entertainment business. "Movies" implied a specific, limited product. This produced a fatuous contentment which from the beginning led producers to view TV as a threat. Hollywood scorned and rejected TV when it should have welcomed it as an opportunity—an opportunity to expand the entertainment business.

Today TV is a bigger business than the old narrowly defined movie business ever was. Had Hollywood been customer-oriented (providing entertainment), rather then product-oriented (making movies), would it have gone through the fiscal purgatory that it did? I doubt it. What ultimately saved Hollywood and accounted for its recent resurgence was the wave of new young writers, producers, and directors whose previous successes in television had decimated the old movie companies and toppled the big movie moguls.

There are other less obvious examples of industries that have been and are now endangering their futures by improperly defining their purposes. I shall discuss some in detail later and analyze the kind of policies that lead to trouble. Right now it may help to show what a thoroughly customer-oriented management *can* do to keep a growth industry growing, even after the obvious opportunities have been exhausted; and here there are two examples that have been around for a long time. They are nylon and glass—specifically, E. I. duPont de Nemours & Company and Corning Glass Works.

Both companies have great technical competence. Their product orientation is unquestioned. But this alone does not explain their success. After all, who was more pridefully product-oriented and product-conscious than the erstwhile New England textile companies that have been so thoroughly massacred? The DuPonts and the Cornings have succeeded not primarily because of their product or research orientation but because they have been thoroughly customer-oriented also. It is constant watchfulness for opportunities to apply their technical know-how to the creation of customer-satisfying uses which accounts for their prodigious output of successful new products. Without a very sophisticated eye on the customer, most of their new products might have been wrong, their sales methods useless.

Aluminum has also continued to be a growth industry, thanks to the efforts of two wartime-created companies which deliberately set about creating new customer-satisfying uses. Without Kaiser Aluminum & Chemical Corporation and Reynolds Metals Company, the total demand for aluminum today would be vastly less.

Error of analysis: Some may argue that it is foolish to set the railroads off against aluminum or the movies off against glass. Are not aluminum and glass naturally so versatile that the industries are bound to have more growth opportunities than the railroads and movies? This view commits precisely the error I have been talking about. It defines an industry, or a product, or a cluster of know-how so narrowly as to guarantee its premature senescence. When we mention "railroads," we should make sure we mean "transportation." As transporters, the railroads still have a good chance for very considerable growth. They are not limited to the railroad business as such (though in my opinion rail transportation is potentially a much stronger transportation medium than is generally believed).

What the railroads lack is not opportunity, but some of the same managerial imaginativeness and audacity that made them great. Even an amateur like Jacques Barzun can see what is lacking when he says:

"I grieve to see the most advanced physical and social organization of the last century go down in shabby disgrace for lack of the same comprehensive imagination that built it up. [What is lacking is] the will of the companies to survive and to satisfy the public by inventiveness and skill." [1]

Shadow of obsolescence

It is impossible to mention a single major industry that did not at one time qualify for the magic appellation of "growth industry." In each case its assumed strength lay in the apparently unchallenged superiority of its product. There appeared to be no effective substitute for it. It was itself a runaway substitute for the product it so triumphantly replaced. Yet one after another of these celebrated industries has come under a shadow. Let us look briefly at a few more of them, this time taking examples that have so far received a little less attention:

☐

Dry cleaning—This was once a growth industry with lavish prospects. In an age of wool garments, imagine being finally able to get them safely and easily clean. The boom was on.

Yet here we are 30 years after the boom started and the industry is in trouble. Where has the competition come from? From a better way of cleaning? No. It has come from synthetic fibers and chemical additives that have cut the need for dry cleaning. But this is only the beginning.

Lurking in the wings and ready to make chemical dry cleaning totally obsolescent is that powerful magician, ultrasonics.

☐

Electric utilities— This is another one of those supposedly "no-substitute" products that has been enthroned on a pedestal of invincible growth. When the incandescent lamp came along, kerosene lights were finished. Later the water wheel and the steam engine were cut to ribbons by the flexibility, reliability, simplicity, and just plain easy availability of electric motors. The prosperity of electric utilities continues to wax extravagant as the home is converted into a museum of electric gadgetry. How can anybody miss by investing in utilities, with no competition, nothing but growth ahead?

But a second look is not quite so comforting. A score of nonutility companies are well advanced toward developing a powerful chemical fuel cell which could sit in some hidden closet of every home silently ticking off electric power. The electric lines that vulgarize so many neighborhoods will be eliminated. So will the endless demolition of streets and service interruptions during storms. Also on the horizon is solar energy, again pioneered by nonutility companies.

Who says that the utilities have no competition? They may be natural monopolies now, but tomorrow they may be natural deaths. To avoid this prospect, they too will have to develop fuel cells, solar energy, and other power sources. To survive, they themselves will have to plot the obsolescence of what now produces their livelihood.

☐

Grocery stores—Many people find it hard to realize that there ever was a thriving establishment known as the "corner grocery store." The supermarket has taken over with a powerful effectiveness. Yet the big food chains of the 1930s narrowly escaped being completely wiped out by the aggressive expansion of independent supermarkets. The first genuine supermarket was opened in 1930, in Ja-

maica, Long Island. By 1933 supermarkets were thriving in California, Ohio, Pennsylvania, and elsewhere. Yet the established chains pompously ignored them. When they chose to notice them, it was with such derisive descriptions as "cheapy," "horse-and-buggy," "cracker-barrel storekeeping," and "unethical opportunists."

The executive of one big chain announced at the time that he found it "hard to believe that people will drive for miles to shop for foods and sacrifice the personal service chains have perfected and to which Mrs. Consumer is accustomed." [2] As late as 1936, the National Wholesale Grocers convention and the New Jersey Retail Grocers Association said there was nothing to fear. They said that the supers' narrow appeal to the price buyer limited the size of their market. They had to draw from miles around. When imitators came, there would be wholesale liquidations as volume fell. The current high sales of the supers was said to be partly due to their novelty. Basically people wanted convenient neighborhood grocers. If the neighborhood stores "cooperate with their suppliers, pay attention to their costs, and improve their service," they would be able to weather the competition until it blew over. [3]

It never blew over. The chains discovered that survival required going into the supermarket business. This meant the wholesale destruction of their huge investments in corner store sites and in established distribution and merchandising methods. The companies with "the courage of their convictions" resolutely stuck to the corner store philosophy. They kept their pride but lost their shirts.

Self-deceiving cycle: But memories are short. For example, it is hard for people who today confidently hail the twin messiahs of electronics and chemicals to see how things could possibly go wrong with these galloping industries. They probably also cannot see how a reasonably sensible businessman could have been as myopic as the famous Boston millionaire who 50 years ago unintentionally sentenced his heirs to poverty by stipulating that his entire estate be forever invested exclusively in electric streetcar securities. His posthumous declaration, "There will always be a big demand for efficient urban transportation," is no consolation to his heirs who sustain life by pumping gasoline at automobile filling stations.

Yet, in a casual survey I recently took among a group of intelligent business executives, nearly half agreed that it would be hard to hurt their heirs by tying their estates forever to the electronics industry. When I then confronted them with the Boston streetcar example, they chorused unanimously, "That's different!" But is it? Is not the basic situation identical?

In truth, *there is no such thing* as a growth industry, I believe. There are only companies organized and operated to create and capitalize on growth opportunities. Industries that assume themselves to be riding some automatic growth escalator invariably descend into stagnation. The history of every dead and dying "growth" industry shows a self-deceiving cycle of bountiful expansion and undetected decay. There are four conditions which usually guarantee this cycle:

1
The belief that growth is assured by an expanding and more affluent population.
2
The belief that there is no competitive substitute for the industry's major product.
3
Too much faith in mass production and in the advantages of rapidly declining unit costs as output rises.
4
Preoccupation with a product that lends itself to carefully controlled scientific experimentation, improvement, and manufacturing cost reduction.

I should like now to begin examining each of these conditions in some detail. To build my case as boldly as possible, I shall illustrate the points with reference to three industries—petroleum, automobiles, and electronics—particularly petroleum, because it spans more years and more vicissitudes. Not only do these three have excellent reputations with the general public and also enjoy the confidence of sophisticated investors, but their managements have become known for progressive thinking in areas like financial control, product research, and management training. If obsolescence can cripple even these industries, it can happen anywhere.

Population myth

The belief that profits are assured by an expanding and more affluent population is dear to the heart of every industry. It takes the edge off the apprehensions everybody understandably feels about the future. If consumers are multiplying and also buying more of your product or service, you can face the future with considerably more comfort than if the market is shrinking. An expanding market keeps the manufacturer from having to think very hard or imaginatively. If thinking is an intellectual response to a problem, then the absence of a problem leads to the absence of thinking. If your product has an automatically expanding market, then you will not give much thought to how to expand it.

One of the most interesting examples of this is provided by the petroleum industry. Probably our oldest growth industry, it has an enviable record. While there are some current apprehensions about its growth rate, the industry itself tends to be optimistic.

But I believe it can be demonstrated that it is undergoing a fundamental yet typical change. It is not only ceasing to be a growth industry, but may actually be a declining one, relative to other business. Although there is widespread unawareness of it, I believe that within 25 years the oil industry may find itself in much the same position of retrospective glory that the railroads are now in. Despite its pioneering work in developing and applying the present-value method of investment evaluation, in employee relations, and in working with backward countries, the petroleum business is a distressing example of how complacency and wrongheadedness can stubbornly convert opportunity into near disaster.

One of the characteristics of this and other industries that have believed very strongly in the beneficial consequences of an expanding population, while at the same time being industries with a generic product for which there has appeared to be no competitive substitute, is that the individual companies have sought to outdo their competitors by improving on what they are already doing. This makes sense, of course, if one assumes that sales are tied to the country's population strings, because the customer can compare products only on a feature-by-feature basis. I believe it is significant, for example, that not since John D. Rockefeller sent free kerosene lamps to China has the oil industry done anything really outstanding to create a demand for its product. Not even in product improvement has it showered itself with eminence. The greatest single improvement—namely, the development of tetraethyl lead—came from outside the industry, specifically from General Motors and DuPont. The big contributions made by the industry itself are confined to the technology of oil exploration, production, and refining.

Asking for trouble: In other words, the industry's efforts have focused on improving the *efficiency* of getting and making its product, not really on improving the generic product or its marketing. Moreover, its chief product has continuously been defined in the narrowest possible terms, namely, gasoline, not energy, fuel, or transportation. This attitude has helped assure that:

○
Major improvements in gasoline quality tend not to originate in the oil industry. Also, the development of superior alternative fuels comes from outside the oil industry, as will be shown later.
○
Major innovations in automobile fuel marketing are originated by small new oil companies that are not primarily preoccupied with production or re-

fining. These are the companies that have been responsible for the rapidly expanding multipump gasoline stations, with their successful emphasis on large and clean layouts, rapid and efficient driveway service, and quality gasoline at low prices.

Thus, the oil industry is asking for trouble from outsiders. Sooner or later, in this land of hungry inventors and entrepreneurs, a threat is sure to come. The possibilities of this will become more apparent when we turn to the next dangerous belief of many managements. For the sake of continuity, because this second belief is tied closely to the first, I shall continue with the same example.

Idea of indispensability: The petroleum industry is pretty much persuaded that there is no competitive substitute for its major product, gasoline—or if there is, that it will continue to be a derivative of crude oil, such as diesel fuel or kerosene jet fuel.

There is a lot of automatic wishful thinking in this assumption. The trouble is that most refining companies own huge amounts of crude oil reserves. These have value only if there is a market for products into which oil can be converted—hence the tenacious belief in the continuing competitive superiority of automobile fuels made from crude oil.

This idea persists despite all historic evidence against it. The evidence not only shows that oil has never been a superior product for any purpose for very long, but it also shows that the oil industry has never really been a growth industry. It has been a succession of different businesses that have gone through the usual historic cycles of growth, maturity, and decay. Its overall survival is owed to a series of miraculous escapes from total obsolescence, of last-minute and unexpected reprieves from total disaster reminiscent of the Perils of Pauline.

Perils of petroleum: I shall sketch in only the main episodes.

First, crude oil was largely a patent medicine. But even before that fad ran out, demand was greatly expanded by the use of oil in kerosene lamps. The prospect of lighting the world's lamps gave rise to an extravagant promise of growth. The prospects were similar to those the industry now holds for gasoline in other parts of the world. It can hardly wait for the underdeveloped nations to get a car in every garage.

In the days of the kerosene lamp, the oil companies competed with each other and against gaslight by trying to improve the illuminating characteristics of kerosene. Then suddenly the impossible happened. Edison invented a light which was totally nondependent on crude oil. Had it not been for the growing use of kerosene in space heaters, the incandescent lamp would have completely finished oil as a growth industry at that time. Oil would have been good for little else than axle grease.

Then disaster and reprieve struck again. Two great innovations occurred, neither originating in the oil industry. The successful development of coalburning domestic central-heating systems made the space heater obsolescent. While the industry reeled, along came its most magnificent boost yet —the internal combustion engine, also invented by outsiders. Then when the prodigious expansion for gasoline finally began to level off in the 1920s, along came the miraculous escape of a central oil heater. Once again, the escape was provided by an outsider's invention and development. And when that market weakened, wartime demand for aviation fuel came to the rescue. After the war the expansion of civilian aviation, the dieselization of railroads, and the explosive demand for cars and trucks kept the industry's growth in high gear.

Meanwhile, centralized oil heating— whose boom potential had only recently been proclaimed—ran into severe competition from natural gas. While the oil companies themselves owned the gas that now competed with their oil, the industry did not originate the natural gas revolution, nor has it to this day greatly profited from its gas ownership. The gas revolution was made by newly formed transmission companies that marketed the product with an aggressive ardor. They started a magnificent new industry, first against the advice and then against the resistance of the oil companies.

By all the logic of the situation, the oil companies themselves should have made the gas revolution. They not only owned the gas; they also were the only people experienced in handling, scrubbing, and using it, the only people experienced in pipeline technology and transmission, and they understood heating problems. But, partly because they knew that natural gas would compete with their own sale of heating oil, the oil companies poohpoohed the potentials of gas.

The revolution was finally started by oil pipeline executives who, unable to persuade their own companies to go into gas, quit and organized the spectacularly successful gas transmission companies. Even after their success became painfully evident to the oil companies, the latter did not go into gas transmission. The multibillion dollar business which should have been theirs went to others. As in the past, the industry was blinded by its narrow preoccupation with a specific product and the value of its reserves. It paid little or no attention to its customers' basic needs and preferences.

The postwar years have not witnessed any change. Immediately after World War II the oil industry was greatly encouraged about its future by the rapid expansion of demand for its traditional line of products. In 1950 most companies projected annual rates of domestic expansion of around 6% through at least 1975. Though the ratio of crude oil reserves to demand in the Free World was about 20 to 1, with 10 to 1 being usually considered a reasonable working ratio in the United States, booming demand sent oil men searching for more without sufficient regard to what the future really promised. In 1952 they "hit" in the Middle East; the ratio skyrocketed to 42 to 1. If gross additions to reserves continue at the average rate of the past five years (37 billion barrels annually), then by 1970 the reserve ratio will be up to 45 to 1. This abundance of oil has weakened crude and product prices all over the world.

Uncertain future: Management cannot find much consolation today in the rapidly expanding petrochemical industry, another oil-using idea that did not originate in the leading firms. The total United States production of petrochemicals is equivalent to about 2% (by volume) of the demand for all petroleum products. Although the petrochemical industry is now expected to grow by about 10% per year, this will not offset other drains on the growth of crude oil consumption. Furthermore, while petrochemical products are many and growing, it is well to remember that there are nonpetroleum sources of the basic raw material, such as coal. Besides, a lot of plastics can be produced with relatively little oil. A 50,000-barrel-per-day oil refinery is now considered the absolute minimum size for efficiency. But a 5,000-barrel-per-day chemical plant is a giant operation.

Oil has never been a continuously strong growth industry. It has grown by fits and starts, always miraculously saved by innovations and developments not of its own making. The reason it has not grown in a smooth progression is that each time it thought it had a superior product safe from the possibility of competitive substitutes, the product turned out to be inferior and notoriously subject to obsolescence. Until now, gasoline (for motor fuel, anyhow) has escaped this fate. But, as we shall see later, it too may be on its last legs.

The point of all this is that there is no guarantee against product obsolescence. If a company's own research does not make it obsolete, another's will. Unless an industry is especially lucky, as oil has been until now, it can easily go down in a sea of red figures—just as the railroads have, as the buggy whip manufacturers have, as the corner grocery chains have, as most of the big movie companies have, and indeed as many other industries have.

The best way for a firm to be lucky is to make its own luck. That requires

knowing what makes a business successful. One of the greatest enemies of this knowledge is mass production.

Production pressures

Mass-production industries are impelled by a great drive to produce all they can. The prospect of steeply declining unit costs as output rises is more than most companies can usually resist. The profit possibilities look spectacular. All effort focuses on production. The result is that marketing gets neglected.

John Kenneth Galbraith contends that just the opposite occurs.[4] Output is so prodigious that all effort concentrates on trying to get rid of it. He says this accounts for singing commercials, desecration of the countryside with advertising signs, and other wasteful and vulgar practices. Galbraith has a finger on something real, but he misses the strategic point. Mass production does indeed generate great pressure to "move" the product. But what usually gets emphasized is selling, not marketing. Marketing, being a more sophisticated and complex process, gets ignored.

The difference between marketing and selling is more than semantic. Selling focuses on the needs of the seller, marketing on the needs of the buyer. Selling is preoccupied with the seller's need to convert his product into cash, marketing with the idea of satisfying the needs of the customer by means of the product and the whole cluster of things associated with creating, delivering, and finally consuming it.

In some industries the enticements of full mass production have been so powerful that for many years top management in effect has told the sales departments, "You get rid of it; we'll worry about profits." By contrast, a truly marketing-minded firm tries to create value-satisfying goods and services that consumers will want to buy. What it offers for sale includes not only the generic product or service, but also how it is made available to the customer, in what form, when,

under what conditions, and at what terms of trade. Most important, what it offers for sale is determined not by the seller but by the buyer. The seller takes his cues from the buyer in such a way that the product becomes a consequence of the marketing effort, not vice versa.

Lag in Detroit: This may sound like an elementary rule of business, but that does not keep it from being violated wholesale. It is certainly more violated than honored. Take the automobile industry.

Here mass production is most famous, most honored, and has the greatest impact on the entire society. The industry has hitched its fortune to the relentless requirements of the annual model change, a policy that makes customer orientation an especially urgent necessity. Consequently the auto companies annually spend millions of dollars on consumer research. But the fact that the new compact cars are selling so well in their first year indicates that Detroit's vast researches have for a long time failed to reveal what the customer really wanted. Detroit was not persuaded that he wanted anything different from what he had been getting until it lost millions of customers to other small car manufacturers.

How could this unbelievable lag behind consumer wants have been perpetuated so long? Why did not research reveal consumer preferences before consumers' buying decisions themselves revealed the facts? Is that not what consumer research is for—to find out before the fact what is going to happen? The answer is that Detroit never really researched the customer's wants. It only researched his preferences between the kinds of things which it had already decided to offer him. For Detroit is mainly product-oriented, not customer-oriented. To the extent that the customer is recognized as having needs that the manufacturer should try to satisfy, Detroit usually acts as if the job can be done entirely by product changes. Occasionally attention gets paid to financing, too, but that is done more in order to sell than to enable the customer to buy.

As for taking care of other customer needs, there is not enough being done to write about. The areas of the greatest unsatisfied needs are ignored, or at best get stepchild attention. These are at the point of sale and on the matter of automative repair and maintenance. Detroit views these problem areas as being of secondary importance. That is underscored by the fact that the retailing and servicing ends of this industry are neither owned and operated nor controlled by the manufacturers. Once the car is produced, things are pretty much in the dealer's inadequate hands. Illustrative of Detroit's arm's-length attitude is the fact that, while servicing holds enormous sales-stimulating, profit-building opportunities, only 57 of Chevrolet's 7,000 dealers provide night maintenance service.

Motorists repeatedly express their dissatisfaction with servicing and their apprehensions about buying cars under the present selling setup. The anxieties and problems they encounter during the auto buying and maintenance processes are probably more intense and widespread today than 30 years ago. Yet the automobile companies do not *seem* to listen to or take their cues from the anguished consumer. If they do listen, it must be through the filter of their own preoccupation with production. The marketing effort is still viewed as a necessary consequence of the product, not vice versa, as it should be. That is the legacy of mass production, with its parochial view that profit resides essentially in low-cost full production

What Ford put first: The profit lure of mass production obviously has a place in the plans and strategy of business management, but it must always *follow* hard thinking about the customer. This is one of the most important lessons that we can learn from the contradictory behavior of Henry Ford. In a sense Ford was both the most brilliant and the most senseless marketer in American history. He was senseless because he refused to give the customer anything but a black car. He was brilliant because he fashioned a production system designed to fit market needs. We habitually celebrate him for the wrong reason, his produc-

tion genius. His real genius was marketing. We think he was able to cut his selling price and therefore sell millions of $500 cars because his invention of the assembly line had reduced the costs. Actually he invented the assembly line because he had concluded that at $500 he could sell millions of cars. Mass production was the *result* not the cause of his low prices.

Ford repeatedly emphasized this point, but a nation of production-oriented business managers refuses to hear the great lesson he taught. Here is his operating philosophy as he expressed it succinctly:

"Our policy is to reduce the price, extend the operations, and improve the article. You will notice that the reduction of price comes first. We have never considered any costs as fixed. Therefore we first reduce the price to the point where we believe more sales will result. Then we go ahead and try to make the prices. We do not bother about the costs. The new price forces the costs down. The more usual way is to take the costs and then determine the price; and although that method may be scientific in the narrow sense, it is not scientific in the broad sense, because what earthly use is it to know the cost if it tells you that you cannot manufacture at a price at which the article can be sold? But more to the point is the fact that, although one may calculate what a cost is, and of course all of our costs are carefully calculated, no one knows what a cost ought to be. One of the ways of discovering . . . is to name a price so low as to force everybody in the place to the highest point of efficiency. The low price makes everybody dig for profits. We make more discoveries concerning manufacturing and selling under this forced method than by any method of leisurely investigation." [5]

Product provincialism: The tantalizing profit possibilities of low unit production costs may be the most seriously self-deceiving attitude that can afflict a company, particularly a "growth" company where an apparently assured expansion of demand already tends to

undermine a proper concern for the importance of marketing and the customer.

The usual result of this narrow preoccupation with so-called concrete matters is that instead of growing, the industry declines. It usually means that the product fails to adapt to the constantly changing patterns of consumer needs and tastes, to new and modified marketing institutions and practices, or to product developments in competing or complementary industries. The industry has its eyes so firmly on its own specific product that it does not see how it is being made obsolete.

The classical example of this is the buggy whip industry. No amount of product improvement could stave off its death sentence. But had the industry defined itself as being in the transportation business rather than the buggy whip business, it might have survived. It would have done what survival always entails, that is, changing. Even if it had only defined its business as providing a stimulant or catalyst to an energy source, it might have survived by becoming a manufacturer of, say, fanbelts or air cleaners.

What may some day be a still more classical example is, again, the oil industry. Having let others steal marvelous opportunities from it (e.g., natural gas, as already mentioned, missile fuels, and jet engine lubricants), one would expect it to have taken steps never to let that happen again. But this is not the case. We are now getting extraordinary new developments in fuel systems specifically designed to power automobiles. Not only are these developments concentrated in firms outside the petroleum industry, but petroleum is almost systematically ignoring them, securely content in its wedded bliss to oil. It is the story of the kerosene lamp versus the incandescent lamp all over again. Oil is trying to improve hydrocarbon fuels rather than develop *any* fuels best suited to the needs of their users, whether or not made in different ways and with different raw materials from oil.

Here are some things which nonpetroleum companies are working on:

☐

Over a dozen such firms now have advanced working models of energy systems which, when perfected, will replace the internal combustion engine and eliminate the demand for gasoline. The superior merit of each of these systems is their elimination of frequent, time-consuming, and irritating refueling stops. Most of these systems are fuel cells designed to create electrical energy directly from chemicals without combustion. Most of them use chemicals that are not derived from oil, generally hydrogen and oxygen.

☐

Several other companies have advanced models of electric storage batteries designed to power automobiles. One of these is an aircraft producer that is working jointly with several electric utility companies. The latter hope to use off-peak generating capacity to supply overnight plug-in battery regeneration. Another company, also using the battery approach, is a medium-size electronics firm with extensive small-battery experience that it developed in connection with its work on hearing aids. It is collaborating with an automobile manufacturer. Recent improvements arising from the need for high-powered miniature power storage plants in rockets have put us within reach of a relatively small battery capable of withstanding great overloads or surges of power. Germanium diode applications and batteries using sintered-plate and nickel-cadmium techniques promise to make a revolution in our energy sources.

☐

Solar energy conversion systems are also getting increasing attention. One usually cautious Detroit auto executive recently ventured that solar-powered cars might be common by 1980.

As for the oil companies, they are more or less "watching developments," as one research director put it to me. A few are doing a bit of research on fuel cells, but almost always confined to developing cells powered by hydrocarbon chemicals. None of them are

enthusiastically researching fuel cells, batteries, or solar power plants. None of them are spending a fraction as much on research in these profoundly important areas as they are on the usual run-of-the-mill things like reducing combustion chamber deposit in gasoline engines. One major integrated petroleum company recently took a tentative look at the fuel cell and concluded that although "the companies actively working on it indicate a belief in ultimate success . . . the timing and magnitude of its impact are too remote to warrant recognition in our forecasts."

One might, of course, ask: Why should the oil companies do anything different? Would not chemical fuel cells, batteries, or solar energy kill the present product lines? The answer is that they would indeed, and that is precisely the reason for the oil firms having to develop these power units before their competitors, so they will not be companies without an industry.

Management might be more likely to do what is needed for its own preservation if it thought of itself as being in the energy business. But even that would not be enough if it persists in imprisoning itself in the narrow grip of its tight product orientation. It has to think of itself as taking care of customer needs, not finding, refining, or even selling oil. Once it genuinely thinks of its business as taking care of people's transportation needs, nothing can stop it from creating its own extravagantly profitable growth.

'Creative destruction': Since words are cheap and deeds are dear, it may be appropriate to indicate what this kind of thinking involves and leads to. Let us start at the beginning—the customer. It can be shown that motorists strongly dislike the bother, delay, and experience of buying gasoline. People actually do not buy gasoline. They cannot see it, taste it, feel it, appreciate it, or really test it. What they buy is the right to continue driving their cars. The gas station is like a tax collector to whom people are compelled to pay a periodic toll as the price of using their cars. This makes the gas station a basically unpopular institu-

tion. It can never be made popular or pleasant, only less unpopular, less unpleasant.

To reduce its unpopularity completely means eliminating it. Nobody likes a tax collector, not even a pleasantly cheerful one. Nobody likes to interrupt a trip to buy a phantom product, not even from a handsome Adonis or a seductive Venus. Hence, companies that are working on exotic fuel substitutes which will eliminate the need for frequent refueling are heading directly into the outstretched arms of the irritated motorist. They are riding a wave of inevitability, not because they are creating something which is technologically superior or more sophisticated, but because they are satisfying a powerful customer need. They are also eliminating noxious odors and air pollution.

Once the petroleum companies recognize the customer-satisfying logic of what another power system can do, they will see that they have no more choice about working on an efficient, long-lasting fuel (or some way of delivering present fuels without bothering the motorist) than the big food chains had a choice about going into the supermarket business, or the vacuum tube companies had a choice about making semiconductors. For their own good the oil firms will have to destroy their own highly profitable assets. No amount of wishful thinking can save them from the necessity of engaging in this form of "creative destruction."

I phrase the need as strongly as this because I think management must make quite an effort to break itself loose from conventional ways. It is all too easy in this day and age for a company or industry to let its sense of purpose become dominated by the economies of full production and to develop a dangerously lopsided product orientation. In short, if management lets itself drift, it invariably drifts in the direction of thinking of itself as producing goods and services, not customer satisfactions. While it probably will not descend to the depths of telling its salesmen, "You get rid of it; we'll worry about profits," it can, without knowing it, be practicing precisely that formula for withering decay. The historic fate of one growth industry after another has been its suicidal product provincialism.

Dangers of R&D

Another big danger to a firm's continued growth arises when top management is wholly transfixed by the profit possibilities of technical research and development. To illustrate I shall turn first to a new industry—electronics—and then return once more to the oil companies. By comparing a fresh example with a familiar one, I hope to emphasize the prevalence and insidiousness of a hazardous way of thinking.

Marketing shortchanged: In the case of electronics, the greatest danger which faces the glamorous new companies in this field is not that they do not pay enough attention to research and development, but that they pay *too much* attention to it. And the fact that the fastest growing electronics firms owe their eminence to their heavy emphasis on technical research is completely beside the point. They have vaulted to affluence on a sudden crest of unusually strong general receptiveness to new technical ideas. Also, their success has been shaped in the virtually guaranteed market of military subsidies and by military orders that in many cases actually preceded the existence of facilities to make the products. Their expansion has, in other words, been almost totally devoid of marketing effort.

Thus, they are growing up under conditions that come dangerously close to creating the illusion that a superior product will sell itself. Having created a successful company by making a superior product, it is not surprising that management continues to be oriented toward the product rather than the people who consume it. It develops the philosophy that continued growth is a matter of continued product innovation and improvement.

A number of other factors tend to strengthen and sustain this belief:

1

Because electronic products are highly complex and sophisticated, manage-ments become top-heavy with engineers and scientists. This creates a selective bias in favor of research and production at the expense of marketing. The organization tends to view itself as making things rather than satisfying customer needs. Marketing gets treated as a residual activity, "something else" that must be done once the vital job of product creation and production is completed.

2

To this bias in favor of product research, development, and production is added the bias in favor of dealing with controllable variables. Engineers and scientists are at home in the world of concrete things like machines, test tubes, production lines, and even balance sheets. The abstractions to which they feel kindly are those which are testable or manipulatable in the laboratory, or, if not testable, then functional, such as Euclid's axioms. In short, the managements of the new glamour-growth companies tend to favor those business activities which lend themselves to careful study, experimentation, and control—the hard, practical realities of the lab, the shop, the books.

What gets shortchanged are the realities of the *market.* Consumers are unpredictable, varied, fickle, stupid, shortsighted, stubborn, and generally bothersome. This is not what the engineer-managers say, but deep down in their consciousness it is what they believe. And this accounts for their concentrating on what they know and what they can control, namely, product research, engineering, and production. The emphasis on production becomes particularly attractive when the product can be made at declining unit costs. There is no more inviting way of making money than by running the plant full blast.

Today the top-heavy science-engineering-production orientation of so many electronics companies works reasonably well because they are pushing into new frontiers in which the armed services have pioneered virtually assured markets. The companies are in the felicitous position of having to fill, not find markets; of not having to discover what the customer needs and wants, but of having the customer voluntarily come forward with specific new product demands. If a team of consultants had been assigned specifically to design a business situation calculated to prevent the emergence and development of a customer-oriented marketing viewpoint, it could not have produced anything better than the conditions just described.

Stepchild treatment: The oil industry is a stunning example of how science, technology, and mass production can divert an entire group of companies from their main task. To the extent the consumer is studied at all (which is not much), the focus is forever on getting information which is designed to help the oil companies improve what they are now doing. They try to discover more convincing advertising themes, more effective sales promotional drives, what the market shares of the various companies are, what people like or dislike about service station dealers and oil companies, and so forth. Nobody seems as interested in probing deeply into the basic human needs that the industry might be trying to satisfy as in probing into the basic properties of the raw material that the companies work with in trying to deliver customer satisfactions.

Basic questions about customers and markets seldom get asked. The latter occupy a stepchild status. They are recognized as existing, as having to be taken care of, but not worth very much real thought or dedicated attention. Nobody gets as excited about the customers in his own backyard as about the oil in the Sahara Desert. Nothing illustrates better the neglect of marketing than its treatment in the industry press.

The centennial issue of the *American Petroleum Institute Quarterly,* published in 1959 to celebrate the discovery of oil in Titusville, Pennsylvania, contained 21 feature articles proclaiming the industry's greatness. Only one of these talked about its achievements in marketing, and that was only a pictorial record of how service station architecture has changed. The issue also contained a special section on

"New Horizons," which was devoted to showing the magnificent role oil would play in America's future. Every reference was ebulliently optimistic, never implying once that oil might have some hard competition. Even the reference to atomic energy was a cheerful catalogue of how oil would help make atomic energy a success. There was not a single apprehension that the oil industry's affluence might be threatened or a suggestion that one "new horizon" might include new and better ways of serving oil's present customers.

But the most revealing example of the stepchild treatment that marketing gets was still another special series of short articles on "The Revolutionary Potential of Electronics." Under that heading this list of articles appeared in the table of contents:

○
"In the Search for Oil"
○
"In Production Operations"
○
"In Refinery Processes"
○
"In Pipeline Operations"

Significantly, every one of the industry's major functional areas is listed, *except* marketing. Why? Either it is believed that electronics holds no revolutionary potential for petroleum marketing (which is palpably wrong), or the editors forgot to discuss marketing (which is more likely, and illustrates its stepchild status).

The order in which the four functional areas are listed also betrays the alienation of the oil industry from the consumer. The industry is implicitly defined as beginning with the search for oil and ending with its distribution from the refinery. But the truth is, it seems to me, that the industry begins with the needs of the customer for its products. From that primal position its definition moves steadily backstream to areas of progressively lesser importance, until it finally comes to rest at the "search for oil."

Beginning & end: The view that an industry is a customer-satisfying pro-cess, not a goods-producing process, is vital for all businessmen to understand. An industry begins with the customer and his needs, not with a patent, a raw material, or a selling skill. Given the customer's needs, the industry develops backwards, first concerning itself with the physical *delivery* of customer satisfactions. Then it moves back further to *creating* the things by which these satisfactions are in part achieved. How these materials are created is a matter of indifference to the customer, hence the particular form of manufacturing, processing, or what-have-you cannot be considered as a vital aspect of the industry. Finally, the industry moves back still further to *finding* the raw materials necessary for making its products.

The irony of some industries oriented toward technical research and development is that the scientists who occupy the high executive positions are totally unscientific when it comes to defining their companies' overall needs and purposes. They violate the first two rules of the scientific method —being aware of and defining their companies' problems, and then developing testable hypotheses about solving them. They are scientific only about the convenient things, such as laboratory and product experiments.

The reason that the customer (and the satisfaction of his deepest needs) is not considered as being "the problem" is not because there is any certain belief that no such problem exists, but because an organizational lifetime has conditioned management to look in the opposite direction. Marketing is a stepchild.

I do not mean that selling is ignored. Far from it. But selling, again, is not marketing. As already pointed out, selling concerns itself with the tricks and techniques of getting people to exchange their cash for your product. It is not concerned with the values that the exchange is all about. And it does not, as marketing invariably does, view the entire business process as consisting of a tightly integrated effort to discover, create, arouse, and satisfy customer needs. The customer is somebody "out there" who, with proper cunning, can be separated from his loose change.

Actually, not even selling gets much attention in some technologically minded firms. Because there is a virtually guaranteed market for the abundant flow of their new products, they do not actually know what a real market is. It is as if they lived in a planned economy, moving their products routinely from factory to retail outlet. Their successful concentration on products tends to convince them of the soundness of what they have been doing, and they fail to see the gathering clouds over the market.

Conclusion

Less than 75 years ago American railroads enjoyed a fierce loyalty among astute Wall Streeters. European monarchs invested in them heavily. Eternal wealth was thought to be the benediction for anybody who could scrape a few thousand dollars together to put into rail stocks. No other form of transportation could compete with the railroads in speed, flexibility, durability, economy, and growth potentials.

As Jacques Barzun put it, "By the turn of the century it was an institution, an image of man, a tradition, a code of honor, a source of poetry, a nursery of boyhood desires, a sublimest of toys, and the most solemn machine—next to the funeral hearse—that marks the epochs in man's life." [6]

Even after the advent of automobiles, trucks, and airplanes, the railroad tycoons remained imperturbably self-confident. If you had told them 60 years ago that in 30 years they would be flat on their backs, broke, and pleading for government subsidies, they would have thought you totally demented. Such a future was simply not considered possible. It was not even a discussable subject, or an askable question, or a matter which any sane person would consider worth speculating about. The very thought was insane. Yet a lot of insane notions now have matter-of-fact acceptance—for example, the idea of 100-ton tubes of metal moving smoothly through the air 20,000 feet above the earth, loaded with 100 sane and solid citizens casually drinking martinis—and they have dealt cruel blows to the railroads.

What specifically must other companies do to avoid this fate? What does customer orientation involve? These questions have in part been answered by the preceding examples and analysis. It would take another article to show in detail what is required for specific industries. In any case, it should be obvious that building an effective customer-oriented company involves far more than good intentions or promotional tricks; it involves profound matters of human organization and leadership. For the present, let me merely suggest what appear to be some general requirements.

Visceral feel of greatness: Obviously the company has to do what survival demands. It has to adapt to the requirements of the market, and it has to do it sooner rather than later. But mere survival is a so-so aspiration. Anybody can survive in some way or other, even the skid-row bum. The trick is to survive gallantly, to feel the surging impulse of commercial mastery; not just to experience the sweet smell of success, but to have the visceral feel of entrepreneurial greatness.

No organization can achieve greatness without a vigorous leader who is driven onward by his own pulsating *will to succeed.* He has to have a vision of grandeur, a vision that can produce eager followers in vast numbers. In business, the followers are the customers.

In order to produce these customers, the entire corporation must be viewed as a customer-creating and customer-satisfying organism. Management must think of itself not as producing products but as providing customer-creating value satisfactions. It must push this idea (and everything it means and requires) into every nook and cranny of the organization. It has to do this continuously and with the kind of flair that excites and stimulates the people in it. Otherwise, the company will be merely a series of pigeonholed parts, with no consolidating sense of purpose or direction.

In short, the organization must learn to think of itself not as producing goods or services but as *buying customers,* as doing the things that will make people *want* to do business with it. And the chief executive himself has the inescapable responsibility for creating this environment, this viewpoint, this attitude, this aspiration. He himself must set the company's style, its direction, and its goals. This means he has to know precisely where he himself wants to go, and to make sure the whole organization is enthusiastically aware of where that is. This is a first requisite of leadership, for *unless he knows where he is going, any road will take him there.*

If any road is okay, the chief executive might as well pack his attaché case and go fishing. If an organization does not know or care where it is going, it does not need to advertise that fact with a ceremonial figurehead. Everybody will notice it soon enough.

Retrospective commentary

Amazed, finally, by his literary success, Isaac Bashevis Singer reconciled an attendant problem: "I think the moment you have published a book, it's not any more your private property. . . . If it has value, everybody can find in it what he finds, and I cannot tell the man I did not intend it to be so." Over the past 15 years, "Marketing Myopia" has become a case in point. Remarkably, the article spawned a legion of loyal partisans—not to mention a host of unlikely bedfellows.

Its most common and, I believe, most influential consequence is the way certain companies for the first time gave serious thought to the question of what businesses they are really in.

The strategic consequences of this have in many cases been dramatic. The best-known case, of course, is the shift in thinking of oneself as being in the "oil business" to being in the "energy business." In some instances the payoff has been spectacular (getting into coal, for example) and in others dreadful (in terms of the time and money spent so far on fuel cell research). Another successful example is a company with a large chain of retail shoe stores

that redefined itself as a retailer of moderately priced, frequently purchased, widely assorted consumer specialty products. The result was a dramatic growth in volume, earnings, and return on assets.

Some companies, again for the first time, asked themselves whether they wished to be masters of certain technologies for which they would seek markets, or be masters of markets for which they would seek customer-satisfying products and services.

Choosing the former, one company has declared, in effect, "We are experts in glass technology. We intend to improve and expand that expertise with the object of creating products that will attract customers." This decision has forced the company into a much more systematic and customer-sensitive look at possible markets and users, even though its stated strategic object has been to capitalize on glass technology.

Deciding to concentrate on markets, another company has determined that "we want to help people (primarily women) enhance their beauty and sense of youthfulness." This company has expanded its line of cosmetic products, but has also entered the fields of proprietary drugs and vitamin supplements.

All these examples illustrate the "policy" results of "Marketing Myopia." On the operating level, there has been, I think, an extraordinary heightening of sensitivity to customers and consumers. R&D departments have cultivated a greater "external" orientation toward uses, users, and markets—balancing thereby the previously one-sided "internal" focus on materials and methods; upper management has realized that marketing and sales departments should be somewhat more willingly accommodated than before; finance departments have become more receptive to the legitimacy of budgets for market research and experimentation in marketing; and salesmen have been better trained to listen to and understand customer needs and problems, rather than merely to "push" the product.

A mirror, not a window

My impression is that the article has had more impact in industrial-products companies than in consumer-products companies—perhaps because the former had lagged most in customer orientation. There are at least two reasons for this lag: (1) industrial-products companies tend to be more capital intensive, and (2) in the past, at least, they have had to rely heavily on communicating face-to-face the technical character of what they made and sold. These points are worth explaining.

Capital-intensive businesses are understandably preoccupied with magnitudes, especially where the capital, once invested, cannot be easily moved, manipulated, or modified for the production of a variety of products—e.g., chemical plants, steel mills, airlines, and railroads. Understandably, they seek big volumes and operating efficiencies to pay off the equipment and meet the carrying costs.

At least one problem results: corporate power becomes disproportionately lodged with operating or financial executives. If you read the charter of one of the nation's largest companies, you will see that the chairman of the finance committee, not the chief executive officer, is the "chief." Executives with such backgrounds have an almost trained incapacity to see that getting "volume" may require understanding and serving many discrete and sometimes small market segments, rather than going after a perhaps mythical batch of big or homogeneous customers.

These executives also often fail to appreciate the competitive changes going on around them. They observe the changes, all right, but devalue their significance or underestimate their ability to nibble away at the company's markets.

Once dramatically alerted to the concept of segments, sectors, and customers, though, managers of capital-intensive businesses have become more responsive to the necessity of balancing their inescapable preoccupation with

"paying the bills" or breaking even with the fact that the best way to accomplish this may be to pay more attention to segments, sectors, and customers.

The second reason industrial products companies have probably been more influenced by the article is that, in the case of the more technical industrial products or services, the necessity of clearly communicating product and service characteristics to prospects results in a lot of face-to-face "selling" effort. But precisely because the product is so complex, the situation produces salesmen who know the product more than they know the customer, who are more adept at explaining what they have and what it can do than learning what the customer's needs and problems are. The result has been a narrow product orientation rather than a liberating customer orientation, and "service" often suffered. To be sure, sellers said, "We have to provide service," but they tended to define service by looking into the mirror rather than out the window. They *thought* they were looking out the window at the customer, but it was actually a mirror—a reflection of their own product-oriented biases rather than a reflection of their customers' situations.

A manifesto, not a prescription

Not everything has been rosy. A lot of bizarre things have happened as a result of the article:

☐
Some companies have developed what I call "marketing mania"—they've become obsessively responsive to every fleeting whim of the customer. Mass production operations have been converted to approximations of job shops, with cost and price consequences far exceeding the willingness of customers to buy the product.
☐
Management has expanded product lines and added new lines of business without first establishing adequate

control systems to run more complex operations.
☐
Marketing staffs have suddenly and rapidly expanded themselves and their research budgets without either getting sufficient prior organizational support or, thereafter, producing sufficient results.
☐
Companies that are functionally organized have converted to product, brand, or market-based organizations with the expectation of instant and miraculous results. The outcome has been ambiguity, frustration, confusion, corporate infighting, losses, and finally a reversion to functional arrangements that only worsened the situation.
☐
Companies have attempted to "serve" customers by creating complex and beautifully efficient products or services that buyers are either too risk-averse to adopt or incapable of learning how to employ—in effect, there are now steam shovels for people who haven't yet learned to use spades. This problem has happened repeatedly in the so-called service industries (financial services, insurance, computer-based services) and with American companies selling in less-developed economies.

"Marketing Myopia" was not intended as analysis or even prescription; it was intended as manifesto. It did not pretend to take a balanced position. Nor was it a new idea—Peter F. Drucker, J.B. McKitterick, Wroe Alderson, John Howard, and Neil Borden had each done more original and balanced work on "the marketing concept." My scheme, however, tied marketing more closely to the inner orbit of business policy. Drucker—especially in *The Concept of the Corporation* and *The Practice of Management*—originally provided me with a great deal of insight.

My contribution, therefore, appears merely to have been a simple, brief, and useful way of communicating an existing way of thinking. I tried to do it in a very direct, but responsible, fashion, knowing that few readers (customers), especially managers and leaders, could stand much equivocation or hesitation. I also knew that the colorful and lightly documented affirmation works better than the tortuously reasoned explanation.

But why the enormous popularity of what was actually such a simple pre-existing idea? Why its appeal throughout the world to resolutely restrained scholars, implacably temperate managers, and high government officials, all accustomed to balanced and thoughtful calculation? Is it that concrete examples, joined to illustrate a simple idea and presented with some attention to literacy, communicate better than massive analytical reasoning that reads as though it were translated from the German? Is it that provocative assertions are more memorable and persuasive than restrained and balanced explanations, no matter who the audience? Is it that the character of the message is as much the message as its content? Or was mine not simply a different tune, but a new symphony? I don't know.

Of course, I'd do it again and in the same way, given my purposes, even with what more I now know—the good and the bad, the power of facts and the limits of rhetoric. If your mission is the moon, you don't use a car. Don Marquis's cockroach, Archy, provides some final consolation: "an idea is not responsible for who believes in it."

1. Jacques Barzun, "Trains and the Mind of Man," *Holiday*, February 1960, p. 21.

2. For more details see M. M. Zimmerman, *The Super Market: A Revolution in Distribution* (New York, McGraw-Hill Book Company, Inc., 1955), p. 48.

3. Ibid., pp. 45–47.

4. *The Affluent Society* (Boston, Houghton Mifflin Company, 1958), pp. 152-160.

5. Henry Ford, *My Life and Work* (New York, Doubleday, Page & Company, 1923), pp. 146-147.

6. Jacques Barzun, "Trains and the Mind of Man," *Holiday*, February 1960, p. 20.

At the time of the article's publication, Theodore Levitt was lecturer in business administration at the Harvard Business School. Now a full professor there, he is the author of six books, including The Third Sector: New Tactics for a Responsive Society *(1973) and* Marketing for Business Growth *(1974). His most recent article for HBR was "Dinosaurs among the Bears and Bulls" (January–February 1975).*

Service Boom— No End In Sight

by Frances Huffman

Janet, 35, is married, works full time, and has a 3-year-old son. Each morning, she drops her son off at a day care center. While she's at work a maid service cleans her home, and a personal shopper does some of her errands and grocery shopping.

Henry, 77, lives with his son's family. On weekdays, while his son and daughter-in-law are at work, Henry goes to a senior day care center.

Gus, 56, and his wife Jean, 52, visited a financial planner before taking early retirement to ensure financial security. The couple plan to fill their golden years with leisure activities and travel, and have already booked trips to Canada and Hawaii through their local senior travel agency.

Janet, Henry, Gus, and Jean have something in common with a growing number of Americans: They are turning to service businesses to take over some of their personal chores. As individuals and families find themselves with more work to do and less time to do it, they have little choice but to find someone else to do the work for them. This dilemma is adding up to big profits for service businesses that lighten the load for busy people.

Service industries are changing the face of America. Cheryl Russell, editor-in-chief of *American Demographics* Magazine, predicts that businesses providing services which help people save time or spend their leisure time will thrive in years to come. Service-producing industries already bring in billions of dollars in revenues and accounted for more than two-thirds of our gross national product in 1985.

Leaving behind its industrial past, America is leaping towards a new, service-dominated future. In fact, the Bureau of Labor Statistics estimates that as early as the year 1995, as many as nine out of 10 new jobs will be created in the service industries.

And if you have trouble believing that, just take a look at your checkbook and see how many checks are made out to hairdressers, dry cleaners, gardeners, florists, shoe repair shops, plumbers, theaters, lawyers, auto repair shops, babysitters, health clubs, food delivery services, insurance companies, and so on.

"Affluence," says Russell, "is really behind the greater demand for services." Also contributing to this trend, she notes, are a number of shifting demographic patterns, such as the aging of America, the increasing number of working mothers, and the recent baby boomlet. People in each of these rapidly expanding segments of society are becoming major consumers of services.

America Goes Gray

The baby boomers, who recently began celebrating their fortieth birthdays, will soon be graying the face of America. By the year 2020, when the boomers begin to retire, the number of Americans over the age of 55 will peak at 59 million, according to the U.S. Census Bureau.

As our population matures, atti-

Senior citizens are spending more and more money on services that let them maintain independence and have fun.

---

tudes about the elderly are changing drastically. No longer do people expect seniors to be sedentary, destitute, and ailing. Instead, the elderly are golfing,

running marathons, and traveling. Betty Ransom, senior coordinator at The National Council on the Aging, explains that we're already seeing a healthier, more affluent, more educated group of old people.

Seniors who don't think they're past the prime of life are looking at retirement in a new way. "With the elimination of mandatory retirement in a lot of sectors, you're going to see a larger proportion of older people who will continue to work for longer periods of time," says Ransom. At the same time, Ransom says she sees a lot of older people who say, "Hey, I want to take advantage of this time. I have some money put away for retirement and I want to go ahead and enjoy it."

These active seniors want all kinds of services—travel, entertainment, personal care, health care, financial services, and educational resources. While they once revelled in purchasing material things—their first house or car—seniors have now graduated to the service market. Willing to spend more money to maintain independence and to have fun, they are more likely to hire chauffeurs, gardeners, or even companions than in the past.

And soon, seniors will have more years of retirement to enjoy than ever before, since the average life expectancy is rising. In the 1950s, people could expect to live perhaps 10 years after retiring; today, with early retirement still imposed in many U.S. companies, retirees can often expect to live another 25 to 30 years.

Ensuring financial security during these later years is one of the major concerns facing today's baby boomers. More and more of the aging boomers are turning to financial planners to help them stretch their money over their retirement years. One occurrence that can deplete an elderly person's savings quickly is one that many seniors don't plan for—illness.

Although the aged, as a group, are becoming healthier, Ransom expects the number of seniors needing some kind of care to rise. In fact, Ransom explains, "We're receiving reports from states that are already direly short on nursing home beds. I anticipate that there will be an increase in the need for nursing-home care, as well as other community-based senior services like day care and home care."

However, two things are making older adults choose day care centers over traditional nursing homes: the high cost of nursing homes and the desire to remain independent. "Most people would choose to have some support either in the home or in the community rather than having to move into a nursing home," explains Ransom.

Senior day care centers have multiplied from just 12 centers in 1970 to more than 1,200 today, and Ransom sees no end to this trend. Day care centers operating for profit, such as

---

"Working mothers look for help wherever they can find it. That's why they buy services aimed at making their lives easier."

Adult Day Clubs of America in Baltimore, Maryland, are already benefiting from the aging of America.

Affluence also plays a role here, according to Russell. "Once, a family would have to take care of their relatives in their home because they couldn't afford anything else. Today, however, many families can afford to have their elderly relatives taken care of outside their homes."

Where Will I Find the Time?

Before women started working outside the home, they were usually in charge of taking care of their ailing parents or in-laws. Now, with more than half the female population in the work force, day care centers for the elderly represent an opportunity to match the phenomenal success of child-care centers.

Like their venerable parents, working mothers are major service consumers, but for different reasons. "It

sounds like a cliché, but finding the time to balance their lives is the greatest challenge working mothers face," says Betty Holcomb, senior editor of *Working Mother* Magazine. "Working mothers, by definition, are trying to do two jobs at once and they aren't getting a lot of help. They're looking for help wherever they can find it and I think that's why they immediately began to buy all the services aimed at making their lives easier—like child care."

Working mothers are not a rare species in the United States, and all reports show that even more mothers will be joining the work force in the future. The Bureau of Labor Statistics shows that in the 1950s, only 4.6 million mothers worked outside the home while 15.4 million stayed at home. Today, more than 65 percent of all mothers work outside the home, constituting some 21.4 million women. And by the year 1995, the Bureau of Labor Statistics projects that 82 percent of all mothers will be working.

As the number of working mothers skyrockets, so does the need for services. Since work outside the home leaves a woman with little or no time to do traditional household chores, she is almost forced to buy services that can perform those duties for her. Holcomb thinks that's why "service businesses are taking off and doing such a big business." Proof of this industry's phenomenal growth finds its way to Holcomb's desk every day in the form of press releases detailing successful service businesses that cater to the working mother.

Housecleaning, says Holcomb, is one service that's booming thanks to working mothers. In just three years, the number of housecleaning companies has more than doubled, jumping from 669 in 1985 to 1,621 in 1988, according to the U.S. Department of Commerce. Revenues in this field have more than tripled during this time, going from a meager $41 million in 1985 to $127 million in 1988.

Numerous other service businesses have surfaced to help working mothers, many of them started by women who were mothers themselves and wished they had some help. For example, Sharlene Martin, of Wilton, Connecticut started a nanny placement service, Helping Hands Inc., to help mothers find qualified live-in nannies.

When Martin started her company in 1984, there were no agencies that offered quality live-in nannies. Today, Martin estimates that "there are more than 200 such agencies around the nation, and most of them have been modeled after Helping Hands." Martin, who thinks Helping Hands is a perfect example of a business born out of necessity, hopes the service boom will last "forever."

Another service that appeals to the harried, frazzled working mother is Drive'Em, a child transportation service in Georgetown, Texas headed by Bonnie M. Riley. In just three years, Drive'Em's customer list has increased from 10 to more than 100 regular, daily customers. Riley thinks the success she has found in her small town is proof of a "need all over the nation for services that help working parents."

Helping working couples cope with their busy schedules is what makes the service boom exciting for Holcomb. "These new businesses are providing support for working mothers and helping them balance and enrich their lives," she says. "Working mothers are actually living better personal lives, thanks to services."

Taking Care of the Kids

One service industry that has already helped millions of working mothers is child day care. But now that there's a veritable baby boomlet on our hands, Holcomb and Russell see mothers crying out for more child care centers. Figures from the National Center for Health Statistics show that the birth rate jumped 3 percent last year to 3,829,000—the highest level since 1964. According to *USA Today*, the number of kids under 5 years old soared by almost 9 percent during the first half of the 1980s and is expected to continue growing.

The climbing birth rate, combined with the fact that today's working parents are opting for outside child care in record numbers, has made child care an $11 billion industry. Martin, at Helping Hands, explains that child care is one area where parents are willing to spend a *lot* of money for quality service. According to a 1986 survey conducted by Yale University, parents are shelling out an average of $87 per week for approximately 34 hours of care for infants and toddlers, and about $68 per week for 32 hours of care for preschoolers.

Though child care centers have spread like wildfire, they have yet to peak. Child care operators, such as Kinder-Care Learning Centers Inc. in Montgomery, Alabama, see a rosy future ahead of them. Kinder-Care, founded by Perry Mendel in 1969, has grown from a single location to the number-one child-care chain in the nation, with 1,150 centers, and expects to keep on growing as the birth rate rises.

On the Business Side

In addition to the demographic changes, Russell cites another reason why service industries are thriving: "It's very difficult to import services. Because of that, services have to be provided by American workers. Meanwhile, our manufactured products don't have to be provided by American workers. So, as companies export their manufacturing jobs overseas, services become a larger share of what's left. And I think that's going to continue to happen, so services will increasingly dominate the economy."

While Russell has no doubts that service industries will indeed dominate our economy in the years to come, she says that the aging population will af- fect the type of services provided. "Twenty years from now, we'll see a profound change in services—from helping people save time to helping people use time." She advises entrepreneurs who want to be on the cutting edge of the service boom that success will depend not on service alone, but on the *quality* of service given. So whether you're meeting with clients, fixing someone's faucet, or delivering your first pizza, do it with style! ∎

6 ☆☆☆☆☆☆ Services

by Frances Huffman

☆ Dining Out . . . At Home

When Southern Californians order food "to go," they can bypass the hamburger and fries in favor of coq au vin, pheasant under glass, or even filet mignon. Restaurant Express, a one-of-a-kind delivery service based in Newport Beach, California, has been delivering fine cuisine from local restaurants to clients' dining rooms since February, 1987.

John Pugsley, a self-proclaimed entrepreneur at heart, says he originally designed the business for his daughter, who was looking for a job at the time. Pugsley recalls, "I had gotten some takeout [from my favorite restaurant] a few months earlier and I thought, 'Boy, it would be nice if somebody would deliver from that restaurant to the home.' Then I started playing with some numbers in my mind and by the time I'd finished tumbling the numbers, I realized there was the potential here for a major industry."

After seeing the profit potential involved, Pugsley decided to keep the business for himself. From the begin- ning, Pugsley knew how the operation would work: "We'd take the orders over a computer and send them to the restaurants by modem." From there, delivery people dressed in tuxedo shirts and bow ties would deliver the meal (kept warm in a Styrofoam chest) to the client.

Clients who want something tasty but don't have the time to make elaborate meals make up the company's target market, which includes singles, retirees, professional couples, and dinner party hosts. Basically, "anyone who likes convenience" is a potential customer, says Pugsley. The meals cost the same as they would in the restaurant, plus a $4 delivery fee.

With such reasonable prices, it's no wonder Restaurant Express has served between 60,000 and 70,000 meals in its first year of business. During the next year, Pugsley expects to make about 2,000 deliveries per week, accounting for some $30,000 in gross revenues weekly. The company's profits are derived solely from the delivery charge and the discounts Pugsley receives from the 40 restaurants participating in the service.

After months of experimenting, "We've finally come up with a very, very effective formula," notes Pugsley, who plans to go public and franchise the operation in the near future. This entrepreneur, who thinks takeout and delivery services are the way of the future, says he "looks forward to becoming the Federal Express of the restaurant business."

☆ Suds & Sweat

Most people would agree that doing the wash at a laundromat is one of their most-hated household chores. After all, it takes away precious weekend time and basically immobilizes you for the hour or so your clothes spend spinning, rinsing, and drying. But just imagine being able to put your laundry in the washing machine, then make your way to the gym, work out, and still get back to the laundromat in time to put your things in the dryer. One young entrepreneur in Vista, California has figured out a way to let his customers do just that.

Greg Trabert, president of Clean & Lean Inc., thinks his unique laundromat/fitness center combined under one roof "will revolutionize the laundry and fitness businesses." In Trabert's one-stop wash and workout center, glass partitions separate the laundry facilities from the fitness area, allowing customers to keep an eye on their wash.

While the marriage between laundromat and gym seemed an obvious one to Trabert, creating this one-of-a-kind business was far from trouble-free. The Southern Californian ran into a number of stumbling blocks along the way, such as obtaining insurance and a building permit. Trabert recalls, "The day before our grand opening, the city informed us that we weren't allowed to open this particular facility in this location. So we had to run down [to city hall] . . . but they finally approved it."

Once Clean & Lean opened its doors in June, 1987, success was no sweat. Thanks to some articles published in local newspapers and magazines, customers started pouring into the facility. "I'd say there are between 60 and 80 people a day now," says Trabert. And while Trabert won't disclose exact figures, Clean & Lean's revenues have jumped 88 percent since their first three months in business.

Convenience, low prices, and a clean facility are some of the reasons customers prefer Clean & Lean to more traditional gyms and laundromats. Compared to other health clubs, Clean & Lean's prices are reasonable, consisting of either a per-visit charge or a monthly fee—no year-long contracts or initiation fees. This explains why many people come to Clean & Lean just to use the fitness center.

Clean & Lean has also attracted some customers that Trabert never expected to see. Says Trabert, "We have customers who have laundry facilities in their homes, but they still come in because they like coming down to exercise and get five or six loads of laundry done at the same time, instead of coming home and doing laundry every night."

After witnessing the growing popularity of Clean & Lean, Trabert plans to start franchising the operation. In fact, after only 10 months in business, Trabert says that some 680 people have contacted him about franchise possibilities, "and that's from word-of-mouth, without any advertising."

☆ A New Wrinkle In Day Care

By the end of the century, adult day care is expected to mirror the phenomenal growth that turned children's day care into a billion-dollar industry. Hoping to lead the way in this industry is Maurice "Tommy" Thompson, president and CEO of Senior Service Corp., based in Wilton, Connecticut.

Deeply disturbed by the declining health of his parents and the lack of care services for the elderly, Thompson says he thought to himself, "I'd better invent adult day care." Putting his experience working in child care to use, Thompson bought an ailing Baltimore, Maryland day care center in 1987 and transformed it into a center for the elderly that's profitable on both a social and a monetary level.

According to a 1984 survey conducted by the National Center for Health Statistics, 3.2 million elderly people received some sort of long-term care that year, but 3.3 million healthy elderly didn't have anyone to care for them should they need care

someday. These 6.5 million people represent potential clients for adult day care centers in the 1990s.

While only 12 adult day care centers existed in the United States in the 1970s, statistics compiled by the National Council on the Aging show that there are between 1,200 and 1,400 such centers operating nationwide today. And if that number keeps doubling every four to five years, as it has been, Thompson expects to see about 10,000 adult day care centers in the United States by the year 2000.

Thompson notes a number of advantages of day care as opposed to residential nursing homes. "Adult day care gives the client a larger measure of the most precious asset that any of us has—our freedom, our independence," explains Thompson. "The second major advantage is that the average nursing home now costs about $26,000 a year, while the average day care experience costs under $5,000 a year."

While 90 percent of adult day care in

this country is provided on a non-profit basis, Adult Day Clubs of America, a subsidiary of Senior Service Corp., is one of the few companies operating for profit. The Baltimore center was losing about $6,000 per month when Senior Service bought it. In just one year, Senior Service turned the center around and was bringing in profits of over $11,000 a month.

Despite the healthy sales figures, Thompson says Adult Day Clubs of America is still in the development stage. Several hundred seniors have participated in the program so far, but Thompson expects to multiply this and reach hundreds of thousands of seniors by the year 2000.

Inevitable is the word Thompson uses to describe the growth in senior day care centers. "I think the outlook for the industry in general is that it will *become* an industry. It will become a major service segment, eventually providing several billions of dollars worth of input. The real question is how rapidly that is going to occur."

☆ *The New Space Saver*

Although computerization has cleared up much of the paperwork that used to clutter offices, "there will never be a paperless office," says Melissa Anderson. "Companies are trying to do away with a lot of the paper," she adds, "but in doing computer printouts, you generate a lot of paper, and what do you do with it?" In 1984, Anderson decided to help rid companies of some of that paper overload by creating En-Sure, a data retention service in Trenton, New Jersey.

Storing both paper documents and computer backups, En-Sure does more than just increase office space—it ensures the safety of valuable files in case of catastrophe. "Automation made [data retention] a necessity," says Anderson, because it "made people aware of how valuable certain

records are." Anyone who has lost files due to equipment failure or natural disaster can see the advantages of an off-site storage space.

What makes En-Sure better than a simple storage space are the additional services it provides, such as organizing and retrieving files. Anderson says organizing files is one of the more popular services En-Sure offers, since it's usually a low priority in busy offices.

According to Anderson, data retention offers something for every business, whether it's a one-person operation or a large corporation. "There is a great need for this type of service," she contends.

Making companies aware of that need, however, has taken some effort. Since data retention is a relatively new concept, Anderson has had to spend

quite a bit of time convincing local businesses to give her service a try. But now, the four-year-old company stores documents for attorneys, doctors, prominent corporations, and government organizations. En-Sure has already had to expand its original 3,500 square foot facility to 6,000 square feet to accommodate all the documents. And although Anderson won't disclose exact sales figures, she expects 1988 revenues to be at least 50 percent higher than 1987's.

As awareness of off-site storage grows, Anderson plans to open other data retention centers throughout New Jersey. "I think we'll stay in this area because the growth potential is phenomenal," she says, adding that data retention is one service that's "really going to take off."

☆ *What They Didn't Teach You In Grade School*

Nearly 20 percent of all school-age children are significantly behind their grade-level norms in reading and math, according to a report published by the U.S. Department of Education. And as public schools across the country are being forced to cut their budgets, little can be done within the schools themselves to remedy the situation.

Taking over after the final school bell rings, Sylvan Learning Corp. offers supplemental education for both children and adults. The most successful franchisor in the field, Sylvan had system-wide revenues of more than $38 million last year, and projections for 1988 figures exceed $65 million, says Gene Montgomery, president and CEO of the 9-year-old company.

Montgomery explains that Sylvan is not trying to replace public education, merely enhance it. Courses at Sylvan include reading, math, algebra, college prep, study skills, and a readiness program to help prepare four- and five-year-olds for beginning school.

Sylvan's latest program, a writing enrichment course, is geared toward adults, who are expected to be the company's future target market, as well as children.

Sylvan isn't just for remedial assistance, though, says Montgomery. Average and above-average youngsters enroll in the Sylvan programs for enrichment. However, Montgomery expects the company's latest target market— adults—to become its greatest source of profits in the future. Obtaining government contracts and corporate clients who want extra schooling for their employees will be Sylvan's main goal in years to come.

In the supplemental education field, Sylvan is virtually unrivalled. The company began franchising in 1980, and by January, 1985, there were 85 centers in operation. Today, Sylvan boasts some 450 centers nationwide, and is adding about 100 franchises per year. However, franchise sales are not expected to be the biggest moneymaker for the company in the future. According to Montgomery, "In two to four years, I think the contract market—both government and corporate—will be bigger for us than the franchise sales." Despite the rapid growth the company's enjoyed, Montgomery says, "We haven't scratched the surface yet."

☆ The Love Broker

Making dating easy for the more than 60 million single adults in the U.S. has become a very profitable business for Jeffrey Ullman. As president and founder of Great Expectations in Los Angeles, California, Ullman has developed a unique video dating service. No longer do singles have to spend hours hanging around in crowded, smoky nightclubs, vainly hoping that Mr. or Ms. Right will show up.

Great Expectations offers a secure environment for singles who "hate wasting their time, energy, and money trying to find somebody to spend their lives with," says Ullman. He adds, "Great Expectations members are doing something that Americans are doing in greater numbers than ever before . . . turning to services to save them their most precious commodity—time."

In 1976, Ullman opened the first Great Expectations center on a shoestring budget, working with a used video camera and VCR in a small, windowless office. Undaunted, the entrepreneur quickly set out to tell singles that there was now a better, faster, safer way to meet and date quality singles.

Now, 12 years later, Ullman is still busy encouraging singles to take charge of their love lives by joining Great Expectations, where they can actively seek their perfect mate without a lot of the guesswork that's usually involved in dating. However, Ullman stresses, "We're not a computer dating service, we're not a personal matchmaker who fixes you up with someone, we're not some astrological matchmaking." Individuals meet only through mutual consent—there are no blind dates and no surprise phone calls.

Great Expectations is far from a lonelyhearts club—attractive professionals, executives, and university graduates are lining up to buy annual or lifetime memberships. Concentrating on upscale, quality singles, Great Expectations guarantees that none of its members are married. And most want commitments; they're not looking to play the field, says Ullman.

Although there are a number of other types of dating services on the market, Ullman notes proudly, "We are absolutely the romantic giants of the industry." To date, 60,000 singles have signed on and almost 2,000 marriages [including Ullman's] have resulted from Great Expectations meetings.

Ullman is proof positive that love and money do mix. The first Great Expectations location met with such success that Ullman decided to franchise the operation almost immediately. This year, Great Expectations' 23 Membership Centres throughout the nation are expected to bring in about $35 million in membership sales alone. And the high-tech dating system is growing phenomenally, according to Ullman, who plans to have 8 more franchises operating by the end of this year. His plans for expansion aren't confined to the U.S., either—the Orient, Australia, and Europe have all expressed an interest in dating, video-style.

Though Great Expectations has never advertised for franchises, Ullman says he receives some two dozen inquiries about franchising every week. Some potential franchisees have heard about the company through the media, while others have been running mom-and-pop matchmaking services that failed.

Keeping up with the business's growth and building credibility for video dating are the two biggest challenges Ullman faces in this business. But the love and profits he's received from the venture have far surpassed Ullman's own great expectations. ■

Information is Power

Introduction by Bonnie Knutson

There's a story about Marshall Field, the great retail pioneer. It goes: In the early days of his Chicago department store, a young newspaper reporter supposedly asked Mr. Field, "Sir, why is it that your store is so successful?" To which Mr. Field replied, "It's simple, my good lad. I ask the lady what she wants and then I sell it to her."

In today's jargon, "asking the lady" is market research. Successful marketers ask questions. They constantly conduct market research -- by themselves and/or using outside professional help. Because once they know what consumers need, want, and expect, marketers have a better chance of developing a product consumers will buy, at the price consumers will pay, and promoting it in a way that will get consumers' attention. In other words, they have a better chance of turning consumers into customers.

Bill Gillespie shows how you can use guest surveys to "ask the lady" and learn more about your customers in "Do-It-Yourself Research". He also shows how to get market information in other less-traditional ways.

Knowing what questions to ask and how to ask them are important vehicles in developing your power of information. Bonnie Knutson's "Guide to Questionnaire Construction" and "The $64,000 Question" will give you some of these tools.

Analysis of market research is also used to identify the needs of various market segments. Knutson's "Profile of the Frequent Traveler..." demonstrates the use of research to discover the differences among the economy, mid-price and luxury-hotel segments.

All research must, however, be viewed in the framework of the overall picture of today's and tomorrow's marketplace. This picture is aptly painted in "31 Major Trends Shaping the Future of American Business."

DO-IT-YOURSELF
RESEARCH

Guest surveys are an excellent, inexpensive way to learn about your customers.

BY BILL GILLESPIE

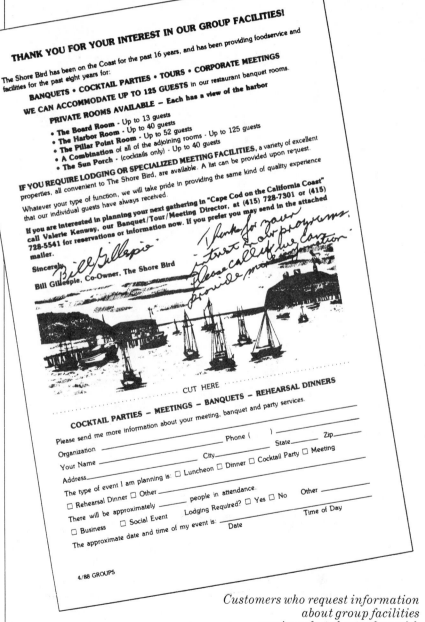

THANK YOU FOR YOUR INTEREST IN OUR GROUP FACILITIES!

The Shore Bird has been on the Coast for the past 16 years, and has been providing foodservice and facilities for the past eight years for:

BANQUETS • COCKTAIL PARTIES • TOURS • CORPORATE MEETINGS

WE CAN ACCOMMODATE UP TO 125 GUESTS in our restaurant banquet rooms.

PRIVATE ROOMS AVAILABLE – Each has a view of the harbor

• **The Board Room** - Up to 13 guests
• **The Harbor Room** - Up to 40 guests
• **The Pillar Point Room** - Up to 52 guests
• **A Combination** of all of the adjoining rooms - Up to 125 guests
• **The Sun Porch** - (cocktails only) - Up to 40 guests

IF YOU REQUIRE LODGING OR SPECIALIZED MEETING FACILITIES, a variety of excellent properties, all convenient to The Shore Bird, are available. A list can be provided upon request.

Whatever your type of function, we will take pride in providing the same kind of quality experience that our individual guests have always received.

If you are interested in planning your next gathering in "Cape Cod on the California Coast" call Valerie Kenway, our Banquet/Tour/Meeting Director, at (415) 728-7301 or (415) 728-5541 for reservations or information now. If you prefer you may send in the attached mailer.

Sincerely,

Bill Gillespie

Bill Gillespie, Co-Owner, The Shore Bird

Thanks for your interest in our programs. Please call if we can provide more information.

CUT HERE

COCKTAIL PARTIES – MEETINGS – BANQUETS – REHEARSAL DINNERS

Please send me more information about your meeting, banquet and party services.

Organization _____ Phone (___) _____

Your Name _____ City _____ State ___ Zip ___

Address _____

The type of event I am planning is: ☐ Luncheon ☐ Dinner ☐ Cocktail Party ☐ Meeting
☐ Rehearsal Dinner ☐ Other _____

There will be approximately _____ people in attendance.

☐ Business ☐ Social Event Lodging Required? ☐ Yes ☐ No Other _____

The approximate date and time of my event is: Date _____ Time of Day _____

4/88 GROUPS

Customers who request information about group facilities receive a fact sheet, often with a handwritten note.

Contrary to popular opinion, effective market research need not be complicated or expensive. There are some techniques that are well within the capabilities of even the smallest operations. One of our favorite methods is in-house guest surveys. In addition to identifying first-time guests, such surveys address an often overlooked, but extremely important source of extra business: your established customer base. Most successful operators and managers have a "feel" for who their guests are and why they return, but even in the best of operations there is room for improvement.

The Shore Bird, with 140 dining room seats and another 100 in the lounge, will generate $2.5 million to $2.6 million in sales this year, on an average check of $12.90 at lunch and $19.25 at dinner. Our goals have been quite specific with regard to the consumer-research program. Although we have used surveys periodically since we first opened in 1973, the current one has become the longest running and most productive of all. Our current survey was begun with the following purposes in mind:

• To develop a market profile on a continuing basis.

• To solicit both positive and negative customer feedback.

• To "sell" additional products and services, such as banquets, to our existing market.

• To increase our in-house mailing lists.

Our current survey was begun in October 1985, and has operated continuously since then. The survey forms are given to each table with the check, every day, at every meal. The completed forms are batched by day, date, and meal, and processing of these forms begins almost immediately. The end result is a continuing picture of how many new guests have discovered us and why, how often our regulars visit us, what they like best and least about us, and where they live.

GUEST FEEDBACK. The first information extracted from the surveys is guest feedback. We are, of course, very concerned with negative comments, but positive ones are of importance as well, especially in evaluating a particular server, menu item, or policy. All comments are copied, batched by day and meal, and circulated to all owners and managers for discussion and action at our weekly management meetings.

All serious complaints are responded to immediately, by telephone, a note, or in really bad cases, a certificate for free meals. The positive responses, especially those about service, are noted and copied to the respective employee's personnel file. Over the years, this kind of feedback has been of great assistance in planning changes within our operation, as well as pinpointing and rewarding the best employees in our organization. Guest response to our rapid follow-up on their complaints has been excellent, and has definitely "saved" many of them.

The "product" that we are currently promoting on the surveys is banquets. To this end, we have a place on the form where guests can request information about our banquet program. The next step in processing is to sort out all of these banquet leads and to follow up on them. Our response letter is preprinted because of the volume involved, but it does allow for a handwritten signature and personal note to be added.

In addition to basic information about capacities, descriptions of our banquet rooms, and the events that we specialize in, there is also a reply card that can be returned to us for more specific details and reservations. We currently respond to an average of 450 of these leads per month. For higher-volume mailings, the names and addresses are typed onto special computer cards and added to current mailing lists.

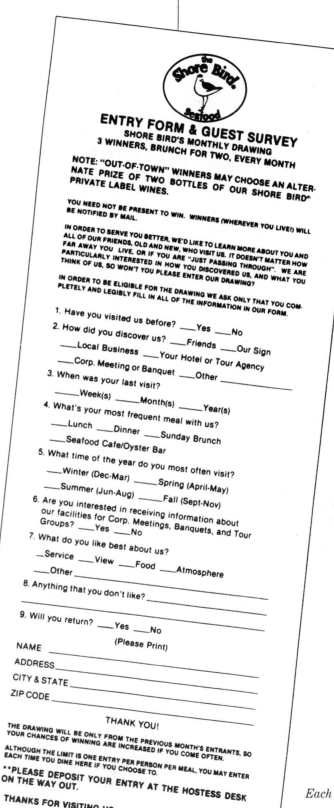

Each customer is given a comprehensive survey to fill out when the bill is presented.

Thank You For Visiting Us!

It has been brought to my attention that you recently had your first visit to the Shorebird.

My partners and I are delighted that you decided to come to see us and we hope that your first experience was a pleasant one.

We have operated the Shorebird since 1973, and we take great pride in the fact that most of our guests are "repeat customers" who come from all over Northern California. Many have been dining here since we first opened.

Because we have always worked hard to provide the best possible dining experience for everyone who visits us, we are also proud of the fact that the vast majority of our guests return because of our food and service, not just our location or ambience.

We hope that you will return soon, and perhaps even bring along a special friend to "discover" us.

My partners and I look forward to your next visit.

Sincerely,

Bill Gillespie — Dear Mr Jones!
Thank you for your visit!

Bill Gillespie, Rob Buckley, Nick Dunn, & Bill Main

Please return soon!

12/87

To maintain contact, preprinted, personalized thank-you notes are sent to new customers.

Mailing lists are, of course, one of the most valuable by-products of our guest-survey program. The completed forms are separated into *return guests* and *new guests* categories and tallied, usually by the serving staff during slow periods. The new guests are then sorted for duplicates, while members of a single family are combined under one address.

A thank-you note—preprinted but personalized as much as possible with handwritten signature and handwritten address—is sent to each new address. In cases where new local residents are involved, we usually add an additional personal note at the bottom to welcome them to the community.

Obviously, the thank-you note can be even more effective and impressive if the entire note can be handwritten, or, better still, be handled through a personal telephone call. If, however, you are dealing with too large a volume or too little time, try at least to add a few personal touches to your notes, even if it is only your signature. We average about 1,000 new customers per month who respond to our surveys, but we do try to personalize the response as much as possible.

Again, don't forget how important it is to follow up with a note or call, especially to acknowledge a complaint, as soon as possible after that first visit. If you can get a customer to return quickly, your chances of developing another loyal regular are excellent. Needless to say, anyone would have to be favorably impressed with a foodservice operation that took the time to thank them for coming in.

MAINTAINING CONTACT. Armed with names and addresses, you can continue to maintain contact with your guests on a regular basis. Instead of having to rely on customers to remember you on their own, you can periodically remind them about returning. Remaining in contact with everyone who comes through your door gives you a decided edge on your competition. Suggestive selling via newsletters or other mailers will bring customers back more often and fuel word-of-mouth recommendations.

Although there is a wide range of computerized address list programs, I prefer to keep my system as simple as possible. All addresses are on computer-sized cards that are easy to use in a typewriter, and easy to sort. They can then be fed through a computer at a local mailing services company to produce labels or listings as you need them. If you have a small operation, you would be smart to keep things simple, at least until you get a good feel for your survey program.

The size of your operation, your available resources (including time as well as money), and what you specifically want to gain from a survey will determine how you approach such a program.

Before instituting an in-house survey, be sure to plan your approach

It is extremely important to process surveys in a timely fashion, and to respond to customer feedback with a call or letter.

carefully and thoroughly.

1) Decide what you want to find out about your market.

2) Decide what you want to "sell" on the survey.

3) Keep the form simple and easy to fill in.

4) Control the handling of completed forms to ensure that all comments, including negative ones, will get to you. A drop slot at the front door is a good solution.

5) Provide a real incentive to complete the survey form. We use a monthly drawing for three prizes of a champagne brunch for two. For out-of-town guests, the prizes are specialty items that we can mail to them.

Use the survey to encourage more frequent repeat business by scheduling frequent drawings and allowing as many entries as possible during each drawing period. This requires additional processing time when tallying the forms, but should be justified by the extra business produced.

Be certain that the prize drawings are held on time, as promised. We post the winners' names and hometown cities (never full addresses) next to the drop box at the front. Our regulars, especially, appreciate this.

6) Design your survey form so that it is simple to process when complete. You can then use your staff whenever possible, to sort and tally the forms during "slow times" on shift.

7) Use the survey to inform the guests of special services or products, as well as to gain information from them.

8) Continue to review and revise the format as your objectives change.

9) Don't ever "sell" your address list to someone else unless you have made it perfectly clear on the form that you will do so. Most guests won't mind *your* use of their addresses, and in fact most will assume that their names will be used this way. If you have additional users in mind, however, avoid potential problems and give the guest the option to decline such use of their address.

10) Finally, be prepared to process and use your data on a timely basis. For example, immediate follow-up on complaints or requests for information, or to thank new guests for their patronage, is essential in order to get maximum value out of your efforts. "Months later" doesn't count.

THE SIMPLE APPROACH. There are, of course, some drawbacks to such a simple approach.

The surveys and resultant data are not "scientific." They are useful for basic information, but any detailed analyses and results would be skewed by potential errors in tallying, duplication of entries, varying response rates per meal and according to server, and so forth. It is a good idea, by the way, to keep a record of responses as a percentage of the total number of covers, in order to keep the information as accurate as possible. Although our response rate varies widely, from 2% of covers to 63%, depending on such factors as volume, night of the week, and season, we are able to generate an *average* response rate of about 20%.

There is some lack of control over the completed forms, especially the ones with negative server comments. Even though we instruct the guest to deposit the form in a special box on the way out, many of these are left on the table and, I suspect, are "deep-sixed" by the offending server. The box does offer an anonymous way for the guest to complain if he uses it, but a cashier could also help to eliminate the problem by simply accepting the form along with payment of the check.

Unless closely monitored, the staff will sometimes neglect to hand out the survey forms, especially if they are busy. As a result, figures on some of your busiest and most important meals may be seriously distorted. Monitoring the percentage of responses versus actual covers will alert you to this problem. I also have a supervisor list the names of the servers on each shift so I can follow up on any poor response.

The best way to insure uniform distribution of the forms is to have the cashier or a floor manager monitor the program at all times. There is a natural loss of momentum in every long-running program, so monitoring would be essential in any case, no matter how good the servers are.

No matter how simple the form, surveys can be annoying and intrusive, especially for regulars, if not handled correctly. We simply present the form with the check, and provide a brief explanation if necessary.

Whether you computerize the process or not, a certain amount of handling of the forms is unavoidable in sorting out duplicates and illegible addresses, as well as in tallying the information. Keep it simple and let the staff do as much as possible during slow periods.

Finally, there is a tendency to allow unprocessed surveys to pile up, especially during busy periods. Timely processing is a must, however, if you are to obtain maximum value from your information. Although tallying of some information can be delayed for a while, follow-up with new guests, product/service leads, and reponse to guest feedback should occur as quickly as possible. If you delay too long, you will be buried in useless information, which will effectively negate your efforts.

Remember, there is no substitute for the presence of the owner or manager out front, walking and talking with guests and the staff. Surveys or any other kind of market research serve to supplement, not replace, the basic knowledge gained from years of experience, and can, if handled properly, be valuable tools.

Market research is an extremely valuable tool when it is used correctly. And not all market research is complicated or expensive: If you are seeking simple, straightforward information, just ask your customer! ▨

Bill Gillespie is a founder and co-owner of The Shore Bird, a multi-million dollar dinner house located in Half Moon Bay, CA. The material for his article was assembled from actual customer surveys in use at the restaurant.

A Guide To Questionnaire Construction
Bonnie J. Knutson, Ph.D.

Anyone who has ever worked with a computer knows ... "garbage in; garbage out." It's the same with market research. If you don't ask the right questions, in the right way, you don't get the right [translate: accurate, valid, meaningful, helpful] answers on which to base sound [translate: profitable] marketing decisions.

In market research, surveys are probably the most used and most abused means of getting primary data. They're the most used because they are a very flexible method of getting information about behaviors and attitudes of people. They're the most abused because many surveys are conducted where questions are biased or poorly stated, where interviewers are poorly trained, or the sample being interviewed is not representative of the market.

Regardless of what survey method you use -- telephone, self-administered [such as mail or comment cards], personal -- some type of a questionnaire has to be developed. What follows, then, is a concise step-by-step guide to producing a good questionnaire.

Step 1 - <u>Know what you need to know</u>.

One of the saddest things I hear is, "I wish I had asked..." Once the telephone interviews are conducted or the questionnaires are mailed out, it's too late to reword a question or include another question. So <u>before</u> you sit down to write the questionnaire, ask yourself...

> * What am I going to do with the information;
> i.e. what market or marketing decisions am I going to make after I do the research?

> * What information do I need to make these decisions?

You may be a hotel manager thinking about adding a complimentary continental breakfast for guests. So you need to know things like how often people eat breakfast when they're on the road? What do they usually eat? How much more, if any, would they be willing to pay for a room if breakfast were included? Would the perceived value of staying in your hotel go up? Et cetera.

If you first make a list of the specific information you need to meet your survey objectives, it will be much easier to decide what questions you have to include and how to phrase them.

Next, ask yourself...

> * How are you going to analyze the data?

Simple frequencies? Crosstabulations? Or more high powered statistical tests such as chi-squares, multiple regression or factor analysis? Too many times, people don't think about these issues ahead of time. So they don't get the data in a form that's suitable for the analytical technique they want to use. Remember, answering these questions <u>before</u> will save you from "I wish I had..." after.

Step 2 - Find the best survey method for your research.

Telephone. Mail. Face-to-Face. There is no one best interview method. The best one is the one which "works" best for you in a particular research situation.

A Brief Comparison Of The Three Survey Methods

	Mail	Telephone	Personal
Handle complex questions	Poor	Fair	Good
Collect large amount of data	Poor	Fair	Good
Control effect of interviewer	Good	Fair	Poor
Control effect of respondent	Good	Fair	Fair
Degree of sample control	Poor	Good	Good
Time required to administer	Poor	Good	Fair
Probable response rate	Poor	Good	Fair
Cost/survey	Poor	Good	Fair

Deciding which method to use is tied to the type of information you need, who you are going to survey and how much time and money you are willing to spend on the research.

* Information -- Can the information be obtained through a traditional, structured questionnaire or should it be a more open, unstructured, in-depth questioning process?

*   Who and Where -- Who will you survey and where are they located? The geographical scope, their accessibility and willingness to participate all have to be considered.

*   Cost and Time -- What you would like to do may differ greatly from what you are able to do because of cost. You may want to conduct in-depth personal interviews with meeting planners of a number of large firms but can't afford the necessary travel expenses. Time is also a crucial factor since the data may have to be obtained within the week. In this case, you may opt for telephone interviews.

Step 3 - Decide on the general types of questions.

When you do research, you are asking people to give you two of their most valuable possessions. Their time and their opinions. So don't waste space with questions that would be "fun" to know but won't help you make your marketing decisions.[1] Make sure that every question carries its weight. Suppose, for example, you are planning an advertising campaign to promote your newly added "Express Business Lunch". You would want to ask respondents about their radio listening habits while on the way to work in the morning. But if you're wondering whether you will sell more desserts if

---

[1] The exception would be in a situation where a seemingly useless question is included at the beginning of a questionnaire for the sole purpose of enticing people to participate.

you used a cart, a tray, or a special menu, don't waste valuable survey space with radio questions.

Remember, too, you can only get meaningful answers if the questions you ask are within a person's memorable experiences. "Which appetizer do you like most -- chilled shrimp, oysters on the half shell, or caviar?" If the person has never had to opportunity to taste, let alone order, caviar, the question is out of his experience and his answer won't be valid. Also, an event may have happened so long ago that the accuracy of the answer is limited. "What was the first drive-thru you ever went to?" Who remembers?

Don't include questions that take a lot of effort on the part of the respondent to answer. Suppose you asked a banquet manager, "What was the sales volume, in numbers and dollars, of your catering department in 1980?" One look at this question, and the manager would probably throw the questionnaire away or at least skip that particular item before he spends the time searching the files for the correct answer. Remember that the people you survey are doing you a favor by giving you their time and opinions. Make it easy for them to do so.

Step 4 - <u>Choose your words carefully</u>.

Use the KISS Principle in writing any question.[2]

---

[2]KISS is an acronym for "Keep it simple, stupid."

*   Use easily understood language.[3]   Use feel not perceive. Menu not Bill of Fare. Attractive not enchanting.

*   Ask one question at a time. "How would you rate our food and beverage?" The food might be great but the beverages awful. How would a respondent be able to answer accurately?

*   Be explicit. For instance, "What brand of cola do you buy?" might confuse the respondent. Does the question mean "buy regularly" or "buy occasionally"?

*   Don't be biased. In other words, don't phrase your question in such a way that you "suggest" the "correct" answer. It might get you the answer you want but it won't you an true answer. Recall that garbage in gives you garbage out.

*   Open-ended, multiple-choice or dichotomous. Again, which type question you use depends on many factors. And each type has advantages/ disadvantages. These benefits and shortcoming are too long to detail in this brief guide, but they are clearly spelled out in most research texts.

I have included, however, a list of categories which can be used in to measure degrees in some multiple-choice questions. They are shown on the following page. These categories are tried and true through years of

_____

[3]If the survey is going to a specific group such as engineers, attorneys or accountants, the language can be more technical.

research use. If possible, use them instead of trying to develop your own.
Why reinvent the wheel?

Step 5 - <u>Order of the questions</u>

The opening questions are like an invitation. They attract attention and set the tone for what follows. Therefore, the first few questions should be interesting and fairly easy to answer. "In an average week, about how many times do you buy your lunch at a fast food restaurant?" is an example. Place the stuff you really want to know -- the more "meaty" questions -- in the body. These are usually more difficult or sensitive and might take some thought to answer. The final section contains the socio-demographic and classification questions. These questions are of lesser importance and people are sometimes touchy about such things as their age or income. If they become "turned off" by these questions and choose not to answer any more, you will not have lost data on the important issues.

Naturally, the questions should be in a logical order, and this means logical to the respondents. Does the questionnaire flow smoothly from one question to another; from one section to another? Are all questions about similar subjects grouped together? Have you "introduced" each section? Using a brief introduction for each section is like a roadmap; it lets the respondent know where he or she is going.

Measurement Categories For Rating Scales

Quality

Excellent	Very	Good	Fair	Poor
		Good		

Excellent		Good	Fair		Poor

A	B	C	D	F

Importance

Very		Somewhat		Not At All
Important		Important	Important	

Very	Fairly	Neutral	Not So	Not At All Important	Important
	Important	Important			

Interest

Very		Somewhat		Not At All
Interested		Interested		Interested

Satisfaction

Very	Quite		Somewhat		Not At All
Satisfied	Satisfied		Satisfied		Satisfied

Very		Neither	Dis-	Very Dis-
Satisfied	Satisfied	Satisfied	Satisfied	Satisfied
			Nor Dis-	
			Satisfied	

Frequency

Always	Often	Sometimes	Rarely	Never

All Of	Most Of	Some Of	Just Now
The Time	The Time	The Time	And Then

Truth

Very	Somewhat	Not Very	Not At All
True	True	True	True

Agreement

| Strongly Agree | Agree | Neutral | Disagree | Strongly Disagree |

Step 6 - <u>Maximize the questionnaire's appeal and use.</u>

"The eye buys what the eye sees." So make sure your questionnaire is laid out in such a way that it is easy for either the interviewer (telephone or face-to-face) or the interviewee (mail, comment cards) to follow the sequence of the questions. This is especially important with self-administered questionnaires.

Many of the rules which apply to menu design apply here. Use a lot of white space. Use at least 14-point type. Stick with lower-case letters, using capital letters only as you would in regular grammar -- i.e. beginning a sentence, proper name, etc. Italics, bold type, and underlining will emphasize a word or phrase, but use them sparingly! And don't use them to bias a question.

Step 7 - <u>Pretest! Pretest! Pretest!</u>

I can't emphasize pretesting strongly enough. A pretest will check whether the ideas in each question are clear to the respondent. It may show that some questions should be reworded, or in the case of multiple-choice questions, different or additional alternatives may have to be included. The pretest will also let you know whether the questionnaire flows as logically for the respondents as you think it does.

And, of course, the people interviewed (a sample of 30 will due) in the pretest have to be similar to those who will be included in the final project.

It does no good to pretest with 30 college students when you plan to survey the "mature market."

When no further revisions are needed, the questionnaire can be structured, printed and put into the field. Now, you're asking the right question, in the right way to get the right [translate: accurate, valid, meaningful, helpful] answers on which to base sound [translate: profitable] marketing decisions.

A Caveat

The steps involved in developing questionnaires were each described very briefly. Developing a good questionnaire is actually a very difficult and time consuming task. There are entire chapters and whole books written on "how to..." You may want to refer to them for more complete directions in writing a questionnaire.

A Postscript

You know who you want to survey and you know how you want to survey. Your task now is deciding how large the sample should be. While there are many factors to consider in deciding how many people you need to survey, a you can use the SAMPLE SIZE CALCULATOR shown on the next page for a "rule of thumb" estimate.[1] To use the calculator:

> Scale A - is graduated proportionally to the percent of favorable responses received (or expected) in a sampling survey. Values from 1% to 50% are graduated on the left side of this scale, and values from 50% to 99% are graduated on the right side of the scale.

> Scale B - is graduated proportionally to sample sizes ranging from 30 to 10,000.

> Scale C - is graduated proportionally to the sampling error (+ or -) in the percent of favorable responses. Graduation on the left side of this scale are for 95% probability of being correct (i.e. 95% confidence), and graduations on the right side of the scale are for 99.7% confidence.

To use the chart, lay a straightedge to connect known values on any two of the scales. Read the unknown value where the straightedge intersects the third scale. You can use the chart to determine proper sample size from an expected favorable response rate and desired maximum error level; or determine expected (or actual) error levels with an expected (or actual) favorable response rate and a given sample size. Note: If you do not have an expected favorable response rate, you will have to assume a 50-50 probability.

---

[1] The SAMPLE SIZE CALCULATOR is reprinted from Marketing Problem Solver by Kenneth Barasch and originally published by Cochrane Chase & Company.

SAMPLE SIZE CALCULATOR

An easy method of obtaining approximate answers to a variety of sampling problems.

To use the chart, lay a straightedge to connect known values on any two of the scales. Read the unknown value where the straightedge intersects the third scale.

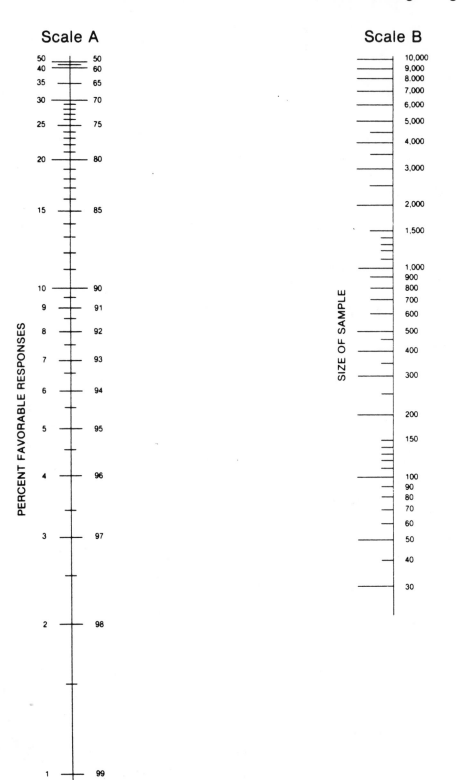

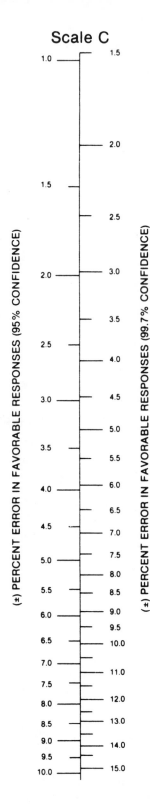

THE $64,000 QUESTION:
JUST WHO IS MY COMPETITION?

Bonnie J. Knutson, Ph.D.
School of Hotel, Restaurant and Institutional Management
Michigan State University

Today, it's "Wheel of Fortune" and "Jeopardy". It seems like almost everyone wants to spin that wheel or learn to talk in "jeopardize". In the earlier days of television, the game show of interest was "The $64,000 Question." Then, people dreamed about the opportunity to climb into a soundproof box, listen to the clock tick away the allotted time, and then, just as the final seconds sounded, confidently give the correct answer to the BIG question.

No matter how game show formats might change over time, the design remains the same: If you answer the question correctly, you win a prize. There's a strong correlation between this game show design and doing business today -- especially as it relates to identifying your competition. If you can answer the BIG question, you can win the prize! And the BIG question is: Who really is your competition? The prize, of course, is increased sales and increased profits.

Unfortunately, many managers and owners don't know who their competition actually is. Oh, they confidently give you an answer when you ask them. But, more often than not, that answer is not correct or only partially correct. Why? Because the company or companies which management identify as competitors are identified from management's perspective, not from the perspective of the only people who truly know who the answer; that is, customers!

A case in point: A seafood restaurant company had seven units in the Detroit area. When I began working with them to develop a new three year marketing plan, one of my first questions to management was, naturally, "Who is your competition?"

Their reply came quickly and confidently. "On, that's easy. We're up against 'The River Crab,' 'The Golden Mushroom,' and places like that." "Are you sure?" I asked. "Oh yeah. Our competitors are all the fine dining seafood restaurants in town."

When we asked their customers (through market research studies), however, the answer to the competition question was quite different. To them, the competition was NOT " 'The River Crab,' 'The Golden Mushroom,' and places like that". It was Red Lobster!

Red Lobster? For years, this restaurant company had been planning, strategizing and marketing under a wrong premise. All the resources (financial, time, personnel) which they targeted against the competition were targeted against the wrong enemy; the "troops and artillery" were not aimed in the right direction. They weren't as effective as they should have been. And while the overall business was profitable, how much higher could the bottom line have been if its decisions had been based on the reality of the customers' perception rather than illusion of management's perception.

Unfortunately, this scenario is duplicated in far too many companies. Banks. Furniture. Office Supply. Tool and Die. You name it. No industry is immune to this potential gap between management perspective and customer perception. If the customer is always right, and you, as owner or manager, don't see exactly what your customer sees, then you are always wrong. It's as simple as that. Perception is Reality! If your customer believes your prices are too high, then they are too high (even though your prices are the same as everyone else's). If your customer believes your salespeople aren't attentive, then the salespeople aren't attentive (so what if they shower your customer with telephone calls, follow-up meetings and lunches). And if the customers of the Detroit seafood restaurant believe the competition is Red Lobster, then the competition is Red Lobster. Perception is Reality!

The only way management can find out who the competition really is to ask the customers. While a full market research study can give you a myriad of valuable in-depth information about your business and/or its competition, there is a an easy way for you to immediately begin to identify your competitors. And that is, the next time you or your employees are talking with your customers (or potential customers), ask then the business version of The $64,000 Question:

IF YOU HADN'T COME HERE TODAY (OR BOUGHT PRODUCT "X" FROM US), WHERE WOULD YOU HAVE GONE (OR BOUGHT IT)?

Then, follow with:

WHY?

The first part of this question will identify who your customer sees as the top-of-mind alternative to purchasing from you. It will identify your major competitor(s). Visualize a group of ladders in your customer's mind. Each ladder represents a different product category -- for example, seafood restaurants in the Detroit area. Each rung represents places where your customer believes he/she can go to buy that particular product - "The River Crab," "The Golden Mushroom," "Red Lobster," or your restaurant. When you ask your customers where they would have gone if they hadn't come to you, they name the place which, in their minds, is on the rung closest to you; i.e. who they think of as your competition. And, Perception is Reality!

A company may, of course, have several major competitors depending on product line and market segment. Stratifying your customers' answers along these dimensions will give you a clearer picture of who you are really up against in each category.

Customers' responses to the second part of business's $64,000 Question -- the "WHY" part -- will tell you what your customers see as your competitors' strength(s). In the Detroit restaurant case, Red Lobster's strengths were seen as a place for which you could dress casually and a wide variety of foods on the menu. Once you know, then, what your competition's perceived good points are, it's easier to develop effective operational and/or marketing strategies positioning you as the best solution to your customer's (and potential customer's) needs.

In the increasingly competitive business environment of the '90s, management can't afford to use the shotgun method of marketing. Even the rifle approach is becoming obsolete. Tomorrow's successful companies will be using a laser technique to better aim their product and message at their customers' needs, wants and expectations. Knowing who your competitors really are is a necessary component of successfully, and profitably, hitting your target markets.

PROFILE OF THE FREQUENT TRAVELER:
PERCEPTIONS OF THE ECONOMY, MID-PRICE AND LUXURY SEGMENTS[1]

Bonnie J. Knutson
School of Hotel, Restaurant and Institutional Management
Michigan State University

When preparing to write this article, two adages kept popping into my mind. The first is often credited to Marshall Field, a pioneer in the retail industry. The story goes that, when someone asked him to what he attributed the great success of his Chicago department store, he replied, "Simple. I ask the lady what she wants and then I sell it to her."

The other adage tells us that "80 percent of our business comes from 20 percent of our customers." While this statement certainly doesn't imply that we can or do ignore the 80 percent of our customers who provide us with the other 20 percent of our business, it does help focus our attention on those who contribute most to our sales.

It makes sense, then, that in an increasingly competitive industry like the lodging industry, hotel managers should ask their regular customers -- i.e. frequent travelers -- just what they really do want in the way of hotel facilities, services and room amenities.....and then sell it to them! Peters and Waterman summed it up well in their 1982 best seller, In Search of Excellence, by reminding us that the excellent -- and successful -- companies anticipate then satisfy or exceed their customers' wants and expectations.[2] They "stay close to their customers."

In this article, I'll share with you the results of a recent national research project specifically designed to "stay close to" frequent travelers.

Because the hotel industry has three major segments -- economy, mid-price, and luxury -- the intent of the study was to look at travelers who predominantly stay in each.[3]   Two major questions of interest to hotel managers and operators were addressed. First, what are the reasons people select a hotel in the first place, or go back? More importantly, what makes them decide not to return to a hotel?   Secondly, when guests stay in a hotel, what services do they expected and use? Similarly, what personal care items/room amenities do they expect and use? The answers given by the frequent travelers suggest several opportunities for property management to increase guest satisfaction in lodging facilities across all price levels.

"BIRDS OF A FEATHER FLOCK TOGETHER"

As highlighted in Exhibit 1, frequent travelers do not necessarily limit their stays to one price category of hotels. Mid-price travelers display the greatest degree of loyalty to their segment, spending seven out of ten nights away from home in mid-price lodging properties. On the other hand, those primarily using luxury or economy hotels tend to move among the three segments more, spending less than six out of ten nights in their respective lodging categories.

The average room rates paid by both business and pleasure travelers correlate to the three hotel price segments, and, nearly doubles in each case, rising from an economy $31 to a mid-price $53 then to a luxury $93 for business travelers and from $32 to $54 to a high of $101 for pleasure travelers.

Further, frequent travelers generally spend more nights in a hotel room when they travel for vacation or other pleasure reasons than when travelling on business -- with economy and mid-price travelers averaging two additional nights while luxury travelers average one additional night.

EXHIBIT 1
Important considerations in initial hotel selection

	Business Travelers		
	Economy	Midprice	Luxury
Clean/Comfortable Room	92%	92%	92%
Convenient Location	87	91	92
Safety & Security	79	82	80
Prompt, Courteous Service	78	83	85
Friendliness	69	69	73
Room Rates	72	57	**

	Pleasure Travelers		
	Economy	Midprice	Luxury
Clean, Comfortable Rooms	91%	91%	96%
Safety & Security	85	90	89
Room Rates	83	81	65
Prompt, Courteous Service	77	85	89
Convenient Location	75	80	78
Friendliness	71	79	82
Recreation Facilities	**	50	56

**Cited by fewer than 50 percent of respondents.

EXHIBIT 2
Important considerations in a return hotel selection

	Business Travelers		
	Economy	Midprice	Luxury
Clean Room	91%	93%	94%
Comfortable Room	90	92	93
Convenient Location	86	89	89
Safety and Security	81	84	84
Prompt, Courteous Service	80	86	88
Friendliness, Hospitality	79	80	82
Room Rates	74	60	**
Staff Makes You Feel Special	59	60	64

	Pleasure Travelers		
	Economy	Midprice	Luxury
Clean Room	95%	96%	96%
Comfortable Room	93	95	95
Safety and Security	90	90	90
Room Rates	83	78	68
Friendliness, Hospitality	79	86	86
Convenient Location	79	79	74
Prompt, Courteous Service	77	86	86
Staff Makes You Feel Special	60	68	72
Recreation Facilities	**	51	56

**Cited by fewer than 50 percent of respondents.

"DECISIONS, DECISIONS, DECISIONS"

Where Will I Stay?

Exhibits 2 and 3 reveal that, regardless of hotel segment, frequent travelers give the same reasons for initially selecting or returning to a hotel:

* Clean, comfortable, well-maintained rooms
* Convenient location
* Prompt and courteous service
* Safe and secure environment
* Friendly and courteous employees

In addition to citing convenient location, approximately two out of five business travelers also look for the availability of meeting/convention facilities.[1] On the other hand, recreational facilities were named as important considerations by the pleasure groups.

Of particular note is the importance guests place on safety and security. While a significant consideration to all groups, how safe travelers believe they will be is especially critical to persons selection a property for leisure travel. It may be suggested that this additional concern stems from the fact that pleasure trips usually involve family and most of us have a heightened sensitivity of what might occur around us when our families are involved.

Survey findings indicate that, overall, room rates become less important as frequent travelers tend to stay in higher priced hotel properties. This may be due, in part, to the fact that business travelers staying in luxury hotels are assumed to have more generous expense accounts than those

EXHIBIT 3
Most frequent reasons given for not returning to a hotel

	Economy	Midprice	Luxury
Room Not Clean	56%	41%	—
Poor Maintenance, Repair	54	45	23%
Do Not Feel Safe, Secure	45	—	—
Poor Temperature Control	43	37	—
Too Noisy	43	38	24
Uncomfortable Bed, Room	—	32	—
High Room Rates	—	—	33
Unfriendly, Discourteous Staff	—	—	28
Slow Service	—	—	26

*Responses are from business and leisure travelers who indicated that, during the past year, they had stayed in a hotel to which they would not return: economy travelers: 53% (n = 379); midprice travelers: 52% (n = 667); luxury travelers: 54% (n = 496).

EXHIBIT 4
Expectations and use of hotel services and amenities

	All Travelers					
	Economy		Midprice		Luxury	
	(E)	(U)	(E)	(U)	(E)	(U)
Bar of Soap	95%	94%	95%	94%	96%	95%
Two + Bath Towels	52	83	80	85	96	88
Wake-Up Call	70	75	91	79	95	83
Direct-Dial Phone	60	79	87	84	95	90
Personal-Care Items	13	68	61	77	95	85
Room Service	11	42	73	52	93	63
Swimming Pool	39	64	83	65	92	67
Free A.M. Newspaper	8	58	39	65	90	77
Cocktail Lounge, Bar	8	45	73	53	88	60
Check Cashing	24	37	64	39	87	43
Valet Dry Cleaning	*	*	34	27	87	36
Exercise, Health Room	*	*	32	32	83	39
Turn Down Bed	*	*	13	32	83	45
Pay, Cable TV	49	67	76	66	81	67
Valet Parking	*	*	9	22	80	33
Concierge	*	*	12	23	77	35
In-Room Refrigerator	5	41	27	47	74	55
VIP Floors	*	*	6	12	73	19
VIP Kit	*	*	8	23	73	30
Complimentary Breakfast	11	52	42	54	71	59
Tennis Courts	*	*	15	13	70	17
Complimentary Happy Hour	*	*	31	36	66	38
Fresh Flowers in Room	*	*	*	*	64	25
Bathrobe	*	*	*	*	63	26
Secretarial Services	*	*	*	*	61	7
In-Room Coffee Maker	24	45	46	47	54	46
Game, Video Room	14	0	45	14	45	12
Iron, Ironing Board	6	12	19	17	42	20
Coin Laundry	26	22	48	19	32	14

E = Expected; U = Used

staying in lower priced properties. The pleasure travelers selecting luxury properties may be thought to have higher household incomes, in general, and more discretionary income for leisure experiences, in particular.

Pleasure travelers place greater importance on the price they pay for a guest room than do their business counterparts. Because pleasure trips generally come out of the traveler's own pocket rather than being covered by a business expense account, rates would naturally be of greater concern to the pleasure market.

Should I Stay Here Again?

As previously mentioned, in deciding whether to return to a hotel, all groups tended to name the same factors as being significant to them. In general, however, the proportion calling the hotel characteristic important was somewhat larger than for the initial selection process. This supports the belief that personal experiences are a strong influence on developing long term guest loyalty.

I'll Never Come Back Here!

More than half of the frequent travelers in all three segments said that, during the previous year, they had stayed in a hotel to which they would not return.[5] This finding presents an attractive opportunity for guest-oriented properties to capture new business from those hotels which do not

"ask and sell the lady what she wants."

Looking at the reasons given for not returning, shown in Exhibit 4, two overall patterns become evident. First, frequent economy travelers had stronger feelings about why they wouldn't go back to a hotel than did the other two groups. In other words, a higher percentage of travelers who regularly patronize economy hotels indicated more reasons why they would not return. Agreeing with their mid-price counterparts, economy travelers listed unclean and/or poorly maintained guest rooms and facilities as the primary reasons for not returning to a hotel. Those staying a luxury properties, however, named high room rates as the paramount reason for not going back.[6]

Whereas several characteristics were clearly identified as reasons to try and/or return to a hotel, no such clear list emerged when respondents were asked why they would not return to a hotel. In other words, no single strong cause for not going back to a hotel was identified by a large percentage in any of the three markets. This second pattern suggests that the total accumulation of all experiences at the hotel (or hotel chain) is more decisive in building long term guest loyalties than any one individual factor.

"MAKING MY DAY"

Expectation and use of both hotel services and personal care items/room amenities vary by traveler categories. These variations are detailed in Exhibits 5 and 6.

Those staying in economy hotels expect very little in the way of either services or room amenities. However, they do use them far more frequently than their expectation level would suggest. As examples, only one in ten said they expected to have personal care items provided in their economy hotel rooms, but seven out of ten stated they use them when provided; while half expected two or more bath towels, more than four-fifths indicate they use the additional towel.

While varying item by item, overall, travelers staying in mid-price lodging tended to use hotel services and room amenities in a similar proportion to that which they expected mid-price hotels to provide. For instance, more expected shower caps, wake-up calls and pay/cable television than used them. Conversely, more said they would use a complimentary morning newspaper along with a wider assortment of personal care items, notably hand and body lotion, than expect them.

Of 29 hotel services, 26 were expected by more than half of the luxury market; of 18 personal care items, 15 were expected by this same proportion. Although the luxury travelers have these high expectations when it come to the number of service and room amenities offered by top priced hotels, they use them far less frequently. For this affluent market, then, it is important for the hotel to offer the service or amenity whether or not it is used. It is the availability, i.e. the option, which attracts this market.

The overall expectation and use patterns of the three frequent traveler groups, for both hotel services and personal care items, may be characterized as:

	Expectations	Use
Economy	Low	High
Mid-Price	Moderate	Moderate
Luxury	High	Low

It should also be noted that, for travelers within each of the three hotel segments, there was a clear correlation between the type of packaging expected and the hotel price category. Economy travelers only expected the personal care items found in their rooms to be plainly packaged.[7] While the mid-price group expected the personal care items to be packaged in what might be called a moderately fancy wrapping, the luxury segment indicated they expected packaging more comparable to their luxury rooms.

"AND THE WINNERS ARE"

In-depth review of the responses from these 1853 frequent travelers will yield a multitude of possible marketing/operations opportunities for the astute hotel manager. Though it is always necessary to tailor any national research information to the specific needs, wants and expectations of your own guests, several opportunities are clearly available to all hotels. Based upon survey results, then, the following recommendations to increase guest satisfaction (and, in turn, new as well as repeat business) are offered.

For Hotels in All Segments

*Don't Spare The Elbow Grease Cleanliness is definitely Number One in the minds of today's traveler. Therefore, a total commitment by the entire hotel staff to keeping every element of the property spotless is mandatory.

*Test for Lumps, Bumps and Worn Spots A corollary to clean is good repair and maintenance. Encourage everyone from housekeeping to general manager to monitor and report any aspect of the hotel which needs repair or replacement.

*Stress Consistant Attention to Detail in All Aspects of Operations This is crucial to building guest loyalty and repeat business. Guests don't comb back, not because of one overriding factor, but because of the accumulation of little things that go wrong.

*Check Lighting and Locks With the importance placed on safety and security, management must evaluate every dimension of the hotel from the perspective of guest protection. Beyond providing a safe environment as a reason for travelers to stay in your hotel, management also needs to reduce chances for any guest injury and potential litigation.

In addition to these four universal recommendations, findings from the study indicate additional opportunities which are more segment specific. These encompass:

For the Economy Hotel Travelers who predominantly stay in economy properties apparently know they are paying for, and thus only expect, the basic, "no-frills" hotel experiences. Therefore, hotels which offer what their guests perceive as "extras," can only exceed expectations.

*Include Shampoo Not only will the addition of shampoo capitalize on the 1-to-4 Expectation:Use ratio, but it provides the hotel with a chance to send a bit of promotion home. Many economy-minded guests might take the shampoo with them, and, if the small bottle has the hotel's name/logo on it, you've furnished a potential repeat guest with a reminder of your property.

*Add Another Bath Towel If you've ever been on the road and decided to take an "extra" shower, then discovered you have to use that damp bath towel you used the first time because the hotel only put one in your room, you understand the value of a second bath towel. Yet, only half of the economy travelers even expect that additional towel.

*Offer Coffee and a Donut When you pay to stay in one of the 14 properties of a midwestern economy hotel company, you not only get an inviting room and a friendly, helpful staff, but you also get a continental breakfast.[8] In a small area off the main lobby, overnight guests help themselves to a brought-in selection of juice, rolls, milk and coffee. Whether they eat at one of the few small tables available, or take it back to their rooms, the guests love the "free" breakfast. Other economy hotels may not be able to offer this variety, but an urn of piping hot coffee and a selection of donuts can exceed the expectations of nine-tenths of economy travelers.

For Mid-Price Hotels Management in mid-price hotels have an opportunity to capitalize on the basic loyalty these travelers show to their hotel segment by converting the more generalized segment loyalty to a specific hotel (or chain) loyalty. Examples suggested from the research data include:

*Emphasize Service Training Promptness, courtesy and, friendliness are service elements which are very important to mid-price travelers. A hotel whose staff anticipates and/or quickly responds to guests' needs, in a genuine caring manner, can position itself for repeat business. The next story illustrates this point.

A family (mom, dad, and two grade-school children) offered to take two cousins (also grade-school age) along on a recent cross country auto trip. At the end of the second day's driving, the weary sixsome checked into their hotel. A few minutes after they got to their room there was a knock at the door. Opening it, they found Sarah, one of the hotel's housekeepers with an armful of extra towels, soap and shampoo bottles. Smiling broadly, she said, "I was down the hall when I saw you come in with all those kids, so I thought you could use some extras. I have four (children) myself and know how fast they can go through stuff." Sarah's one act of anticipation made two loyal guests...not to mention two good advertisers.

*<u>Increase the Number of Personal Care Items</u> Nearly four out of five mid-price travelers use the personal care items provided by hotels. Those which are used significantly more than they are expected include shampoo, hand and body lotion, complexion soap and hair conditioner.

*<u>Furnish a Complimentary Newspaper</u> Whether placed outside the room door or available in the lobby, providing a complimentary morning newspaper would be a welcome service for at least two-thirds of this mid-price group. As people become more accustomed to reading either a local or a national A.M. newspaper at home, guest appreciation of this additional service can only escalate.[9]

<u>For the Luxury Segment</u> The old maxim that we generally don't miss something until we don't have it seems to be applicable to the luxury group. Travelers opting for top-priced hotels expect almost everything whether or not they ever use it. For managers in this segment, the question is how can you exceed these expectations. The answer is, of course, first meet the expectations then meet them with a unique flair. Survey findings prompt these possibilities:

*Place Fresh Flowers in the Guest Room   Fresh flowers say "you are special" to me. We give flowers for birthdays and anniversaries; we have a centerpiece on our holiday table; we send an arrangement to thank our weekend host and hostess. A simple bud vase with a carnation (long lasting) or two will tell your guest that he/she is special as well as add to the perception of luxury in the guest room.

*Provide In-Room Refrigerator and/or Coffee-Maker   Decoratively incorporating these mini appliances into rooms offers guests both convenience and time. Most travelers enjoy a cup of steaming hot coffee/tea first thing in the morning; many also enjoy a beverage and/or snack before dinner or going to bed at night.   Their addition may also help to competitively position your hotel against the increasingly popular all-suite properties.

*Add Some of the 16 Personal Care Items Expected   Within the list of 16, management can increase the array of amenities provided each guest, based upon the individual characteristics of your particular hotel: sun tan lotion (especially at resort properties), hair dryer or a comb are examples. With the hotel name/logo, a comb (or emery board) taken home will provide a reminder of your hotel for the guest's next visit.

31 Major Trends
Shaping The Future Of American Business

In this special issue of The Public Pulse, *we put forth our forecasts of 31 key trends that will shape the American business environment of the late 1980s. These trends cut across virtually every facet of American society and point to major changes in consumer lifestyles, working habits, public attitudes toward business, and political beliefs. These are the trends with true staying power—the harbingers of the emerging social and economic landscape in which American business will operate. These are not merely changes of degree but significant new departures in the way people look at their lives—and hence the products they buy, the services they use, the work that they do, and the major issues that concern them.*

Time Control

Americans are increasingly placing a premium on their time and seeking greater control over how it is used. They are segmenting their time, allocating it more efficiently, looking for ways to stretch their leisure hours.

The desire for time control is more than just a quest for convenience, although convenience stores, fast foods, microwave ovens, and similar products and services have been prime beneficiaries. More importantly, it reflects a new determination among consumers to tailor daily schedules to *their* needs rather than having schedules *imposed* on them.

This is why the VCR is so enormously popular: program schedules on television are managed by the individual, rather than by the network. The consumer becomes an active viewer, allocating his or her viewing time, instead of being a passive one. It also lies behind the growing use of ATMs: customers are no longer constrained by "bankers' hours." And it is fueling the boom in home shopping.

Because time will be increasingly controlled by individuals and less by outside structures, the nature of work in the "information economy" will change. More and more employees will demand *flexibility*: the organization of their responsibilities around tasks to be completed rather than hours spent in the office.

Americans' new emphasis on time control is largely the result of two developments: the revolution in electronic technologies, and the growth of two-income households. The microchip has made "democratic technologies"—ones that permit individuals to exercise greater control over their own lifestyles—*possible*. The relative scarcity of free time for working couples, who are a fast-growing majority of married households, has made such heightened control *necessary*.

Component Lifestyles

Because of the greater control that consumers can exercise over their time and the more numerous *choices* available to them, old patterns of consumer demographics and psychographics are increasingly meaningless. Consumer behavior is becoming more individualistic and less defined by reference to easily identified social groups.

Americans are piecing together "component lifestyles" for themselves, choosing products and services that best express their growing sense of uniqueness. A consumer may own a BMW but fill it with self-serve gasoline. Buy takeout fast food for lunch but good wine for dinner. Own sophisticated photographic equipment and low-priced home stereo equipment. Shop for socks at K-Mart and suits or dresses at Brooks Brothers.

This lifestyle fragmentation is most noticeable among affluent consumers. While they still seek social status and prestige, they feel less constrained by social custom and rigid standards. Instead, they are emphasizing *individual* style and taste—self-expression that combines class with the desire for convenience. But even less affluent people are behaving in less predictable ways. They, too, are pursuing greater choice and ways to express their individuality.

In the next few years, the trend is *away* from social conformity and *toward* the component lifestyle. New and surprising combinations of consumer interests, spending patterns, buying habits will be the rule rather than the exception. This means that market research and marketing strategies in general must pay closer attention to *actual* behavior and less to *presumed* psychographic categories. Successful selling tactics must recognize the product-specific and occasion-specific nature of the emerging consumer environment.

The Culture Of Convenience

The fast-rising number of two-income households lies behind the take-off of the "convenience industry," and almost all indicators beyond simple demographics point to further, sustained growth for services and products that give consumers more time for themselves.

Convenience stores, of course, have been prime beneficiaries of this consumer quest for more "disposable time" —time that consumers can spend as they see fit. Convenience stores are so popular, in fact, that consumers would like to see more of them—in gas stations, for instance.

Other types of services will profit as well. Weekend and evening deliveries of large appliances, furniture, and other merchandise are already in considerable demand; that demand will grow. Supermarkets, grocery, liquor stores may find that home deliveries and phone-in orders attract customers.

The spreading culture of convenience also explains the tremendous potential of prepared take-out foods and of appliances like microwave ovens (already owned by more than half of all households).

In the more upscale markets, private daycare services for children of two-income baby-boom households should see growing clienteles. So too might private transportation services between schools and home. Housecleaning services, laundry services, yard services, and others that perform routine household tasks will also benefit from growing demand among two-income households.

In general, what were once considered "do-it-yourself" chores will increasingly become marketplace transactions. Consumers are willing to pay for convenience and that precious item it brings them: more free time.

Home Shopping To Grow Dramatically

One area in which consumers will seek greater control over their time and how it is spent lies in shopping habits. Rising frustration about time wasted in check out lines, for service in stores will fuel the boom in home shopping.

The already-huge mail order industry will experience sustained growth. But a caveat here: mail-order "clutter" is beginning to turn consumers off. The typical reaction of the mail-order industry, and particularly its creative professionals, has been to intensify the sales pitch—even overpromise. Yet the time may have come to focus efforts elsewhere, especially on stimulating graphics and visual presentations.

The most promising area for home shopping is television shopping. The televised home shopping networks are already proven successes. Their sales will continue to soar, and their success will spawn imitators. Local merchants will increasingly get into the act, perhaps via cooperative arrangements with other merchants on local TV stations.

Further down the road, videotext and computer shopping are likely outlets. At the moment, electronic shopping terminals placed in malls, airports, and other locations hold great potential. But as home PCs proliferate, so too will this kind of shopping activity move inside the home.

All these forms of home shopping are based on an implicit trust in high-quality service offered by the vendors. Also appealing is that home shopping is quick, clean, painless. No long lines. No annoying sales pitches. No pressures. It is "active," as opposed to "reactive," shopping. Consumers thus control their shopping environment, as well as the time spent in it.

Traditional retailers should take note. It may be impossible to stem the home shopping tide, so they should quickly adopt new strategies. And to keep customers coming in, vast improvements in service may be required.

Shopping Habits Of The Sexes To Converge

One of the key factors contributing to the decline of brand loyalty in recent years has been the increase in the number of men who shop regularly for food and other items. As a rule, men are much less likely than women to know which product brand they want when they go into a store. They thus have a more pronounced tendency to shop around, or to simply take the first brand that comes to sight.

Many women, at the same time, find themselves with less and less time to do the family shopping—or even shopping for themselves. The reason? More of them are working. Working women, in their search for convenience, tend to look for products that they know will do the job. They are less likely than homemakers to identify personally with the products they use.

Working women are adopting many of the shopping habits of men. They make more decisions on the spot in stores, draw up fewer shopping lists, clip fewer coupons, go shopping more frequently but for shorter, less-planned trips. Simultaneously, men are gaining greater experience in supermarkets and stores, which will breed greater familiarity with specific brands and probably greater loyalty to them.

"Convergence" is the key word. And convenience. The stereotypical roles of the sexes are fading (albeit more quickly among women than among men). The consumers of the future will not be "unisex," but they will have many more—rather than fewer—characteristics in common.

Escalation Of The Home Entertainment Boom

The consequences of the boom in the home entertainment market are only beginning to be felt. The driving force behind the boom—the fantastic surge in VCR ownership—continues unabated. New products and services are just beginning to take advantage of what promises to be an enormous change in Americans' lifestyles.

The movie and film industry, of course, will be in the middle of everything. The downside here is a continuing shrinkage in the number of consumers who go out to movie theaters. The upside is the opportunity to reach huge new markets (older people, for instance) via films targeted for video/cable distribution—markets that beforehand were left outside the industry's main focus.

Look for major changes in eating habits. Take-out foods should be a primary beneficiary, as more and more people order food to eat in—in front of their home video movie.

Home furnishings and appliances—the integrated entertainment center—will increasibngly be forced to adapt to the new environment or suffer loss of market share.

Greater control over the entertainment environment that the VCR permits should lead to diversification in other leisure activities. People can segment their leisure time more effectively, feeling less constrained by what is on television during any particular evening. For instance, there is now a high correlation between people who are "VCR-active" and those who read regularly. Hypothesis: the rapid market penetration of the VCR could carry, in its wake, higher sales and profits for book and magazine publishers.

Market Segmentation In Physical Fitness Activities

The "fitness market" is being divided into progressively smaller niches as mass activities like jogging lose popular appeal. Specialized fitness products and programs, in tune with consumers' growing penchant for individual expressions, are the wave of the future. Jogging may be down, but aerobics is up. Look for aerobics itself to become increasingly segmented: non-impact aerobics, aquatic aerobics.

The proliferation of specialty fitness programs will affect a wide variety of manufacturers. Products like rowing machines, stationary bicycles, and cross-country ski machines will be in greater demand. Also, further growth lies ahead for specialty athletic/exercise shoes and clothing.

Dress For Success

There is a widespread return to attention to fashion and concern for the way one looks now under way. More people believe that it is important to dress properly for certain occasions, and they think that physical appearance can be an important factor in creating the right personal impression.

This resurrected sense of stylishness, however, does not imply a sudden formalization of fashions—the "black-tie" mentality—or even a return to mass fashions—when hem lengths rose and fell in lockstep. Instead, it presages greater demand for individualistic styles of clothing that are attractive and of good quality.

This trend will favor small-scale clothing manufacturers with distinctive lines, large-scale manufacturers that can successfully expand their product lines and compete against their own products, and boutique-type retail outlets. More generally, it might even aid American producers in their bitter battle with Far East Asian competitors.

Spread Of The Diversified Diet

Consumers are not just eating better; they're eating *different*. A key trend for tomorrow's food and restaurant industries is the growth of the diversified diet, incorporating a wider variety of ingredients and cuisines. People are fleeing from the blandness of traditional American cooking.

The popularity of beef products, already down, will continue to fall. Consumers will increasingly buy poultry products, fish, and seafood for their main courses. More creative use of green vegetables will also be a feature.

Certain ethnic cuisines will find larger markets. Italian and Chinese cooking have long been perennial favorites. Mexican food has recently joined their ranks—and the people's fancy for Mexican food should continue. "Dark-horse" cuisines with growing popularity include Japanese, Thai, Spanish, Carribean, Indian, Middle Eastern.

Except for the upscale market, the accent will *not* be on "gourmet" cooking. Instead, the diversified diet is becoming a mass phenomenon—with emphasis on convenience, nutrition, choice, and reasonable prices.

Self-Imposed Prohibition Of Alcohol

The consumer trend toward "light" drinks—vodka instead of bourbon, light beer instead of regular beer—points to more far-reaching trend: a further decline in the number of alcohol users and an ultimate decline in overall consumption.

New, heightened emphasis on health and fitness is likely to endure. This acts to the detriment of products widely perceived as unhealthy, particularly cigarettes and alcohol.

The analogy with cigarettes is significant. Smokers first moved to "light," low-tar cigarettes—before an ultimate consumption decline set in. Further, smoking became a *social* issue, not a strictly personal one, as demonstrated by the growth of no-smoking areas in public places.

The same is happening now with alcohol—especially its move into the social terrain via campaigns against drunk driving. Intensifying social pressures on drinkers could lead large numbers of them to abandon alcoholic products.

The Lightest Drink Of All: Water

Bottled water is one product that seems likely to profit from changes in consumer habits and lifestyles. Two factors underlie the growing appeal of this product.

First, sparkling water is considered chic by the young, affluent market—the "yuppies." It's attractiveness as an alternative type of cocktail fits perfectly with their emphasis on fitness, their desire to be different, and their growing avoidance of alcohol. Second, large numbers of consumers—almost two-thirds—are worried about possible contamination of their everyday drinking supplies. Such worries will probably grow, not fade, in step with increasing environmental concerns. This is the market for the gallon jugs of bottled water.

So both up-market waters and mass-consumption ones look poised for good growth. Perhaps there are lessons to be learned from the European marketplace, which has long been inundated by bottled water products.

The Bifurcation Of Product Markets

In addition to an accelerated segmentation in many product markets, there is another process at work that will reshape markets in coming years. That is the growing bifurcation of markets—an increasing distance between high-priced, up-market goods and low-priced, mass-market ones.

At the low end of the market, the decline in consumer

brand loyalties is feeding price competition. Particularly for non-durable goods, price is becoming a larger factor in people's purchase decisions. But also contributing to consumers' price sensitivity is the massive influx of foreign imports. While consumers may believe that American-made products are generally superior to others, they have few hesitations today about buying lower-priced competitive products from almost any part of the world.

In upscale markets, however, another phenomenon will largely influence the nature of competition. That is, affluent consumers will seek products that reflect and express their sense of individualism. Product quality will not be the determining factor, because these consumers assume that the quality of most products in their price range is equal. Instead, appeals to status, style, taste, reliable service, and so forth will be more persuasive.

In general, companies must differentiate their products or services from those offered by competitors by referring to features *other* than performance. At both the low end and high end of the marketplace, the current performance standards of most products are already above most consumers' standards of acceptability.

Market bifurcation also means that companies or products caught in the middle will probably fare poorly. It signals the collapse of the middle market—where products are neither competitively priced nor particularly individualistic. In part, this is what has been happening to certain general department store merchandisers, like Gimbel's.

High volume or high price: these strategies hold the best potential for future profits.

Product And Service Quality: More Important, If Not Everything

The bifurcation of many product markets is based on two key social developments: some consumers' heightened sensitivity to price, and others' increased desire for individual self-expression. In both areas, product and service quality are more or less taken for granted.

Yet it is important here to issue a warning: Products or services that fall below acceptable quality standards in the future will be treated more mercilessly. Consumers' standards have risen significantly, in step with new technological developments. And while most products or services can fairly be said to equal or surpass these standards, the ones that do not meet them will face grim prospects.

As the globalization of the American economy gathers speed, a renewed emphasis on quality will have the most severe practical consequences. It is not the key to marketing success so much as the necessary *prerequisite* for it.

Advertising And Marketing: Heightened Importance Of Visuals

The impact of the VCR revolution on consumers' television viewing habits is accelerating. Commercial "zapping" is a popular pastime. The new challenge for advertisers and marketers is to make messages seen, not heard.

Visual recall will be key. Corporate and product logos need to be strong, eye-catching, given longer display time. Creative efforts should turn increasingly to dramatic staging, exciting images, bold graphics and away from copy.

New forms of advertising, while now unorthodox, may hold solutions. "Framing" programs with short messages or logos and using video overlays—similar to station identification techniques—are possibilities. Pre-recorded video cassettes will play more important roles in broadcasting commercial messages, with their contents sponsored by individual or multiple advertisers.

VCR technology could also lead to the return corporate-sponsored programs (like the old GE Theater, or Westinghouse Playhouse 90) on network TV. Sponsoring televised movies, in entirety or in part, helps clear up the commercial clutter that encourages zapping—and lets messages be seen.

Note, too, that advertising time once considered unattractive—very late night, early morning hours—could draw greatly increased numbers of viewers, thanks to VCR recordings. Progam sponsorship in these time slots should not be neglected as 24-hour television takes on a new meaning.

VCRs Will Improve Image Of TV

Perhaps the least expected side-effect of the VCR boom will be a measurable improvement in public attitudes toward television. People today have a generally ambivalent view of TV: they derive enormous satisfaction from the hours they spend in front of it but are simultaneously annoyed—even angered—by the violence, sex, and commercials on it. While they look to television as their primary source of entertainment, consumers are also highly critical of the quality of much programming.

These attitudes should change—even if actual TV programs do not—because of the VCR. By giving viewers greater control and allowing them to be more selective, the VCR will encourage a more active involvement with the television set. Viewers will get more of what *they* want. Because their desires are being met more satisfactorily, they will think that the quality of television is improving.

So at the very least, the VCR will foster an *illusion* that everything associated with television is getting better. But it will also probably promote *actual* improvements as well, inasmuch as it catalyzes even further competition in the television industry.

Fragmentation Of Media Markets

Stiff new competition in the media is both the cause and effect of changing consumer habits. This trend is now most apparent in the television industry, where new sources of programming—from cable programs and, in the future, direct satellite transmissions—have profoundly altered the competitive environment.

One result has been fading loyalty to the major television networks. With more choices available—and *accessible*, thanks to VCR recording technology—viewers have turned easily to independent and cable channels. This has been particularly pronounced in late-night viewership markets. And keeping with the general social trend to greater self-expression in consumer tastes, it is notable that cable TV receives high marks for its diversity of programs.

Viewers are becoming more selective and directed. While there will always be the "channel hoppers," the underlying tendency is for growing numbers to know *what* they want to watch and *when* they want to watch it. Among other things, this means that detailed audience demographics for specific programs become more and more vital to advertisers and marketers.

The fragmentation of the television market is something of a replay of what has already happened to radio. The old national networks, like the Red or Blue Network, have been replaced by hundreds of local and specialty stations. And, contrary to expectations, radio did not die but has prospered.

Similar trends have long been at work in the magazine publishing industry. Specialty books that cater to specific interests have superceded national publications, such as *Life* and *Look*. In newspaper publishing, the growing number of one-paper cities has been offset by the proliferation of local and community-based newspapers.

The trends thus point to increasing specialization, diversity, and localization. Media markets will continue to be sliced into smaller and smaller niches.

The Family Is Back

Despite persistent public worries about the decline of family values, the evidence suggests future vitality of the family structure. The family is seen as something to *join*.

Partly this is due to simple demographics. The fact that the baby boom generation is now in its family-forming and child-raising years has significantly influenced the current debate. The nature of the modern family, however, will be irrevocably different from the "traditional" family. First, most families will have both parents working. Second, the average family size will be smaller than in previous generations. Third, a concern for a growing number of families will be the care of elderly relatives—the grandparents.

The major challenges for the future will revolve around balancing the competing demands of work and home when both spouses are employed. At the moment, working women still bear most of the responsibilities for homemaking and child-rearing in two-income households. But increasingly, men will adapt to the circumstances of the "working marriage"—which will no doubt alter their perceptions of themselves as husbands, fathers, and employees.

New Employee Benefits For Two-Income Families

To meet the needs of the modern, two-income family, employers will feel growing pressures to modify current employee benefits programs.

Flexible work hours and schedules, part-time jobs, and job sharing will be increasingly important for two-income families with young children. Demand for daycare services —especially on employer premises—should accelerate.

Controversial issues like providing maternity/paternity leaves with full job protection—and continuation of health benefits—will *not* go away. Now the focus is on unpaid leaves; in the future, activists will enjoy substantial public backing if they press for *paid* leaves.

Problems about which worker is covered by which benefits plan, when both husband and wife work, will multiply. There will be increased pressure for companies to offer "cafeteria" plans, in which workers can pick and choose—so as not to duplicate benefits already obtained by the other spouse.

This is generally quite expensive for companies, however, which leads to another consideration: The insurance industry itself may have to adopt new strategies. Insurance companies might become benefits brokers, offering membership in large, pre-designed benefits programs to corporate participants instead of custom tailoring specific plans for each individual company. Such membership schemes would allow companies' individual employees to choose from a wider menu of benefits options than any one company could afford, while giving employees from two-income households what they need: *flexibility*.

Growing Appeal Of Homework

Executives, many of whom are now familiar with personal computers and how they can improve efficiency, had better start looking at how PC and telecommunications technologies will affect the current structure of the workplace—and even the structure of entire industries.

Large and growing numbers of employees would like to learn jobs that allow them to work at home on their own computers. And as the "information economy" matures, a growing number will actually be able to do such homework: secretaries, typists, data processors, programmers, analysts, as well as professionals in a wider variety of fields.

There will be huge implications for things like flexible work schedules, corporate overhead, accountability for time worked at home, redefinition of numerous job descriptions. As telecommuting spreads, employees increasingly will be organized around tasks to be completed rather than *time* on the job. Yet another result should be a growing supply of labor, as homemakers are recruited to do tasks once reserved for office workers. Further, entire industries might move into the home—high-tech versions of the old "cottage industry" tradition. Key punch/data entry and temporary secretarial services are two prime candidates.

Older Americans: The Next Entrepreneurs

The next major wave of entrepreneurial activity will include an unusually high proportion of older Americans, aged 60 and up. Though this runs counter to the stereotypical image of the young, dynamic entrepreneur, numerous forces at work in our society today indicate the emergence of a new, older class of businessmen and women.

First are attitudes toward retirement. Large and growing numbers of older employees want to keep working after "normal" retirement age. They have the *motivation* to go into business for themselves. Second, older Americans have high levels of disposable income. They have the *resources* to invest in their own enterprises. Third, developments in medicine and health have not only increased average life expectancy; they have also vastly improved the physical fitness of older Americans. These people thus have the *energy* to run their own businesses.

Types of businesses that seem ripe for older entrepreneurial activity: numerous kinds of consulting, financial management, community services. Also a growing "older" presence in the retail trade—boutiques, shops, restaurants.

The Young American: A New Kind Of Conservative

The current generation of young Americans, between 18 and 29 years-old, embodies a unique blend of economic and political conservatism while also being socially liberal.

Politically, this is the most conservative group in this age bracket since the 1950s. They face stiff competition for jobs and a more somber economic environment than did older baby boomers. They are likely to heed calls for strict limits on government spending, because they feel they benefit little from government largesse and are skeptical of the efficacy of government programs. The political implications, as might be expected, favor the Republican Party.

Socially, however, the young have accepted—and profited from—the general changes in social mores since the 1960s. They have no qualms about living with someone of the opposite sex without being married. They support the ERA and favor free choice for abortions. They tolerate the off-beat lifestyles of various minorities.

Yet at the same time, the young stand out as bucking the current trend toward greater individualism and pluralism. There is a pronounced tendency, instead, toward conformity and belonging—which should only grow as this generation ages. Hence the greater emphasis they place, compared to past generations, on dressing appropriately for specific occasions. Or on acceptable manners, proper discourse, and creating the right impression of oneself in public.

After the next few years of heightened individualism, therefore, business should probably prepare for a reaction. That reaction will entail renewed desires to belong to the mainstream community.

Public Relations: Tough Times Ahead For Business

Business has failed to build on the immense foundation of public good will that has been evident during the recent upturn in the economy. While general attitudes toward business are still favorable, people remain deeply suspicious about how business operates.

Business has received virtually no credit for the millions of new jobs created in the past few years or the very low inflation rate. Instead, public opinion gave it all to the Reagan Administration. Thus, the ultimate irony: when the free enterprise system *works*, *government* gets the credit.

Despite public receptivity to more education about business issues and a desire to be better informed, American companies have not been seen as taking the lead. Business does a good job promoting itself to the investor community but a poor one in solidifying its relation with consumers and voters. Result: potentially massive swings in public sentiment on issues like regulation, taxation, the environment.

For too long, business has relied on a popular, pro-business President to carry the flag with the public. This leaves business quite susceptible to changes in the political environment—without its own solid base of public support. After President Reagan, a reaction to the pro-business mood of the past few years is likely to occur.

The Personal Face Of Business

A forthcoming deterioration in public attitudes toward business will provoke a damage-control reaction from business. What strategies might prove effective?

Stressing the human side of business and, especially, putting a personal face on business itself would be good bets. Think of Americans' current love affair with entrepreneurs. Their popularity stems in part from their perceived contributions to the economy, of course. But more important in terms of public psychology, entrepreneurs are dynamic *individuals* that people can relate to.

The example of Lee Iaccoca, while much publicized, is nevertheless important. Companies as large as Chrysler can materially benefit by personalizing their images.

Business knows how to react well under pressure, and the likelihood is that public pressures on business will build in the future. Traditional reliance on lobbyists will no longer be enough—and might backfire if seen as secretive and only for "special interests." It's time for business leaders—people with the knowledge *and the charisma*—to take an active role in public relations. Not just any CEO, but particularly articulate, personable ones.

Improvement In Labor's Image? Yes, But Ultimately Meaningless

Ever since President Reagan broke the air traffic controllers' strike—with massive public support—labor unions have been fighting a rearguard action to maintain influence. In the future, however, the situation could change.

The images of unions and their leaders appear to have "bottomed out," and the public is beginning to express greater tolerance of them. Recent large-scale lay-offs and furloughs in major corporations tend to encourage people to think of their common interests as workers, and to provoke sympathetic reactions toward the embattled workers' unions.

But the real problem for the labor movement is not its image. It is the risk of becoming *irrelevant*.

Unions continue to lose members, and there is no evidence that they have started to reverse this trend. Their concentration in heavy smokestack industries is a big part of the problem. Their general failure to make inroads in the white collar workforce is even more significant.

Too often, labor unions as institutions incorporate precisely the same faults as the industrial companies they deal with. They are hierarchical, bureaucratic, unresponsive to their constituents' needs. They are at odds with the entrepreneurial spirit and, more importantly, with Americans' quest for more individual control over the workplace.

Unless the labor movement responds aggressively to the immense changes underway in American society, it will increasingly be seen as anachronistic.

Growth Of Environmentalism

Contrary to the expectations of many analysts, attention to environmental issues has *not* peaked; it is still gathering momentum. In fact, public attitudes toward a wide variety of environmental issues today point to a steady growth in the power of environmental movements in coming years. And that growth in power could become an outright explosion if some spark—an incident like Chernobyl or Bhopal—ignites in this country.

Problems of toxic wastes and nuclear energy rank very high on the list of public priorities. People are distrustful of business in these areas, and they support greater government regulation and control. What's more, these environmental concerns are both broad and deep—profoundly held beliefs by a very wide cross-section of American society. The appeal of the environmental movement is not limited to a lunatic fringe or a few kooks.

Throughtout the 1980s, environmental issues that directly affect business have been fought at local levels more than at the national level. But the general image of environmentalists today is highly favorable—and environmental issues will increasingly provide an attractive platform for political candidates. In the future, more wide-ranging calls for tighter safeguards and for stricter standards will be heard.

Permanent Damage To Nuclear Energy Industry

Growing environmental concerns in general, combined with the Chernobyl disaster, have retarded further developments in nuclear energy for the foreseeable future.

Public worries and opposition to new nuclear plants are high and rising. There is increasing willingness even to close down existing nuclear plants, much less build new ones. The recent drop in oil prices has created an economic environment altogether unfavorable for nuclear power—and has made consumers much less concerned about energy independence or self-sufficiency.

The nuclear power industry probably cannot recover in the short term. U.S. nuclear capabilities will therefore fall behind other countries, especially those in Europe. Any revival of nuclear power in this country may ultimately depend on further government intervention, particularly associated with quality control in plant construction phases.

Government Regulation To Increase

One of the hallmarks of the Reagan Administration has been the emphasis on deregulation of business. Entire industries—from airlines to financial services, telecommunications to the oil industry—saw their competitive environment radically altered by the lifting of government controls.

As consumers, Americans tend to support deregulation as long as prices decline. But as voters, Americans are *not* wedded to the principle of deregulation. To the contrary, in many vital areas concerning business, the public desires even stricter government rules—for instance, toxic waste disposal, general environmental standards, workplace safety, and even the accuracy of advertising.

Two forces should propel the trend to more regulation. The first one is rather ironic: Although President Reagan is a champion of free enterprise, perhaps his most important contribution has been to restore peoples' faith in government institutions. Second, specific developments over the past year—the insider trading scandal, for example—could spark increased demand for regulation.

More likely than not, however, the regulatory environment of the future will be more industry specific. The New Deal belief that government can oversee all aspects of business—in practically any business—has been irrevocably replaced by a more pragmatic, limited approach. Increasingly, business and government will be encouraged to become partners, not adversaries separated by regulatory barriers.

The Budget Deficit Won't Go Away

While virtually everyone agrees that the huge budget deficits of the Federal government threaten our nation's future prosperity, the problem is that no one is willing to do anything about them. Blame is typically laid at the door of Congress—because of its "pork-barrel" politics—or the Reagan Administration—because of its defense build-up and tax cuts. But the truth is that the public *itself* is not prepared to see decisive action taken.

The income tax cuts of recent years have been so popular that any talk of future tax increases is almost political suicide. Yet at the same time, most people desire even more government spending for all the major social programs. Americans want to have their cake and eat it, too.

Underlying these contradictory desires is a serious misunderstanding of the economics involved. The public has an extraordinarily exaggerated notion of the inefficiencies in the public sector—and thus of the tax dollars that could be saved by cutting back on government.

Political support for low income taxes and high social spending will remain a "given." It will probably take an economic crisis—or, perhaps, strong leadership—to change the situation. But then efforts to balance the budget might come at precisely the *wrong* time in the economic cycle, accentuating difficulties rather than alleviating them.

Defense Spending More Vulnerable

If important cuts in government spending *are* eventually to be made, the political consensus will support a reduction in the defense budget over most other spending items. The very success of the Reagan Administration in pushing through its massive defense build-up set the stage for retrenchment. The defense build-up, in a word, *worked*. The public now feels psychologically secure about America's position in the world.

And the future of the Strategic Defense Initiative, or "Star Wars," is becoming increasingly tenuous. While the plan appeals to Americans' imagination—the promise of a homeland shielded from nuclear attack is a powerful one—public desire for negotiations with the Soviet Union is strong and growing, especially after the Reagan-Gorbachev summit. Star Wars is a chip that might be bargained away.

Reversal Of Tax Cuts For Wealthy

Americans are still more pleased than displeased by the passage of the Tax Reform Act of 1986—mainly because that bill cut many individuals' tax liabilities.

Yet there is good reason to believe that favorable opinions of the new tax system might fade. For one thing, the two-tier structure, with only two tax brackets, runs against Americans' desire for a progressive system of taxation. For another, the new code was not simplified in terms of reducing the average taxpayer's annual paper work—to the contrary.

If indeed Washington finds the political courage to tackle the deficit problem by increasing Federal revenues—which certainly cannot be taken for granted—then income taxes paid by the affluent are likely targets. Political reality and public preferences dictate that this will be so.

The Nation's Mood: The New Reality

During the mid-1980s, Americans felt great about themselves, their prospects, and their country. The peak of the Reagan era, to exaggerate only mildly, was marked by public euphoria and a kind of zealous boosterism.

Partly this was a psychological reaction to the troubles of the 1970s. After Watergate, Vietnam, OPEC, Iran, high inflation, soaring interest rates, and other problems, Americans felt a deep need to put such disturbing memories behind them. Ronald Reagan—with his cheerful brand of personal optimism—helped accomplish that goal.

But this euphoric public mood was, in its latter stages, becoming curiously divorced from economic realities. For instance, consumers' real incomes, after adjusting for infla-

tion, did not make the heady progress that their psychological mood might have suggested. Developments in the stock market illustrated precisely the same point: The unprecedented bull market of the 1980s did not take its clues from trends in the general economy, such as GNP growth, but from its own euphoric optimism. That bubble burst dramatically, of course, on October 19, 1987.

What lies ahead? First, the "go-go" years of the mid-1980s are now over, both on Wall Street and on Main Street. If the stock market crash in itself did not decisively change the face of the American economy, at the very least it changed people's *perceptions* of the economy. Americans are much more sober today about their own—and their country's—economic prospects, and it is highly unlikely that they will go on a psychological binge again any time soon.

Yet in one important sense, a legacy of the mid-1980s will endure. There is a renewed national determination to make things *work*, and a fundamental confidence in our institutions and our leaders that was so sorely lacking in the 1970s. The new reality is not nearly as cheerful as it appeared during the height of the Reagan era, but, even so, people are not cowed.

After euphoria comes relative austerity—a sobering-up period. For marketers, this new mood possibly will restrain the level of consumer confidence and the willingness to incur debts for major expenditures. For business generally, it raises a challenge to play an aggressive role in a national *partnership*, with government and labor, to attempt to correct our nation's economic problems.

You're nobody 'til somebody loves you ... and not everybody will love you.

Introduction by Ken McCleary

In our society we are all competing constantly. Students are competing for grades, athletes for medals and recognition, and all of us are competing for jobs, promotions and the attention of a "significant other". Hospitality businesses are functioning in one of the most highly-competitive industries there is. Entry into the field is still relatively easy, and that results in a continuous stream of new competitors. Smart executives keep constant watch on the competitive environment and the individual players in it.

William C. Hale in *Strategic Planning: How to Hold a Market Profitably* underscores the value of assessing competition. He not only outlines how competitive information can be used to help you plan strategy, but provides specific checklists for evaluating competitors to see where you stand. Be sure to add the term "area of dominant influence (ADI)" to your marketing vocabulary.

While it is important to assess your competition in the current environment, it's also important to look to the future. In *Competitive Environment* Hale notes that competition will probably become even stiffer down the road, and that you'll need to consider the "software" side of the business more carefully than in the past. In a companion piece, Raymond Daniel discusses some economic variables that may affect the future. *Economic Outlook* emphasizes the need to monitor the larger competitive environment. It may also provide some insight as to why hospitality management students need to study economics.

K. Michael Haywood, in *Scouting the Competition for Survival and Success*, quotes from *In Search of Excellence: Lessons From America's Best-Run Companies* where Peters and Waterman say, "The excellent companies clearly do more and better competitor analysis than the rest." Haywood not only echoes Hale, but he provides a framework for keeping an eye on competitors, and identifies specific benefits which accrue from so doing.

Clearly, you can't be all things to all people. You have a chance to be something special to some group(s) of people, but only if you compete successfully for the opportunity.

Strategic Planning:
How to Hold a Market Profitably

William C. Hale

In the first article of this series, we focused on the results of an executive survey concerning strategic planning. The survey identified the five most important strategic issues facing the industry in the 1980s:

1. Improving cost controls;
2. Attracting an adequate labor force;
3. Improving productivity;
4. Managing in an intensified competitive environment; and
5. Responding to market saturation.

This article explores how management might approach resolution of these Market Share/Penetration issues, or *How can our chain hold a market profitability in a highly competitive environment?*

The reason for linking the requirement for holding a market with market penetration is quite simple. As a market becomes highly competitive (normally a symptom of a mature industry), management must make a basic decision. Do we:

Abandon the market because it is unprofitable; we have a very weak position; and, long term it does not fit our development scheme;

Trim back the number of units to the most profitable units or niche, and reinvest capital in the remaining units;

Maintain the current level of effort, i.e. same number of units, marketing effort, etc.; or

Penetrate market so as to increase share of market and improve overall operating efficiencies.

In or out

In most of the geographic markets Technomic has evaluated over the past few years, maintenance has not been a viable strategy. The question comes down to, are we *in* or *out* of the market. If we are *in*, then we either implement a niche penetration (trim back to few most profitable); or implement a broad market penetration. This is a principle way to hold a market in a highly competitive environment.

The basis for gaining a strong market position through a market penetration strategy is tied to economics. The chains with the high-market-share positions will tend to be the most efficient operators, and generally, the efficiencies realized increase with share. The economics come in the form of more efficient marketing and advertising; better utilization of supervisor management; lower costs of distribution, among other efficiencies. Also, most chains can point to a sizable increase in average unit sales as the overall market share increases, since per unit sales are significantly lower in a low share market than in a high share market.

Define market

The first step in deciding whether to penetrate or abandon, (let's not consider maintenance as a viable option), is to define the market. How do we want to define our markets: by the way operations has structured its field management?; or by the way consumers' life patterns, and purchasing patterns are structured and defined?

We would strongly suggest that consumers provide the clues to how markets are described. In fact, one convenient way to describe a market is by an Area of Dominate Influence (ADI) of a TV signal. Each ADI is defined by the configuration of the beamed TV signal. Each ADI can be further defined by demographic characteristics, growth, and most important, by expenditure patterns. (For example, *Restaurant Business* tracks the eating and drinking sales for each of the 212 ADIs in the U.S.)

As we move forward, it is important that we have a means to measure effort-input against results. ADIs will allow us to do that.

The next step is to develop a good understanding of the market. Most management teams do not know their markets well! For example, how many of these questions could you answer for your major competitors? (See *Figure 1* for checklist of competitive factors.)

Competition

How many units do your competitors have in each of your ADIs?

What is their average unit volume in your market area?

What is their share of the market?

What is their menu/pricing strategy?

What is their cost structure (operating costs)?

Where are the units located (location strategy); how old are the units?

What has been the expansion or renewal activity over the last four years? Cost of new unit construction?

How is their management organized and what are their strengths and weaknesses?

What is known about the competitors supply system?; operational systems?

What is their marketing thrust in terms of: new products, new services, consumers targeted, and profile of users, advertising budget?

What is the competitors' overall strategic direction in this market?

What does the consumer like and dislike about the competitors?

What is known about the competitors supply system?; operational systems?

Answers to the above questions are among the major factors that should be mapped out for each of the major competitors. The information can be readily assembled for analysis. Some of the information sources are shown in Figure 2.

Consumers

What do you know about the consumers in your markets?

How many are there in the market and what is their: age distribution, household structure, consumer expenditure patterns, income levels, employment status, and labor force composition?

What are the dynamics of the population in terms of: growth, movement, life style shifts and other shifts?

What do your customers as well as non-consumers think about your concept and execution?

What are the consumer trends operating in your markets that will have an adverse or positive impact?

What can be done to minimize or accentuate those impacts?

Industry trends

The last set of questions that management should be able to answer concern the industry structure and other institutional factors. For example:

What are the trends within the foodservice industry that will impact my business in terms of: new concepts or competitors; new products/service or technology; procurement practices and raw material market trend; labor practices; and unit design?

What are the institutional factors that will impact the business in terms of: cost and availability of capital; government regulations; and economic situation?

Business review

In addition to market informa-

tion on the competition, and the state of the industry, management should take an *objective* look at their business:

What has been the unit sales, traffic count, and operating margin history?

What has been the return on capital employed?

What is the market share by ADI (company and licensed)?

What is the product sales mix and contribution by item?

What is the pricing history and

relationship/effect on customer traffic counts?

What is the consumer profile of user and non-users?

What has been the marketing thrust and its effectiveness?

What is your cost of unit construction?

What has been your expansion history?; renovation history?; and its payback?

What is your cost of raw material?

Figure 1.

CHECKLIST OF COMPETITIVE FACTORS	
☐ LOCAL MARKET PENETRATION	☐ G&A STRUCTURE AND COSTS
☐ CONSUMER IMAGE/ PREFERENCES	☐ UNIT MANAGER TRAINING & EXPERIENCE
☐ SALES PER UNIT	☐ BACKWARD/ HORIZONTAL INTEGRATION
☐ CHECK AVERAGE	
☐ FOOD COST RATIOS	
☐ LABOR COST RATIOS	
☐ UNIT GROSS MARGINS (%)	☐ FRANCHISEE STRENGTHS
☐ UNIT CONTRIBUTIONS ($)	☐ AVAILABLE CAPITAL FOR EXPANSION/RENEWAL
☐ AGE OF UNITS	
☐ LIFE CYCLE OF CATEGORY	☐ MARKETING
☐ LIFE CYCLE OF CONCEPT	☐ "SECRET WEAPONS"

Figure 2.

COMPETITIVE ANALYSIS INFORMATION SOURCE CHECKLIST	
☐ ANNUAL REPORTS	☐ TIME SERIES OF PRINTED MENUS
☐ 10-K	
☐ D&B, CREDIT AND OTHER PURCHASED REPORTS	☐ DIRECTORIES
	☐ TELEPHONE BOOKS
	☐ RESEARCH REPORTS
☐ TRADE PUBLICATIONS/ FINANCIAL PAGES	☐ SUPPLIERS
	☐ PERSONAL OBSERVATION
☐ ANALYSTS' REPORTS	
☐ TRACKING SERVICES	☐ COMMISSIONED RESEARCH

What is the status of your franchising program (if appropriate)?

What are your human resource programs—recruiting, training, promoting?

How effective is your research and development effort?

What is your real estate situation and strategy?

What are the strengths and weaknesses of your concept, management and operations?

Depending on the specific chain and its unique characteristics, there will be other questions that need answers However, the key point is, managers should base the *in or out* decision on facts, not feel—facts about the competition, market conditions, industry dynamics, institutional factors and your own business situation.

Penetration strategy

With the above information in hand, business managers should perform an *objective* analysis to see how their chain stacks up to competitors in each of the ADIs.

Let's assume that a fairly rigorous analysis of the chain's strategic position relative to competition, the industry's development, the market/consumer perceptions was conducted. The results of that analysis suggest that in the core ADIs, management believes the market should be retained and, in fact, penetrated. The steps to implement a penetration strategy are:

Step 1. Rank ADIs—Establish a ranking of ADI in terms of the order they are to be developed/penetrated.

• It is difficult to focus on all ADIs at once, focusing on a few at a time may be easier to manage and more effective.

• Do not necessarily attack the most difficult or largest ADIs first, since that may be frustrating to management. Take the ones that are most likely to succeed first. This develops a track record and moves management along the learning curve faster.

Step 2. Develop share measurement mechanism—Develop a means to determine and track share of market trends for your chain and major competitors.

• Before you attempt to *gain* share, make sure you know your current share and have a way to monitor changes in share over time. This can be done with published data—such as the *Restaurant Business* Restaurant Growth Index. Data (See *Restaurant Business,* September 15, 1981) on ADIs might be based on number of units and traffic surveys as well as Crest (Consumer Reports on Eating Share Trends) data on a regional basis, or some other scheme.

• The tracking mechanism will be important in monitoring and managing the strategy.

Step 3. Establish share target and determine the share gap for each ADI—Analyze the current share information and determine what share is required to place you among the top three chain operators. The share target should be for each ADI, and the competitive set you should compare your chain with might be described as "close-in competitors" (same menu and service).

• In mature markets, there will be two or three major players and a few other niche players. Other chains will tend to shake-out. Therefore, to hold a market, the chain should be aiming at the 1, 2 or 3 position.

• If management thinks that it will be impossible to be in the top three, then a niche-strategy should be considered.

• Given the chains *current share* and *targeted share,* management can readily determine the difference, or *gap.* If the market is mature and the share gap is quite large, management may want to consider a niche strategy.

Step 4. Delineate a market development plan for each ADI—For each ADI, a specific detailed plan of action describing how the share gap will be filled should be established. In most cases, this will be a multiple year plan. The plan should address the role each marketing element will play:

Product/service features—Will new menu items be needed? Will new service be offered? Can the current menu items and services be improved?; differentiated?; expand-ed? Can the quality image be enhanced? Will remodeling help build traffic?

Price—What should be the pricing strategy?; premium?; or discount? Can new pricing points be added to make the overall package more attractive?

Promotions—What will be the promotion strategy?—games, premiums, tie-in, cents-off? Are special promotions needed to attract non-current users? What promotions can be employed to increase usage by current users?

Distribution—How many new units are needed to achieve better market coverage, i.e. more convenient for customers? Where should these be located? Can existing buildings be purchased/leased and converted to your chain's image?

Communications—Is there a need to alter signage? What will be the advertising strategy and level? What other publicity campaigns must be employed? Can other in-store/point of purchase displays add to sales?

The market development plan should say what is to be done; who is to do it/be responsible for implementation; when it is to be done; the estimated budget; and the expected results.

Step 5. Management review—The ADI market development plans should be reviewed by management and accepted or modified. The review should include:

(1) Completeness;

(2) Cost of implementation versus expected results/return;

(3) Resource needs—people, capital, outside services;

(4) Reasonableness, i.e. ability of planned actions to fill the share gap; and

(5) Assurance that the individual in charge is aware of responsibilities and expectations.

Step 6. Implementation and monitoring—The implementation calls for the orderly roll out of the actions delineated in the plan. This should be coordinated by one individual. This individual would have management's support and be able to call upon all the impact functional areas, i.e. research and development, marketing, operations, personal, financial.

Management reports should be established specifically to review the implementation and results. Otherwise, the experience gained in the early ADIs targeted for penetration will be lost. Also, without a monitoring system, management will not know how it is progressing toward its share object.

Managing the strategy

Once the planning is completed and the decision to implement given, the successful penetration of the market will be the result of *good, solid blocking and tackling*. While there is a need for creativity in the design of the strategy, a steady competent management team is required to make it happen.

COMPETITIVE ENVIRONMENT

BY WILLIAM C. HALE

Unless restaurant operators get better at managing the intangibles of their business, it'll be a long haul through the 1990s. During the past two decades operators have necessarily stressed the "hardware" side of the business—building and maintaining restaurants in good locations, and adding to and rearranging menus in order to keep pace with consumer demand. These things won't be inconsequential in the 1990s, but alone they won't be enough.

In fact, it's the "software" side of restaurants that will matter most in the next decade, the subtler, often elusive touches that all too frequently go ignored. Those who'll prosper in the next decade will have more than just hard-

William C. Hale is president of The Hale Group, Danvers, MA, a management consulting organization serving the foodservice industry.

ware: They'll have, for one thing, managers who are adaptable, who are comfortable with doing anything it takes to please the customer. There are several elements of "software":

- Brand
- Service
- Convenience
- Price/Value
- Management of Intangibles

BRAND. We're now entering an era of "hyperchoice" in which consumers will have less time and more choices. Because of this, brand names should take on greater significance. The operator should communicate to consumers certain things about his restaurant's brand:

- discrete areas of competence the brand commands;
- descriptive standards of performance the consumer can expect; and
- the definition of ambience and product presentation.

The ability to create a strong consum-

er franchise for the brand will provide the "equity" to fund growth in the 1990s and beyond.

SERVICE. The great number of options consumers have means they'll avoid restaurants that provide a low level of service. Good service will go a long way toward developing a competitive edge, superior service being the trademark of successful operators.

Operators able to achieve premium service levels won't, in many cases, need to rely on superficial special promotions to maintain sales. Rather, long-term service strategies will attract loyal customers, and superior service must be built into the fabric of the operation.

CONVENIENCE. The consumer of the 1990s will seek the path of least resistance when looking for ready-to-eat foods for at-home consumption. In the 1990s, products and services that help consumers improve their lifestyles will clearly be big winners. These products should be aimed at reducing stress and assisting consumers in enjoying the free time they have. They should offer:

- Simplicity
- Accessibility
- Efficiency
- Consistency

PRICE/VALUE. The consumers of the 1990s will be even more price-sensitive than the consumers of the past two decades; they'll be quite willing to "trade off" to food products that meet their immediate needs. Since consumers will have more options available to them—whether that be eating at home or in a restaurant—they will be able to be far more selective. Consumers will be able to get what they want at "discounted" prices, too, as large numbers of foodservice suppliers chase fewer, or a static number of, buyers.

The successful concepts will be efficient and willing to share some of these efficiency benefits with the consumer. This will provide value to the consumer and the operators/suppliers.

INTANGIBLES. The final basis of competition deals with management's ability to be comfortable with and adaptable to successfully managing the software, or intangibles, of the business.

The hardware elements of a foodser-

The Winners

BRAND

MANAGEMENT OF INTANGIBLES

CONVENIENCE

STAR PERFORMERS

PRICE

SERVICE

SOURCE: The Hale Group

Chart by Peter Niceberg

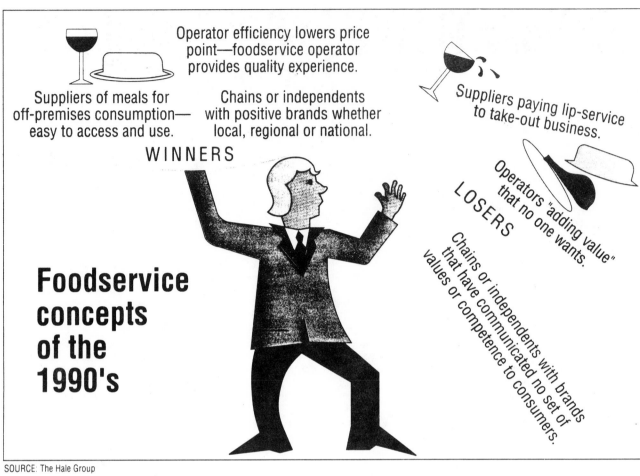

Operator efficiency lowers price point—foodservice operator provides quality experience.

Suppliers of meals for off-premises consumption—easy to access and use.

Chains or independents with positive brands whether local, regional or national.

Suppliers paying lip-service to take-out business.

WINNERS

Operators "adding value" that no one wants.

LOSERS

Chains or independents with brands that have communicated no set of values or competence to consumers.

Foodservice concepts of the 1990's

SOURCE: The Hale Group

vice concept are easier to monitor and manage because there are readily available measures of performance (like costs, number of units, and covers). Software elements—brand, service levels, convenience, and value—are more difficult to measure with existing systems, although it is not impossible. Successful managers will find ways to measure the intangible elements to assure they are operating as planned and promised.

ENVIRONMENTAL CONDITIONS. The new basis of competition will be implemented in an environment that will have the following characteristics:

Supply-side segmentation. Segmentation of the market by supply-side participants will drive competition in the future. At-home dining will most certainly detract from away-from-home eating decisions. The desire for convenience will drive off-premise business. Off-premise foodservice can be a major new business for restaurant operators if they design convenient systems with efficient, consistent service.

Consumer brand equity leveraged

by noncommercial feeders. Branded concepts will be implanted in institutional/noncommercial segments, e.g., hospitals, colleges, schools, and in-plant/in-office settings. Consumers want foods they like and trust.

Lower price point concepts will drive the 1990s. Concepts that deliver a quality dining experience at a reasonable price will enjoy higher customer traffic and broader acceptance than those that depend solely on the tactics of ambience and product quality.

National chains no longer have the upper hand. The national chains will find further expansion difficult as the regional and local chains fight back. Regional chains can now achieve many of the economies of scale in purchasing, training, managing, and advertising that were previously enjoyed only by national and multi-regional chains. Information exchange, miniaturization of systems, and localized, targeted communication will all assist in strengthening the regional chains.

The 'software' side of the business will count just as much as the 'hardware' in the decade to come.

88

ECONOMIC OUTLOOK

BY RAYMOND DANIEL, PH.D.

A year ago, the prospects for the U.S. economy looked uncertain at best. The financial market convulsions leading to the 1987 stock market crash brought the bears out of the closet, and forecasts of a recession rebounded. Forecasts that the economy would grow by 2.5% in 1988 were considered overly optimistic. The reality, of course, was that the forecasts underestimated the strength of the U.S. economy last year.

GROWING RAPIDLY. Why was 1988 so much stronger than expected? Several reasons come to mind. First, the U.S. and world economies were growing rapidly prior to the crash. This, combined with the almost negligible wealth effect, meant that growth did not slow significantly. Second, the U.S. Federal Reserve (Fed) and other central banks acted swiftly and in concert to offset the potential impacts of the crash on the real economy.

Third, monetary stimulus abroad meant that Japan, Europe, and the rest of the world grew at a 4% rate, setting the stage for strong export growth in the U.S. Fourth, despite the strong growth in the U.S. and abroad, there was enough slack on a worldwide basis that inflation rose very little.

The extra strength experienced in the U.S. economy was concentrated in the consumer sector, which grew twice as fast as expected, in capital spending, which grew about 25% faster, and in exports, which rose nearly twice as fast as anticipated. Inventories also accumulated at a quicker pace than was projected. As a result of this faster growth, interest rates were also higher.

During the first half of 1989, the story was little changed: job growth remains strong; consumers appear willing to keep spending; the trade gap continues to narrow, albeit slowly; factory output is growing at a de-

Ray Daniel is senior vice president of The WEFA Group, Bala Cynwyd, PA, directing food industry consulting services.

cent clip; inflation, though edging up, remains fairly tame; and the Fed continues to nudge interest rates upward.

ECONOMIC FEARS RISING. Fears about the economy are again emerging as they did at the beginning of 1988. Is the U.S. growing too fast? Will there be a boom-bust in 1989-90? Will wages and prices finally begin their upward spiral? Will the Federal Reserve be able to slow the economy down without triggering a recession? Will the twin deficits (trade and fiscal) continue to cause problems for the economy?

While real Gross National Product growth in the fourth quarter of 1988 was at an acceptable 2.5% rate, the nonfarm economy grew more than 3% and domestic demand rose at a rate close to 4% because of strong growth in consumer expenditures, government spending, and housing.

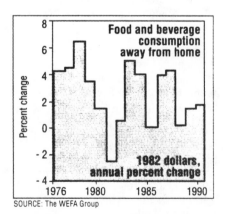

SOURCE: The WEFA Group

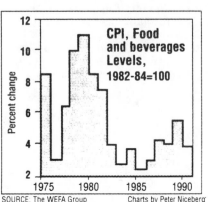

SOURCE: The WEFA Group   Charts by Peter Niceberg

There are a couple of ironies in this performance. First, strong economic growth, now considered to be bad, increases the risk of a traditional boom-bust economic recession. Second, by raising interest rates, the Federal Reserve wants to slow the growth of domestic demand, but it does not appear to be succeeding. Rather, the most visible impact of higher interest rates has been increasing the value of the dollar and, in part, stagnating any improvement in the trade deficit.

STRENGTH OF DEMAND. Given rising interest rates, what accounts for the strength of domestic demand? The three most interest-sensitive categories of domestic demand are consumer durables (primarily autos), housing, and business fixed investment. In each of these, both because of financial deregulation and the recent behavior of lending institutions, the impact of higher interest rates has been cushioned.

The household sector in the U.S. is a net creditor. Specifically, interest earnings by households exceed interest payments by more than $400 billion. So, interest rate increases actually benefit this sector as a whole. Moreover, consumers have yet to feel the bite of higher rates. Automobiles, appliances, and other durable goods have not been affected because of incentives like cut-rate loans and the lengthening of financing periods.

The housing sector has yet to feel the pinch, largely because of the pervasive use of adjustable rate mortgages (ARMs). Roughly two-thirds of home buyers now use adjustable rate mortgages, and 25% to 30% of all outstanding mortgages are ARMs. The teaser rates for ARMs are near 8.5% (compared to more than 10% for fixed-rate loans), which means that many households that would otherwise not qualify for fixed-rate mortgages are qualifying for ARMs.

Moreover, interest rates on fixed-rate loans have begun to rise only recently. Thus, home sales and starts have not been affected much by the rate increases so far.

Consequently, financial deregulation and the willingness of many U.S. businesses to absorb interest rate increases mean that the Fed has not yet succeeded in slowing the growth of domestic demand.

How much longer can U.S. business "buy down" interest rates and how much further will the Fed have to raise rates to slow down domestic demand? We expect that the inflation increase due to these higher rates will be over this year; therefore, the Fed will not have to engineer major increases in interest rates. However, the risks of much higher interest

The economy has been surprisingly healthy this year, but we may be in for a slowdown ahead.

rates and a contraction in domestic demand—i.e. a recession—are substantial enough that they cannot be ignored.

THE BUST OF 1990? Looking ahead, the risk of a booming economy followed by a bust in 1990 seems greater, perhaps twice as great, as a hard-landing recession this fall triggered by a loss of confidence by foreign private investors in the U.S. The *sine qua non* of a boom-bust scenario is a rise in inflation, especially wage inflation.

The biggest puzzle about the outlook centers on the very tame behavior of wages, labor unions, and prices in the face of tight labor markets and high capacity utilization. Will 1989 be the year that potential re-inflation in the U.S. is finally realized?

The tameness of current U.S. inflation vis-à-vis the double digit rages of the 1970s can be attributed to two factors. First, the U.S. is a more open economy now than it was 10 years ago. Operationally, this means that many more companies and unions now feel the pressure of foreign competition. Second, the world is still characterized by excess supply and over-production.

This is not only true in commodity markets like oil, but also in goods markets that have been hit by a wave of relatively low-price and high-quality goods from the newly industrialized economies of Asia. This combination of a more internationalized U.S. economy and a world of glut means that there are constraints on how much U.S. wages and prices can rise.

It's still too early to quantify the extent to which these factors account for the very slow rise in U.S. inflation. However, there is evidence that supports this general hypothesis:

• As the dollar fell, foreign producers raised their prices by only a fraction of the decline and, in an attempt to maintain their market share in the U.S., allowed their profit margins to narrow;

• Productivity gains in U.S. industries have held down wage increases, allowing these industries to sharpen their competitive edge;

• Job security, not higher wages, is still the major issue for much of the U.S. labor force;

• Evidence from wage data across the U.S. and Europe suggests that when goods and/or workers move freely across borders between countries, rapid wage increases in one region or country cannot be sustained unless they are pervasive across regions and countries.

THE BIGGEST SINGLE RISK. Nevertheless, wage inflation is still the single biggest risk to the U.S. outlook in 1989, and will be closely monitored by the Federal Reserve. There are, however, a number of uncertainties clouding the outlook for 1990. If the expected upward adjustment in monthly adjustable rate mortgage payments has a big enough impact on consumer finances and spending, a dramatic slowdown in domestic consumer demand would ensue. Likewise, if foreign investors lose confidence in dollar-denominated assets, both U.S. interest rates and inflation would rise.

Upward pressures on interest rates could also come from other sources. So far, the potential for inflation in the U.S. economy has not been fully realized. If either wage or price inflation picks up on any sustained basis, the Fed is likely to take harsher actions to stop it. With GNP growth continuing to surpass the Fed's target of 2.5% annually, both short- and long-term rates are likely to rise in the coming months. The predominant risks will fall on the long

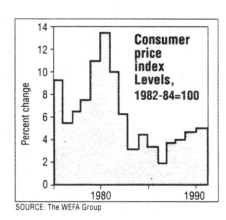

SOURCE: The WEFA Group

SOURCE: The WEFA Group

Over the longer term, operators must control costs until restaurant sales rebound.

end, where a sharp sell-off should move Treasury bond yields back up to 9.5%.

Also, the weakness in business fixed investment and the worsening net export picture in the fourth quarter of 1988 do not bode well for the adjustment process that the country's economy has really just begun. Higher interest rates and a higher dollar would further hurt the prospects for improvement in the savings/investment balance and the trade deficit.

COUNTERING THE RISKS. The counterweights to these risks are the Federal Reserve and the foreign central banks. While the Fed is determined to preempt any rise in inflation in the U.S., it is unlikely to raise rates rapidly for fear of exacerbating the Savings and Loan crisis, hurting the highly leveraged corporate sector, or precipitating a default of Less Developed Country loans.

Similarly, the foreign central banks want neither a sharp appreciation of the dollar (for fear of inflation in their countries) nor a sharp depreciation (for fear of a recession). They will therefore intervene heavily if needed to make any necessary adjustments smooth.

Spending for consumer nondurables rose a healthy 0.2% in January in real terms, though food and beverage purchases were flat. Flat food purchases were likely related to rapid price increases resulting from last year's drought. However, the food sector appears to represent an area of actual weakness in consumption spending.

In the months ahead, we expect a resumption of growth in consumer spending. Car sales have already recovered moderately from the abysmal levels of early January. Though first-quarter sales will be lower than sales in the fourth quarter of 1988, the decline will not be as severe as indicated by the January figures alone.

Although there will be continued gains in personal income, the pace will slow markedly. Wage rates will

contribute more to this growth than they have in the recent past, and less is likely to come from strong job growth as the economy begins to slow. Interest income will continue to expand briskly as short-term interest rates spiral higher. The combination of higher inflation and slower job creation will result in slower real growth in disposable income.

Higher interest rates, higher infla-

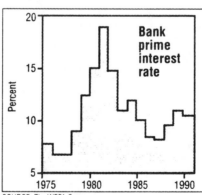

SOURCE: The WEFA Group

SOURCE: The WEFA Group   Charts by Peter Niceberg

tion, and weaker real disposable income growth will soon begin to exact a toll on consumer confidence. Following a rise in the first half of this year, we expect the index of consumer sentiment to post a second-half decline. As consumers become more wary, their spending will slow and the savings rate will hover between 5% and 5.5% for all of 1989, compared with 4% in 1988.

ADDITIONAL CONSTRAINTS. Real consumer spending will slow from the 3.5% to 4% pace of the second half of last year to 2.2% to 2.4% in the first half of this year, then decline further to 1.5% in the final quarter of 1989. We anticipate that real disposable income growth, and consequently real consumer spending, will be additionally constrained by tax increases in 1990 and 1991. Real disposable income growth will slow from 3.8% in 1989 to just under 2% in 1990 and 1991.

Meanwhile, consumer purchases will advance 2.7% this year (in 1982 dollars) before slowing to 2.2% in 1990 and recovering moderately to 2.6% in 1991.

Away-from-home restaurant sales will subsequently slow dramatically in 1989 and 1990, increasing by only 1.5% to 2% annually in real terms, compared with the 4% annual rate experienced since 1983.

Inflation is projected to increase by 4% to 5% annually compared to only 3% to 4% in 1987 and 1988. Labor wages within the restaurant industry will escalate this year to 5% to 6% annually, and food raw material costs are projected to increase also by 5% to 6%, compared with 2% to 4% in 1988. The largest increase in food costs will be in beef, fruits, and vegetables, due to short supplies.

This projected slowdown in restaurant sales and acceleration in wages and food raw material costs will significantly reduce profits in 1989 and 1990. The major task of restaurant owners and managers during the next two years will be to control cost until the economy strengthens again in 1991. $\mathbb{R}$

Scouting the Competition
for Survival and Success

"Putting the book" on your competition is a sound business strategy. Here is what to look for and where to look

by K. Michael Haywood

LATE IN the 1929 baseball season, Connie Mack, manager of the Philadelphia Athletics, was convinced of three things. The A's would win the American League pennant, the Chicago Cubs would cop the National League flag, and Howard Ehmke needed a rest. Ehmke, a right-handed pitcher with a sore arm, had won only seven games for the A's. Mack told Ehmke: "Take the rest of the year off, and go watch the Cubs."

When the Cubs met the A's in the first game of the world series, they faced Mack's surprise weapon—Howard Ehmke. He struck out 13 Cubs that day, and the A's went on to win the series in just five games.

Ehmke is sometimes credited with being the first advance scout in major-league baseball. Today, al-most all sports teams "put the book" on their opponents, often through complex computer charting.[1]

You can, too. Businesses also put the book on competitors, as Peters and Waterman reported in their survey of top-notch businesses: "The excellent companies clearly do more and better competitor analysis than the rest."[2] Competitive analysis is one secret of success for many firms. This article will explain why your firm should make competitive analysis a regular practice, how you can start a program

[1] Phil Patton, "Baseball's Secret Weapon," *The New York Times Magazine*, July 8, 1984, pp. 25–27, 49–52.

[2] Thomas J. Peters and Robert A. Waterman, Jr., *In Search of Excellence: Lessons from America's Best-Run Companies* (New York: Harper & Row, 1982), pp. 197–198.

of monitoring competitors' activities, and the types of information that should go into a competitive audit.

A Link to Strategy Development

Many hospitality businesses cast an occasional eye on competitors, but they do not always seek in-depth information about them. Competitive analysis entails the *systematic* retrieval and evaluation of information about competitors for use in developing competitive strategies. Michael Porter observed that the lodging and food-service industries are so fragmented that a competitive advantage can be gained only after a company's management

K. Michael Haywood is an associate professor at the School of Hotel and Food Administration at the University of Guelph.

thoroughly understands the structure of the industry and the position of competitors.[3]

Denny's Restaurants, for instance, used competitive analysis as part of its decision earlier in this decade to aim for the mid-price market. Denny's determined that all major players in the coffeeshop sector were saddled with problems, so the firm set out to reposition itself as a family restaurant. It expanded by acquisition in certain geographic regions, stepped up its renovation and design program, redeveloped its menus, and boosted its marketing and advertising budget. In this instance, intelligence efforts led Denny's to develop a strong offense.

Constraints

Few hospitality firms are inclined to conduct this type of competitive analysis, however. The nature of the hospitality business fosters a focus on daily operations and immediate customer contact. But exclusive attention to internal operations may create a short-term point of view as well as a false sense of confidence, even when competitors are about to overtake a business.

Some hospitality companies—particularly small operators—assume that the costs of competitive analysis are beyond their financial capabilities. The expense of competitive analysis is no reason to assign it low priority, because it can yield invaluable information.[4] But as I shall show, much competitive information can be obtained for little or no cost.

Although gathering information on competitors smacks of spy rings and shady deals, competitive analy-

sis has nothing to do with corporate espionage. Most of the information you'll gather is public, and much of the rest is freely available through informal contacts. After all, Ford and Chrysler are said to be GM's first two customers for any new car that rolls off the assembly line.

Benefits

There are compelling reasons for conducting competitive analysis.

- It enlarges a company's understanding of the customer, and sheds light on how customers—faced with multiple choices—make decisions about which hospitality businesses will best fulfill their needs.
- It is a source of new ideas and a confirmation of an operator's own ideas. It fosters product development and innovation.
- It facilitates better predictions about the future, and helps an operator prepare contingency plans for future crises.
- It enforces discipline in playing the competitive game, forcing an operator to evaluate any prospective course of action in the light of possible responses by competitors.
- It focuses an operator's attention on the need to choose which points of the operation will be emphasized.
- It fosters an acceptance of change—a realization that the business will necessarily be different tomorrow and that complacency is the surest road to failure.

- It helps point up competitors' weaknesses. A company that builds strength in the areas in which its competitors are weak is likely to expand its market share.

Bits and Pieces

Uncovering information on competitors is not as difficult as it might first appear, although the information generally comes in bits and pieces. You can start by reading the trade press, which publishes industry statistics, biographies of industry leaders, new-product information, profiles of companies, news of marketing efforts, financial results, and much more. The local business press might also print news of building proposals, new openings, and the like. Most companies seem to like publicity, although one industry leader, McDonald's, generally shuns company profiles and other revealing publicity.

National and local trade associations are also sources of information, both in the published information they supply and in the personal contacts that you can make during their meetings. Sometimes people reveal in conversations sensitive information that they would never want printed. You can also sometimes pick up information on competitors' plans during seminar presentations and discussions.

Firms that do business with your competitors usually have an excellent sense of their strengths and weaknesses. Vendors will probably not disclose privileged information, but they can tell you about general buying trends, levels of new-product use, experiences with new kinds of kitchen equipment, and so on.

[3]Michael E. Porter, *Competitive Strategy* (New York: Free Press, 1980).

[4]Robert Hershey, "Commercial Intelligence on a Shoestring," *Harvard Business Review*, September–October 1980, pp. 22–24, 50.

Professional recruiters and personnel agencies might give some indication of the labor situation in a given company. Local trade schools, colleges, and universities will know when companies are recruiting, and what positions are being filled. Simple help-wanted advertising will tell you a great deal about what kinds of jobs competitors are filling. Personnel announcements also give you a clue as to the level of talent a company has. Whether appointments are being made from within or from outside can also reveal much about a company's philosophy and personnel situation.

Propriety's edge. A common information-gathering tactic is simply to hire persons who have worked for competitors. While these people will not necessarily reveal all of their former employers' secrets, they will certainly bring a fresh perspective to their new employer.

You can also analyze competitors' advertising and marketing programs, taking note of media used, timing, type of offers, and prices. An understanding of the messages communicated, their continuity, and the relationship of the messages to other competitive information can be strategically valuable. Some media firms specialize in gathering and selling this sort of data.

Consultants. Consulting firms, government agencies, and college faculty members conduct analyses of the food-service and lodging industry and of specific sectors and firms. Some consulting firms monitor certain parts of the industry, making their data available to others (often at substantial cost). Since your competitors often use the same consultants, you (and they) may learn additional information through direct contacts with these firms.

Publicly traded companies must issue reports to their stockholders and to analysts on Wall Street. If you hold some of your competitors' stock, you will receive this information—which is, of course, public. Statements by corporate executives reveal management attitudes and values, trends, performance, and future directions. You can compare annual financial disclosures to those of years past. Information held by the U.S. government can be obtained through the Freedom of Information Act, but, under this law, your request itself becomes a public document. (A firm in Rockville, Maryland, FOI Services, specializes in making requests under this law to shield the identity of those seeking information.)

Customers. One of the best sources of information is your customers, who also patronize your competitors' establishments. You can talk to your customers in informal conversations, or learn their views through more formal structured interviews or surveys. A market survey of patronage habits in your community can be conducted via mail or telephone. Many firms engage college marketing students to gather this type of information.

You can also assess your competitors' products firsthand, by eating at their restaurants and staying at their hotels. You can determine price-value relationships, ingredients, costs, and a variety of performance measures. But developing an objective evaluation of competitors' customer demographics, staff competency, and product strengths and weaknesses requires far more than the simple collection

of brochures and menus.[5] Moreover, since observations like these are a good way to collect information on competitors, many companies have discontinued plant tours. (Companies can go too far in protecting their concepts; I recall a colleague's being booted out of a small dessert eatery simply for photographing the interior.)

Framework for Competitive Analysis

You must pursue competitive information in a methodical fashion, if it is to be useful to you. Large firms will benefit from the five-step program I will explain next; smaller firms need not use such a sophisticated approach. The steps are as follows:

(1) Set up a structure for gathering competitive information;
(2) Identify direct competitors;
(3) Gather competitive information through a competitive audit;
(4) Evaluate competitive information; and
(5) Feed this information into your planning processes.

Creating a structure. Without top-level support, a company probably cannot maintain a useful competitive-intelligence system. Once management decides to proceed, it should create a structure for gathering and using the competitive information. To begin with, management should decide why the information will be gathered and what kind of information is needed. From these decisions will follow the assignment of responsibility for maintaining the information system. Because the type and extent of competition may vary from one locale to the next, the best

---

[5]For example, see: K. Michael Haywood, "Assessing the Quality of Hospitality Services," *International Journal of Hospitality Management*, 2, No. 4 (1983), pp. 165–177.

plan is usually to have each unit manager be responsible for collecting his or her own competitive information. Chains operating regional clusters of units may want to vest responsibility for disseminating information in an area manager. Ultimately, one person in the head office will compile all reports from the field.

The degree of importance attached to competitive analysis will determine the amount of time to be spent on this activity. Regardless of the time involved, employees must be committed to the process, and understand why competitive analysis is essential. You can work out with your employees an arrangement for gathering, storing, and disseminating the information.

At minimum, your information-gathering system should include, for each competitor, a file that is kept up to date, a useful format for recording information, a way to disseminate the key information, regular meetings to discuss the information, and a security system to prevent the release of sensitive information.

Identifying rivals. The process of determining your direct competitors can be complex. To begin with, you can list all the hospitality businesses operating in your geographic area. Because you are not competing directly with all the restaurants and hotels in town, however, you should then classify these businesses, distinguishing the primary competitors from firms that affect your business only tangentially. Use such measures as type of establishment, target market groups, type and timing of patronage, and location.

Your trading area—the vicinity from which you draw most of your customers—depends on your market niche. A luxury center-city ho-

tel might define its competitors as other high-ticket hotels within a five-mile radius. But airport hotels might present some direct competition, and must be included even if they are farther away or if their pricing structure seems different. Moreover, the hotel's management should take note of whether some potential customers are selecting university facilities for conferences.

For a fast-food restaurant, the competition might easily be defined as other fast-service restaurants within three or five miles. But all other restaurants with a $3 to $6 dinner check might be competing for the same customers and should also be included.

Functions and benefits. The most effective way to identify competitors is by matching the hotels or restaurants with the specific needs their customers are trying to fulfill, or by the benefits each competitor is offering the customers. Say that you want to attract well-to-do, dual-career couples who are entertaining important business clients during the evening. Consider the competitive choices these people have: a meal prepared at home by the hosts, a catered meal eaten at home, a catered meal served at a facility like a bed-and-breakfast inn, a fancy hotel restaurant, an exclusive independent restaurant, the company's executive dining room, or a country club. All the firms that can meet this demand are your direct competitors.

The process of identifying competitors can be likened to mapping a battlefield. By locating the relative positions of the major competitors on the "map" relative to target groups of customers, you can gain a better understanding of the stra-

tegic and tactical decisions that may be necessary to outfox the competition. Once you have identified your competitors, you can focus your attention on gathering information about them.

Dynamics. The problem with identifying your major rivals is that the field is always changing. One company may be ascendant this year; next year, it's been purchased and its components sold piecemeal. The really important competitors are those that can meet the needs and wants of customers now and in the future. Identifying rivals is a matter of determining which firms the customer will choose to patronize, because the customer makes the final determination of business success. For this reason, you must watch new and existing businesses and regularly reassess the question of which ones are your direct competitors.

Competitive Audit

After you have identified your competitors, you start gathering information. This could involve an in-depth analysis of competitors' product and market mixes, pricing policies, promotional techniques, positions in the product life cycle, and their past, present, and anticipated behavior. You can also assess how well each competitor is doing and their strengths and weaknesses.

Clearly, it is possible to gather reams of data on each competitor. You must, therefore, conduct an early "triage" operation on the information, deciding exactly what is worth keeping. All the effort you spend on data gathering is wasted if you cannot answer the essential questions about your competitors. The many kinds of information you should consider collecting are listed in the accompanying box.

Location. Note each competitor's location and size in relation to those of your firm. If a market is

Keeping Track of Competitive Information

A complete competitive-information system will comprise a wide variety of information. The lists below suggest what such a system should include.

Location:
Location of competitor
Advantages and disadvantages of the site
Proximity to other competitors
Effect of location of head office

Size:
Number and size of units or properties
Typical per-unit sales volume
Number of employees

Background:
Company founders: biography, business philosophy, management style
Evolution of company: periods of glory, setbacks
Problem-solving methods
Type of ownership
Financial performance: sales, profitability, market share, occupancy, turnover

Executives:
Personal traits: energy level, perseverance, self-discipline, initiative, level of enthusiasm, leadership skills, reputation, age, management style
Job history: length of service, degree of commitment
Knowledge, experience, judgment: managerial ability, skill levels, education, savvy, business judgment

Market status:
Current rank or standing
Trend of company business
Status as market leader, trend setter, or follower
Penetration of market with units, properties, sales personnel, products or services
Strength of company's loyalty among specific customer groups
Dependency on current customers or market groups (noted seasonally)

Corporate objectives:
Desired internal performance: market share, growth, profitability, cash flow, return on investment
Desired levels of customer satisfaction, product quality, and performance
Strength of company's objectives and degree to which they are communicated
Past successes in achieving objectives
Possible future choices of products, services, markets
Priorities and guidelines in allocating resources
Competitive intentions regarding each component of the business
Identifiable events that have triggered company's intense retaliation
Means company uses to detect market trends
Structure of company; appropriateness to mission and objectives
Company's ability, speed, and response to activities of market competitors; adaptability and flexibility

Customers:
Typical customer mix and variation over time
Average customer expenditures for different time periods
Actions designed to attract specific kinds of customers and success thereof
Strength of company's grip on specific market area: coverage and penetration, company or brand-name awareness, media coverage
Customers' view of company's products, services, facilities, reputation, price-value relationship, strengths, and shortcomings
Ways in which other firms have enticed competitors' customers away

Physical facilities:
Age of units, maintenance levels, state of obsolescence
Size or capacity of units, appropriateness, and need for expansion or renewal
Cost-efficiency of units in regard to maintenance and energy use
State of repair and attractiveness of interior design, decor, furnishings, and equipment
Overall ambience, unique features
Efficiency of service-delivery systems

Performance of products and services:
Extent to which products create desired effect or perform intended function (atmosphere, comfort and convenience, appropriateness, flexibility, tastefulness, presentation)
Consistency, dependability, and safety (speed, waiting time, cleanliness, neatness, attention to detail)
Efficiency (operational systems, customer flow, policies and procedures, services, delivery systems, checkin and checkout)
Tradeoffs customers might make when purchasing

Salability of product or service:
Physical and functional attractiveness and distinctiveness
Unique selling proposition, or any other important, exclusive, or promotable feature
Price in relation to competition
Demand for product or service

Defensibility of product or service:
Protection of company's name, facilities, product line (e.g., menu) by copyrights, licenses, franchise agreements
Proprietary advantages, access to special sources of supply or trade secrets

Functional factors:
Overall labor situation: costs and rates, employee attitudes, union activities, job-classification flexibility, fringe benefits, access to skilled employees, training programs, skill level and technical expertise, recruitment and selection policies, degree of employee loyalty, turnover, and absenteeism
Age and appropriateness of equipment
Equipment limitations
Technological sophistication
Competitive edge in production methods
Relationships with suppliers, access or control of sources of supply
Location of major suppliers
Use of special buying practices
Adaptability and flexibility of production space
Adequacy of capacity
Management ability to keep quality up and costs down
Extent and use of research in menu development, cost control, kitchen design, concept development, facility evaluations, etc.

Marketing prowess:
Management: number of people, size of budget, existence of annual marketing plan, distribution of marketing expenditures, effectiveness of decision-making, effectiveness of forecasting
Products and facilities: Current product-service-facility mix, and contribution of each to sales and profitability, existence of program of product development and deletion, management concentration on a given product or service, stage of product life cycle, distinguishing features, advantages, or benefits, image presented by current decor and furnishings
Pricing: methods and image, leadership role, reaction to other companies' price changes, objectives and strategies, elasticity of demand, sensitivity of customers, credit policies and payment plans
Promotion: Sufficiency of advertising budget in relation to marketing objectives, use of campaign objectives for promotional expenditures, use of outside marketing agencies (e.g., travel agencies, advertising agencies), creative and media strategy, frequency of advertising and type of media used, use of direct mail, point-of-sale, or cooperative promotions, use of public relations, staff training in suggestive selling

Finances:
Means of financing growth: external, internal, or both
Debt load
Credit rating
Seasonal and cyclical cash requirements
Short- and long-term borrowing capability
Extent of any past financial difficulties
Effectiveness of physical control of food, beverage, and other items
System of monitoring costs and cost performance
Effectiveness of accounting systems

Who Needs It? We're Doing Fine!

Competitive analysis is often thought to be irrelevant to an operation's success. Many restaurateurs or hoteliers have been heard to claim, "I have no competitors, because my restaurant (hotel) is unique." This rationalization may have been appropriate when the demand for hospitality services was rapidly expanding. With the tremendous increase in competitive activity and the slackening of the growth in demand, it has become more difficult to achieve expected sales and profit growth relative to historical performance. This means that any growth in market share will have to come from competitors. Outdoing competitors is impossible if you are ignorant of their place in the market.

Many hospitality businesses do keep an eye on competitors, but do not seek in-depth information about them as part of strategic planning. For example, in a medium-size city in Ontario, Canada, the owner of a 20-seat pizza restaurant worries about the arrival of a Pizza Hut in his market, but does nothing about it, outside of changing the pizza from round to square and pinning his hopes for continued success on customer loyalty. The operator of Muldoon's, a casual drinking and dining spot, is concerned about a sudden "invasion" of Irish-named roadhouses, but does no more than visit each operation once and make a few price adjustments on his menu. A fried-chicken franchisor sees no direct competition at all, but is unaware of a slow sales erosion caused by the addition of chicken-by-the-bucket at supermarket deli counters. Within the year, all these businesses will be forced to sell or go into receivership.

On a much grander scale, hark back to the 1960s and '70s, when virtually all the food-processing giants had a stake in the high-flying fast-food industry and were intent on becoming the segment leader. When security analysts threatened saturation, companies like Burger King slowed their rate of expansion. None of these companies understood how McDonald's would react, and they were caught completely off-guard when McDonald's solidified its preeminent position by continuing with its aggressive expansion program—a carefully crafted competitive strategy that has helped to establish its profitability and sustained its position.

As an operator, you can't afford to be a mere spectator in the battle for customer patronage. —*K.M.H.*

dominated by large firms or chains, small firms might find it difficult to compete effectively. In a market consisting of small firms that cater to distinct tastes, larger firms might check for reasons that large firms are not competing in the market.

Philosophy. You should also record competitors' prevailing philosophy and approach to business, as a function of history and as it is currently expressed. A study of a company's history can provide clues to its reactions to future market changes.

The personal traits, know-how, experience, and ambitions of current managers affect a company's success or failure. While it may not be possible to evaluate all the managers in a firm (particularly a large company), a profile of key executives is essential.

Guessing Game

Wouldn't it be marvelous to know the precise corporate objectives, strategy, and positioning of your competitors? Unfortunately, that is an unrealistic goal, because no company will knowingly present its game plan to its rivals or define exactly what it intends to do or become, or to specify the kinds of results it seeks. Nevertheless, by studying what a competitor can or might do, you can develop a counter-strategy that might blunt your competitor's moves.

To release a customer from a competitor's grip, you need to know as much as you can about each competitor's customers, and the reasons for their purchase decisions. You should also examine the facilities and environment maintained by each competitor. At the same time, you should evaluate each competitor's products for performance, salability, and "defensibility."

After completing a product analysis, you also should assess the labor, equipment, and technology involved in production. Next, keep track of the competitors' marketing programs, to determine how well the marketing mix is managed. Last, you should consider competing firms' financial resources, taking note of their access to money and their management of existing capital.

Evaluating Data

As you can see from the lists on the preceding page, you'll have much information to assess. It must be sorted and judged according to the credibility of its source. Then you can draw inferences and make interpretations. The major problem is that of compiling good information and applying it to decision-making. Many factors can interfere—namely, the initial information may be inaccurate, distorted, garbled, or deliberately ignored (if it doesn't fit the management's preconceptions); information sources may be unreliable; or the information may not be relevant, timely, or in a useful form.

One way to reduce the amount of bad information going into the system is to evaluate the source and content of each item. The following letter-numeral scheme used by military intelligence is one excellent way to make this evaluation.

Source reliability:

A—completely reliable
B—usually reliable
C—fairly reliable
D—not usually reliable
E—unreliable
F—reliability cannot be judged

Information accuracy:

1—confirmed
2—probably true
3—possibly true
4—doubtful
5—improbable
6—accuracy cannot be judged

After judging the accuracy of each item, some companies put the information into one of three categories: background or basic description, current activities, or future speculation. Basic descriptive information contributes to the in-depth profile of the competitor. A major U.S. hotel chain, for instance, keeps a file on each of its major competitors, including an exhaustive description of personnel, holdings, performance, strategic thrusts, room-rate policies, and the like.

Current-report information gives you an idea of what is occurring at the moment. Executives in the hotel chain I just mentioned meet regularly to discuss current industry and competitive developments identified through their competitive-information system. They use this information to speculate on competitors' possible future actions.

Speculative information is difficult to process. In a perfect grand strategy, the unexpected should never happen. But information gathering has not yet approached such perfection, so it is necessary to develop a set of indicators or essential information points that allow operation of an effective forecasting or warning system. Examples of indicators in such a warning system could be the hiring of a new vice president for real-estate development or a staff expansion in the franchise division. Depending on past events, each of these hirings may signify a renewed emphasis on expansion or a strategic change in unit- or property-ownership patterns. Other indicators of renewed vigor or a change in direction could be new senior management, a switch of advertising agencies, an increased marketing budget, or a major recruiting drive. These indi-cators, added to the usual financial- and resource-based indicators, may have real significance when viewed in the light of existing knowledge of the competitor's specific capabilities and weaknesses.

The value of an integrated collection plan is that it is a first step in the development of sound estimates or forecasts of a competitor's capabilities and intentions. The essence of the competitive-intelligence process is the creation of a set of indicators that can be applied to a competitor's actions. To be valid, such indicators can be established only on a base of accurate descriptive studies, coupled with current information. Predictions based upon bias or hunch are of little value, as are those based on the premise of "what we would do if we were in their shoes."

Gaining Competitive Advantage

Merely gathering information on competitors does not provide the answers needed to outperform them. By researching the competition, you can gain information that allows you to follow them closely. But you still need to answer such "what-if" questions as: How can we increase our share of the market? What should we do if competitor X cuts prices? What can we do that we're not doing now? The answers to these questions involve integrating competitive information with a clear vision of your firm's strengths and weaknesses.

But competitive information can take you only so far. It can show you your competitors' strengths, but if you choose to match them in these areas of strength, you merely meet them head on. The best use of competitive information is to ascertain the competition's weaknesses, so that you can build strength against those weaknesses and gain an upper hand in that portion of the market. Patronage is not necessarily won by offering excessively appealing benefits to customers. It results from skillfully outmaneuvering your competitors to gain a patron's purchase.

Identifying your competitors' Achilles' heel is not easy, however. In some markets, most operators will have the same weaknesses. This is particularly likely when no operators are conducting adequate market research, and everyone is simply following the leader. These operators may not be aware of products and strategies being tried in other markets. An operator who regularly visits other areas or reads trade magazines might be exposed to new competitive tactics and benefit therefrom.

You may see the limitations of the competition, and the consequent opportunities for you, relatively early in the competitive-analysis process. As an opportunity becomes clear, you should determine your firm's ability to fulfill that need. You may soon observe that some of your competitors are failing to deliver on the promise of their concepts or that they are simply missing a market opportunity. On the other hand, you may discover that your competitors are in such a strong position that you cannot justify continuing with your present strategy.

Although many operators neglect it, competitive intelligence is an essential ingredient in the strategic-planning process. The difference between good and bad decisions often lies in the information available to the decision-maker and the decision-maker's ability to make sound judgments about the eventual consequences of competitors' current moves. □

You have to be at the right place ...
at the right time ...
with the right stuff.

Introduction by Ken McCleary

George Burns, America's favorite nonagenarian comedian, has often noted that "Timing is everything." Well, George, that may be true for comedians, but it's only part of the story for hospitality firms. Consumers are becoming more and more sophisticated every year, and are demanding more and more from hotels and restaurants. Key to success is understanding the needs and wants of potential customers, and then providing the *stuff* to satisfy those needs and wants better (in the minds of those potential customers) than anyone else does. This *stuff* includes appropriate location, conducive hours of operation, a good price/value relationship, and any number of other amenities and services.

The hard part, then, becomes figuring out what customers want. *Consumer Behavior in the Hospitality Industry* discusses the importance of understanding your customer, and describes (in a general sense) how consumer purchase decisions are made.

The Hilltop Steak House in Saugus, Massachusetts has by far the highest gross (annual sales) of any restaurant in America. In *Top of the 500* Michael Sanson chronicles the history of the Hilltop's owner who has always provided the "right stuff". You should probably note that this has occurred without paying any attention to any of the genius in any of the articles in this book.

Consumer Behavior in the Hospitality Industry

Ken W. McCleary

Does being a good manager of an operation which offers a quality product guarantee success? Not necessarily. Consumers are complex beings whose reactions vary from situation to situation. Because of this, marketers have learned the importance of considering consumer reactions to marketing decisions and have developed a field of study called consumer behavior.

" 'Consumer behavior' may be defined as that behavior exhibited by people in planning, purchasing, and using economic goods and services."[1] The purpose of studying consumer behavior is so that you, as a manager, will be able to understand how and why people select a hotel or restaurant. This understanding will aid in designing a product that is appealing and then persuading potential customers to buy it.

A hospitality manager who understands what motivates consumers and how they arrive at their decisions will be able to develop a marketing strategy which influences consumers at each step in their decision process, and develop products that provide the satisfaction necessary to ensure repeat business. The *marketing concept* indicates that the most successful business is one that matches its product with consumer needs and wants. In order for an operator to follow the marketing concept, he must first understand consumer needs and wants. Studying consumer behavior develops the skills necessary to gain this understanding.

The Consumer Decision Process

All of us, when making a purchase, go through several steps or phases before actually deciding exactly what product we will buy. In some instances, such as when we purchase an item we have used before, each phase in the decision process is completed rapidly, almost unconsciously. At other times, especially when purchasing a new, expensive product, the decision process is long and involved.

Consider two different purchases: a student's decision as to where he should eat lunch, and a family's decision of where to go for a week's vacation. Both decisions are similar in that they involve a hospitality product but are quite different in how they are made. The first decision will probably be made rapidly with little deliberation. This is because buying a lunch is not a major purchase and the consumer probably has little time to search for alternative places to eat. The decision regarding a vacation, on the other hand, may take weeks of planning and involve the whole family. Nevertheless, both decisions involve basically the same steps and are subject to the same kind of influences.

The consumer decision process can be broken down into five phases:[2]

*Problem recognition
*Search for alternatives for solving the problem
*Evaluation of alternative solutions to the problem
*Actual purchase decision
*Postpurchase evaluation

How long it takes a consumer to complete these phases depends on his personality, the type of product involved, familiarity with the product, and external constraints such as time and income. In some circumstances, such as repeat buying or impulse buying, steps may be passed over rapidly or even skipped. To illustrate the decision process, let us look at the example mentioned earlier, which involved selecting a restaurant for lunch.

Frank Furter, the student in the example, feels hungry, thus recognizing the problem, a need to satisfy his appetite. Since Frank lives in an apartment off-campus, he limits his options to commercial restaurants and begins to think of places where he might like to eat. Possible choices include a fine dining restaurant and three fast food restaruants.

At this point, Frank's external constraints influence his choice. Since he has no car and little money, he selects a fast food restaurant near his apartment, goes to the restaurant and orders his food. The purchase decision has been made, but the purchase process is not completed. As Frank waits for his order, eats his meal, and leaves the restaurant, he will be evaluating the service, surroundings, and quality to determine if he has received value for his money. This postpurchase evaluation will be stored in his memory for use in determining future purchases.

At each step in the decision process the consumer is susceptible to influences which help him arrive at his final decision. Some influences come from within the consumer and are called *internal influences*. Internal influences come from factors such as the consumer's basic beliefs, values, and attitudes, his personality and previous experience with the product. Although there is little that can be done to change internal influences, marketers can develop strategies which appeal to already established internal influences. For example, a restaurant which builds a luxury image may appeal to some consumers' basic personalities which dictate a need for esteem.

External influences include any limitations placed on the consumer by environmental factors such as income, and sources of information such as friends or advertising. It is the manipulation of external influences that provides the hospitality manager with the best opportunity for attracting new customers.

Consumer Behavior and Marketing Strategy

A *marketing strategy* is a general plan which is aimed at attracting and satisfying customers. Central to the development of marketing strategy is the consumer. Because consumers have diverse needs and wants, it is nearly impossible for a hospitality firm to appeal to all types of consumers. To make strategy development more manageable, marketers divide the total market into smaller homogeneous portions based on common characteristics. For example, *Institutions* magazine determined that households with incomes over $30,000 a year eat out nearly twice as often as households making less than $12,000.[3] This eating out pattern would be a useful behavioral dimension for dividing the market. The process of dividing the market is called *market segmentation*.

Market segmentation cannot be accomplished in a meaningful manner without an understanding of consumer behavior. Based on what influences consumers, the marketer can select one or several segments on which to concentrate marketing effort. This concentration of effort is called *target marketing*.

Once a target segment has been selected, it should be studied in detail to discover how best it can be attracted and serviced. Since strategy provides a broad guide, it is necessary to also make specific decisions on how strategy will be implemented using marketing variables such as pricing, advertising, location, and product offerings. These specific decisions involve the selection of marketing tactics. Thus, *tactics* are marketing techniques which are applied on a day-to-day basis to achieve specific results.

After the hospitality firm has examined the market, selected a target segment and determined decision process characteristics of the target, strategy is planned and tactics are developed. At each stage in the decision process, consumers are likely to be susceptible to different tactical appeals. Understanding what appeals are most effective during each decision phase allows the marketer to become more effective in spending scarce marketing dollars and gives the firm a competitive edge.

An Example of Using Marketing Tactics in the Decision Process

Assume that you are the marketing manager for a Hyatt hotel property which is targeted towards an affluent clientele.[4] Your hotel has further divided its clientele into subsegments, one of which is the market for meetings. Your job is to determine what marketing tactics to use in persuading potential customers to hold meetings at the property you represent.

The first step is to make meeting planners aware of the need for your hotel services (problem recognition). This can be done by using specific tactics such as advertising in trade publications or sending direct mail to corporations. After a need has been established, tactics should be designed to help the consumer through the remainder of the decision process to a final selection of Hyatt as a meeting site. Familiarizing meeting planners with the Hyatt name and the projecting of a quality image through general advertising and merchandising may be effective as potential customers search for alternatives.

During the alternative evaluation phase, you must make sure that Hyatt compares favorably with your competition. Since Hyatt understands the needs of those who plan meetings, the property has been designed to meet those needs. Personal sales calls may be an appropriate tactic to use so that the benefits of the property can be pointed out and questions answered. Personal or telephone selling can be used to expedite the actual purchase decision. A positive postpurchase evaluation is enhanced by friendly, efficient service and a followup letter thanking the meeting planner for his business. These are some possible tactics that could be used for attracting the meetings segment. However, these tactics may not be effective for other segments which the hotel wishes to attract. For example, it would not be efficient to use personal selling to gain individual restaurant business, whereas targeted radio advertising may be an effective tactic.[5] Thus, the hotel marketer needs to consider behavioral characteristics for each major segment and use tactics which elicit the most favorable response.

A Decision Model for Restaurant Selection

A hospitality manager who understands the decision process can develop conceptual models to aid in selecting effective marketing tactics. Figure 1 illustrates how this might be done for a fine dining restaurant's non-group dinner business. Note that different marketing variables are used at each stage in the decision process. Restaurant marketers will find it useful to develop a decision model for each of their market segments. Not only does a model help develop tactics, but also helps management understand why certain marketing decisions were made.

Modifying Consumer Choices

Nearly all hospitality operations rely on repeat business. For the hotel or restaurant which has developed customer loyalty, the marketing task is easier since positive attitudes have already been formed. These operations need to concentrate on continuing to give good service during the purchase phase.

The task of attracting new customers is more difficult because it entails modifying current behavior patterns. In order for hospitality firms to alter patterns, it is necessary for managers to determine what motivates consumers to select various operations. Once this is determined, marketing tactics can be designed to appeal to identified motivations. For instance, many consumers are motivated by an opportunity to save money. Some fast food restaurants use discount coupons to appeal to the economy motive and to encourage switching from one restaurant to another.

An examination of the consumer decison process helps managers understand the need for reminder advertising during the postpurchase evaluation phase. It also points out that the best opportunity for modifying choices occurs during the search for, and evaluation of, alternatives. The "correct" marketing appeal can be used at these times if underlying purchase motivations are discovered.

Conclusion

Knowledge of consumer behavior is essential to all aspects of hospitality marketing, from the design of the product offering to the development of marketing strategy. No amount of accounting, finance, and other skills can compensate for a failure to identify what the consumer wants and what motivates him to buy. The consumer is central to all hospitality operations. It is only through

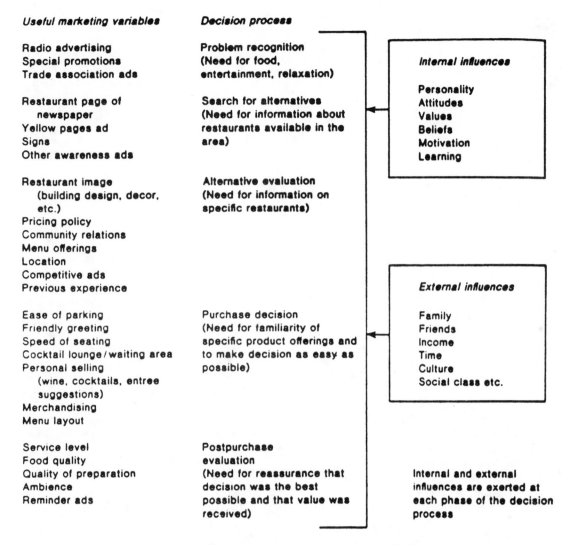

Useful marketing variables	Decision process	
Radio advertising Special promotions Trade association ads	Problem recognition (Need for food, entertainment, relaxation)	**Internal influences** Personality Attitudes Values Beliefs Motivation Learning
Restaurant page of newspaper Yellow pages ad Signs Other awareness ads	Search for alternatives (Need for information about restaurants available in the area)	
Restaurant image (building design, decor, etc.) Pricing policy Community relations Menu offerings Location Competitive ads Previous experience	Alternative evaluation (Need for information on specific restaurants)	
Ease of parking Friendly greeting Speed of seating Cocktail lounge/waiting area Personal selling (wine, cocktails, entree suggestions) Merchandising Menu layout	Purchase decision (Need for familiarity of specific product offerings and to make decision as easy as possible)	**External influences** Family Friends Income Time Culture Social class etc.
Service level Food quality Quality of preparation Ambience Reminder ads	Postpurchase evaluation (Need for reassurance that decision was the best possible and that value was received)	Internal and external influences are exerted at each phase of the decision process

Figure 1. Decision process for restaurant selection.

understanding consumer behavior and providing consumer satisfaction that we can bring people into our operation and keep them coming back.

NOTES

1. Kenneth E. Runyon, *Consumer Behavior*, Second Edition, Charles E. Merrill Publishing Company, Columbus, Ohio, 1980, p. 48.
2. Kenneth E. Runyon, Ibid., p. 61.
3. "Tastes of America," *Institutions*, November 15, 1980, p. 50.
4. Denise M. Garbedian, "Hyatt Hits New Heights," *Restaurant Business*, October 1, 1980, p. 145.
5. Harry A. Egbert, "Radio Advertising for Hotels," *The Cornell Hotel and Restaurant Administration Quarterly*, May 1980, pp. 31–36.

Central Michigan University

Courtesy of Ken W. McCleary.

It's no secret why customers sometimes wait up to two hours for a seat at Hilltop Steak House.

Top of the "500"

By Michael Sanson

It's 5 p.m. on a typical Friday night in Saugus, Massachusetts and "the wait" begins. The seasoned veterans have brought their playing cards, their knitting needles and their books knowing all too well how the game is played. So, they wait, patiently playing cards, knitting sweaters and reading books with the hope that a table will soon become available at Hilltop Steak House, the highest grossing single-unit restaurant in the country.

On Saturdays, and frequently during the week, the waiting game begins all over again. Some customers may be in line for up to two hours before they ever reach a table, yet week in and week out motorists cruising down Rt. 1 will see Hilltop customers stretched along a glass-enclosed hallway leading to the restaurant's front door.

A line of eager customers is not a rare sight in the restaurant industry, particularly at new, trendy hot spots. But this thing in Saugus has been going on now for 28 years, and Hilltop, with its "howdy partner" western motif and its outlandish, 60-foot neon cactus sign, is anything but trendy.

What makes this Hilltop waiting game so mind boggling is its size. We're talking about the Hoss Cartwright of restaurants here, folks—a whopping 1,500 seats in five dining rooms on two levels.

So, what gives? Frank Guiffrida gives. He's the owner, and to the casual observer,

he's giving away the house. The highest-priced item on the menu is Lobster Pie at $13.95. The pie includes the meat of two lobsters and is served with a bowl of salad, a huge potato or rice and rolls. The next priciest item is a 16-ounce filet mignon for $12.95. Just about everything on the menu comes with the full battery of side dishes.

> *"I'm no college man, it's easy to see that. But I do know people and I know what they like."*

It would be easy to dismiss Guiffrida as overly generous until you remember two things—those long lines of customers and Hilltop's sales figures. This year it's expecting sales in excess of $25 million. That's not taking into account the $25 million or so expected from Hilltop's butcher shop next door.

You liked those statistics, didn't you? Try these on for size: On any given Saturday, Hilltop rustles up over 7,000 meals. That comes to about 40,000 meals a week or nearly 2.4 million annually. During a typical week, Hilltop sells 20,500 pounds of beef, 8,000 pounds of fish, 17,500 pounds of baked potatoes, 120,000 rolls, 3,500 pounds of butter, 14,500 pounds of lettuce, 4,000 pounds of tomatoes and

550 pounds of coffee. It also gives away three million doggie bags.

The doggie bags tell you something. The portions are so large here that a good many customers end up carting away what they can't finish. Large portions, small prices, big lines, even bigger profits.

"I've learned that if you give value and be generous, your customers will reward you with loyalty," says Guiffrida.

That's it. He has no gimmicks, no elaborate marketing plan, no advertising, no other explanations for his success.

If Guiffrida's philosophy for success sounds oversimplified that's only because Guiffrida is a simple, down-to-earth man, a point he'll readily admit to. We're not talking about someone armed with degrees in restaurant management from Cornell University. What we have here is a street-smart butcher from Lawrence, Massachusetts who, in 1961, got together $7,000 and bought a small gin mill outside Boston to convert into a 125-seat restaurant.

"I was running a butcher shop and my brother had a restaurant," he says with a gruff voice that reminds one of a boxing trainer. "He was doing less work than I was and making more money, so I decided to open my own restaurant."

Guiffrida explains that he opened a steak house because that's what he knew—steaks and meat. He also knew a lot about human nature. Offer people top quality at a low price and they'll be back and they'll pass the word on.

Guiffrida's comments about top quality are not an overstatement. He insists that Hilltop's steaks are "the very" best he or anyone else can buy. No meat soaked in tenderizer here. He says he's so committed to quality that he'll go out of the way to get it, including importing black pepper. This commitment to quality also helps explain why his food costs run "in the high 40s."

When Guiffrida opened Hilltop at the age of 43, he and his soon-to-be wife, Irene, operated the place with a handful of employees. "Back then I was the cook, cashier, tablewasher, you name it." But that didn't last long because success came immediately.

The large crowds of customers soon required an expansion from 125 seats to 400 seats. Later, as the crowds kept growing, another expansion took place and the number of seats were doubled. A third expansion later added 350 more seats, to make 1,500.

To ensure crowd control and security on weekends, four local police officers are on duty. Hilltop, including the butcher shop, now employs about 800 people. Guiffrida had no intentions of ever operating a butcher shop again when he opened the restaurant. But customers fell in love with his product and soon began making special requests—"Hey, Frank, sell me a few steaks for a party I'm having." Those types of requests kept growing, so Guiffrida began to put five-pound bags of hamburger in the beer cooler near the door. Every day the bags were quickly snatched up and it soon became apparent that a demand existed that Hilltop was only half-heartedly trying to meet.

A full-scale butcher shop was eventually opened at the rear of the steak house. There was little need for advertising or promotion. After all, its customers had already tasted the fully-cooked product and were standing in line at the restaurant to do so. The butcher shop's prices, which are 20 to 30 percent below that of local grocery stores, is also a strong lure. The butcher shop was recently relocated next door to a larger building.

With all this talk about lines of customers, one might get the impression that diners are run through Hilltop in assembly line fashion. Well, the turnover is fast—45 minutes. But Guiffrida is quick to point out that the speedy turnover is a reflection of a well-oiled operation. The wait staff is assigned only three or four tables, not six or eight like many operations, and no less

than 70 servers are on the floor at any one time. Also, orders are deftly handled by the two kitchens, one on each floor.

Compared to food costs, the cost of labor is low at 13 percent. Yet, in a labor-tight economy like New England's, Hilltop has a list of people longing to work there. While the check averages are low ($7.50 for lunch and $12 for dinner), the fast turnover provides a solid tip income.

Along with quality and value, Guiffrida cites a couple other variables that have contributed to Hilltop's success. Location is one. Route 1 is a commercial magnet that has attracted mini-malls, liquor marts, muffler shops, restaurants—you name it. "Before I built here," he says, "I counted the cars driving along Route 1 and saw a business opportunity." Cash is another factor in Hilltop's success. That's all Hilltop accepts—no credit cards, thank you.

Hilltop also appeals to all types of customers, Guiffrida adds. At any given time, you'll find "young executive types" sitting next to blue-collar workers, who are sitting next to senior citizens, who are next to young families. Hilltop has such a wide appeal, and offers such great value, that it's not unusual for customers to drive 40 or 50 miles to eat here, he says.

Hilltop's menu evolved over the years to appeal to a wider base of customers. What was mainly a steak-based menu is now one that also offers chicken (Broiled Half

Chicken—$7 and Baked Boneless Breast of Chicken—$9.95) and several fish entres, including Broiled Haddock, Broiled Shrimp, and Broiled Swordfish Steak, all $10.95. One thing that has never changed over the years is portion size.

"The size of the portions we give customers will never change. That, along with the quality of the food we serve, is the reason why people go out of their way to come here," Guiffrida emphasizes. "It all boils down to value."

Although he's still actively involved with the operation of Hilltop, Guiffrida admits that he's spending more time these days smelling the roses. The chairman of the board (that's his official title with Hilltop) has become quite a gourmet cook over the years, and spends a lot of hours in his own kitchen at home.

Guiffrida readily admits that he would have a much more difficult time trying to start the business today. The competition is much more fierce and sophisticated. But Guiffrida isn't starting the business—he is expanding it. A second Hilltop Steak House recently opened in Nashua, New Hampshire and plans call for up to 10 more restaurants in New England within the next 10 years.

"I'm no college man, it's easy to see that. But I do know people and I know what they like," Guiffrida said. "And they know me too. They know I'm honest and that I'm giving them the best value they can get. What more do you need to know?" 🍵

Selling Sizzle and Getting People to Come

Introduction by Bonnie Knutson

We   live in an information society -- an over-communicated information society. How can you hope to have consumers notice, let alone act upon, the message in your advertising when it must compete with the power of McDonald's, Domino's, Red Lobster's, and Pizza Hut's? Among Hyatt's, Hilton's, Marriott's and Holiday Inn's?   How can you be the next Bartles and Jaymes?

The answer -- if there is one -- is to rise above or cut through the clutter. To present your message in a way that is different and better than the competition, and, above all, believable. Betsy Gerkman's "Moving Your Audience to Action" gives some tips for doing just that in print media.

In "Restaurant Advertising: Coupons, Clowns, and Cadillacs," Michael Lefever draws on his years of hospitality experience to describe the advertising and marketing strategies most frequently employed in the food service industry. He warns us, however, that while effective advertising can bring customers in the door, it's up to operations to bring them back by providing them with a positive experience.

Advertising and Marketing

The Sandwich Board Approach

I suppose most of you have taken a marketing course or attended a seminar on advertising. Here are some terms that should sound familiar: perceptual maps; cross tabs; psychographics; geo-demographics; discriminant analysis; factor analysis; cluster analysis; positioning; market segments; the four Ps; AIDA; KISS; regression analysis; product-service mix; and sales blitz. They are all valuable concepts and not particularly difficult to use. Unfortunately, you probably will forget these marketing luxuries in the real world of restaurants. You will be too busy with the everyday basics of attracting and keeping your customers.

I will always remember the two magnetic signs Joe had made for the doors of his Cadillac. They advertised the name of the restaurant, which incidentally was the same as Joe's last name. Every time Joe drove down the street, the whole town knew it. Everyone knew where he shopped, where he bought his gas, where he lived, and how often he visited the dentist. They also knew his daily habits: when he went to work, when he went home, and when he took the money to the bank. People knew too much about Joe.

One afternoon Joe took his wife to another local restaurant for lunch. He parked his Cadillac in front, near the street, where he could keep an eye on it from their reserved window seat. Suddenly another car pulled up alongside the Cadillac and the driver, a former waitress Joe had recently fired, jumped out. She pried open the locked lid to the Cadillac's gas tank and unscrewed the cap. Then she took a book of matches from her purse, lit one, and tossed it down the tank. Nothing happened, so she did it again.

Joe grabbed his wife and ran to the rear of the restaurant in case the Cadillac exploded. The sheriff arrived a few minutes later and found her still stuffing matches down the gas tank. According to the sheriff, she was intoxicated, recognized Joe's Cadillac with the magnetic signs, and had decided to get even.

That was enough for Joe. He did not have any privacy, and then someone had tried to blow up his car. He removed the signs the same afternoon. But the sun had noticeably faded the paint on his car—except for the surfaces underneath the signs. Each door had an obvious and permanent impression exactly the same size and shape as the signs. Joe was furious and considered having the car repainted. He bought a new Cadillac instead, because it was more convenient.

Then one of Joe's bartenders asked if he could borrow the signs to put on his own car. Joe agreed, thinking he would get some free advertising. The bartender was happy because people might think he was the new owner of the restaurant.

One morning I saw the bartender cruising the streets with the lopsided signs stuck to the doors of an ancient, oversized, rusted car. It was like watching a parade. The unshaven bartender, wearing dirty coveralls and sitting low in the seat, drove slowly along the busiest street with a cigarette dangling from his lips. Everyone turned to watch as the car approached, with thick blue smoke belching from a dragging muffler.

The bartender parked his car in front of every local tavern and finally was involved in a multiple-car accident. Joe's signs made the front page of the newspaper, and he fired the bartender. But he retrieved only one of the signs from the police impound lot. Early one morning Joe received a phone call from an excited neighbor who said he had seen the missing sign stuck on the back of a city garbage truck.

Even without the magnetic signs, Joe had ways to advertise his restaurant. He always wore white cook's pants, a starched white shirt, a white apron, and big, comfortable black shoes that squeaked when he walked. He wore that same uniform whether he was working in the restaurant or doing errands around town. He also bought a new Cadillac every year and liked to smoke expensive cigars. It was easy to recognize him. His appearance and positive attitude attracted more customers than the restaurant could feed.

Joe was proud of his restaurant. It had one of the most modern kitchens available. He also had a small fortune invested in two tall, freestanding signs and an array of blinking neon lights on the outside of the building. One day a city inspector came to the restaurant and told Joe he had to rewire the neon lights to make them stop blinking, because of a new sign ordinance. That was not the worst part; the new ordinance also limited the height of freestanding signs.

After spending another small fortune to rewire his lights and reduce the height of his signs, Joe finally was in compliance with the new law. He liked to remark how advertising was just an "expensive privilege."

Soon afterward, another official-looking person came to the restaurant.

He was a process server. Joe was being sued by the owner of a well-established restaurant with a well-known name in another part of the state. Both restaurants just happened to have exactly the same name, and the other owner contended that Joe was advertising illegally. The bitter legal battle continued for years, costing Joe another fortune. In the end Joe had to add his first name to all his signs and other forms of advertising. No one talked much about signs around Joe after that.

One of Joe's more traditional forms of advertising was a gigantic window, which allowed people walking by or waiting outside the building to look into the kitchen and watch the cooks. Our indiscreet and downright foul behavior forced Joe to replace the glass with a solid piece of colored plastic. People could not see in and we could not see out. But it was successful at preventing the cooks from nauseating the customers before they even got in the door.

Besides the original outside window, Joe designed his open kitchen with a pass-through shelf that allowed the customers sitting or standing in the foyer to watch the team of "trained chefs" flipping and flaming the house specialties. But as you already know, we flipped and flamed more than the food, so Joe closed the restaurant for an entire month to remodel and block the kitchen and cooks from public view.

I learned from Joe that advertising, whether it is traditional or unique, works only if you have the right kind of employees. I think most small, independent restaurant owners and large international chains keep forgetting this rule. I wonder how many businesses actually try to match their advertising and promises to what their employees can deliver?

Joe's most powerful form of advertising was the fact that he was always at the restaurant. He called it his personal goodwill. Customers often came in just to see Joe; eating and drinking were secondary. He would listen from his favorite corner seat in the lounge for the front door of the restaurant to swing open. Before the door swung shut, Joe would greet the customers with a big .smile and a warm handshake. He made everyone, whether a new or regular customer, feel equally special. I would hear him say, "I'm going to have Mikey fix you something extra nice tonight." And I would be thinking, "Yeah, right, Joe. Fix it yourself."

The company for which I worked as a unit manager had its own standard forms of advertising. Our marketing department spent millions of dollars on television spots. I always thought they did more harm than good, because the sparkling facilities, inviting food, and friendly actors did not resemble our operations at all.

We had to close one of our model regional training units and clean for two days before it was camera ready. The food props were prepared in the quality control laboratory by technicians and touched up with dyes and wax. We never saw any of our own employees or customers in the spots. I suppose our own employees were not attractive or friendly enough, and our own customers would not smile, sing, and dance.

We had one continuous form of print advertising. It was our corporate logo, pressed into everything the customer might see, touch, eat, walk on, or sit on. All those logos even advertised our garbage. They helped nearby home owners identify the source when someone dumped our cups, bags, and wrappers on their front lawns during the night. Almost every morning I would get a phone call from an irate neighbor complaining about our litter on his or her property. I always asked where the property was located, because there were eight other units in the city and our number just happened to be listed first in the telephone directory. Sometimes I would refer the callers to the unit manager nearest their property. Other times I would recite my lukewarm apologies. If they were obnoxious, I would offer them a complimentary lunch if they returned the litter. That usually took care of the problem one way or another.

Once we had a "professional" litter complainer. He called me and the district manager every day. I even had an employee begin inspecting his lawn early each morning. He would not stop complaining, so I had my employee start dumping litter from several of our nearby competitors on his lawn. The complaints stopped instantly. We later found out that our competitors had been dumping our litter on his lawn for the same reason.

About once a month we would have a special marketing promotion in the unit. It often consisted of a reduced price for a single menu item or a combination of items. Sometimes we would even offer two for the price of one. The major problem with those special promotions was that they did not encourage the customers to come back. We had to cook and assemble the products faster because of the increased business, which reduced the quality even further. Our hamburger production area was such a mess that I could not distinguish a bun top from a bottom. At least I was beginning to know how the customers felt.

Special promotions also caused a constant state of confusion at the cash registers. Cashiers often were not sure how to calculate the discounts or enter them into the registers. The amount of the discounts often would change from shift to shift, depending on the interpretation of the assistant manager in charge. Inventory and cash reconciliations were virtually impossible during promotions, which meant we had a higher incidence of employee theft to top everything off.

I doubt if the special promotions ever helped our profit margins. They did, however, make us all work harder and made it possible for part-time employees to get full eight-hour shifts and more. The real problem came after the typical week-long promotions. Most of the employees had to return to their part-time schedules, causing some of them to quit. That created a revolving employee crisis, and we continually scrambled to hire new people.

The monthly promotions did reduce our food costs. It was not because we were carefully portioning and weighing every menu item. Rather it was because we did not have any spoilage or waste. We sold every scrap of food in the restaurant as fast as we could, and the employees did not have time to eat, which helped matters too.

Our company regularly advertised by offering the public a special purchase item. The most popular special purchase item was a Christmas drinking glass. If a customer bought a sandwich and a drink, he or she could also purchase the glass for a small additional amount. Some customers enjoyed collecting a set of glasses as a gift for a special relative.

A week before the promotion, we filled our storeroom, office, freezer, refrigerator, and even attic with cases of Christmas glasses. We carefully trained our employees how to sell them. It was one of the most successful events of the year, and everyone got geared up for it.

On the first day of the promotion, we would start selling dozens of glasses with the early breakfast orders. By noon we were selling hundreds of glasses, and there were piles of empty cases stacked around the outside of the building. Halfway through the dinner rush on the first day of the one-week promotion, we would sell out of glasses and be unable to get more. It happened exactly the same way each year I was with the company.

When Renee and I bought our first restaurant, it had a large sign on the roof. The nicknames of the previous owners and the name of the restaurant were painted on it. One of the first things I did was call a sign painter and ask if he would change the nicknames to "Mike and Renee's." Renee mumbled something so I reminded her that *M* precedes *R* in the alphabet. I was eager to get the sign changed because it did not seem as if we really owned the restaurant with the previous owners' names still on the roof.

The painters arrived and I watched as they quickly covered the old names with whiteout paint and neatly lettered our names over the top. It worried me to see how easy it was to change owners on a sign. I wondered how long we would own the restaurant and how thick the whiteout paint would be in twenty years. I finally realized I was more concerned about having our names, especially mine, on the sign than the name of the restaurant. Since it was at one of the busiest intersections in town, thousands of people a day would see our names and know we were the proud new owners. I suddenly understood why Joe was so sensitive about his signs. They are a very personal and strange source of pleasure.

Years later Renee and I had a new sign made for the roof. It did not include our names. It was a simple but tasteful sign that just advertised the name of our restaurant. I felt good about the new sign, because I had begun to be embarrassed about our names continually assaulting every passing motorist. But it was a great way to advertise. Everyone, including tourists, knew that Mike and Renee owned the restaurant. In fact, most of our customers just called the restaurant "Mike and Renee's."

One day my father-in-law, Ozzie, told me a story about his dad, who had also owned a few restaurants. He said, "Dad was a great one for advertising. He'd put on his clean white pants, white shirt, white apron, and white cook's hat and start walking down one side of the street and up the other. It was obvious what he did for a living from the way he dressed. He'd stop and say hello to everyone he saw and invite them to his restaurant. Dad called it sandwich-board advertising, and he always had the busiest restaurant in town."

Ozzie said most people do not like to advertise using the old-fashioned sandwich-board approach because they are either embarrassed about what they do for a living or just plain lazy. He also told me that my pride had destroyed one of our cheapest and most effective forms of advertising when I had our names taken off the sign on the roof.

I tried to overcome my pride by wearing a clean white cook's apron every time I left the restaurant. I could not force myself to wear the hat. I even started walking up and down the streets saying, "Hello. We haven't seen you in the restaurant for a while. Come in and see us when you have a chance." We ended up having more customers and friends than we could manage. Ozzie's dad was right about what it took to advertise. It was a continual effort and we could not stop for a moment, but the results were immediate, measurable, and overwhelming. The sandwich-board approach was not a surprise, though; Joe used it too.

We had several other forms of advertising. They all seemed to work, some better than others. The most effective form was customer word of mouth and it was not easy to accomplish. In a word, everything in our restaurant had to be perfect. It was possible, because we defined the *perfect* condition for our customers. In other words, we trained them into anticipating only the products and services we could deliver with perfection.

We did very little media advertising because word of mouth took all our time, attention, and energy. We noticed that many restaurants relying on media advertising were not doing a good job in the first place and already had made too many mistakes in their kitchens and dining rooms. It was like begging people to come back. I know there are many exceptions to this thinking, but the basic premise is correct.

Renee and I regularly invited the local hotel and motel owners to our restaurant for complimentary meals. Most of the other restaurateurs made the mistake of inviting that important support group only once, usually right after the restaurant opened, when the employees were still unfamiliar with the operation. We never used the telephone to invite them. They were very special people, so we made personal visits once a month. If they could not or would not come to the restaurant, we would have one of our employees deliver a homemade pie.

In return we always had a crowd of tourists in our restaurant, which surprisingly did not annoy our regular customers. All the customers enjoyed each other because our employees always maintained control of the dining room. They would not hesitate to ask customers to restrain their children or extinguish a cigar. Restaurants that allow the customers to control the employees are always unpredictable and often unmanageable.

That brings me to another form of advertising. It was employee word of mouth. Many restaurateurs fail to realize how much damage employees can inflict on the reputation of their business. Employees tend to be either full-time allies or nonstop enemies, and they constantly advertise their feelings. Our employees were much more valuable than our most loyal customers when it came to word-of-mouth advertising.

Two other forms of advertising I would like to mention are somewhat controversial. First, I always made sure our parking lot was full of cars. Critics might argue that customers would not be able to find a parking place. But customers can always find a place to park if they think a restaurant is worth it. I would tell my employees to park their own cars in the front parking lot until it got busy. It was hilarious to watch the reaction of the customers when all our employees would walk out together, get in their cars, and move them to the rear lot.

Second, we would purposely run out of food every weekend. Most restaurateurs say it is the worst thing that can possibly happen. But it was an effective form of advertising for us. Town gossip characterized our restaurant as the best and the busiest because it was the only one that ever ran out of food. It is worth noting, however, that this risky form of advertising worked because we were *already* one of the best and busiest.

We always had our house in order before advertising. The corporate chains seemed to do just the opposite, hoping advertising would get their house in order.

Sometimes our advertising did not work. We spent hundreds of dollars sponsoring a bowling team. Once the players had our check, we never saw them again. I followed the bowling scores in the local newspaper, and our team, along with the name of our restaurant, was always at the bottom of the list. One day a customer told me our team had acquired quite a reputation. The players were the champion beer drinkers of the league.

As a district manager, I was impressed with our corporate marketing department. It had seven full-time staff members and its own modern building next to corporate headquarters. The director of marketing was a kind and perceptive person. I was equally impressed with his knowledge of the industry. He had also been a restaurant owner for twenty years.

He invited me to lunch soon after I joined the company. We went to a cafeteria-style restaurant and watched the operation while we ate. I learned more about restaurants in those two short hours than at any other time in my career. He told me our company definitely needed a marketing department to create an image by taking advantage of its financial and professional resources. He thought many of the unit managers were overworked and did not have the time, energy, or commitment to think about advertising. He said, "How can people think about advertising, which involves creativity and good human relations, when they're totally preoccupied with protecting their present job and fighting for a better one? We also have a problem with middle- and upper-level management. They think they've been promoted out of the restaurant. So they hire an office full of marketing personnel responsible for attracting and keeping their customers. It's difficult to understand after being a restaurant owner."

Consequently, management blamed the marketing department for flat sales and declining customer counts. Marketing responded by noting that something had to happen in the units. The solution to those regular bouts of passing the buck was for the president periodically to replace the director of marketing with some "new blood." The director of marketing once told me, "Just remember that working for a large corporation is almost the opposite of working for yourself. While you're here, more attention will be focused on the worker, including yourself, than on the customer." He was asked to resign the next day, and he graciously helped a new director of marketing move into his old office.

One of the first advertising campaigns I supervised as a district manager consisted of printing up ten thousand fliers for each of my units. The flier announced the date and time of a super-big discount on all our sandwiches.

I delivered the fliers to the unit managers and instructed them to have their employees place the fliers under the windshield wipers of cars parked in nearby shopping centers.

I think the managers tossed most of the fliers in the dumpster as soon as I was out of sight. The employees probably tossed out the rest of them so they would not have to wander around parking lots in their silly uniforms.

But a few of the fliers actually ended up under the wiper blades of potential customers. I got a half-dozen phone calls from people threatening to sue the company if we did not immediately replace their damaged wipers. I always wondered how both wipers on a car got damaged. It was always much cheaper just to have the people send us a bill rather than fight it out in court. They knew it too. The next calls were usually from the shopping centers, demanding that we send over a crew to clean up their parking lots.

I remember one of our employees getting into an argument with the owner of a car after sticking a flier under his wiper. The owner demanded that the employee remove the flier and apologize. The employee removed it but would not apologize. So the car owner started punching the employee in the face. The serious thing about the whole incident was that our employee won the fight. He got fired, and the car owner got a speedy cash settlement.

We also used a marketing tool called *time-fused couponing.* A perforated sheet of nine coupons would appear in the Sunday newspapers. The first row of three coupons was valid immediately, the second row of three was good the following week, and the third row the third week. We hoped the customers would save and use the coupons for three weeks.

Unfortunately, the coupons were too confusing for our customers. A family of six would come into a unit and shove all nine at the cashier, or an elderly couple would bring in coupons with the wrong dates. Sometimes the company authorized the units to honor all the coupons all the time, and sometimes it did not. That confused the customers and employees even more.

The continual couponing caused a rather interesting dilemma. Customers did not like the confusion of the coupons, and they did not like paying the full price without them. Couponing backfired, and we started honoring any fast-food coupons, regardless of the company or the dates. It rapidly got out of control, and our accounting systems became a disaster. We finally gave up and started leaving stacks of coupons on the counter so the customers could help themselves. But the customers finally gave up too and would say, "Don't bother trying to figure out my discount; I'd rather pay the full price and get my sandwich while it's still warm."

Sophisticated corporate marketing would not be complete without a company mascot. Each district had its own clown costume, and each unit could borrow it for one weekend every other month. We would buckle, button, zip, and even staple an employee inside. On hot summer days, an employee could not stay inside the heavy costume more than twenty minutes without collapsing from the heat. Most employees stuck in the costume wore only their underwear, if that, and secretly drank beer.

One Saturday our clown gave away two hundred free french fry coupons to children at a local park, and the nearest unit set a company record for the highest sales volume in a single day. The next week another unit borrowed the clown and gave away another two hundred coupons. That time the coupons did not work. Only six were redeemed.

One bright Sunday we stationed the clown next to the road outside a unit, waving at cars. Inside we were giving away helium-filled balloons. All day the dining room was a solid mass of kids trying to grab a floating balloon. We did not sell one sandwich, because all the employees were tying balloons and helping control the crowd. When we ran out of balloons, the dining room emptied out as quickly as it had filled up. It took several days before the regular customers returned.

One morning I was asked to bring some cooked products to a local television studio. Our company was making a new thirty-second commercial, and it needed fresh props. I rushed the products to the studio in my company car, hoping they would not get cold and soggy. I raced in the front door with my Styrofoam carrying case as if I were bringing lifesaving blood to a dying patient. Someone from the studio intercepted me and said, "Slow down; this stuff doesn't have to be fresh. We can fix it up later."

It was amazing what they did with their lights and cameras. Even more amazing was watching them "fix up" the products. They took the warm soft drinks and dropped imitation ice cubes in them. Then they added a wafer that made them fizz and sprayed the outside of the cups with water to make them look frosty. They coated the hamburger buns with hair spray to give them a healthy shine and melted the corners of a piece of cheese over the meat patties with a cigarette lighter. The cold french fries were given a blast of penetrating oil from an aerosol can so they would look fresh out of the fryer. Finally, they squirted white all-purpose glue on the sandwiches, because it was more photogenic than mayonnaise.

I did not have to worry much about couponing or television commercials when I was a regional vice-president for a full-service chain. Our standard building design was unusual but stylish, and it attracted everyone's attention. We enhanced its distinctiveness even further by adding a "deluxe garden" landscape package and camouflaging typical restaurant eyesores such as dumpster areas and rooftop equipment.

Colors were also very important. We had an interior designer, a lighting engineer, and several other professionals harmonize all the interior and exterior finishes. Even the lighting was coordinated. We ordered special incandescent bulbs and fluorescent tubes from a half-dozen companies. The kitchen had three different types of fluorescent tubes so the cooks would look healthy. All the interior lights were designed to make the food look more appealing by adding reds and other warm colors of the spectrum. The exterior lights were designed to make the building look special and alive without being garish. The entire building was our logo and sign.

We always located our restaurants in high-traffic areas, usually at the intersection of two major arteries in front of large shopping centers. Access in and out of our parking lots was always easy, and we positioned our restaurants so they were highly visible to an approaching driver. Our restaurants had built-in advertising.

The high visibility also kept us on our toes when it came to outside maintenance. The lawns were mowed twice a week, dead flowers and burned-out light bulbs were immediately replaced, and litter was seldom seen around the buildings. We even picked up most of the litter from adjacent parking areas so it would not blow into our own perimeters.

Another form of advertising we used was staying open twenty four hours a day, every day of the year. It helped establish an image of convenience, dependability, goodwill, and permanence.

We did not spend large sums of money on advertising. In fact, it was just the opposite. We often made money while doing our own advertising. One of the best examples of this doubly profitable advertising was the way we hired our managers and hourly employees. We always hired management teams from the local community and preferred candidates from respected, well-liked, influential families. Once they were hired, we sent them to another restaurant for training. While they were away, my district managers would visit the local businesses and ask the owners or managers if they could recommend someone who might be interested in a restaurant job. Many recommended their own children, and that is exactly what we wanted. We also concentrated on churches and public service companies for prospective employees, because they had very extensive, active, and powerful communication networks.

Our goal was to have an employee from each significant "market nest" in the community. That is how we quickly established a core of regular customers and why the entire community became our personal, full-time advertising firm.

The major problem with the community-driven advertising system was the risk of amplifying negative characteristics through the same free and efficient channels. That is why we had to be extremely cautious when we fired someone. One of our restaurants was boycotted by the entire community until we rehired an employee who had been fired for stealing.

When Renee and I bought our third restaurant, advertising and marketing became less a portfolio of clever strategies and more an everyday test of endurance. We struggled again to memorize the names of our customers, including spouses and children. We listened to their problems, told them funny stories, and did everything in our power to make them comfortable and happy. I walked the streets wearing my apron, shaking hands like a politician, and smiling until my mouth hurt.

Since our restaurant was in a historic tourist area, we had to get written permission from the historical society, city council, and merchants' association before displaying any outside signs. Our restaurant had two approved signs, but I wanted another one near the front door. I applied for the new sign, but the request was denied because of a two-sign limit. I discovered from another business owner that the two-sign limit pertained only to permanent signs, which made it possible to hang banners and flags during special events.

I went ahead and had another sign made in the shape of an A-frame. While we were open, I would place the sign on the sidewalk near the front door. After we closed in the evening, I would drag the sign inside. The historical society threatened to confiscate the sign, even though it was "temporary." Therefore, I began chaining the sign to an adjacent light post while it was outside. It was not long before I saw other "temporary" signs appearing in front of businesses up and down the street.

We also tried advertising in the telephone directory. About four months after the new telephone directories were distributed, we wanted to change our hours and the credit cards we honored. But we had to wait another eight months for the new directories. We later called the telephone company to ask when someone planned to get in touch with us about the changes. The person said the new books were already at the printer's and we had already agreed to keep our new ad exactly the same. We did not remember renewing the ad or even talking with a telephone representative. But then again, it was easy to say anything on the telephone when we had a restaurant full of employees and customers. We also did not remember that the advertising rates had doubled.

We tried advertising our "early bird" specials, half-price dinner entrees between 4:00 and 6:00 P.M. on weekdays, in the local newspaper. We would get dozens of phone calls from people asking if they could still have the reduced price if they were "only an hour or so late." On Friday and Saturday nights we always would get a few customers who had "driven for hours just for the 'early bird' special." The thing I remember most about our "early bird" ads was the account executive. For several weeks after we stopped advertising, she would appear every afternoon and ask if we would like to start again. We would say "No," and she would give us a cold, penetrating stare that clearly meant, "You'll be sorry." Unfortunately, we already were.

We joined a "dine out" club soon after we bought the restaurant. It consisted of a coupon book containing discounts at more than a hundred local restaurants, including ours. Anyone could purchase the coupon books for a modest amount. Most of the coupons were two-for-one offers with various types of restrictions. We offered a two-for-one champagne buffet brunch on Sundays.

"Dine out" clubs were a popular and successful form of advertising. The coupon books were advertised, along with the participating restaurants, in all the local newspapers. Many loyal and regular customers first came to our restaurant because of the club. It was doubly profitable because many couples with two-for-one coupons brought friends who did not have them. We could make a respectable profit even if every couple had a coupon.

There were, however, a few minor drawbacks to the "dine out" club. Many of the club customers were our biggest complainers. They acted like restaurant critics irritated that they had to pay anything at all. They also had a tendency to leave a tip based on the one paying guest or half the bill. Our servers were known to avoid tables when they saw customers sit down and pull out their coupon books. Some customers got smart and waited until they finished their meals before displaying the coupons, so they would not get half the service.

Early one Sunday morning at the restaurant, we started getting phone calls from friends telling us to look in the entertainment section of the newspaper. Our restaurant had a nice write-up describing it as one of the city's ten best. Once each year the newspaper sent out a survey to the readers asking them to nominate the best restaurants. It was exhilarating, even though a close friend admitted she bought extra newspapers and collected enough blank survey forms from friends and neighbors to nominate us a hundred times herself.

Moving Your Audience to Action:

Remember the key elements of advertising that get results. The requirements of print, radio, and TV are very different, but if you keep the basics in mind, an effective advertising campaign can be achieved.

BY BETSY GERKMAN

Whatever your product or service, in order for the cash register to ring, a purchaser's mind must be moved from attention to interest to conviction to action. Ads that produce results—in print, radio, and television—move the reader or listener through these four steps to a sale.

Grabbing Attention in Print

Your ad will have to compete with some 200-300 other messages in a single day. What will make it stand out from the rest?

First, keep in mind a few layout basics. Remember the simpler the graphic the more powerful it can be. Plan white space in the ad to focus attention and invite reading. Dark letters on light background have been proven to have the highest readability. Limit letter styles—no more than three is a good rule of thumb.

Your headline has a big job to do. It has to stop the reader *and* draw him into reading the copy that will sell him. In copy research, the "conversion ratio" measures how many headline readers are drawn into reading copy. What would you guess? Half? A third? It's actually only 20% for the average ad. That means out of five persons reading your headline, only one will probably read your copy. So get your message out front in the headline!

When writing a headline, come at it from the reader's point of view, focusing on the benefit to him—the need it answers, the want it satisfies. Be specific, honest, believable.

Questions are often effective.

A guarantee sparks interest too.

Whatever the headline, it should work with the layout and illustration, reinforcing your message visually and verbally.

Copy that sells convincingly

Copy that sells continues and reinforces the interest you created in the headline. Write it just as if you were talking to a potential customer—one on one.

You don't "con" a customer; you *convince* them. So convince the reader with the unique features of the product—tied to benefits, its performance records, test results, leadership position in sales. Use testimonials. Stress the quality or performance guarantee. Don't generalize; use precise, honest words.

Close with a call for immediate action of some sort on the reader's part. Make it urgent, compelling... phone now, come in today, don't wait to grab this opportunity. You can add to the urgency with activators such as "limited-time savings," "three-day introductory offer," "free demonstration," or "0% financing available this week only."

To strengthen your position in the marketplace and add to the consistency and recognition of your name and image, try to create your ad to be a part of a series, designed around a central theme. Create a consistent campaign by applying the following principals to each ad of the series: Deliver your campaign keynote in each ad for unity of message. Make each ad distinctively yours so that all carry a familiar look. Keep interest and attention high by varying and reinforcing your selling message within that familiar format.

Grabbing attention in radio

Winning a listening audience is very different from a reading audience. Often advertisers make the mistake of thinking that print copy can simply be read to a listening audience. Not so!

You *can* capture their attention with *dialogue*—two or more voices talking to each other and/or the listener It can be upbeat and interesting, and it can still pack a wallop of a sales message..

The addition of *music*—particularly a jingle for your company or product—is an excellent attention-getter. While producing an original, professionally produced jingle can be an expensive endeavor, it can be used over a long period of time to reinforce your image and name through various campaigns.

Sound effects are ideal for the stage you are setting on radio. By enticing the imagination of your listener, you are using the medium of radio to your best advantage.

No matter how you choose to capture your audience, be quick with stating your benefit, and make it personal. Remember that radio has the distinct advantage of creating a personal relationship with the listener—a kind of intimacy not achieved through other media. So present your benefit in a personal way, speaking directly to the listener if possible.

Validate the value of your product with numbers, a guarantee, a comparison, history of satisfaction—there are a number of ways to create conviction.

Then wrap it up with a clincher—free trial, special introductory price, or any technique to create action.

Sign off with your company identification and any last minute instructions.

Plan to repeat your company name throughout the spot, a minimum of two times.

Each of these steps will strengthen your radio campaign by using sound effectively.

Grabbing attention on television

Unless television is well timed, well placed and very well made, it can backfire faster and to a far larger audience than other media. Combining audio and visual is an art, and capturing the TV audience is one of the most creative challenges to be faced by advertisers. The competition for attention is fierce!

Always try to use sight, sound, motion and color when you select television for your message.

Create a strong central sell message, and go right to the unique benefit. It may be a life-style benefit, a product guarantee, or the product itself in demonstration.

Become an ad watcher, and tune in to music videos often. Here you will see how attention is being captured and you will become more familiar with the film and video techniques being used today.

Perhaps most importantly, don't overdo special effects. Insist that every word, every motion, every sound pass this test: Does it put across the message? Does it heighten interest and understanding? Does it add to the appeal? If not, it doesn't belong in a 30-second commercial.

Show your product in action or in demonstration if possible. Or have your "customers" act out the benefits. But be sure to make the tests real and the people believable.

Display and say what you want your audience to do. Be sure to give them a specific action to take as the commercial closes.

A bit of warning

Listen and watch for good local advertising if you're considering a campaign and the selection of an advertising agency to assist you. Listen or watch for *attention, interest, conviction, and action,* and then call the media to find out who produced the ad. That may be the first step to developing a working relationship.

The purchase of space or time in print, radio, or television is a large investment that demands careful attention. Each of these can be powerful conveyers of your message, if it is produced effectively. ■

Betsy Gerkman is president and executive creative director for Riversedge Marketing Incorporated.

What's on the menu?

Introduction by Pete Stevens

Menu has two meanings for us: First, it represents a restaurant's *product mix*. [What's on the menu? Steaks, some seafood ...] Second, it represents a *merchandising medium* for that product mix. [Would you like to see the menu now?] Though the articles in this section all focus on food service, I suggest that you translate the messages for hotels, airlines and tourist destinations as well. All organizations have *menus*.

Any restaurateur who understands that the customer is boss (smart restaurateurs), would agree with the National Restaurant Association's *Accuracy in Menus* position paper, so it's included here. Further, it would seem that Tom Feltenstein's customer-focused approach to new product development makes some sense if the customer is boss. And then, my reading is that particularly educated travelers and executives are increasingly demanding nutritious as well as tasty, etc., meal choices. Beth Carlson's article can give us some guidance there.

A number of models for evaluating menus and improving performance have come down the pike in recent years, some simple, some complex, some better than others (in my opinion). Lendal Kotschevar provides a survey of the models, some discussion *vis-a-vis* their merits, and some wisdom to help in choosing among them.

Finally, *The Groesbeck Club: A Case Study* describes the beginning stages of a consulting project. There's marketing research, market segments, positioning, promotional strategy, menu analysis and more. There's much to chew on and discuss. You should bring much of what you've read to bear on recommending what club management should do. It'll help you integrate the *stuff* you've been reading.

Meeting consumer needs — the basis for successful marketing of nutrition in foodservice

Beth L. Carlson

Division of Hotel, Restaurant and Institutional Management, Virginia Polytechnic and State University, Blacksburg, VA 24061, U.S.A.

In this paper the need to base the design and marketing of nutrition in the hospitality industry upon consumer segmentation of the market is discussed. Characteristics of existing programs are summarized as are the factors contributing to their success or failure. An understanding of how to market nutrition programs successfully in the hospitality industry is essential, as nearly all hotel chains and many independent and chain restaurants have developed nutrition promotions or will be implementing nutrition programs in the next two years.

Key words: marketing   nutrition programs   hospitality   consumer   foodservice

Introduction

In the past, the role of nutrition in foodservice was to give a 'clinical' slant to menu planning. Little thought was given to consumer attitudes and behavior and the role these play in food habits and preferences. The nutrition market was believed to be a homogeneous group of consumers who were mostly calorie-conscious dieters. Their needs were met with a standard 'diet' plate. Most restaurateurs believed that these consumers would 'go off their diet anyway' when eating away from home (Sibley, 1986).

Today, not only have changes occurred within this market but restaurateurs are beginning to realize that it is a growing and increasingly complex one. This shift from 'low-cal' to 'healthful' holds great opportunity for restaurateurs. Providing nutrition programs is now considered to be essential in remaining competitive in the hospitality industry (Carlson, 1986). This article is concerned with how the market can be segmented on this dimension and with examples of how different sectors of the industry have responded in addressing these markets.

Consumer segmentation of the nutrition market

In segmenting the nutrition market in the hospitality industry, one must consider the consumer's perception of nutrition and diet concomitant with trends occurring in the 1980s. Five current trends relating to nutrition include: (1) concern over the future and use of long-term preventative measures; (2) increased emphasis on communication and the availability of pertinent information rather than protection by regulation; (3) desire for flexibility, pluralism and choice; (4) commitment to science and technology; (5) changing social themes, family structure and increasing value placed on fitness and vitality (Skelly, 1982).

The American consumer is at present mature, self-confident and knowledgeable about food, diet, health, fitness and nutrition (Bukos, 1983; Campbell Soup Company, 1984; McRobbie, 1984). Seventy-seven per cent of consumers are more interested in nutrition than they were a year ago. This interest is reflected not only in the decision of whether to eat out, but where to eat out, and what food to select when eating out. Nutritious food was rated by 75–85% of patrons as being 'somewhat' to 'very' important in their decision to eat out. The consumer most interested and knowledgeable about nutrition has the same demographic characteristics as those of the frequent patron (Anon, 1983; Sherwood, 1984).

Nutritional awareness has inspired the following changes: (1) avoidance of certain foods; (2) avoidance of certain food substances and ingredients; (3) altered methods of food preparation, and (4) increased consumption of foods 'perceived' to be healthy. Restaurant patrons thought that nutritional responsibility rested primarily on the consumer when dining out (Bukos, 1979). However, 65% of restaurant patrons believed that restaurateurs do have a responsibility to provide their patrons with a variety of properly prepared offerings (Bukos, 1983).

Consumer attitudes about nutrition have changed eating habits both at home and away. These changes, undertaken by 60% of consumers, include eating more fruit, vegetables and whole grains; and eating less refined sugar, animal fats and salt (Gallup Organization, 1983; Wren, 1986). These dietary changes, which are in accordance with the U.S. Dietary Guidelines, are maintained by 40% of consumers when eating away from home. The percentage of patrons reporting specific changes both at home and in restaurants are: increased consumption of fish or seafood (20%), vegetables (18%) and salads (18%), and decreased consumption of sugar (20%) and salt (25%) (Gallup Organization, 1983). Furthermore, the segment of the population which must modify its diet for health reasons is growing. Twenty-two per cent of all consumers live in a household in which someone is on a special diet (Riggs, 1980). Over 50% of restaurant patrons have indicated that they would be more likely to order entrée items if they had the choice of smaller portion sizes, low sodium or low calorie options (Gallup Organization, 1983).

Based on their attitudes toward food, consumers can be segmented into four groups. The largest group (32%) places nutritional value over taste, convenience or caloric value when making food choices (CREST, 1983). The importance that nutrition plays for patrons in selection of menu items varies with restaurant type. Table 1 indicates the importance of nutritious food selections to restaurant patrons in fast-food, family and atmosphere restaurants. Sixty per cent of restaurant patrons feel that the nutritional value of meals provided by restaurants is good to excellent. Only 8% felt that it was poor (Sherwood, 1984).

Consumer food attitudes can be grouped into four main categories: these include: (1) nutrition/fitness (32%), (2) conventional taste (26%), (3) convenience (22%) and (4) dieter (20%) consumers. It is important to remember that no one person is fixed in a single attitude group and that a single attitude group may consume more than one type of food (Runyon, 1977; Kramer, 1980; Engel and Blackwell, 1982; Lipske, 1984). It is important to remain aware of the fact that consumer attitudes are not always translated into and exhibited as consumer behavior.

The food selections by these attitude groups can be grouped into five categories of food consumption: (1) natural foods (23%), (2) meat and potatoes (20%), (3) sophisticated foods (10%), (4) kids' foods (16%) and (5) diet foods (26%). In addition, these 'attitude' groups prefer certain restaurant types and desire certain foods to be served by those restaurants (Lipske, 1984) (see Table 2).

The attitude and behavior segmentation of the restaurant industry suggests why it is so difficult to predict acceptance and desire for nutrition in restaurants. It also helps to explain why contradictory trends, such as a market for elegant desserts, can exist concurrently with a diet/health market. First, different consumer segments (such as nutrition/fitness and conventional taste consumers) are eating in the same restaurant. These groups desire different types of foods. No restaurant is catering to a single 'market segment'.

Second, a single consumer attitude group may exhibit different types of behavior, particularly under different situations and circumstances. For example, the nutrition/fitness consumer may eat natural, diet and sophisticated foods. He/she may make different food selections based upon the purpose of the meal (business or social). Even the courses of the meal (entrée vs dessert) may alter the type of food chosen (heavy or light).

If we consider who comprises the nutrition market (i.e. fitness-oriented, restrictive dieters, health-

Table 1. Importance of availability of nutritious foods to restaurant patrons at different restaurant types

| Importance rating | Type of restaurant | | |
| | Fast-food | Family | Atmosphere |
	Restaurant patrons (%)		
Very important	24.4	34.7	30.6
Important	29.3	35.5	32.9
Somewhat important	22.7	18.6	22.3
Slightly important	9.8	4.4	4.8
Not at all important	12.4	6.6	9.2

Source: Sherwood (1984).

Table 2. Major type of food preferred by the primary and secondary attitude groups for restaurants			
Market segment and food desired	Restaurant type		
	Fast-food	Midscale	Upscale
Primary market segment Food type desired	Conventional Meat and potatoes	Convenience Diet foods*	Nutrition/fitness Natural foods
Secondary market segment Food type desired	Nutrition/fitness Natural foods	Nutrition/fitness Natural foods	Conventional Meat and potatoes

*This is their home food preference. The mid-scale restaurant patron in the primary market segment is the only consumer group whose away from home (A–F–H) eating behavior contradicts their at-home (A–H) eating behavior. When A–F–H, they are 'treating' themselves to foods they are not supposed to be eating (Lipske, 1984).

conscious, vegetarians and the elderly), we can understand the large diversity of attitudes and behaviors that we might expect from these groups. Because these market segments cannot be expected to make all the same food choices, a single type of food should not be expected to satisfy all of these groups' food preferences. However, there may be a 'convergence in the market' in the purchase of certain items which are perceived differently yet positively by two different groups (Lowe, 1979). For example, a menu item such as a natural fruit shake may represent a healthy, low calorie food to a nutrition/fitness consumer and be seen as a novel food item by a convenience consumer.

The segmentation of attitude and behavior raises several questions for restaurateurs: (1) What types of patron comprise their major market segments? (2) What types of 'convergence in the market' might occur for menu items in their restaurant? (3) What types of menu item substitution or trade-off are patrons likely to make and how should their menu be modified to meet these needs? (4) What implications does this have for food placement and categorization on the menu? (5) What effects will 'ear marking' have on the consumer perception and acceptance of certain menu items?

Types of nutrition program in the restaurant industry and their success or failure

Nutrition and health are addressed in varying degrees throughout the hospitality industry. Addressing nutrition is no longer a faddish promotion of 'natural' or 'health foods' (as in the 1960s and 1970s) but rather the widespread marketing of 'healthy' menu items by a broad spectrum of foodservice operators.

The following summary of nutrition programs is based on a phenomenological qualitative research study of 33 corporate food and beverage directors in the hospitality industry. The individuals inter-

viewed were all directly involved in the design, implementation and marketing of the nutrition programs. Twenty-three of the organizations currently had implemented their nutrition program and ten were currently in the process of designing their programs. The organizations involved in the study are listed in Table 3 (Carlson, 1986).

Table 3. List of participants surveyed on the design, implementation and marketing of nutrition in the hospitality industry

Hotels
  Best Western International
  Days Inn
  Fairmont Hotel Company
  Four Seasons Hotels Ltd.
  Holiday Inns
  Hyatt Hotels Corporation
  Loews Hotels
  Marriott Corporation
  Radisson Hotels
  Ramada Inns
  Sheraton Hotels
  Stouffer Hotels
  Thunderbird/Red Lion Inns
  Westin Hotels

Restaurants
  Burger King Restaurants
  D'Lites America
  Dobbs Houses, Inc.
  Four Seasons Restaurant
  General Mills Restaurant Group
  The Good Earth
  Jerrico Inc.
  McDonald's
  Noyes Lodge, Cornell University
  Popeye's Fried Chicken (Copeland Industries)
  Red Lobster Inns
  21 Management Company
  Wendy's

Business–industry–health-related foodservice
  Dobbs Inc.
  Eastman Kodak Company
  Greyhound Foodservice
  Ogden Foodservice
  Marriott Corporation
  Szabo Foods

(a) Hotels

The most extensive nutrition programs in the hospitality industry are those developed by hotel chains. These programs have recognized the demand for nutrition programs by the business traveler, the convention and upscale tourist markets. Many of these consumers have frequented resorts and spas and many have a regular fitness routine which they do not want disrupted when they are away from home.

Hotels with extensively developed programs provide a separate menu consisting only of their 'healthy' items or have added at least three new nutritious entrées to the menu. In addition, they usually have added special accompaniments, appetizers, soups, salads and desserts. They are more likely to have created new menu items rather than have simply altered existing menu items. Special menu items are likely to be available at all meal periods within at least one restaurant within the hotel. The nutritional menu changes are often integrated in some way with the spa and exercise facilities of the hotel.

Sales (in dollar amounts) of nutritious menu items in extensive programs have exceeded those of other promotions. In general, sales are highest for those items: (1) directed toward the frequent traveler, (2) creatively and attractively designed and presented and (3) served for lunch rather than dinner. Success of these items also depends greatly on the geographical area of their introduction. The areas where they have achieved their greatest success to date are: the West Coast, Arizona, Florida, St Louis and Denver. These areas have also received greater consumer demands for more nutritious menu items, prior to and during the implementation of nutrition programs. In general, nutritious menu items have been found to be as or more profitable than the regular items (higher contribution margins).

Incorporating nutrition into menu items increases desirability and perceived value even though consumers do not necessarily choose such items. Evidently consumers like having the choice made available to them. The single greatest advantage of the programs has been the consumer goodwill generated toward the hotel chain. It is claimed by corporate food and beverage executives that nutrition programs are the single most valuable marketing programs ever developed by these hotel chains. They are also extremely important in maintenance of market share and have increased repeat business by the frequent patron.

Less extensive programs have been implemented by many hotel chains. These programs involve the addition of only a few menu items that are slightly altered variations of regular menu items. These programs are usually the result of frequent requests from both local patrons and frequent travelers. In many instances the hotel owner's personal health concerns have been the impetus for initiating the program.

The target market of the less extensive programs are individuals on special diets for health concerns. The sale and profitability of nutritious menu items in the less extensive programs are similar to other menu items. Many chains have not closely followed the sales of these items. Consumer perceptions of the quality of these menu items are similar to those of standard menu items. Many of the hoteliers are not concerned about how these items are perceived by the consumer, as they are being offered more as a service to meet the special dietary needs of these restaurant patrons.

Hotels that have implemented nutrition through special menu offerings rather than through programs generally placed the nutritious menu items on the main or regular menu. The major emphasis of the menu revisions is minor adaptations of currently existing regular menu items. These items are frequently placed on the menu to give the restaurant patron a choice, they are usually not marketed or promoted and whether or not the items sell well does not appear to be important.

In most cases however, the sale and profitability of nutritious menu items have been similar to those of standard menu items. These items are often priced lower than regular menu items to maintain their 'value' to the consumer as portion sizes are frequently reduced. Consumers perceive these items as being of as good quality as the standard menu items.

The most extensive programs currently being designed by hotel chains will provide new and modified menu items throughout daily meal periods. The emphasis of these programs will be upon: (1) drastically increasing the number of menu options, (2) their flexibility to meet various consumer nutritional needs, and (3) implementing the programs in more of the restaurant operations of the hotel. In general, these programs extend beyond food items to include development of innovative beverages to meet the demands of the nutrition market. The programs will be integrated with the existing food and beverage program of the hotel.

The major focus of the new programs is upon flexibility in order to allow guests to put together a diet that meets their individual needs. Most of the program designers plan on providing the guest with detailed nutrition information about the menu items upon request. The programs are being designed to meet the nutrition needs of restrictive dieters, health-conscious and fitness-oriented consumers.

Less extensive nutrition programs and menu revisions are being developed by some hotels in order to maintain their market share. These programs are designed to meet the needs of the special diet consumer. The developers of these programs are limiting the number of nutritional factors that they will address. The main emphasis will be upon the restriction/addition of specific menu item components to meet special health-related diet concerns (cardiovascular, diabetes).

(b) Restaurants

Nutrition has been implemented at all levels of the restaurant industry (fast-food to upscale dining) and often reflects greater creativity than any other segment of the foodservice industry. The focus of nutrition in restaurants is more likely to reflect the owner's personal concerns and has frequently been integrated to enhance the theme of the property.

Restaurateurs in upscale foodservice operations want to build on trends toward healthier foods and menus that enhance their clientele's lifestyles, rather than focus on fads. These restaurateurs not only know their markets extremely well, but they have identified the 'power brokers' of their market. In general, the power brokers who 'control' the restaurant offerings are: affluent, well-educated, prominent, middle-aged, male professionals. These consumers want nutrition to be integrated with a high quality meal and the menu items must meet the needs of their active lifestyles. They do not want 'diet foods' which connote a restriction but rather elegant, lighter, healthier foods. These menu items must first be established as 'good to eat' rather than 'good for you'. These patrons want something that is special for them as well as 'healthy'.

The nutritious items are almost always part of the main menu and are frequently emphasized for the lunch meal period. Nutrition information is available to the guest, but is, in general, presented only upon request by the restaurant patron. Very 'subtle' marketing, which rarely emphasizes nutrition is used. Emphasis is usually placed on quality and perceived value by using more 'exotic' ingredients, more novel presentations, and charging higher prices. The labor intensiveness and higher priced ingredients justify the higher menu prices charged for these items. These menu items are usually the best selling items on the menu. They are perceived as being of very high quality and increase repeat patronage.

Midscale (family style) restaurants are more likely to have a broader market than that of the upscale restaurants and therefore have less defined nutritional goals for their market segment. The 'nutrition market' is a smaller proportion of the midscale restaurant's total market than for upscale restaurants. Therefore, the primary focus of midscale restaurants is to give the consumer a choice by offering a limited number of nutritious menu items. The major nutrition market of midscale restaurants is diet and health-conscious restaurant patrons of middle income, holding white-collar jobs.

For midscale restaurants, the sales volume of nutritious menu items depends on the location of the restaurant. The sales are comparable to other menu items. They are profitable (in dollar contribution margins) but not by a large margin. These items are of the same or higher perceived quality than the regular menu items. 'Light and healthy' does not mean 'cheap' to the consumer. The configuration of the product determines its perceived value.

Nutritious menu items are extremely important in maintaining market share in midscale restaurants. These menu items help to increase repeat patronage. Designing, implementing and marketing nutrition also helps to generate enthusiasm within the organization and enhance the organization's quality assurance efforts. However, there is often a stigma associated with 'health foods' and these menu items often have only a small core group of users that is not large enough to support their promotion on the menu. Further, the demand for these items is often very regional. The items are frequently given more 'lip service' than actual purchase by consumers. The menu requires constant updating for these items to remain current yet care must also be taken that such menu items do not reach the market before their time (i.e. before they are desired by a large enough group of consumers to make them profitable).

The best timing for introduction of the new menu items can be very difficult to determine, especially in midscale restaurants. The market is not homogeneous; and fitness, health, and diet-conscious segments have different needs.

Nutrition programs and menu revisions in fast-food restaurants focus on product specifications and menu items that may be substituted. There is no emphasis on rapidly changing consumers' eating habits. These restaurants emphasize the use of menu items such as chicken that are already accepted in the fast-food sector and also are perceived as being nutritious.

Nutrition information is most often provided as a defense for menu offerings. The nutrition information is provided to reflect a positive image of the products. Poor nutrient information (negative in nature) is carefully avoided. The products are developed first to meet consumer sensory expectations, second to meet cooking and preparation requirements and third to consider nutrient quality. The fast-food industry is clearly divided in their future approach to product development for both nutritious and regular menu items. Some will emphasize menu item proliferation to include a greater variety of lighter menu items, while other fast-food restaurants will seek to develop a limited number of specialized menu items.

Fast-food restaurants are introducing menu items that are substitutes for 'typical' fast-food menu items. These restaurants are promoting salads and introducing 'health foods' that meet the fast-food image. Nutritious menu items are a very small percentage of total sales in the fast-food foodservice segment. They are in general, lower in profitability because of greater food cost inherent in their more perishable nature and higher inventory requirements associated with these menu offerings.

Nutrition promotions enhance the image that the company does care about the consumer's needs. These promotions are also important in maintaining a competitive edge over other fast-food and family-style restaurants.

Until there is a greater demand for certain products by the consumer, the fast-food restaurants will not introduce them to a large extent. Fast-foods are not selected on the basis of nutrition information; rather the nutrition information is used to support (or justify) the selection after the fact.

(c) *Business, industry and health*

The implementation of nutrition in the business, industry and health (B–I–H)-related foodservice segment is largely a result of management's recognition of the need to meet special dietary needs of employees or patrons with health problems and to promote wellbeing. Because most of these programs are geared toward enhancing the health of corporate executives and white-collar workers, they have been very successful. The programs are frequently integrated with the company's health and fitness plan.

The nutritional value of meals is very important to a 'captive audience'. The extensive information provided is most likely to be aimed at educating the consumer and in integrating the areas of fitness, health and diet. The foodservice operations do not, in general, initiate these programs as 'a big splash' as is often the case for hotel/restaurant chains. Consumer interest is obtained slowly and gradu-

ally. This is possible for these operations as a result of their rather stable, repeat clientele.

The marketing emphasis is placed on the program itself rather than focusing on particular menu items. This may be a result of the frequent use of cycle menus and frequently changing menu items to please the extensive repeat patronage. Promotions are done on a large scale via an employee newsletter, menu clip-ons, table tents, posters, and information sheets in the fitness/health clubs and medical/health departments. Frequently, the sales volume forecasts for these items are over-estimated for the cafeteria-style dining areas.

In corporate dining facilities, nutritious items are the best selling of the menu items and are highly profitable. These items have a high perceived value by the consumer, they are viewed as an employee benefit and increase repeat patronage.

Future of nutrition promotions in our industry

Nutrition will be an integral part of the menu and marketing of tomorrow's restaurant. This will result from the increasing consumer interest in nutrition, health and fitness. Further development of products and ingredients by food processors and manufacturers will have enhanced nutritional and sensory properties that will encourage development of nutritious menu items. The incorporation of nutrition into the training of tomorrow's chefs will also encourage the role and marketing of nutrition in the foodservice industry.

The emphasis on nutrition in restaurants will continue to shift away from reduced caloric needs to integrating total or holistic health-related concerns. It will no longer be sufficient to offer a few nutritious menu items. The consumer's nutritional needs will need to be met throughout the food and beverage outlet, including the bar. Hospitality properties will meet consumer's health, fitness and wellbeing concerns by integrating all the means and resources available. Further, restaurants and hotels will need to do a better job of segmenting their markets, identifying the needs of those market segments, developing programs to meet these needs and communicating what is available and how it will meet the guests' needs and goals.

Designing, implementing and marketing nutrition in programs throughout the foodservice industry will continue because of the many advantages and benefits this holds for both restaurateurs and consumers. Nutrition is a trend that must be addressed in the foodservice industry because it is part of current consumer lifestyle changes that place an emphasis on health and physical fitness.

Table 4. *Characteristics of successful nutrition programs in the hospitality industry*

(1) The extent and type of patrons' nutrition concerns have been well researched.

(2) Menu items have been created that fulfill not only the consumers' nutritional needs but also meet their overall menu item quality expectations.

(3) The promotions clearly communicate to the restaurant patron 'how' the items meet their needs.

(4) The menu items are novel and creative. They convey a desirable image.

(5) The menu items fit with the overall theme of the restaurant. They do not appear to be an after-thought appended to the menu.

(6) The menu items are addressing more than restrictive dieters (low-calorie, low-cholesterol, low-fat, low-sodium diets). They are emphasizing health, fitness and wellbeing advantages of nutritious menu items.

(7) They are not only addressing current nutrition needs but also have the built-in flexibility to adapt to future nutrition concerns.

(8) They are promoted 'in house' to the staff (production and service) as well as to the restaurant patron. This generates enthusiasm for the program.

(9) They review and revise the menu and program to remain current with changing consumer desires and to continually upgrade their quality.

References

Anon (1983) Americans show healthy preference for nutritional foods. *NRA News* **3**, 30–31.

Bukos, J. B. (1979) Is dining out nutritious? *Restaurant Business* **78**, 16.

Bukos, J. B. (1983) A nutritional message. *Restaurant Business* **82**, 20.

Campbell Soup Company (1984) Food preferences changing — national study shows. *Microwave World* **2**, 7–9.

Carlson, B. L. (1986) Analysis of Nutrition in the Hospitality Industry, pp. 198–298. Cornell University Thesis. Ithaca, NY.

Consumer Reports on Eating Out Share Trends (CREST) (1983) Eater Occasions by Food Item. National Dairy Purchase, GDR-CREST Enterprises.

Engel, J. F. and Blackwell, R. D. (1982) Alternative evaluation: beliefs, attitudes and intentions. *Consumer Behavior*, Chapter 15, p. 439. Dryden Press, New York.

Gallup Organization Inc. (1983) *Changes in Consumer Eating Habits*. National Restaurant Association, Washington.

Jacoby, J., Olsen, J. C., Szybello, G. I. and Hart, E. W. (1981) Behavioral science perspectives on conveying nutrition information to consumers. *Criteria of Food Acceptance*, pp. 12–26. Forster, Zurich.

Kramer, A. (1980) Food codes and habits. *Food and the Consumer*, p. 105. AVI, Westport, CT.

Lipske, S. N. (1984) *The Eating Out Public's Interest in Nutrition*, Position Paper and Research Summary, pp. 1–58. GDR-CREST Enterprises.

Lowe, M. (1979) Influence of changing lifestyles on food choice. *Nutrition and Lifestyles*, pp. 141–148. Applied Science, London.

McRobbie, J. J. (1984) Know thy consumer. *Progressive Grocer* **63**, 25–27.

Riggs, S. (1980) How to serve special diet customers. *Food Business* **86**, 90–94.

Runyon, K. E. (1977) *Consumer Behavior and the Practice of Marketing*, chapter 3, p. 51. C. E. Merrill, Columbus.

Sherwood, K. (1984) Nutrition and Food Service. *NRA Current Issues Report*, pp. 1–21. National Restaurant Association, Washington, D.C.

Sibley, F. L. (1986) Preventative medicine and the restaurant industry. *Restaurants and Institutions* **96**, 12.

Skelly, F. R. (1982) Attitudes of the consumer. *Nutrition Reviews* (Suppl.) **40**, 35–39.

Vanlenten, C. V. (1983) Serving up health. Nutrition in today's restaurant. *NRA News* **3**, 11–14.

Wren, J. J. (1986) The future of food processing: matching production technology to consumer demand. *Chemistry and Industry* **7**, 227–230.

About the Author

Beth L. Carlson holds a Ph.D in Hotel Administration, an M.S. in Food Chemistry from Cornell University and a B.S. in Nutrition Sciences. She is an Assistant Professor of Food and Beverage Management and Hospitality Information Systems at the Division of Hotel, Restaurant and Institutional Management at Virginia Polytechnic Institute and State University. As president of Better Living Concepts Inc., she designs and markets 'healthy' food and fitness concepts for resorts, hotels and foodservice companies. She is a member of the American Diatetic Association and a board member of the Virginia Chapter of the American Heart Association.

New-Product Development in Food Service:
A Structured Approach

New menu items can help expand a restaurant firm's market share. But these new products must fit in with the restaurant's existing menu and with the company's overall goals. Here's a methodical way to make sure new menu items are right for your firm

by Tom Feltenstein

LIKE THE hotel industry, the restaurant business is mature. The days when you could expand sales and market share merely by building more locations are gone. But the maturity of the market does not mean growth must stop. In fact, restaurant chains that do not grow will probably be left behind by those that are expanding. But the growth I am speaking of is not just a matter of building new restaurants. Instead, this growth depends on developing and introducing new menu products.

Today, restaurant companies of all shapes and sizes are jumping on the new-products bandwagon. Some are spending enormous sums to rush their newest taste sensations to the marketplace and into the mouths of consumers, who are constantly hungry for something new and different. Many of the largest chains are spending small fortunes on introductory media campaigns.

For these large chains, however, the money spent on product development and advertising is small compared to the gains to be won and the sales that might be lost if they do not innovate.

A flurry of new products have been rolled out by fast-food restaurant chains during the past two years. Some of the more prominent introductions are:

- Burger King's Croissan'wich line of breakfast products, its improved Whopper, and Chicken Tenders;
- Wendy's breakfast menu, its Lite menu, and chicken nuggets;
- McDonald's McDLT, breakfast biscuits, and Chicken McNuggets;
- Kentucky Fried Chicken's chicken nuggets; and
- Church's Crispy Nuggets and Southern-fried catfish.

In this brief list, you can see evidence both of innovation and "me-too" product introductions. Innovative products can expand a company's market, while "me-too" products are intended to preserve a company's market share by providing a product similar to that of competitors. In either case, the chains have aggressively supported their new products with heavy advertising and promotional campaigns. In 1985, Burger King spent nearly $50 million to announce its Croissan'wich and the new Whopper. Wendy's spent $14 million to announce its breakfast menu, and, according to industry

*Formerly the owner of a chain of four family restaurants, **Tom Feltenstein** is founder and president of the American Restaurant Marketing Group. His clients have included the U.S. Marine Corps, Federated Department Stores, Chi-Chi's, Popeye's, Arby's, and Ponderosa. He is also chairman and chief executive officer of the Franchise Institute of America.*

sources, Church's spent $5 million introducing catfish to selected regional markets.

This is not to say that new-product development and introduction cannot be reasonably priced. Restaurant firms of all sizes can put new products on their menus and advertise them on an appropriate scale.

The evolution that is occurring now in the restaurant industry has occurred in other industries— home appliances, packaged foods, and automobiles, to name three. In these industries, new-product introductions have been a key strategy for expanding or maintaining companies' market share. In this article, I will present a systematic method for product development typical of the methods used by big companies that regularly introduce new products. This step-by-step process is designed to maximize the chances for a successful introduction. It includes observation of the industry and the competitive environment, careful screening of potential opportunities, thorough evaluation of ideas and resulting new products, and substantial operational and market testing.

How-to. While actual methods of product development differ to some degree from firm to firm, the basic framework presented here will work for most companies. An outline of the procedure is presented in Exhibit 1.

Assemble a Task Force

New-product development requires the expertise of individuals from different departments within the organization, including marketing, operations, accounting, and finance. These individuals should form a new-products task force, which will conduct the development process, lend necessary expertise, and act as communicators between the task force and the departments it represents. The task force should hold regular meetings to make assignments, provide timely updates, and facilitate research efforts. You should appoint a new-products coordinator to lead the task force. The coordinator should ideally have previous experience in new-product development and be familiar with the techniques necessary to complete the effort.

Set Priorities

It is essential to start your product-development process by setting priorities. By doing so, you establish guiding principles that the task force will follow, and you ensure that the product will mesh with overall company goals. Clear priorities also neutralize personal biases among task-force members, so that company needs become the decision criteria, and not personal tastes. Finally, a list of priorities ensures that all ideas receive an equitable evaluation against common standards.

The best way to set priorities is to use a worksheet, putting the basic framework for product-development planning on paper. On the worksheet, task-force members review corporate goals, audit existing test items, and list opportunities or threats to the chain. The worksheet may be completed as a group effort, or task-force members can complete the sheet individually and compile their answers.

Reviewing corporate goals. The first item on the worksheet and the first step in setting new-product priorities is a review of corporate plans for growth to determine the overriding needs for product development, and to ensure the product will mesh with overall corporate strategy. Is the purpose of the product to acquire new customers, increase the frequency of customer visits, or increase the average check size? Is the goal to maintain market share by responding to the actions of a competitor? Or does management wish to use facilities more productively, round out menu offerings, or target a specific market? The answers to these questions will guide the task force in developing products that will contribute to the firm's financial objectives.

Auditing current test items. As an initial part of new-product development, the task force should audit the items currently in testing or development. This audit is a check of the status and progress of these products that will help keep them performing on schedule and on budget. The audit also will help determine the availability of resources for further new-product development.

When the audit is complete, the task force should move immediately to "clear the decks" for further development. Obvious new-product winners should either be moved to test marketing or to a rollout, depending on the extent of testing they have received. Products that need additional work should be improved or adjusted as needed, but the task force should set a clear deadline for a decision on any questionable items. It is unlikely that every test product will be a success. The firm should withdraw the obvious failures to free up resources for development of other new products.

Deletion or redevelopment. The next step is a review of the current mix of menu items to determine whether some should be deleted or redeveloped. You may have to delete poor performers to make room for promising new items, as this will simplify operations and reduce the pressure on company resources.

Base your deletion decisions on such objective performance measures as research results, sales levels, profit contribution, levels of complaints or returns, and production efficiencies. But don't be in a hurry to delete an item. If it rounds out the menu or if a substantial minority of customers regularly purchase it, keeping the item may be advisable regardless of generally poor performance.

Sometimes products require redevelopment, not deletion. You can resurrect some low performers by taking them back through the product-development process. This involves first isolating the problems and then reformulating the product as needed. However, if improvement remains unlikely, the product should be phased out permanently.

If you are deleting a product, develop a complete withdrawal strategy. Perhaps you can promote a new menu item to draw attention from the deleted item. Items that are to be redeveloped should be incorporated into the new-product development pipeline under the task force's jurisdiction.

New-Product Roles

There are essentially three types of new food products: entrees, side dishes, and new-category products. Each type plays a different role on the menu.

A new entree is an additional meal offering that expands, extends, or enhances the menu, without departing from the operation's basic concept. It rounds out and maintains the menu's competitiveness, particularly when it matches a competitor's offering. For instance, the McDLT was added by McDonald's to defend its menu against Burger King's Whopper. The goal for the new entree is to bring in new customers, to increase the average ticket by trading up customers, and to increase the frequency of customer visits by providing variety on the menu. Although it is different from the Big Mac and the Quarter Pounder, the McDLT does not really depart from the basic McDonald's "meat-and-potatoes" menu concept.

A side dish usually extends or enhances the current menu. Its purpose is to increase the average check by adding to existing entrees or to differentiate an operation from direct competitors. McDonaldland cookies, Popeye's corn on the cob, and KFC's baked beans are examples of side dishes that differentiate one fast-food restaurant from another.

New-category products are outside the scope of the current menu, but they address important consumer needs that the restaurant has not met. A new-category product is a departure from existing menu concept. The goal is to

Virtually all the growth that has occurred recently in the restaurant industry has come through product development.

EXHIBIT 2
Qualitative screening worksheet

1. Proposed new product _____
2. General description _____
3. Company objectives it will meet _____
4. Role it will play: new entree   side dish   new product category
5. Key strengths or opportunities _____
6. Key weaknesses or threats _____
7. Expected impact on sales: increase traffic   increase frequency
   trade up   draw new customer group(s)   increase average check
8. Yearly sales goal _____ Profit-impact goal _____
9. Items it will cannibalize _____ To what degree _____
10. Target customers _____
11. Day part(s) affected _____
12. Target price _____ Target portion size _____
13. Key ingredients _____
14. Estimated food costs _____
15. Expected production required _____
16. Current equipment required _____
17. New equipment required _____
18. Space required _____
19. Labor required _____
20. Additional employees required _____
21. Special training required _____
22. Negative effects on current production _____
23. Negative effects on staff _____
24. Similar competitive items _____
25. Likely competitive response _____
26. Key benefits _____
27. Key disadvantages _____
28. Required for development:
    a. facilities _____
    b. budget _____
    c. personnel _____
    d. special expertise _____
    e. time _____

broaden the customer base and increase the visit frequency of existing customers. McDonald's Chicken McNuggets, baked potatoes at Wendy's, and Church's catfish are new-category products.

Before developing specific products, the task force should set priorities among these product types—determining whether the existing menu should be extended with new entrees, rounded out with new side dishes, broadened with new-category products, or some combination of the three. The direction depends on your company's current position and an analysis of market forces.

SWOT team. A critical step in establishing priorities for new products is to examine the market and your firm for strengths and opportunities you can capitalize upon, and weaknesses or threats you can overcome as a result of new-product development. Because this analysis is an inventory of strengths, weaknesses, opportunities, and threats, it is called SWOT analysis. In a SWOT analysis, your task force should take into account the company's position with regard to the industry, the competition, the customer, the economy, and the government. The outcome of this analysis provides yet another set of guidelines for the development of new products.

In your SWOT analysis, you should consider the results of recent competitive actions you've taken, changes in economic conditions, new legislation, current consumer trends, changing demographics, and recent company successes and failures.

Opportunities. Six areas have recently afforded prime opportunities for new menu products. These are:

- breakfast foods,
- light or nutritious foods,
- new taste sensations (ethnic or regional recipes),
- foods that cannot be prepared easily at home,
- foods that lend themselves to takeout, and
- delivered food.

These opportunities have arisen from the demands of customers who are older, better educated, more convenience-oriented, and more nutrition- and weight-conscious than restaurant customers of the past.

Each area of opportunity holds unique advantages. Breakfast, for instance, is an opportunity for incremental sales, and it holds few barriers to entry, because physical plants are, in most cases, already in place. The increasing demand for foods with fewer calories and greater nutritive value creates the opportunity for such menu additions as salads, baked or broiled items, and whole-grain breads and pastas. American consumers' desire for something new creates a demand for ethnic and regional taste sensations. With the advent of the microwave oven, prepared frozen foods have proliferated, and cooking basic foods at home is now simpler than ever. As a result, foods that are difficult or time-consuming to prepare are ideal for restaurant menus. Takeout food is a substantial growth area that offers operators a way to expand sales without significantly affecting current traffic. Takeout traffic increased by one-third from 1982 to 1984, while eat-in traffic declined slightly during the same period. Finally, as the success of Domino's pizza and other operators attests, delivery is the biggest development in the food-service business today. Many restaurant companies are testing delivery in their operations.

Generate Ideas

When your new-product priorities have been specified, the task force can commence generating goal-directed ideas. This is a brainstorming process in which participants list all new-product ideas that are in basic alignment with company priorities. Ideas may come from task-force members or from anywhere in the company.

Screening Ideas

When all the possible ideas—no matter how farfetched—have been listed, the task force should evaluate them, using a formal, customized screening method. The purpose of using a set method for idea selection is to make sure each idea receives the same consideration and an unbiased evaluation.

Screening method. Screening normally involves a qualitative analysis and a quantitative analysis. Qualitative analysis involves answering a series of pertinent, open-ended questions about the prospective menu idea. Quantitative analysis involves numerical ratings of ideas. Exhibits 2 and 3 show examples of worksheets you might use in your qualitative and quantitative analyses.

Qualitative analysis. The questions to be considered in qualitative analysis should shed light on how the product will meet company priorities. A typical questionnaire might include the following questions:

EXHIBIT 3
Quantitative screening worksheet

CRITERIA	RATING (A)	WEIGHT (B)	TOTAL (A × B)
Image			
Menu approach			
Overall company goals			
Company strengths			
Company opportunities			
Desired role			
Level of quality			
Pricing			
Current customers			
Targeted customers			
Services			
Specialties			
Menu voids			
Day-part voids			
Production procedures			
Labor content			
Equipment			
Space availability			
Suppliers			
Developmental capabilities			
Total			

Each new product idea is rated on a scale of 1 (low) to 5 (high) on each of the criteria. Then a weight of 1 to 5 is assigned to each criterion. The product of the rating and the weight gives a total score for the product on each criterion. The sum of these scores gives a final grand total for comparison with other proposed products.

- Will the new product affect one meal period more than others? If so, which one?
- Will the new product increase customer counts or trade up the customer? What are the realistic goals for these increases? What are realistic sales and profit targets?
- What kind of customer will the new product attract, and at what price? (Setting a general target price will help forestall creating a product with a price that is too high for the target customer. It also helps set guidelines for food costs.)
- What strengths and opportunities will the new product capitalize on?

- What weaknesses and threats will work against it? Will it cannibalize other products? If so, which ones? Will customers and employees accept this product as fitting in with the company's current image?
- What negative effects will the new product have on production?
- Does the competition offer anything similar? How does it compare?
- Does our firm have the capability to develop and produce this item? What will it take in terms of time,

The risks of ignoring a growth strategy are far greater than those of developing and introducing new products.

expertise, facilities, labor, and budget?

• Will the new product require new equipment? If so, what kind and at what cost? Will the restaurant's labor needs be changed? If so, in what way?

Quantitative analysis. Prospective product ideas that survive qualitative analysis should be rated quantitatively. In quantitative analysis, each new-product idea is scored according to criteria based on the company's priorities. Proposed products suitable for development can be selected from those ideas receiving the highest scores. The rating criteria should include such issues as image, quality, equipment, day-part voids, menu voids, and developmental capabilities. You can use any scale you wish for the ranking; I prefer using a five-point scale, in which 1 is low and 5 is high.

You should also rank the importance of each criterion, using the same scale you applied to the product ranking. To get a final score for each idea, multiply each idea's rating by its criterion weight, and then tally the scores.

Selecting ideas. Based on the benchmarks, qualitative judgment, and quantitative scores, the most promising ideas are selected for development. The task force should pursue more than one product idea at a time, because some ideas will inevitably fail during testing. The number of ideas selected should be realistic, however, so that the company's facilities are not overtaxed.

At this point, the task force should set developmental objectives and plans for each idea. These plans should include a timetable, a budget, task assignments, and expected results. The progress of each idea should be controlled through a procedural checklist that includes regular reports to management.

Product Development

For the products selected for development, the task force must oversee recipe formulation, operational specifications, unit operational testing, and market testing.

Recipe formulation. All food-related issues should be included in the task force's consideration of recipes. This includes ingredients, portions, waste, prep times, holding times, storage, production procedures, and food specifications and costs. Your firm should use consumer taste panels to adjust the recipe while it is still being formulated in your test kitchen.[1]

Operational specification. While the product is still in the test kitchen, you should determine what it will cost to get the product to the customer. Assess equipment needs and costs, presentation, plating, packaging, production flow, inventory needs, supplier needs, and labor needs and costs. You should also determine menu price and profit expectations, choose a product name, and prepare in-store promotional material.

Testing unit operations. Test the product in one or two operating units to make sure that the expectations created in the test kitchen can be realized in actual production. During this test, you can determine the feasibility of your plans for storage, preparation, and serving the new item. Staff-training methods and materials should be outlined and refined during this test. Evaluate the impact of the new product on current operations within the unit, and make note of all problems it might cause. You

---

[1]For more information on taste panels, see: Marilyn Skelton, "Sensory Evaluation of Food," *The Cornell Hotel and Restaurant Administration Quarterly*, 24, No. 4 (February 1984), pp. 51–57.

should also monitor employees' and unit managers' reactions to the new item.

To check whether the product meshes with the chain as a whole, you might expand the test to several units, after the first two or three weeks of testing in isolated units. It is essential to expand the test to several markets if there are regional variations in your menu, or if there are substantial differences in sales, management, or training at different locations.

Preliminary test marketing. Before you take the new item public in a formal market test, you should conduct preliminary consumer research on the item. This will help you firm up the product's name, its recipe, and its advertising appeal. You may want to observe consumers' reactions to the product, conduct focus groups,[2] send out questionnaires, or conduct taste tests.

In addition, you should conduct a mini-market test by offering customer trials at the operational test units. You can run trials at one or all of the operational test sites. The best way to run this test is to add the item to the menu, give free samples, and, if possible, use in-house and external promotions of the same type you plan for the formal test marketing. Track item sales, profits, and product mix changes during this mini-test. You may also solicit consumers' reactions through interviews or questionnaires.

The information gleaned from the preliminary test will guide your formal market test. When the initial trial is complete, the task force can plan for the final, broad-based market research.

Market test. Your formal market test should reveal whether the

product will perform as anticipated. During a market test, the item is introduced into selected, representative markets, just as if it were already part of your product line. In this test, you use the marketing, advertising, and promotional tactics that would be applied in an actual product rollout. You should measure the consumer response to the market test, so you can get an accurate sense of consumer acceptance.

The market test should last at least six months, so that you can get an adequate amount of information on which to base the final decision on whether to roll out the product. Particularly when the product is a major item or a costly one, it is critical that the market test be of sufficient length. The disadvantage of a lengthy market test is that you have tipped your hand to competitors, giving them a chance to move along any products that they might have in their development pipeline to defend against your innovation. (In fact, some package-goods marketers are dropping the formal test-marketing step altogether, to roll out their products ahead of the competition.)

During your market test, you should collect the following information:

- Consumer feedback on quality, price, value perception, intent to repurchase, customer profile, and regularity of patronage;
- Sales statistics: sales, customer counts, average check, day-part

counts, meal-occasion mix, and product mix for the test period, compared to a base period; and
- Profit and loss performance during the test period, compared to a base period.

Any unusual promotional effort should also be analyzed in relation to sales to determine the additional effect the promotion had on top of the impact of the introduction of the product itself.

From the test-market information, you can determine whether to roll out the product as planned, alter your rollout plans, or abandon the product.

Go for It

Once the decision has been made to roll out the product, plans for introducing the product should be completed and implemented. These plans should spell out the timing, support, and tactics for introducing and marketing the product. You will probably have to amend existing marketing plans to accommodate the new effort.

No Guarantees

Even if you apply the most disciplined of product-development methods, many factors beyond your control might doom a product that looked great during the test. Competitors might retaliate. Legislative and economic changes might alter the market. Your test results might have contained an unseen bias; consumers might have responded to the promotion, and not the product, or competitors might have rigged the results by running specials that altered the true sales pattern.

No matter how carefully orchestrated the process, developing new products is risky business; there are no guarantees of product success. In today's marketplace, however, the risks associated with ignoring a growth strategy are far greater. □

[2]See: Joe L. Welch, "Focus Groups for Restaurant Research," *The Cornell Hotel and Restaurant Administration Quarterly*, 26, No. 2 (August 1985), pp. 78–85.

Introduction

Every foodservice operator is acutely aware that success is based upon providing customer satisfaction. A keystone in this effort is the accurate representation of the products served. This truthful representation involves not only the printed menu but also photographs, graphic illustrations and other printed materials, as well as verbal depiction by employees.

The founders of the National Restaurant Association recognized this in 1923 when adopting its Standards of Business Practices. These Standards appearing on the inside front cover, have been repeatedly endorsed and employed by NRA members in the conduct of their business. In February, 1977, the NRA Board of Directors reaffirmed the position by adopting the statement "Accuracy in Menu" reproduced on page eight.

This publication has been developed to assist the foodservice operator in properly representing the foods offered for sale in their restaurant. The specific types of errors are limitless and this guide describes some of the most likely kinds of mistakes.

The ultimate responsibility for accuracy in representing your menu offerings rests with you. Creativity and appealing merchandising is in no way restricted, but description and phrases must accurately reflect the food served. Be certain you can substantiate your written and spoken words with product, invoice or label.

Representation of
Quantity

Proper operational procedures should preclude any concerns with misinformation on quantities. Steaks are often merchandised by weight, and the generally accepted practice of declared quantity is that prior to cooking.

Obviously, double martinis are twice the size of the normal drink, and if jumbo eggs are listed it means exactly that—as "jumbo" is a recognized egg size. Petite and super-colossal are among the official size descriptions for olives. However, the use of terms such as "extra large salad" or "extra tall drink" may invite problems if not qualified. There is no questions about the meaning of a "3-egg omelette" or "all you can eat". Also remember the implied meaning of words—a bowl of soup contains more than a cup of soup.

Reprinted by permission of the National Restaurant Association. 1977.

Representation of
Quality

Federal and state standards of quality grades exist for many restaurant products including meat, poultry, eggs, dairy products, fruits and vegetables. Terminology used to describe grades include Prime, Grade A, Good, No. 1, Choice, Fancy, Grade AA and Extra Standard.

Care must be exercised in preparing menu descriptions when these words are used. In certain uses, they imply certain quality. An item appearing as "choice sirloin of beef" connotes the use of USDA Choice Grade Sirloin of Beef. One recognized exception is the term "prime rib". Prime rib is a long established, well understood and accepted description for a cut of beef (the "primal" ribs, the 6th to 12th ribs) and does not represent the grade quality, unless USDA is used in conjunction.

Because of our industry's volume use of ground beef, it is well to remember the USDA definition: Ground beef is just what the name implies. No extra fat, water, extenders or binders are permitted. The fat limit is 30 percent. Seasonings may be added as long as they are identified. These requirements identify only product ground and packaged in Federal or State inspected plants.

Representation of
Price

If your pricing structure includes a cover charge, service charge or gratuity, these must be appropriately brought to your customer's attention. If extra charges are made for requests such as "all white meat" or "no ice drinks" these should be so stated at the time of ordering.

Any restrictions when using a coupon or premium promotion must be clearly defined.

If a price promotion involves a multi-unit company, clearly indicate which units are participating.

Representation of
Brand Names

Any product brand that is advertised must be the one served. A registered or copywritten trademark or brand name must not be used generically to refer to a product. Several examples of "brand" names of restaurant products are:

Armour Star Bacon, Sanka, Log Cabin Syrup, Coca-Cola, Seven-Up, Swifts Premium Ham, Pepsi-Cola, Starkist Tuna, Ry-Krisp, Jello, Heinz Catsup, Maxwell House Coffee, Chase and Sandborn Coffee, Kraft

Cheese, Tabasco Sauce, Ritz Crackers, Seven and Seven, Miracle Whip.

Your own "house" brand of a product may be so labeled even when prepared by an outside source, if its manufacturing was to your specifications. Containers of branded condiments and sauces placed on a table must be the product appearing on the container label.

Representation of Product Identification

Because of the similarity of many food products, substitutions are often made. These substitutions may be due to non-delivery, availability, merchandising considerations or price. When such substitutions are effected, be certain these changes are reflected on your menu. Common substitutions are:

Maple syrup and maple flavored syrup
Boiled ham and baked ham
Chopped and shaped veal pattie and veal cutlet
Ice milk and ice cream
Powdered eggs and fresh eggs
Picnic style pork shoulder and ham
Milk and skim milk
Pure jams and pectin jams
Whipped topping and whipped cream
Turkey and chicken
Hereford beef and Black Angus beef
Peanut oil and corn oil
Beef liver and calves liver
Cream and half & half
Margarine and butter
Non-dairy creamers or whitners and cream

Ground beef and ground sirloin of beef
Capon and chicken
Standard ice cream and french style ice cream
Cod and haddock
Noodles and egg noodles
Light meat tuna and white meat tuna
Pollack and haddock
Flounder and sole
Cheese food and processed cheese
Cream sauce and non-dairy cream sauce
Bonita and tuna fish
Roquefort cheese and blue cheese
Tenderloin tips and diced beef
Mayonnaise and salad dressing

Representation of Points of Origin

A potential area of error is in describing the point of origin of a menu offering. Claims may be substantiated by the product, by packaging labels, invoices or other documentation provided by your supplier. Mistakes are possible as sources of supply change and availability of product shifts. The following are common assertions of points of origin.

Lake Superior Whitefish	Bay Scallops
Idaho Potatoes	Gulf Shrimp
Maine Lobster	Florida Orange Juice
Imported Swiss Cheese	Smithfield Ham
Puget Sound Sockeye Salmon	Wisconsin Cheese
Danish Bleu Cheese	Alaskan King Crab
Louisiana Frog Legs	Imported Ham
Colorado Brook Trout	Colorado Beef
Florida Stone Crabs	Long Island Duckling
Chesapeake Bay Oysters	

There is wide spread use of geographic names used in a generic sense to describe a method of preparation or service. Such terminology is readily understood and acepted by the customer and their use should in no way be restricted. Examples are:

Russian Dressing	French Toast
New England Clam Chowder	Country Fried Steak
Irish Stew	Denver Sandwich
Country Ham	French Dip
French Fries	Swiss Steak
Danish Pastries	German Potato Salad
Russian Service	French Service
English Muffins	Manhattan Clam Chowder
Swiss Cheese	

Representation of Merchandising Terms

A difficult area to clearly define as right or wrong is the use of merchandising terms. "We serve the best gumbo in town" is understood by the dining-out public for what it is — boasting for advertising sake. However, to use the term "we use only the finest beef" implies that USDA Prime Beef is used, as a standard exists for this product.

Advertising exaggerations are tolerated if they do not mislead. When ordering a "mile high pie" a customer would expect a pie heaped tall with meringue or similar fluffy topping, but to advertise a "foot long hot dog" and to serve something less would be in error.

Mistakes are possible in properly identifying steak cuts. Use industry standards such as provided in the National Association of Meat Purveyors *Meat Buyer's Guide.*

"Homestyle", "home made style" or "our own" are suggested terminology rather than "homemade" in describing menu offerings prepared according to a home recipe. Most foodservice sanitation ordinances prohibit the preparation of foods in home facilities.

If using any of the following terms, be certain you can qualify them.

Fresh daily
Fresh roasted
Flown in daily
Kosher meat
Black Angus beef
Aged steaks
Milk fed chicken

Corn fed porkers
Slept in Chesapeake Bay
Finest quality
Center cut ham
Own special sauce
Low calorie

Representation of
Means of Preservation

The accepted means of preserving foods are numerous, including canned, chilled, bottled, frozen and dehydrated. If you choose to describe your menu selections with these terms, they must be accurate. Frozen orange juice is not fresh, canned peas are not frozen and bottled apple sauce is not canned.

Representation of
Food Preparation

The means of food preparation is often the determining factor in the customers selection of a menu entree. Absolute accuracy is a must. Readily understood terms include:

Charcoal broiled
Sauteed
Baked
Broiled
Roasted
Fried in butter

Deep fried
Barbecued
Smoked
Prepared from scratch
Poached

Representation of Verbal and Visual Presentation

When your menu, wall placards or other advertising contains a pictoral representation of a meal or platter, it should portray the actual contents with accuracy. Examples of visual misrepresentations include:

- The use of mushroom pieces in a sauce when the picture depicts mushroom caps
- The use of sliced strawberries on a shortcake when the picture depicts whole strawberries.
- The use of numerous thin sliced meat pieces when the picture depicts a single thick slice.
- The use of five shrimp when the picture depicts six shrimp.
- The omission of vegetables or other entree extras when the picture depicts their inclusion.
- The use of a plain bun when the picture depicts a sesame topped bun.

Examples of verbal misrepresentation include:

- If a waiter asks "sour cream or butter with your potatoes" when in fact an imitation sour cream or margarine is served.
- A waitress' response — "the pies are baked in our kitchen" when in fact they are a purchased prebaked institutional pie.

Representation of Dietary or Nutritional Claims

Potential public health concerns are real if misrepresentation is made of the dietary or nutrutional content of food. For example "salt free" or "sugar free" foods must be exactly that to assure the protection of your customers who may be under particular dietary restraints. "Low calorie" or nutritional claims, if made, must be supportable by specific data.

**A POSITION STATEMENT OF THE
NATIONAL RESTAURANT ASSOCIATION**

Accuracy in Menu Offerings

The foodservice industry has long recognized the importance of accuracy in describing its products, either on menus, and through visual or oral representation, both on ethical grounds and from the standpoint of customer satisfaction. The National Restaurant Association incorporated standards of accuracy in all representations to the public in its Standards of Business Practice, originally adopted by the Association in 1923. We reaffirm and strongly support the principles therein expressed.

"Truth in dining" or "truth in menu" laws and ordinances have been proposed in some government jurisdictions, and in a few cases adopted, in the belief that representations on restaurant menus present a unique problem in consumer protection. The National Restaurant Association believes that such legislation is unnecessary as Federal, state and many local governments have laws and regulations prohibiting false advertising and misrepresentations of products, and providing protection from fraud. In an industry such as ours, where economic survival depends upon customer satisfaction, misrepresentation is most effectively regulated by the severe sanction of customer dissatisfaction and loss of patronage.

To be equitable, the complexity of such legislation would be staggering. It is conceivable that standardized recipes for each menu listing would be required if regulatory refinement followed its logical course. The problems of enforcement, and proof if due process is observed, would be monumental, if not impossible.

The "truth in dining" movement is not confined to the proposition that restaurant menus be absolutely accurate in their representations. Legislation and ordinances have been proposed that would require the identification of a specific means of preservation, method of preparation or statement of food origin. Such requirements could unjustly imply that certain foods, processes or places of origin are unwholesome or inferior.

Government action must be confined to problems where its intervention can be effective and at a cost commensurate with the benefits to gained.

Adopted February, 1977

Menu Analysis: Review and Evaluation

by
Lendal H. Kotschevar
Distinguished Professor
School of Hospitality Management
Florida International University

*Various methods are used to evaluate menus. Some have quite different
approaches and give different information. Even those using quite similar
methods vary in the information they give. The author attempts to describe
the most frequently used methods and to indicate their value. A correlation calculation is made to see how well certain of these methods agree
in the information they give.*

Menus are often examined visually through the evaluation of various
factors. It is a subjective method but has the advantage of allowing
scrutiny of a wide range of factors which other methods do not. The
method is also highly flexible. Factors can be given a score value and
scores summed to give a total for a menu. This allows comparison between menus. If the one making the evaluations knows menu values, it
is a good method of judgment.

A favorite way of keeping cashiers busy was to have them keep a
tally of menu items sold in addition to their taking cash. Often one would
see a cashier taking counts of items from sales slips and tabulating them
by placing marks after menu items. These were summed for each item
to give management valued information on sales. It is an easy and simple way of getting good information on how well menu items are doing.

A popularity index can be made from a menu count by just summ-
ing all items sold of a group and calculating the percent the sales of each
item are of this total. Thus, instead of a numerical count, a percentage
is obtained which management can study to see how well various menu
items are doing compared with each other. Thus if 10 of one item sold
of a total of 50 overall items, the popularity index would be 20 percent
(10/50).

Both menu counts and popularity indexes give information that is
informative and valuable. Volume or number of items sold is an important factor in the successful operation of a food service, and, if other factors are also favorable, can indicate good patronage satisfaction and profitable operation. If records are maintained, one has a historical file which
is helpful in indicating good menu items to offer.

A disadvantage of popularity index is that it is difficult to compare
values between menus when the percent is based on a different number
of items studied. If five items are studied one time and then eight the
next, items among five have a better chance of having a higher index than

Reprinted with permission of *FIU Hospitality Review*, © 1987.

145

one in a group of eight. If the five are equally popular, their index is 20 percent, whereas if all eight are equally popular, their index is 12 1/2 percent.

Hurst's menu score[1] is a value obtained by multiplying the percent of patrons selecting items being studied of all similar items offered on the menu by the average gross profit of the items studied. Thus, if there were 340 patrons selecting entree items and 143 selected menu items being studied, the percent would be 42. If the average gross profit of these items was $4.90, then the menu score would be 2.06 (0.42 times $4.90). Hurst's method tests for the combined effect of items such as volume, selling price, food cost, and gross profit. It is highly flexible and sensitive to even slight changes in any factor. It lends itself well to simulation and checking ahead for possible beneficial or undesirable effect in price, food cost or other changes. It is not difficult to do and comes readily from quickly available data. The effect of changes in individual menu items is not available but it does test their effect on the whole which is an important consideration.

Kotschevar's Menu Factor Analysis[2] studies individual items, assigning them a numerical value which indicates how well they come up to management's expectations in food cost, gross profit, dollar sales, and volume. It lends itself to simulation. A factor is derived as follows: a menu item has a popularity index of 15 percent but management expects it to be 18 percent. A factor based on the actual percentage and the expected one is calculated by dividing the expected into the actual percentage (A/E), i.e., 15/18 = 0.83. Such a factor can also be calculated for dollar sales, gross profit, or food cost. Thus, if an item is 22 percent of dollar sales and management expects it to be 20 percent, the factor is 22/20 or 1.10. Any factor over 1.0 indicates a menu item is doing better than expected, while anything below 1.0 indicates it is not meeting management's expectations, except for food cost, where the opposite is true: over 1.0 being bad and under, good. It is possible by studying how various menu items come out when combined together to see the effect they have on each other and how well they compete with each other.

Break even is a tool which can be used to see how much income a menu must bring in before a profit is made. It can also be used to indicate how many items must be sold or patrons served before this occurs. It assumes a linearity in costs, pricing, etc., which may not always occur. It also does not analyze individual menu item performance but it can be helpful in setting goals.

Miller[3], Smith and Kasavana[4], and Pavesic[5] have developed menu analysis methods using matrix techniques. Miller studied the performance of menu items ranking most desirable as those having a (A) low dollar cost and (B) a high volume. Smith and Kasavana ranked them according to their (A) gross profit and (B) volume. Pavesic ranked items on a (A) food cost percent and (B) weighted gross profit.

Each established a standard based on the combined performance of the items studied and then ranked each item individually as to whether they were equal to, above, or below the standard.

The calculations for the standards used in these three matrix methods are shown in Table 2. They are drawn from data given in Table 1. Table 3 indicates how these three matrix methods would evaluate the four menu items. The actual value minus the standard gives the menu item's rank value. One standard and item value have the same value and this is called "low" (L) or below standard and therefore not a particularly desirable item on the menu.

Table 1
Operating Data on Four Menu Items

Menu Item	# Sold	% Sold	Item $ Food Cost	Total Food Cost	Selling Price	Total Sales	% Food Cost	Item Gross Profit	Total Gross Profit
1 Steak	20	29	4.75	95.00	11.90	238.00	40	7.15	143.00
2 Chicken	24	35	1.75	42.00	6.95	166.80	25	5.20	124.80
3 Sole	9	13	3.65	32.85	8.70	78.30	42	5.05	45.45
4 Shrimp	16	23	2.60	41.60	7.50	120.00	35	4.90	78.40
TOTALS	69			$211.45		$603.10			$391.65

Table 2
Standard for Three Matrix Methods

Miller

A. $ Food cost = total $ food cost/total no. items sold
$ Food cost = $211.45/69 = $3.06

B. Volume = total items sold/no. of menu items
Volume = 69/4 = 17.25

Smith and Kasavana

A. Volume = 1/no. of items sold x 70%
Volume = 1/4 times .7 = 17.5

B. Gross profit = total gross profit/no. sold
Gross profit = $391.65/69 = $5.68

Pavesic

A. Food cost % = total $ food cost/total $ sales
Food cost % = $211.45/$603.10 = 35%

B. Gross profit = total $ gross profit/no. items
Gross profit = $391.65/4 = $97.91

Table 3
Results of Three Matrix Analyses of Four Menu Items

		A.	Item $ Food Cost	B.	Volume
Miller		A.	Item $ Food Cost	B.	Volume
	(1)		$4.75 - $3.06 = 1.69 H	(1)	20 - 17.25 = 2.75 H
	(2)		$1.75 - $3.06 = -1.31 L	(2)	24 - 17.25 = 6.75 H
	(3)		$3.65 - $3.06 = 0.59 H	(3)	9 - 17.25 = -8.25 L
	(4)		$2.60 - $3.06 = -0.46 L	(4)	16 - 17.25 = -1.25 L
Smith and Kasavana		A.	Volume	B.	Gross Profit
	(1)		20 - 17.5 = 2.5 H	(1)	$7.15 - $5.68 = 1.47 H
	(2)		24 - 17.5 = 6.5 H	(2)	$5.20 - $5.68 = -0.48 L
	(3)		9 - 17.5 = -8.5 L	(3)	$5.05 - $5.68 = -0.63 L
	(4)		16 - 17.5 = -1.5 L	(4)	$4.90 - $5.68 = -0.78 L
Pavesic		A	% Food Cost	B.	Gross Profit
	(1)		40 - 35 = 5 H	(1)	$143.00 - $97.91 = 45.09 H
	(2)		25 - 35 = -10 L	(2)	$124.80 - $97.91 = 26.89 H
	(3)		42 - 35 = 7 H	(3)	$ 45.45 - $97.91 = -52.46 L
	(4)		35 - 35 = 0 L	(4)	$ 78.40 - $97.91 = -19.51 L

All three methods used terms such as "winner," "dog," or "standard" to indicate the standing of a menu item after analysis. The following table gives these names for the various values of each system:

Table 4
Terms Used to Indicate Values in Matrix Analysis

Miller	High volume (HV)	-Low food cost (LFC)	Winner
	High volume (HV)	-High food cost (HFC)	Marginal 1
	Low volume (LV)	-Low food cost (LFC)	Marginal 11
	Low volume (LV)	-High food cost (HFC)	Loser
Smith and Kasavana	High volume (HV)	-High gross profit (HGP)	Star
	High volume (HV)	-Low gross profit (LGP)	Plowhorse
	Low volume (LV)	-High gross profit (HGP)	Puzzle
	Low volume (LV)	-Low gross profit (LGP)	Dog
Pavesic	Low food cost (LFC)	-High gross profit (HGP)	Prime
	High food cost (HFC)	-High gross profit (HGP)	Standard
	Low food cost (LFC)	-Low gross profit (LGP)	Sleeper
	High food cost (HFC)	-Low gross profit (LGP)	Problem

The four menu items make every category in both Miller's and Pavesic's methods, but Smith and Kasavana find no puzzle. As one can see there is little agreement as to what some of these menu items are - good or bad. They agree on only one item and that is sole. It is bad.

Hayes and Huffman[6] developed a menu analysis method, Goal Value Analysis, which is designed to include more variables than possible in a two-way matrix method. It is largely a quantitative method of

Table 5
Menu Item Values in Three Matrix Analyses

| Menu | Miller | | Smith and Kasavana | | Pavesic | |
	Volume	Food Cost	Volume	Gross Profit	Food Cost	Gross Profit
1 Steak	H	H	H	H	H	H
	(Marginal 1)		(Star)		(Standard)	
2 Chicken	H	L	H	L	L	H
	(Winner)		(Plowhorse)		(Prime)	
3 Sole	L	H	L	L	H	L
	(Loser)		(Dog)		(Problem)	
4 Shrimp	L	L	L	L	L	L
	(Marginal 11)		(Dog)		(Sleeper)	

study. They establish a mathematical model: A times B times C times D = Goal Value; the following are assigned:

A = (1 - food cost %)

B = volume or number sold

C = selling price

D = (1 - variable cost % + food cost %).

They use consolidated data to arrive at a standard which is used as a measure to decide if a calculation using this same formula for individual menu items is equal to the standard, below it or above it. If above the standard, the menu is doing well; if below it, it is not. If it is equal to the standard, it is neither desirable or undesirable.

Using the data given in Table 1, an evaluation can be made on its four menu items with the Goal Value method. The following figures are used to calculate the standard:

Average food cost	211.45/603.10 = 35%
Average no. sold	69/4 = 17.25
Average selling price	603.10/69 = 8.74

A variable percent cost of 32 was selected. The calculation of the numerical standard follows:

A		B		C		D	Numerical Standard
(1 - .35)	times	17.25	times	8.74	times	(1 - [.32 + .35])	= 32.3

The same mathematical model is used to calculate the values for the individual four items. The results follow:

Menu Item	A	Times B	Times C	Times	D	Numerical Score
(1) Steak	(1-.40)	20	11.9		(1-[.32 + .40])	= 40.3 H
(2) Chicken	(1-.25)	24	6.95		(1-[.32 + .25])	= 53.8 H
(3) Sole	(1-.42)	9	8.7		(1-[.32 + .42])	= 11.8 L
(4) Shrimp	(1-.35)	16	7.5		(1-[.32 + .35])	= 25.7 L

The Goal Value method indicates that chicken is the best performer with a score of 53.8 compared with the standard of 32.3. Steak is also an approved item, while shrimp does poorly and sole very poorly.

The three matrix methods and Goal Value Analysis give somewhat similar information about the same menu items. All four methods agree only on one menu item and that is sole. If paired rank correlations are made, Miller and Hayes and Huffman have the highest correlation (r = .7). Kendall's test for coefficient of concordance was used to obtain a value to indicate whether there was any correlation between these four methods as a whole. A value of w = .4 was obtained. Spearman's rank correlation and a test by Friedman were also made to check against Kendall's. They both agreed with Kendall's finding which indicated some but not a high correlation. These tests would have been stronger had we been comparing more data.

It is readily seen in reviewing and evaluating these different methods for analyzing menus that they can yield a wide variety of valuable information to management. The kind depends upon which method is used. All these methods discussed here lend themselves to computerization, which can considerably simplify compilation of the information.

Menu analysis is a good way to focus management's attention on what menus or menu items are doing or should do; they force management to scrutinize, study, and evaluate menus or menu items. Numerical values can be developed that make possible comparisons which are helpful in making evaluations. They also can allow pretesting or simulation without actually running the menu.

Of these different methods of analysis one might wonder which is best. There is probably no best one because each gives rather specific and different information. Perhaps the best one is the one that suits the conditions and needs of the user. All have value.

Probably the preferred situation in using menu analysis is to use a combination of methods. Certainly any menu needs scrutiny by the subjective method. It is a good way to get at factors which one in no other way can check. Using the Hurst scoring method gives a numerical factor which can be used to compare menus given subjective evaluation. Various tests are available which give detailed information on individual menu items. All three matrix methods have their champions. However, the Hayes-Huffman seems preferable over these because it covers more variables. Combing several or more can certainly be helpful and revealing in indicating how well a menu is doing or should do, or how menu items are doing or should do. Certainly they are better than nothing.

References

[1] Lendal H. Kotschevar, *Management by Menu*, 2nd ed., (Dubuque, IA: Wm. C. Brown Publishers, 1986), pp. 182-88.

[2] *Ibid.*, pp. 179-82.

[3] Jack Miller, *Menu Pricing and Strategy*, 2nd ed., (New York: Van Nostrand Reinhold, 1986), pp. 185-193.

[4] D.I. Smith, and M.L. Kasavana, *Menu Engineering*, (Okemos, MI: Hospitality Publishers, 1982), pp. 142-158.

[5] D.V. Pavesic, "Prime Numbers: Finding Your Menu's Strengths," *Cornell Quarterly,* (November 1985), pp. 71-77.

[6] David K. Hayes, and Lynn Huffman, "Menu Analysis: A Better Way," *Cornell Quarterly*, (February 1985), pp. 65-69.

The Groesbeck Club: A Case Study

Peter J. Stevens

INTRODUCTION

The Groesbeck Club is located in a planned community
in northern Indiana. This bedroom community is 10 to 15
miles from each of three cities where most residents work.
Many also return to these cities when dining out in the
evening. Groesbeck, with its home sites lining three
lakes and 18 fairways of beautiful golf course, is popu-
lated with 1300 single-family households each of which
automatically holds membership in and pays annual fees to
the Groesbeck Property Owners Association. The POA owns
and operates the Clubhouse/Restaurant, six tennis courts,
the 18-hole golf course, olympic-sized swimming pool and
adjacent "Teen Center" (candy, soft drinks, hot dogs),
Nineteenth Hole (beer, wine, distilled spirits, sandwiches), small marina near the Clubhouse, and three small
picnic parks. The community has 24-hour security staff
at its only entrance/exit and employed vehicle patrol.
All of this, along with street maintenance, is supported
by POA fees. The elected nine person POA Board of Directors employs a full-time Community Manager, who in turn
employs a Food and Beverage Director (responsible for the

Clubhouse/Restaurant, Nineteenth Hole, and Teen Center).

The restaurant staff--waitresses, bussers, bartenders, cooks, and kitchen helpers--are unsophisticated, limited in previous experience, and not now well-trained. Most seem loyal and anxious to learn.

The Clubhouse/Restaurant, built twelve years ago by a land development company and since expanded twice by the POA, is located on a peninsula which protrudes eastward into the largest lake. The pool and Teen Center, marina and beach area, and large parking area share this parcel. The Clubhouse/Restaurant is within 3.5 miles of the farthest home site, .6 mile from the Nineteenth Hole, and virtually "on the way" for most residents leaving or returning home.

The building, originally a sales office and place to entertain small numbers of potential home site purchasers with food and drink, now has its kitchen at the east end; 64-seat dining room (south side) and 24-seat cocktail lounge (north side facing the pool) to the kitchen's west; banquet room (south side) and entrance (north side) and restrooms (north side) further to the west; and finally offices at the west end.

The kitchen--the most expensive single room in the building, and the most expensive to move--is located such that serving banquet guests (a) interrupts service to the dining room; (b) disrupts any possible relaxed and convivial atmosphere in the cocktail lounge; (c) interferes with, and is interrupted by, normal member access and egress flow through the Clubhouse door; and (d) is impaired in terms of potential food and service quality.

The relationship among the dining room/cocktail lounge, front door, and rest rooms is such that no measure of privacy can be offered to banquet or meeting guests in the ballroom. This situation is embarrassing and uncomfortable both for them and for dining room/cocktail lounge patrons.

The most attractive and valuable land for customer use--the east end of the building--is occupied by the kitchen, employee parking, refuse containers, and an outbuilding. This space could have provided a dining room with panoramic view to the north, east, and south with all desirable seating, and no dinner-guest discomfort from the glare and radiant heat of the setting sun.

Finally, the design of the golf course placed the 9th and 18th greens so as to discourage use of the Clubhouse by golfers in conjunction with play. The Nineteenth Hole adds to total expenses and still does not serve golfer needs as well as the Clubhouse could. Had the original design placed the 9th and 18th greens on the Clubhouse peninsula, the viability of either the "Teen Center" food and beverage area of the Restaurant, or both could have been enhanced. It is likely that golf course, pool area, and Clubhouse/Restaurant usage would all have been increased.

The dining room has only one-half, the lounge only

one-half, the appropriate table-seating capacity. If, therefore, the Food and Beverage Manager provides quality products and service, and enthusiastically promotes and merchandises the Restaurant, dissatisfaction and ill will result because of waiting lines. Operationally, he has a no-win situation.

The bar and lounge lack decor, lighting, comfortable or attractive furnishings, window view, attractive glassware, enthusiastic and professional service. It looks like what it is: the hallway from the kitchen to the ballroom. It has no personality. The only reason to patronize it is to find a place to wait for seating to become available in the dining room when the ballroom is occupied.

THE MARKETING RESEARCH PROJECT

In the spring of 1982 the Community Manager, with the support of the Board, contracted HRI to determine what the members wanted and what should be done with the Clubhouse/Restaurant. The Clubhouse/Restaurant had for some time been less than financially self-sufficient and, it seemed, was being virtually ignored by many members.

May 19-20 the consultants visited Groesbeck to see the community, the Restaurant, and the surrounding area; to acquire data and information regarding membership and

Restaurant operations; and to anonymously and unobtrusively gather subjective information in the community which would help in focusing a subsequent in-depth Survey.

The Survey was developed, pretested, revised, and refined. Seven people were trained and tested. The consultants and interviewers visited Groesbeck June 4-6, and conducted in-depth personal face-to-face interviews using the Survey instrument at 98 homes randomly selected from within four zones:

    Zone 1   lake-front homes
    Zone 2   golf course fairway homes
    Zone 3   single-family non-lake/non-fairway homes
    Zone 4   Condominium and townhouse homes

The consultants also visited and analyzed dining establishments frequently mentioned by interviewees as their favorites, including the Clubhouse/Restaurant, Nineteenth Hole, and Teen Center again.

Results of the Survey have been analyzed by the consultants both subjectively and by computer analysis. Marketing ideas have been discussed with a number of specialists.

Results of the Survey indicate that some members are quite happy and well-served by the Restaurant. Some care, but are unhappy and not well served. A substantial number are just apathetic, perceiving no particular need for a Club in their lifestyle. The consultants see great potential for better serving the needs and wants of the membership.

The survey provided data and information with respect to:

    (1)   age of respondents;

    (2)   number and ages of children living with respondents

    (3)   family size and occupations, and income level;

    (4)   how often and where respondents have dinner out;

       (a) with just adults;
       (b) with children;

    (5)   how much is typically spent per person

       (a) with just adults
       (b) with children;

    (6)   why respondents choose the restaurants they do

       (a) with just adults;
       (b) with children;

    (7)   what respondents like/dislike about the Clubhouse/Restaurant;

    (8)   what respondents would like to change about the Club; and

    (9)   what would cause the respondent to use the Clubhouse/Restaurant more often.

A summary of the findings follows:

1. <u>Age of the Respondents</u>

under 20	2.0%
20-30	19.4%
31-40	32.7%
41-60	31.6%
over 60	14.3%

2. <u>Number of Children (under 21) Living at Home</u>

0	44.7%
1	9.4%
2	31.6%
3	10.2%
4	2.1%
5 or more	2.0%

Ages of Children Living at Home (Note: percentages
will not total exactly 100% of above because of a few
reported children who are 21 and older.*

Age	1st	2nd	3rd	4th	5th	TOTAL
1	3.1	2.0	0.0	0.0	0.0	5.1%
2	1.0	1.0	0.0	0.0	1.0	3.0%
3	2.0	3.1	1.0	0.0	0.0	6.1%
4	2.0	3.1	1.0	0.0	0.0	6.1%
5	2.0	2.0	1.0	0.0	0.0	5.0%
6	6.1	2.0	1.0	0.0	0.0	9.1%
7	3.1	2.0	1.0	1.0	0.0	7.1%
8	3.1	3.1	0.0	0.0	1.0	7.2%
9	2.0	0.0	0.0	0.0	0.0	2.0%
10	2.0	5.1	0.0	1.0	0.0	8.1%
11	5.1	1.0	1.0	0.0	0.0	7.1%
12	2.0	4.1	3.1	0.0	0.0	9.2%
13	4.1	0.0	0.0	0.0	0.0	4.1%
14	3.1	1.0	1.0	0.0	0.0	5.1%
15	1.0	2.0	0.0	0.0	0.0	3.0%
16	2.0	2.0	0.0	1.0	0.0	5.0%
17	3.1	4.1	1.0	0.0	0.0	8.2%
18	3.1	1.0	1.0	0.0	0.0	5.1%
19	1.0	4.1	0.0	0.0	0.0	5.1%
20	4.1	0.0	0.0	0.0	0.0	4.1%
*	8.0	2.0	2.0	1.0	0.0	13.0%

Note: the last column (TOTAL) means that 5.1% of homes
have a 1-year-old child, 3.0% of homes have a 2-year-
old child, etc.

3. Number of Adults in the Household

1	12.4%
2	80.4%
3	6.2%
4	1.0%

Full-Time Employment

Respondents	56.7%
Spouses of Respondents	67.9%
All Adults	62.8%

Occupations of Full-Time-Employed Adults

Teacher	9.5%
Professional (doctor, lawyer, etc.)	6.0%
Nurse, medical technician	3.4%
White collar business	40.6%
Blue collar business	38.8%
Retired	1.7%

Family Income

under $20,000	6.3%
$20,000-$30.000	29.1%
$30,000-$40,000	29.1%
over $40,000	35.4%

4. Restaurant Dinners per Month

Number	Total	With Spouse, Date	With Friends	With Children
0	1.0%	18.3%	38.5%	35.8%
1	11.2%	13.4%	20.0%	17.9%
2	14.3%	12.2%	12.3%	14.9%
3	12.2%	7.3%	3.1%	6.0%
4	16.3%	11.0%	7.7%	10.4%
5	11.2%	7.3%	6.2%	4.5%
6-10	21.4%	30.5%	12.2%	10.5%
11-15	7.1%	0.0%	0.0%	0.0%
16-20	3.0%	0.0%	0.0%	0.0%
21-25	2.0%	0.0%	0.0%	0.0%
Mean Occasions	5.6	3.7	2.2	2.2

5. Amount Typically Spent per Person for Restaurant Dinner with Adults

less than $5.00	2.1%
$5.00-$10.00	29.2%
$10.00-$15.00	40.6%
$15.00-$20.00	16.7%
more than $20.00	11.5%

Amount Typically Spent for Restaurant Dinner per Person with Children

less than $5.00	16.9%
$5.00-$10.00	49.2%
$10.00-$15.00	20.3%
$15.00-$20.00	10.2%
more than $20.00	3.4%

6. ## Variables Considered When Selecting a Restaurant for Dinner

Variable	Very Important 1	2	3	Very Unimportant 4	5
Atmosphere	26.0%	38.5%	31.3%	3.1%	1.0%
quality of food	83.3%	10.4%	3.1%	2.1%	1.0%
Prompt and courteous service	54.6%	36.1%	6.2%	2.1%	1.0%
Reasonable prices	26.8%	32.0%	32.0%	4.1%	5.2%
Entertainment	6.3%	6.3%	30.2%	29.2%	28.1%
Convenient location	20.6%	28.9%	29.9%	11.3%	9.3%
Menu with wide variety	28.1%	32.3%	31.3%	6.3%	2.1%
Menu with specialty items	19.6%	20.6%	37.1%	13.4%	9.3%

Reason for Choosing Most Frequented Restaurant with Adults

Variable	First	Second
Atmosphere	7.6%	18.5%
Quality of food	59.8%	17.4%
Prompt and courteous service	7.6%	27.2%
Reasonable prices	4.3%	16.3%
Entertainment	0.0%	2.2%
Convenient location	7.6%	10.9%
Menu with wide variety	4.3%	6.5%
Menu with specialty items	8.7%	1.1%

<u>Reason for Choosing Most Frequented Restaurant</u>
<u>with Children</u>

Variable	First	Second
Atmosphere	3.8%	8.0%
Quality of food	28.8%	26.0%
Prompt and courteous service	11.5%	16.0%
Reasonable prices	23.1%	34.0%
Entertainment	1.9%	2.0%
Convenient location	5.8%	10.0%
Menu with wide variety	13.5%	2.0%
Menu with specialty items	11.5%	2.0%

7. <u>Rating of the Clubhouse/Restaurant</u>

Variable	Good 1	2	3	4	Poor 5
Atmosphere	27.8%	21.1%	27.8%	13.3%	10.0%
Quality of food	39.1%	29.9%	17.2%	9.2%	4.6%
Prompt and courteous service	39.1%	26.4%	17.2%	14.9%	2.3%
Reasonable prices	33.3%	35.6%	17.2%	6.9%	6.9%
Kind of entertainment	18.7%	6.7%	29.3%	20.0%	25.3%
Convenient location	88.8%	7.9%	2.2%	1.1%	0.0%
Menu selections	38.1%	27.4%	26.2%	6.0%	2.4%
Management of the restaurant	32.1%	25.9%	28.4%	7.4%	6.2%

(<u>Note</u>: one should compare and contrast these
responses with responses to open-ended questions
which follow. The nature of the questioning was
designed to overcome natural reticence to be frank
and candid. Responses here, and also in the previous
section, suggest the space opportunity costs and
direct expense of the present entertainment offering
might not be justified.)

<u>Sample of Responses by Residents to the Questions</u>

<u>How Do You Feel About the Clubhouse/Restaurant
in General?</u>

<u>What Do You Particularly Like About the Club
Food Service?</u>

<u>What Do You Particularly Dislike About the Club
Food Service?</u>

rundown and lifeless, lack of atmosphere, reasonable
prices, good quality . . . never eaten there--lived
here one and one-half years . . . good place, love
it . . . excellent, prompt and courteous service
. . . like it, but busboys need to be neater, gives
impression of dirty kitchen . . . fairly satisfied,
good food, service only fair . . . should be bigger
. . . mediocre, good food, service is slow . . . do
not cater to senior citizens, open for weekend breakfast and lunch, open earlier for dinner . . . like
the filet, salad bar, brunch, need better furnishings
. . . service is prompt unless crowded, bad house
wine . . . fair, like the menu, dislike noise, need
more room . . . mediocre food, average service, dislike the limited and varying hours . . . don't like
the salad bar and poor lighting . . . like the location, specials are terrible . . . convenient, food
quality and service vary . . . not impressed with
training and actions of employees, bad windows, cold
food on seafood buffet, terrible food on buffet,
unappetizing . . . satisfied . . . never eaten there,
too open--no atmosphere, bar too small . . . under-
staffed, workers efficient and friendly, like comrad-

erie, always accommodated . . . bad, food terrible, needs cleaning in restrooms and carpeting, embarrassed when with friends, convenient, service okay . . . fair, go because it's convenient, improve menu variety, increase activities for teenagers, atmosphere not warm--cliquish . . . has gone down hill . . . okay, cramped, knock out wall between ballroom and eating area, service good, courteous, unattractive bar, needs warmth and charm, lower prices . . . very cold atmosphere, not accessible, overprices for what you're getting, needs expansion . . . enjoy it, convenient, nice atmosphere for entertaining, good food, quality, nice variety . . . not very good, couldn't get a table . . . atmosphere not like a country club, seems like a diner . . . looks like a cafeteria . . . Sunday Brunch is very convenient, no information is communicated (on menus, hours, specials) . . . nice to have access to, good food, prompt, bar service is good, menu is quite limited.

8. Sample of Responses by Residents to the Questions:

What Would You Like to Change About the Club Restaurant?

What Would You Like to Change About the Clubhouse in General?

stick to regular items usually on salad bar, cut items that are "extra" and maybe could make up for it on price on entrees, could expand operating hours . . . more spacious . . . more formal and professional . . . consistent high quality . . . interior

163

decorations, enlarge it, bigger dining area . . .
reservations, furniture and carpeting . . . upgrade
quality of food, clubhouse layout is bad, unclassy,
landscaping in front . . . offer a full menu more
often, redecorate the place, more open for members'
use . . . the service rushing you . . . take reservations on Saturday and Sunday . . . more attention
to variety, better quality food, more fresh food,
served better, offer more events . . . eliminate it,
don't like property owners association feeling of
supporting aristocratic lifestyle . . . enlarge
dining room, very pleased, is friendly, reasonable
rates . . . better utilize the bar, more use of ballroom for dining room overflow . . . open every day,
enlarge building . . . screen doors to take advantage
of breeze instead of air conditioning . . . better
cook, children out of control of parents--should not
be allowed to run around, younger people should be
dressed properly . . . add nonsmoking section . . .
give manager free hand to do what he wants, rearrange
facilities, outside cafe needed, good entertainment
. . . should be at golf course . . . better quality
service and food, take out restaurant and put in
youth center, if not renovate and enlarge, stop catering to over 45 . . . better seating arrangement, needs
booths, dinner lights . . . the atmosphere, make
lounge larger . . . prices are too high, the people
subsidize it and feel prices should be lower, Joe

164

(the manager) and his family are not congenial and
don't do anything . . . atmosphere, make more intimate
and private, it is like a cafeteria, make it bigger
. . . like to have more specials . . . improve food
quality, parking is too far away . . . service must
be speeded up, make sure food is warm when served,
give members price break, upkeep is not sufficient.

9. <u>Sample of Responses by Residents to the Question</u>:

   <u>What Would Cause You to Use the Clubhouse More?</u>
   reasonable prices, gear more toward everyday dinner
   instead of "Sunday dinners" . . . cable TV, special
   events (Holmes fight) promoted and planned through
   the club . . . if I had a car . . . atmosphere (not
   necessarily physical) but type of persons frequenting
   it . . . expand menu and restaurant . . . give members
   discount on prices . . . make it larger with more
   waitresses . . . put on equal par with Rupcich . . .
   if the food facilities were better, extend happy hour
   and include beer . . . the restaurant doesn't have as
   much atmosphere as the ballroom does during parties
   . . . better prices . . . kids never . . . more family
   type atmosphere . . . bigger lounge, good juke box,
   more privacy in restaurant . . . more children's services . . . better food, nearer golf . . . better
   restaurant, seating capacity . . . separate formal/
   informal more family/relaxed . . . wider variety
   throughout week, lower prices, don't compete with high
   priced restaurants . . . a reason to go there other

than dinner . . . just getting into the habit . . .
monthly social event . . . better food . . . don't
put so much smelt on the variety fish platter . . .
upgrade restaurant as a whole . . . lower prices . . .
better quality of food and consistency . . . better
food, more formal atmosphere, more flexibility of
hours . . . bigger dining room . . . maybe lower
prices to suit families . . . if I had more leisure
time . . . awareness and information . . . size, serve
dinners in larger room . . . improve atmosphere,
capitalize on lake, outside dining, cocktail area,
closer parking, booths--privacy update room . . .
different entertainment . . . better advertising,
make it more like a club . . . better restaurant
. . . lower prices . . . limit attendance of children
after 8:00 or on special days . . . improved spirit
. . . better selection of food . . . cleaner place
. . . more time and money . . . nothing there but bar
and restaurant, should offer carry out . . . develop
consistency in food quality and service . . . if I
felt more comfortable, break up clique so people can
feel more at ease . . . breakfast and lunch menu . . .
less formal atmosphere, adjust prices to fit family
pocket book . . . opening facilities on Sunday night,
special events . . . if there were more to do . . .
if it were open more often . . . if it were renovated.

RECOMMENDATIONS BY THE CONSULTANTS

HRI presented recommendations to the Board which in Phase 1 include:

(1) possible addition of 1-3 electrical outlets;

(2) purchase of 2 Cres-Cor portable stand-up convection cooking/holding units, and 1 Cres-Cor portable stand-up cold holding unit;

(3) purchase of 2 hostess, 4 waitress, 4 busser, and 2 bartender uniforms;

(4) allocation of staff time to tabulate food item purchases by item and by time for a thirty-day period, and to compute actual designed food cost for each item on the menu;

(5) purchase of the menu engineering computer analysis service of Hospitality Financial Consultants in Lansing, Michigan;

(6) re-defining the menu mix based upon (4) and (5) above, using one day of consultant time;

(7) use of two days of consultant time to define the service system, and train the manager to train staff;

(8) use of four days of consultant time to design an internal control system to assure effectiveness and efficiency at low ongoing cost;

(9) minor alterations in the item mix, display arrangement, and salad dressing quality level of the salad bar;

(10) change in dining room table placement configuration to permit more options in terms of window-view seating;

(11) addition of distinctive wall-decor items, new bar stools, and two special hors d'oeuvre items in the cocktail lounge;

(12) retaining a menu design consultant to create a new printed menu which informs accurately and concisely, and which effectively merchandises that which management, per (6) above, wishes to feature;

(13) eliminating the process of aging and cutting meat;

(14)   replacing the dining room windows (which fog
        because the seals are broken), making sure that
        each can be used later for access/egress if a
        screened patio addition is added; and

(15)   opening Tuesday night for "family night" with a
        buffet (say $4.95 for adults, $2.95 for child-
        ren; serving inexpensive, but creative well-
        balanced and nutritional meals), beginning in
        the dining room (no regular menu served) and
        expanding to the ballroom when the first
        instance of overcrowding is anticipated. There-
        after, no longer book banquets for Tuesday
        nights.

(16)   set closing hours and then never close earlier.

(17)   replace the monthly calendar with a flyer which
        selectively promotes what is needed (i.e., the
        beginning of "Family night every Tuesday!"
        "Stop by with a friend for the delicious new
        fried mushrooms and a cold one in the lounge!")
        Use a sign near the community entrance/exit to
        promote the Clubhouse/Restaurant. It must be
        changed daily and promote use that night or
        week.

PRIVATE PARTY INFORMATION

Introduction

This brochure has been prepared to familiarize our

patrons with club policies, menu suggestions, and bar

arrangements befitting your social event. Our staff

takes pride in creating a pleasant atmosphere for you

and your guests.

The menu and services listed herein are offered as a

guide; items not listed are usually available upon

advance request. It is our aim to satisfy the most dis-

criminating taste and make your event a pleasant affair.

General Rules and Regulations

Hosts are responsible for the conduct of their guests.

Patrons shall not bring food or beverages into the club, except ceremonial cakes and pastries. Food and beverages remaining at the end of a party are the property of the club, except ceremonial cakes and pastries.

A contract that guarantees the number of guests, all arrangements, and prices is required for all events involving food and/or beverages. This is to be completed and signed at least two weeks in advance of the event, with minor changes 72 hours prior to the event.

We require a non-refundable $100.00 deposit at the time a date is booked for your event. This deposit will be applied to damages, if any. If there are no damages, the deposit will be applied to the final cost of your event.

Cancellations of parties must be in writing and are subject to a 10% penalty charge of the food bill if can-celled within two weeks the event. Events cancelled within 72 hours of the booked date will also forfeit the $100.00 deposit. Patrons will also be required to reim-burse the club for any expenses already incurred.

There will be a $25.00 cleaning charge for throwing rice or other material in the club or club grounds.

Fireplace

There is a $20.00 charge for the use of the fireplace.

Seating Capacity

The Ballroom has a seating capacity for 150 people.

Wines

Wines complement a fine meal. We shall be happy to assist you in the selection of wines and/or champagne. Prices vary as to selection and vintage.

Decorations

Decorations are the responsibility of the host and are to be confined to table centerpieces, unless otherwise authorized by the Food and Beverage manager.

Wedding Receptions

We pride ourselves in working out the most minute details for this memorable occasion and welcome the opportunity to serve in any way we can.

Wedding Cakes

There is a $15.00 service charge if our staff is to cut, serve, or wrap cakes.

Cocktail and Bar Service

Listed are the types of bar service offered:

(1) Cash Bar

The customer pays for a drink on an individual basis, when served. Prices vary with the drink served.

(2) Bottle Bar

The bar is issued a given amount of liquor. At the conclusion of the event, an inventory will be taken of the amount used, and the host will be billed at the quoted prices. Special brands are usually available, if requested two weeks in advance of the event. When applicable, we use liter sizes.

Blends, Bourbon, Scotch, Gin, Rum, Vodka, and Brandy are $30.00 per bottle. Beer is $65.00 per keg. Beer by the pitcher is $3.00. Premium liquor brands are available at $35.00 per bottle as well as Liqueurs.

Prices quoted are for all types of cocktails and mixed drinks, except ice cream drinks. Prices also include all set-ups.

For fifty or more guests, we will provide a separate bar for your event.

The following items are available or we will be happy to make your favorite recipe when requested at least two weeks in advance.

```
Champagne Punch    $30.00 per gallon
Liquor Punch       $40.00 per gallon
Fruit Punch        $12.50 per gallon

Champagne from $6.50
Wines from $4.75
```

Champagne and wine are quoted on a per bottle basis.

Dinners

Sit-Down Dinner

Select one

*Whole Roast Cornish Game Hen	$6.95 per person
*Split Cornish Game Hen	$5.75 per person
*Boneless Breast of Chicken, Bernaise Sauce	$6.25 per person
*Chicken Kiev	$6.25 per person
*Pepper Steak	$5.75 per person
Roast Turkey with Dressing, Cranberry Sauce	$5.75 per person
Roast Top Sirloin of Beef, Mushroom Sauce	$5.95 per person
Broiled Rib Eye Steak 8 oz	$7.55 per person
New York Strip Steak 12 oz	$8.75 per person
Roast Prime Rib of Beef, Au Jus 10 oz	$9.25 per person
Filet Mignon 6 oz	$8.95 per person
Baked or Fried Chicken	$5.75 per person
Rock Lobster Tail 8-10 oz	Market Price
Stuffed Tomato-Chicken, Tuna, or Ham Salad	$5.25 per person
Assorted Fruit Plate (seasonal)	$4.25 per person

* With these entree's, we recommend Rice Pilaf instead of potato.

Family Style Dinner

Select two $7.95 per person
Select three $8.98 per person

Roast Top Sirloin
Fried Chicken
Ocean Perch
Italian Sausage, Mostaciolli
Stuffed Cabbage
Baked Ham
Polish Sausage, Sauerkraut

Buffet

Steamship Round of Beef, Carved - $7.95 per person, plus a $25.00 charge for carving. This entree is available for parties of fifty or more.

Any of the above Family Style Dinners can also be served Buffet style.

With any Buffet, we recommend our Salad Bar at $1.25 extra per person, and includes a wide selection of salads, relishes, etc.

All dinners include the following:

Vegetable

Select one

Green Beans, Almondine	Glazed Carrots
Peas	Baked Beans
Corn	Mixed Vegetables

Potato

Select one

French Fried	Whipped
Au Gratin	Roasted
Parslied	Candied Yams
Baked with sour cream and chives, 25¢ extra per person	

Tossed Salad

Dressing

Select three

French	Thousand Island
Creamy Garlic	Italian
Bleu Cheese, 15¢ extra per person	

Dessert

Select one

Ice Cream: Vanilla, Chocolate, Peppermint
Sherbet: Orange, Lime, Rainbow

Hors D'Oeuvres

We offer the following. In addition, we can usually

accommodate you for other items when requested two weeks in advance. Prices quoted are on a per person basis.

Swedish Meat Balls	$ .90
Rumaki	$ .90
Chicken Mates	$ .85
Deviled Eggs	$ .90
Weiner Wraps	$ .85
Fancy Assorted Cold Canape's	$1.50
Popcorn Shrimp (hot, breaded)	$ .95
Cocktail Franks with or without B-B-Q Sauce	$ .85
Cold Crab	$1.25

Large Decorated Cheese Ball
  (includes crackers) $25.95 each

All Dinners, Luncheons, and Buffets are served with rolls and butter, plus your choice of coffee, tea, Sanka, or milk.

ALL FOOD AND BEVERAGE PRICES ARE SUBJECT TO A 4% SALES TAX AND A 15% GRATUITY AND ARE SUBJECT TO CHANGE, ACCORDING TO MARKET PRICES.

ALL CATERED EVENTS ARE TO BE PAID IN FULL AT THE CONCLUSION OF THE EVENT.

Joe Burns
Food and Beverage Manager

FRIED CHICKEN DINNER

8 quarters
6 dimes
2 nickels
5 pennies

SHRIMP DINNER

9 quarters
5 dimes
9 nickels
5 pennies

PERCH DINNER

7 quarters
10 dimes
4 nickels
5 pennies

PRIME RIB

12 quarters
6 dimes
5 nickels
5 pennies

ALL CHILDREN'S DINNERS INCLUDE THEIR CHOICE OF POTATO. ICE CREAM FOR DESSERT.

HOT DOG

4 quarters
4 dimes
2 nickels

SPAGHETTI, with meat sauce

4 quarters
4 dimes
2 nickels

GRILLED CHEESE

4 quarters
2 dimes
1 nickel

HAMBURGER

6 quarters
3 dimes
2 nickels
10 pennies

CHOPPED SIRLOIN DINNER

7 quarters
8 dimes
2 nickels
10 pennies

SUMMARY - CHILDREN'S MENU

	Item	Selling Price	Cost	Number of Items Sold
1.	Hot Dog	$1.50	$ .27	13
2.	Spaghetti	$1.50	$ .41	8
3.	Grilled Cheese	$1.25	$ .28	8
4.	Hamburger	$2.00	$1.11	10
5.	Chopped Sirloin	$2.45	$1.20	1
6.	Fried Chicken	$2.75	$ .34	15
7.	Shrimp	$3.25	$1.77	7
8.	Perch	$3.00	$1.02	9
9.	Prime Rib	$3.75	$1.50	4

```
TOTAL SALES LEVEL              169.95

POTENTIAL FOOD COST             54.00

FOOD COST PERCENTAGE            31.77

TOTAL DEMAND FACTOR                75

MENU CONTRIBUTION MARGIN       115.95

AVERAGE CONTRIBUTION MARGIN      1.55
```

```
****************************************************************************
*                                  *                                     *
*           PLOWHORSE              *              STAR                    *
*         ---------------          *         --------------------        *
*    HOT DOG                        *    FRIED CHICKEN                    *
*    SPAGHETTI                      *    PERCH                           *
*    GRILLED CHEESE                 *                                     *
*    HAMBURGER                      *                                     *
*    SHRIMP                         *                                     *
*                                   *                                     *
****************************************************************************
*                                   *                                     *
*             DOG                   *              PUZZLE                  *
*         ---------------           *         --------------------        *
*    CHOPPED SIRLOIN                *    PRIME RIB                        *
*                                   *                                     *
****************************************************************************
```

```
 20 :                              .
 19 :                              .
 18 :                              .
 17 :                              .
 16 :                              .
 15 :                              .                          6
 14 :                              .
 13 :                   1          .
 12 :                              .
 11 :                              .
 10 :              4               .
  9 :                              .           8
  8 :            3  2              .
  7 :                           7  .
  6 :                              .
  5 : . . . . . . . . . . . . . . . . . . . . . . . . . . . . 70% MM
  4 :                              .               9
  3 :                              .
  2 :                              .
  1 :                     5        .
  0 :                              .
    -------------------------------------------------------------
                 1.00                    2.00                3
                         AVE CM
```

Menu Name: CHILDREN'S MENU

ITEM ANALYSIS

ITEM NAME	ITEM PRICE	PORTION COST	CONTR. MARGIN	ITEM COUNT
HOT DOG	1.50	0.27	1.23	13
SPAGHETTI	1.50	0.41	1.09	8
GRILLED CHEESE	1.25	0.28	0.97	8
HAMBURGER	2.00	1.11	0.89	10
CHOPPED SIRLOIN	2.45	1.20	1.25	1
FRIED CHICKEN	2.75	0.34	2.41	15
SHRIMP	3.25	1.77	1.48	7
PERCH	3.00	1.02	1.98	9
PRIME RIB	3.75	1.50	2.25	4

MENU MIX ANALYSIS

ITEM NAME	MM COUNT	% MM SHARE	GROUP RANK	% CM SHARE	CONTR. MARGIN	GROUP RANK	MENU CLASS
HOT DOG	13	17.33	HIGH	13.79	1.23	LOW	PLOWHORSE
SPAGHETTI	8	10.67	HIGH	7.52	1.09	LOW	PLOWHORSE
GRILLED CHEESE	8	10.67	HIGH	6.69	0.97	LOW	PLOWHORSE
HAMBURGER	10	13.33	HIGH	7.68	0.89	LOW	PLOWHORSE
CHOPPED SIRLOIN	1	1.33	LOW	1.08	1.25	LOW	<< DOG >>
FRIED CHICKEN	15	20.00	HIGH	31.18	2.41	HIGH	**STAR**
SHRIMP	7	9.33	HIGH	8.93	1.48	LOW	PLOWHORSE
PERCH	9	12.00	HIGH	15.37	1.98	HIGH	**STAR**
PRIME RIB	4	5.33	LOW	7.76	2.25	HIGH	?PUZZLE?

179

-APPETIZERS-

Jumbo Shrimp Cocktail	4.50
Double Jumbo Shrimp Cocktail	8.00
Shrimp De Jonghe	3.95
Sauteed Mushrooms	2.75
Tomato Bread	1.50
Garlic Bread	1.00
Breaded Cauliflower, Mushrooms and Zucchini	2.50

-SALADS-

Chef's Salad Supreme	2.55
Crisp Garden Salad	1.45
Salad Bar (ala carte)	3.95

-POTATOES-

Cottage Fries	.95
French Fries	.95
Hash Browned	.95
Baked	.95
Special Baked	.95
(with Dinner .85)	

**ALL DINNERS INCLUDE OUR FULL HOMEMADE
SALAD BAR AND SOUP WITH CHOICE OF
POTATO, FRESHLY BAKED DINNER ROLLS, AND
YOUR CHOICE OF COFFEE OR HOT TEA**

-HOUSE SPECIALTIES-

Veal Parmegiana	6.95	Country Fried Chicken	5.95
Shish-ka-bob	7.45	Chicken Kiev	6.95
Liver and Onions	6.55	Sauteed Chicken Livers	5.95
Chopped Sirloin	5.95	Pork Chops	6.95
London Broil	6.95	Spaghetti, with meat sauce	4.25

-SANDWICHES-

Hamburger	2.45	Reuben	3.25
Cheeseburger	2.75	Italian Beef	2.65
Stacked Ham on Rye	2.85	Club	2.95
Salad Bar with Sandwich		2.50 extra	

-STEAKS-
We Cut and Age Our Own Beef

Grande Filet 10 oz. .... 10.95   N.Y. Strip Steak 16 oz. .. 9.75

Petite Filet 6 oz. .... 7.75   Rib-Eye Steak, on toast points ... 8.75

Bar B-Q Back Ribs-Slab 9.95

Prime Rib (served Friday and Saturday) 8.95

Chef's Cut 10.45

Steak & Lobster — Market Price

- SEAFOOD -

Broiled Halibut (Dieter's Delight) 6.45

Pan Fried Lake Perch, Boned in Butter 9.25

Deep Fried Shrimp 8.95

Neptune's Platter, crab, shrimp, perch, frog legs,
   clams, scallops & oysters 10.25

Land & Sea (filet & crab legs) 10.95

Broiled Scallops (smothered in spiced butter) 7.95

Single Lobster Tail (8-10 oz.) (with drawn butter)
   twin tails .... market price

Shrimp De Jonghe 8.75

Catfish Filet, Baked in Butter, and chef's spices 6.75

Frog Legs 8.95

Alaskan King Crab 10.25

Seafood Combo (perch and shrimp de jonghe) 8.25

Rainbow Trout Almondine 6.95

Red Snapper 7.95

Service Plate - 2.50

AFTER DINNER,
ASK YOUR WAITRESS ABOUT
OUR SELECTION OF DESSERTS &
ICE CREAM DRINKS

Thank you for joining us -
   we hope you'll come back

SUMMARY - DINNER MENU

	Item	Selling Price	Cost	Number of Items Sold
1.	Chef's SS	$ 2.55	$ 1.47	3
2.	Crisp GS	1.45	.30	3
3.	Salad Bar	3.95	.80	27
4.	Veal P	6.95	1.96	7
5.	Shisk KB	7.45	3.57	20
6.	Liver	6.55	1.89	17
7.	Chopped S	5.95	2.65	12
8.	London B	6.95	1.93	21
9.	C.F. Chicken	5.95	1.61	28
10.	Chicken K	6.95	2.56	18
11.	Sauteed CL	5.95	1.70	22
12.	Pork C	6.95	2.43	16
13.	Spaghetti	4.25	2.14	10
14.	Hamburger	2.45	1.47	11
15.	Cheeseburger	2.75	1.57	43
16.	Ham-R	2.85	1.02	6
17.	Reuben	3.25	.94	4
18.	Italian B	2.65	1.86	20
19.	Club S	2.95	1.28	11
20.	Grande F	10.95	5.10	14
21.	Petite F	7.75	3.43	102
22.	NY SS	9.75	5.10	33
23.	Rib-Eye	8.75	4.10	10
24.	BBQ-Ribs	9.95	4.67	30
25.	Prime R	8.95	4.10	72
26.	Chef's Cut	10.45	5.16	28
27.	Steak & L	20.95	12.56	3
28.	Halibut	6.45	3.29	5
29.	Lake Perch	9.25	2.99	36
30.	Shrimp-DF	8.95	3.87	42
31.	Neptune's P	$10.25	$ 5.86	3
32.	Land & Sea	10.95	4.70	4
33.	Broiled Scallops	7.95	2.72	13
34.	Lobster T-S	16.95	10.05	7
35.	Lobster T-T	24.95	19.18	0
36.	Shrimp De J	8.75	4.59	15
37.	Catfish	6.75	1.97	19
38.	Frog Legs	8.95	2.96	13
39.	A.K. Crab	10.25	6.20	20
40.	Seafood C	8.25	4.07	12
41.	Trout	6.95	3.27	5
42.	Snapper	7.95	2.22	5

```
------------------------------------------------------------------------
                    MENU MIX ANALYSIS- ADULT MENU
------------------------------------------------------------------------
                  MM    % MM   GROUP  % CM   CONTR.   GROUP    MENU
ITEM NAME         COUNT SHARE  RANK   SHARE  MARGIN   RANK     CLASS
------------------------------------------------------------------------
CHEFS SS            3   0.38   LOW    0.10   1.08     LOW    << DOG >>
CRISP GS            3   0.38   LOW    0.10   1.15     LOW    << DOG >>
SALAD BAR          27   3.42   HIGH   2.54   3.15     LOW    PLOWHORSE
VEAL P              7   0.89   LOW    1.04   4.99     HIGH   ?PUZZLE?
SHISK KB           20   2.53   HIGH   2.31   3.88     LOW    PLOWHORSE
LIVER              17   2.15   HIGH   2.36   4.66     HIGH   **STAR**
CHOPPED S          12   1.52   LOW    1.18   3.30     LOW    << DOG >>
LONDON B           21   2.66   HIGH   3.14   5.02     HIGH   **STAR**
CF CHICKEN         28   3.54   HIGH   3.62   4.34     HIGH   **STAR**
CHICKEN K          18   2.28   HIGH   2.36   4.39     HIGH   **STAR**
SAUTEES CL         22   2.78   HIGH   2.79   4.25     HIGH   **STAR**
PORK C             16   2.03   HIGH   2.16   4.52     HIGH   **STAR**
SPAGHETTI          10   1.27   LOW    0.63   2.11     LOW    << DOG >>
HAMBURGER          11   1.39   LOW    0.32   0.98     LOW    << DOG >>
CHEESEBURGER       43   5.44   HIGH   1.51   1.18     LOW    PLOWHORSE
HAM R               6   0.76   LOW    0.33   1.83     LOW    << DOG >>
REUBEN              4   0.51   LOW    0.28   2.31     LOW    << DOG >>
ITALIAN B          20   2.53   HIGH   0.47   0.79     LOW    PLOWHORSE
CLUB S             11   1.39   LOW    0.55   1.67     LOW    << DOG >>
GRANDE F           14   1.77   HIGH   2.44   5.85     HIGH   **STAR**
PETITE F          102  12.91   HIGH  13.14   4.32     HIGH   **STAR**
NY SS              33   4.18   HIGH   4.58   4.65     HIGH   **STAR**
RIB EYE            10   1.27   LOW    1.39   4.65     HIGH   ?PUZZLE?
BBQ RIBS           30   3.80   HIGH   4.72   5.28     HIGH   **STAR**
PRIME R            72   9.11   HIGH  10.41   4.85     HIGH   **STAR**
CHEFS CUT          28   3.54   HIGH   4.42   5.29     HIGH   **STAR**
STEAK/LOBSTER       3   0.38   LOW    0.75   8.39     HIGH   ?PUZZLE?
HALIBUT             5   0.63   LOW    0.47   3.16     LOW    << DOG >>
LAKE PERCH         36   4.56   HIGH   6.72   6.26     HIGH   **STAR**
SHRIMP/DF          42   5.32   HIGH   6.36   5.08     HIGH   **STAR**
NEPTUNES P          3   0.38   LOW    0.39   4.39     HIGH   ?PUZZLE?
LAND/SEA            4   0.51   LOW    0.75   6.25     HIGH   ?PUZZLE?
BROILED SCALLOPS   13   1.65   LOW    2.03   5.23     HIGH   ?PUZZLE?
LOBSTER T-S         7   0.89   LOW    1.44   6.90     HIGH   ?PUZZLE?
LOBSTER T-T         0   0.00   LOW    0.00   5.77     HIGH   ?PUZZLE?
SHRIMP DE J        15   1.90   HIGH   1.86   4.16     LOW    PLOWHORSE
CATFISH            19   2.41   HIGH   2.71   4.78     HIGH   **STAR**
FROG LEGS          13   1.65   LOW    2.32   5.99     HIGH   ?PUZZLE?
AK CRAB            20   2.53   HIGH   2.42   4.05     LOW    PLOWHORSE
SEAFOOD C          12   1.52   LOW    1.50   4.18     LOW    << DOG >>
TROUT               5   0.63   LOW    0.55   3.68     LOW    << DOG >>
SNAPPER             5   0.63   LOW    0.85   5.73     HIGH   ?PUZZLE?
```

Menu Name: ADULT MENU

ITEM ANALYSIS

ITEM NAME	ITEM PRICE	PORTION COST	CONTR. MARGIN	ITEM COUNT
CHEFS SS	2.55	1.47	1.08	3
CRISP GS	1.45	0.30	1.15	3
SALAD BAR	3.95	0.80	3.15	27
VEAL P	6.95	1.96	4.99	7
SHISK KB	7.45	3.57	3.88	20
LIVER	6.55	1.89	4.66	17
CHOPPED S	5.95	2.65	3.30	12
LONDON B	6.95	1.93	5.02	21
CF CHICKEN	5.95	1.61	4.34	28
CHICKEN K	6.95	2.56	4.39	18
SAUTEES CL	5.95	1.70	4.25	22
PORK C	6.95	2.43	4.52	16
SPAGHETTI	4.25	2.14	2.11	10
HAMBURGER	2.45	1.47	0.98	11
CHEESEBURGER	2.75	1.57	1.18	43
HAM R	2.85	1.02	1.83	6
REUBEN	3.25	0.94	2.31	4
ITALIAN B	2.65	1.86	0.79	20
CLUB S	2.95	1.28	1.67	11
GRANDE F	10.95	5.10	5.85	14
PETITE F	7.75	3.43	4.32	102
NY SS	9.75	5.10	4.65	33
RIB EYE	8.75	4.10	4.65	10
BBQ RIBS	9.95	4.67	5.28	30
PRIME R	8.95	4.10	4.85	72
CHEFS CUT	10.45	5.16	5.29	28
STEAK/LOBSTER	20.95	12.56	8.39	3
HALIBUT	6.45	3.29	3.16	5
LAKE PERCH	9.25	2.99	6.26	36
SHRIMP/DF	8.95	3.87	5.08	42
NEPTUNES F	10.25	5.86	4.39	3
LAND/SEA	10.95	4.70	6.25	4
BROILED SCALLOPS	7.95	2.72	5.23	13
LOBSTER T-S	16.95	10.05	6.90	7
LOBSTER T-T	24.95	19.18	5.77	0
SHRIMP DE J	8.75	4.59	4.16	15
CATFISH	6.75	1.97	4.78	19
FROG LEGS	8.95	2.96	5.99	13
AK CRAB	10.25	6.20	4.05	20
SEAFOOD C	8.25	4.07	4.18	12
TROUT	6.95	3.27	3.68	5
SNAPPER	7.95	2.22	5.73	5

```
---------------------------------------------------------------
                 MENU ENGINEERING SUMMARY
---------------------------------------------------------------

        TOTAL SALES LEVEL              5925.50

        POTENTIAL FOOD COST           2571.96

        FOOD COST PERCENTAGE            43.40

        TOTAL DEMAND FACTOR              790

        MENU CONTRIBUTION MARGIN      3353.54

        AVERAGE CONTRIBUTION MARGIN     4.24
```

```
*****************************************************************
*                                *                              *
*           PLOWHORSE            *              STAR            *
*           ----------           *           ----------        *
*     SALAD BAR                  *     LIVER                    *
*     SHISK KB                   *     LONDON B                 *
*     CHEESEBURGER               *     CF CHICKEN               *
*     ITALIAN B                  *     CHICKEN K                *
*     SHRIMP DE J                *     SAUTEES CL               *
*     AK CRAB                    *     PORK C                   *
*                                *     GRANDE F                 *
*                                *     PETITE F                 *
*                                *     NY SS                    *
*                                *     BBQ RIBS                 *
*                                *     PRIME R                  *
*                                *     CHEFS CUT                *
*                                *     LAKE PERCH               *
*                                *     SHRIMP/DF                *
*                                *     CATFISH                  *
*                                *                              *
*****************************************************************
*                                *                              *
*             DOG                *            PUZZLE            *
*           ----------           *           ----------        *
*     CHEFS SS                   *     VEAL P                   *
*     CRISP GS                   *     RIB EYE                  *
*     CHOPPED S                  *     STEAK/LOBSTER            *
*     SPAGHETTI                  *     NEPTUNES P               *
*     HAMBURGER                  *     LAND/SEA                 *
*     HAM R                      *     BROILED SCALLOPS         *
*     REUBEN                     *     LOBSTER T-S              *
*     CLUB S                     *     LOBSTER T-T              *
*     HALIBUT                    *     FROG LEGS                *
*     SEAFOOD C                  *     SNAPPER                  *
*     TROUT                      *                              *
*                                *                              *
*****************************************************************
```

```
200 :                                  •
190 :                                  •
180 :                                  •
170 :                                  •
160 :                                  •
150 :                                  •
140 :                                  •
130 :                                  •
120 :                                  •
110 :                                  •
100 :                                  21
 90 :                                  •
 80 :                                  •
 70 :                                  •        25
 60 :                                  •
 50 :                                  •
 40 :              15                  •           30           29
 30 :                            3         9   22   26
 20 :        18                         5336112378
 10 :......14....11613.......28..41..40..234.33..4238......34..........70% MM
  0 :        12            17           .31              35   32              27
    ----------------------------------------------------------------------------
            1.00      2.00     3.00     4.00    5.00     6.00    7.00     8.00    ?
                                       AVE CM
```

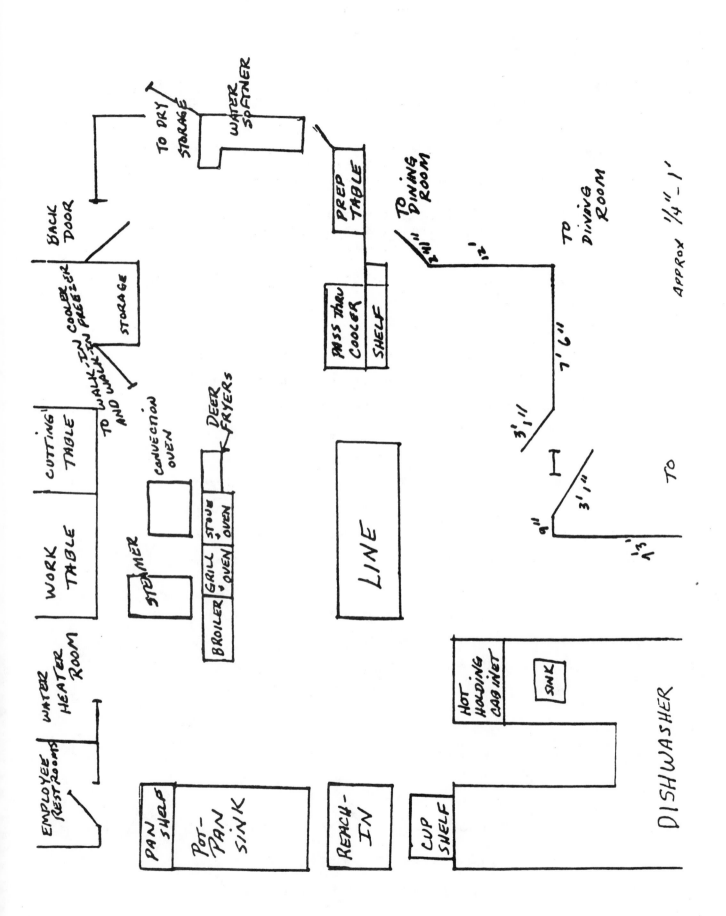

REFERENCES

Kasavana, Michael L., and Smith, Donald I. Menu Engineering. Lansing, Michigan: Hospitality Publications, 1982.

Kreul, Lee M. "Magic Numbers: Psychological Aspects of Menu Pricing." The Cornell Hotel and Restaurant Administration Quarterly (August 1982):70-75.

"Menu Design for Effective Merchandising." The Cornell Hotel and Restaurant Administration Quarterly (November 1978):38-46.

National Restaurant Association. Accuracy in Menus (pamphlet), 1977.

The author acknowledges and is grateful for the assistance of Dr. Ken W. McCleary of Central Michigan University who worked with the author in the design and conduct of the marketing research described in the case; of Dr. Pamela Weaver of Central Michigan University who designed the needed statistics package and analyzed results; of seven undergraduate students in Hospitality Services Administration at Central Michigan University who administered surveys; of Drs. Michael L. Kasavana and Raymond S. Schmidgall of Michigan State University and Hospitality Financial Consultants who provided Menu Engineering Analysis; and of Rick Collamer, Michigan State University MBA student who worked with the author in designing a training program and new control system at the Club.

P.J. Stevens, Ph.D.

Assistant Professor

School of Hotel, Restaurant and

Institutional Management

Michigan State University

Can we talk price?

Introduction by Bonnie Knutson

Price is important. Price is what guests pay to get the products and services you sell. It is also an important variable in the critical "price-value" equation that helps determine guest satisfaction. But price is more than the number of dollars your customer takes out of his wallet; it is more than the number she writes on the credit card form.

For your business, price is a major determinant of profitability. Price is likewise a marketing tool, just as promotion, packaging or place. It helps "position" your product/business in consumers' minds. As such, you need to view price as an extension of the economic principle that the economy responds to the consumer.

This need is examined in Robert C. Lewis's article, "Customer-Based Hotel Pricing." Using hotel examples, he shows how pricing policies run counter to economic wisdom and market realities. He then calls for hotels to set rates with the long-term customer in mind, not the short-term margin.

"Business at Any Price" echoes this sentiment. With the rampant use of discounting and couponing brought on by excess capacity, James C. Makens warns the industry to avoid the temptation to use these pricing strategies.

"Yield Management" is a proven technique for maximizing income, but its use in the lodging industry is relatively new. Walter Relihan discloses how "The Yield-Management Approach to Hotel-Room Pricing" can dramatically increase the property's revenues. But, he cautions, it is not a substitution for good marketing.

For the restaurant industry Lee Kreul reveals how "magic numbers" stimulate sales and influence customer choices. And why restaurateurs should use "psychological pricing" principles more, rather than formula-based pricing strategies.

Business at Any Price

A warning to avoid the temptations of discounting brought on by excess capacity

by James C. Makens

A DEMON has invaded many sectors of industry. No, it's not Lucifer, and it can't be exorcised by incantation. This demon is called "Business at Any Price." The practice of accepting and even promoting business below costs has become commonplace in many industries.

Among those most infected are major players in the much-touted service industry. Lodging, health services, transportation, financial services, and even management consulting have heard the sneering laugh of this demon.

Nothing is more perishable than a ballpark seat, airline seat, or resort-hotel suite. Once the ball game or theater production begins, few seats are sold. Worse yet, once the plane taxis to the runway, the vacant seat has spoiled like a rotten apple. Manufacturers with excess capacity face the same problem. Nevertheless, the perils of succumbing

James C. Makens, *Ph.D.*, *is an associate professor of marketing at the Babcock Graduate School of Management at Wake Forest University. This article is reprinted by permission of* PACE Magazine, *the Piedmont Airlines in-flight magazine, Pace Communications, Inc., Greensboro, NC.*

> I recently asked the general manager of a beautiful hotel in Singapore about occupancy levels. The reply was: "It doesn't matter. We couldn't break even at 100-percent occupancy, given our current rates."

to business at any price are greater than swallowing unsold seats or rooms.

Fixed Costs

How can the service industry serve as the flagship to carry the United States through the rest of this century with a profit formula that says total costs can exceed total revenue? Businesses with heavy fixed costs are particularly susceptible to this approach. When someone mentions fixed costs, such industries as petroleum refining, paper manufacturing, or steel normally come to mind. To that list we can add hotels, airlines, hospitals, convention centers, and many more. Chefs, pilots, hotel managers, doctors, and even maintenance crews are often thought of as variable or semivariable costs, but employers know they function as fixed costs.

Managers who face heavy fixed costs are likely to say, "If I can get business that covers my variable costs and contributes something to fixed, I'll be better off than I am with empty rooms, empty beds, and empty seats." To put this problem in perspective, let's examine a single hypothetical example. Suppose you operate a shoe-manufacturing plant with fixed costs of $4.00 per pair, and variable costs of $6.00, for a total cost of $10.00 per pair of shoes produced. Your plant operates at less than full capacity, and you could easily manufacture an additional 2,000 pairs per day. A retail chain sees your plight and offers to pay $8.00 per pair with a guaranteed contract of 2,000 pairs per day, to be sold under a private label.

Marketing Problem

Analyze the deal. You cover variable costs and contribute $2.00 to fixed. Will you take the offer or politely refuse? It may depend upon marketing. If your sales manager says it's simply unrealistic to sell those extra pairs of

shoes at $10.00 or more, you'll be tempted to take the deal.

The real question in all this is more basic. Why does the firm face extra capacity in the first place? A depressed economy is often the culprit, but not always. In many cases, the problem is lack of marketing planning at two critical points: prior to expansion or development, and prior to annual fiscal operations.

Think Before Building

A thorough and objective assessment of the market is essential prior to expansion or development. The consumer-products industry has learned the benefits of market analysis prior to product development. Unfortunately, sections of the service industry apparently have not.

The hotel industry is a great example. By all calculations, this industry is heavily overbuilt, yet new properties are being developed daily. A rule of thumb for calculating hotel room rates is that each $1,000 of the cost of developing a room must be met by one dollar per night in room rates. A cost per room of $100,000 would mean that $100 should be charged for the room per night.

The United States is filled with new hotel properties that cost well over $100,000 per room. Several of these are in markets, such as second-tier cities, that simply will not consistently support room rates over $100 per night.

Multimillion-dollar hotel developments have been financed and built without the support of thorough market analysis. This results in products that are poorly matched to markets and have little or no chance of operating in the black. With a surplus of rooms, managers decide to cut rates and attract discount groups. This in turn places heavy pressure on competitors to do likewise.

The United States is not the only nation to suffer from this curse. I recently asked the general manager of a beautiful new hotel in Singapore about current occupancy levels at his hotel. The reply was, "It doesn't matter; occupancy is no longer important. We couldn't break even at 100-percent occupancy, given our current rates."

I asked the same question in a competing hotel, and the answer was startlingly different. Occupancy levels in that hotel averaged 80 percent at $250 per night. The difference was marketing. True, there were some product differences, but marketing was the key. The successful hotel had selected CEOs and members of boards of directors from Europe and the United States as targets and had aggressively pursued this population with customized marketing strategies.

A bigger truck. A story is told about two brothers who entered the watermelon business. The brothers knew of a farmer 80 miles away who would sell watermelons at $1.00 each. The brothers made repeated trips to the farm to purchase watermelons. On returning, they sold their product at $1.00 per melon in a fruit stand. After two weeks of paying for gas and oil to fuel the truck, the brothers noted they actually had less money than they had had before entering the business. Each agreed to think about the problem and come up with a solution. Finally, one of the lads shouted that he had the answer: "We need to buy a bigger truck."

Wide sectors of the service industry have arrived at the same answer. Economies of scale are often given as the reason for expansion. However, economies of scale mean little if one operates at 30 percent of capacity with discounted prices. Demand and the cost of marketing to generate demand are often assumed away or ignored in the rush to build an exciting new hotel or office, or to have the outstanding convention center in the region.

Subsidies, Not Segments

Instead of carefully considering probable demand by various market segments, major consideration seems to have been given to depreciation and other tax benefits. Appreciation also served as a major consideration. Costs could exceed income and the venture would still result in nice capital gains. Given the presence of new tax laws in a period of disinflation, marketing planning prior to development or expansion will take on new importance.

Government loans or grants have often been expected to relieve the nonprofit service sector of the realities of the marketplace. A beautiful theater could be developed at a cost of many millions of dollars if only it had historic value and enough town fathers with the right connections in the district or the state capital. Never mind that for the project to be viable, theater tickets would have to run $50.00 and occupancy would have to average 95 percent. Marketplace demand was of secondary consequence.

Annual Planning

The second critical necessity for marketing planning is as a guide for the next fiscal year. The annual marketing plan must identify market potential, targeted segments, sales objectives, the mix of marketing strategies needed to reach these objectives, and the associated cost.

A professional marketing plan can't ensure success if the basic product is mismatched to the market or if costs are too high to permit sufficient sales volume. In some cases, the only answer will be a thorough financial restructuring, bankruptcy, or continuing subsidization by taxpayers, investors, bondholders, or other groups.

The annual marketing plan can greatly assist most companies and organizations. Market segments must be selected that have sufficient size and demand characteristics to offer profitable sales.

Penetration of these segments won't come easy. Your prime customers have already been targeted by a competitor. The loser will be left with discount segments that either cannot or will not pay the price. Certain segments can be attracted only through substantial price reductions.

Lower income is not the only liability connected with these groups. Maintenance and security costs often increase. Breakage and shrinkage may rise, lowering the longevity of fixtures and furnishings.

The most serious side effect is that discount groups sometimes drive away "full-pay" customers. Don't jump to the conclusion that I'm referring to any particular group. People of all kinds can become undesirable customers under certain conditions. Serious businesspeople have been known to be-

come outrageous oafs when placed in a freewheeling convention or party environment.

Strategic mistakes. A popular southeastern U.S. resort community discovered the real price of attracting a large group of middle-class teenagers during the prime season of 1986. Comprising several hundred potential customers, this group demanded and received cut-rate prices. The group also drove away large numbers of full-pay regular customers who found the noise and confusion unbearable. The real cost of selling to this group far exceeded the increase in marketing budgets that might have been necessary to attract greater numbers of full-pay customers.

During a recent trip to the American Virgin Islands, I asked the front-desk clerk of a resort hotel how the summer season was going. The reply was that occupancy was low. Many traditional guests from New York and Chicago just weren't coming. Upon further inquiry, I discovered that this clerk was also the sales manager. "Why are you working the front desk?," I asked.

"We don't have sufficient budget, and anyway we have a hotel rep there," he answered.

Chicago and New York remain large, viable markets, and it wouldn't take many people from either market to fill that hotel. Obviously, the hotel rep wasn't working out, and a new strategy was needed.

The use of a marketing plan might not have brought occupancy levels to 100 percent, but it would never have permitted the use of a sales manager as front-desk clerk. Instead, that person would undoubtedly have been in Chicago or New York.

Service-sector managers have not discovered a new formula for success after all. Total cost cannot exceed total revenue for very long in any industry. If the United States is going to place its hopes on the service industry, that lesson must be learned quickly. Business at any price is not a pathway to profit and progress. □

Customer-Based Hotel Pricing

Many of the hotel industry's pricing policies run counter to economic wisdom and market realities

by Robert C. Lewis

THE REPORT of Laventhol & Horwath's second annual Hotel-Motel Conference, published in the last issue of *The Quarterly*,[1] led me to consider the question that is so often asked of students working on advanced case studies: "What's the *real* problem?" Much of the talk at the conference was of overbuilding. But not *everyone* is complaining about overbuilding. If you look carefully, you'll see some hotel operators aren't saying a thing; they are too busy finding out what the customer wants at which price. These are the operators who will still be around after the industry "shakeout," the one that so concerned people at the conference, is over.

So, what's the real problem? I'll try to answer that question in the following pages.

Growth Opportunities

The hotel industry might take a lesson from the computer business. Right now the computer industry is in a slump: sales are off, discounting is rampant, and budget models are proliferating. (Sound familiar?) But is the real problem too many computers? Hardly. The problem is that the computer makers must find new ways to satisfy customers' needs. Some firms (Apple, for instance) are doing just that. The firms that cannot keep up with the customer will fail.

The same is true of the hotel industry. As Theodore Levitt wisely wrote 25 years ago, there is no such thing as a growth industry, only growth opportunities.[2] A current example of such an opportunity is the all-suite hotels, which so recently seemed like nothing

more than an aberration on the market. Levitt wrote that businesses fail "not because the market is saturated. It is because there has been a failure of management." The dimensions of this failure include the following mistaken management assumptions:

- There is a never-ending, ever more affluent population that will sustain increasing demand for a product.
- There is no competitive substitute for a product.
- Technological advances will maintain the superiority and high prices of a product.

Another reason for failure is that management doesn't understand its business.

None of these factors in business failure involves oversupply. I think oversupply is a scapegoat for poor performance. In fact, there is substantive evidence that overbuilding is a phenomenon of a few specific cities (e.g., Houston), where conditions have caused an imbalance in supply and demand.[3] It may be, as Albert Gomes recently wrote, that people are "confusing competition with overcapacity."[4]

Reverse Relationship

The industry has interpreted the demand for quality accommodations as a mandate to raise prices and add services and amenities of questionable value. Have technological advances at the front desk shortened the lines of guests checking in or out? Have all those bathroom soaps and shampoos made the customer any cleaner? Does a chocolate on the pillow make up for the fact that guests must check out at noon, regardless of their business or conference schedule?

The hotel business can be defined simply as providing accommodations without inconvenience. How many hotels do that? The hotel industry's position seems to be: "Pay your money and see what we can give you in return." But the historic attitude of consumers is the opposite: "Offer me value; if you do, I'll pay the price."

Looking glass. In a retrospective commentary on his earlier article, Levitt noted the problem of selling a complex service like that provided by hotels:

> In the case of the more technical industrial products or services, the necessity of clearly communicating product and service characteristics to prospects results in a lot of face-to-face "selling" effort. But precisely because the product is so complex, the situation produces salesmen who know the product more than they know the customer, who are more adept at explaining what they have and what it can do than learning what the customer's needs and problems are. The result has been a narrow product orientation rather than a liberating customer orientation, and "service" often suffered. To be sure, sellers said, "We have to provide service," but they tended to define service by looking into the mirror rather than out the window. They *thought* they were looking out the window at the customer, but it was actually a mirror—a reflection of their own product-oriented biases rather than a reflection of their customers' situations.[5]

Michael Leven, president of Days Inns, apparently had this problem in mind when he explained why he made his senior vice president of marketing the senior vice president of operations instead:

> The answer lies with the general managers, whose bailiwick has been soap, ashtrays, sheets, and light bills. These product-oriented people have to turn their attention to "creative revenue buildup" in today's high-supply environment and turn away from the technical approach to the hospitality business. It is the job of [the vice president of operations] to make clear to them the customers' capability to deliver revenue if they are satisfied with the services they receive.[6]

Limits to Growth

Many upper-tier operators are complaining about having to discount their rooms to get business. I believe those

[1]Glenn Withiam, "The State of the Industry," *The Cornell Hotel and Restaurant Administration Quarterly*, 27, No. 1 (May 1986), pp. 20–27.

[2]Theodore Levitt, "Marketing Myopia," *Harvard Business Review*, 1960.

[3]For example, see: Marie Griffin, "Is the Hotel Market *Really* Overbuilt?," *Successful Meetings*, March 1986, pp. 49–55.

[4]Albert Gomes, *Hospitality in Transition: A Retrospective and Prospective Look at the U.S. Lodging Industry* (New York: American Hotel & Motel Association, 1985). Gomes found that there are about the same number of hotel rooms per capita today as in 1930.

[5]Robert Blomstrom, ed., *Strategic Marketing Planning in the Hospitality Industry* (East Lansing, MI: Educational Institute of the AH&MA, 1983), pp. 5–18.

[6]Connie Goldstein, *Corporate Meetings and Incentive Travel*, June 1986, p. 6.

Robert C. Lewis, Ph.D., is a professor of hotel, restaurant, and travel administration at the University of Massachusetts, Amherst.

rooms were overpriced in the first place. Recent history bears out this belief.

In a 1982 speech, William Moeckel said:

> The hotel industry has not been bashful in its response to inflationary pressures on its operating expenses. It has simply passed them on to its guests in the form of higher room rates, restaurant checks, and charges for amenities.
> *Successful hotel companies of the future [need] a better understanding of the myriad forces affecting supply and demand relationships in their industry* [emphasis added].[7]

But two years later, the trade press was still recording price increases:

> Nationwide hotel occupancy is expected to rise 1.8 percent in 1984, continuing a 17-month upward trend. Rate hikes for the year will average about 7.5 percent.[8]

Perhaps those price increases finally caught up with the industry, because a 1985 news item noted reduced occupancy:

> U.S. hotel prices rose 5.5 percent in the first half of 1985, says Laventhol & Horwath. *Reduced occupancy rates and sluggish volume at hotel restaurants prompted price increases* [emphasis added].[9]

Seven months later, the same publication reported further increases in price and declines in occupancy:

> Room rates will average $61 this year, a 3.3-percent rise from 1985, predicts Laventhol & Horwath. The overall occupancy rate will dip slightly, to 63.9 percent, the firm projects.[10]

In fact, Laventhol & Horwath trend reports show increases in room rates every month, compared to the same month a year earlier, while occupancy has declined every month but nine for at least the last five years. Room rates have increased more than the consumer price index (a measure of inflation) for at least the last ten years.

The hotel industry is one of the very few that raises its price when its product doesn't sell. At some hotel firms, price increases are actually automatic. Every quarter or every six months, rack rates go up, regardless of occupancy ratios or business trends. Then these same firms are forced to offer discounts that are, at best, confusing,

naive, and unsophisticated. At worst, the discounts are detrimental revenue losers.

The discounts are there if you know how to ask. My concern is that many travelers don't ask, and they are quoted rack rates. Then they make other plans. Many stay with family or friends when they travel. Or they cut short their stays by leaving their conventions a day early. Or they take advantage of commuter-airline flights and conduct their business in one day without ever booking a hotel room.

Many of the people who are shying away from hotels are rate-sensitive, and they constitute a growing group. "All groups in the rate-sensitive category appear to be growing in number, including senior citizens, budget-oriented vacationers, and price-sensitive commercial travelers," according to industry analyst Stephen Brener.[11] Rate-sensitive guests either find a discount price, book a budget hotel, or simply don't use hotels—especially not upper-tier hotels. (In fact, Brener sees high-price guests as composing the smallest group of hotel customers.) And even travelers on expense accounts are feeling pressure to avoid high rates.[12]

The vice president of a national hotel chain was recently asked how many people actually pay rack rate in his hotels. He estimated ten percent. Asked whether these people were getting poor treatment, he answered, "We don't care about them." Are we expanding the market or killing it?

[11]Stephen W. Brener, "Lodging Industry Needs New, Efficient Facilities," *Hotel & Motel Management*, August 1985, p. 69.

[12]See: Robert C. Lewis, "The Basis of Hotel Selection," *The Cornell Hotel and Restaurant Administration Quarterly*, 25, No. 1 (May 1984), pp. 54–69; also see: *Consumer Reports*, July 1986, pp. 472–478. The magazine reports on hotel ratings by 150,000 subscribers. The survey echoes the sense of the author's argument.

Cat and Mouse

It almost seems as if the industry is cutting its own throat. Would you be willing to patronize a company that treated you as it did the person who tells the following story of trying to purchase a room?[13]

> It was June 20, 1986. I had to be in a certain city from Wednesday to Sunday in early August. In a full-page ad in *The Wall Street Journal*, I saw a national hotel chain's offer of a special summer rate of $69 for the property at that city. I called the 800 number, and had the following conversation:
> *Me:* "I'd like to book a room in August. Could I have the special rate of the association I belong to?"
> *Hotel:* "Rooms are available, but not at that rate."
> *Me:* "Why is that?"
> *Hotel:* "Each hotel decides for itself, and we are fairly busy at that time."
> *Me:* "What rate is available?"
> *Hotel:* "$135 per night."
> *Me:* "Is that all?"
> *Hotel:* "Yes."
> *Me:* "What happened to the $69 rate advertised on a full page of *The Wall Street Journal*?"
> *Hotel:* "I don't know anything about that. What did it say?"
> (I retrieved the ad and read it.)
> *Hotel:* "Oh, yes, we have those. Those are class D rooms, but they're all gone."
> *Me:* "How come you didn't know about these rooms before I mentioned them?"
> *Hotel:* "It's because they come up on a different screen. I was looking at the screen for the rate you first asked for."
> *Me:* "How about a weekend rate for Friday and Saturday, anyway?"
> *Hotel:* "Yes, we have a special weekend rate of $84. That's a class E room, but none are available."
> *Me:* "Is a class E room smaller than a class D room?"
> *Hotel:* "Right."
> *Me:* "So my only choice is $135?"
> *Hotel:* "Right." (I had stayed at that hotel before, and it's not worth $135.)
> *Me:* "Thank you, but I will look elsewhere."
> *Hotel:* "Thank you for calling Incommunicado Hotels, and have a good day."

[13]I do not want to single out any chain. At the time of this writing, three other major chains were advertising similarly low weekend rates at all their hotels. When queried about these low rates in random phone calls to their 800-number reservation desks, these firms all said their rooms were sold out. We can only assume that, very suddenly, 67 percent of these chains' hotels are full on weekends. If we also assume that these rooms would otherwise be vacant, a case for discounting is well supported. See: Robert C. Lewis and Christopher C. Roan, "Selling What You Promote," *The Cornell Hotel and Restaurant Administration Quarterly*, 27, No. 1 (May 1986), pp. 13–15.

[7]William G. Moeckel, "Price Sensitivity and Value Relationships in the Hotel Industry," speech to the Travel and Tourism Research Association, 1982.

[8]*Meeting News*, December 1984, p. 1.

[9]*The Wall Street Journal*, September 12, 1985, p. 1.

[10]*The Wall Street Journal*, April 17, 1986, p. 1.

The story is not quite ended. The teller has a friend who has a friend who works at the front desk of the hotel. Out of curiosity, he found out what the projected occupancy was on the days of his proposed hotel stay. Wednesday was 72 percent; Thursday, 68 percent; Friday, 58 percent; and Saturday, 45 percent. Can anyone explain this? Does it pay to play cat and mouse with the customer on prices?

Unknown Forces

This is not the place for a discussion of pricing theory or consumer-behavior theory. But most hotel-room pricing, especially in the upper-tier market that has become so crowded with competing firms, is unscientific and self-defeating. There is abundant evidence that even travelers on expense accounts are unwilling to pay high prices for rooms.[14] They are using lower-priced hotels, so it's not hard to figure out why budget and middle-tier properties are prospering, while upscale hotels are suffering.

Some in the industry seem to believe that "natural demand" or some other unknown force should fill a hotel. Hoteliers still talk about room rates of $1.00 per $1,000 of construction cost, as if this ratio had been engraved in stone from on high. This ratio was an estimation practice that originated in a less-competitive market situation, and it ignores the customer. I know of two hotels that recently opened using this rule of thumb for pricing. Their corporate parents had strict policies against discounting. Three months after opening, the hotels' sales staffs were scrambling—new discount rates in hand—to get customers even to talk to them. Not exactly the way to build customer loyalty.

It doesn't take an economist to determine why occupancies are declining or why hotel food-service covers are off. At $140 per night for the room, $45 for an $8 bottle of wine (plus, for your convenience, a 15-percent service charge and eight-percent sales tax), and $15 for a breakfast of juice, coffee, an egg, and a Danish, is it any wonder that occupancies and covers are down?

The industry often responds: We have to raise rates—look at our occupancy costs; look at our return on investment; look at the demands of the owners. These factors have nothing to do with the essential element of the hotel business—namely, that it is volume-sensitive, like the airline business. And as the airlines have learned, when you increase supply, you also have to increase demand. (In fact, the airlines have taken many steps to do this.)

Pricing, Not Discounting

It might surprise the reader to know that I am not necessarily advocating discounting. I agree to some extent with Abbey's contention that rate cutting is counterproductive.[15] What I advocate is setting rates based on the *customer* as a focal point, and not the demands of owners, corporate guidelines, or returns on investment. My message is this: Set prices fairly, stick to them, and tell customers what they'll get for their money. Then make sure customers get what you promise.

The airlines once believed that expense accounts were unlimited. The greatest number of seats on most planes used to be in first class. But high prices have scared off even many expense-account customers, and the first-class section has shrunk considerably on most planes. Airlines created new seat classifications to get fliers back on the plane. Hotels could do the same.

Robert Hazard, CEO of Quality International, is one hotel executive who seems to understand the pricing problem. He said:

> The secret to success in the lodging business will be to provide guests with higher quality and better value at reasonable prices. Those who improve their price-value perception will tap into a nearly inexhaustible supply of new guests. Those who ignore it will choke on an ever-expanding supply of empty new rooms.[16]

[14]Steven J. Stark, "Biz Travelers Increasingly Being Steered to Budget Hotels," *Business Travel News*, April 14, 1986, pp. 22, 24.

[15]James Abbey, "Is Discounting the Answer to Declining Occupancies?," *International Journal of Hospitality Management*, 2, No. 2 (1983), pp. 77–82.

[16]Robert C. Hazard, Jr., "Bracing for the Changes Ahead in the Hotel Industry," *Business Travel News*, May 13, 1985, p. 26.

[17]Elliot B. Ross, "Making Money with Proactive Pricing," *Harvard Business Review*, November–December 1984, pp. 145–155.

[18]Hazard, loc. cit.

[19]Abbey, loc. cit.

[20]"Room at the Inn Can Be a Bargain for the Insistent," *The Wall Street Journal*, November 18, 1985, p. 33.

First Aid for Choking

Two things need to be done. First, the industry must understand marketing as a customer-focused practice. Pricing is a marketing tool, just as advertising and selling are. Marketing is an extension of the economic principle that the economy responds to the customer. Hotel rates must be set with the long-term customer in mind, and not short-term margin. Much of what the hotel industry now calls marketing is really just advertising and selling.

Success in pricing depends on an understanding of how the industry's pricing works and how customers perceive prices, according to Elliot Ross of McKinsey & Co.[17] He advises "proactive" pricing: "Time price changes to the anticipated reactions of customers and competitors rather than to...analysis of costs."

Second, the industry must develop more sophisticated, integrated marketing and pricing strategies that respond to supply and demand. Computer-based research can provide alert managers with the information needed to evaluate market segments and "consumer demand against the availability and price of competitive rooms," as Hazard put it. Hotel managements must, he continued, "learn how to sell rooms on a discounted demand basis, without committing financial suicide. The key will be to develop a flexible rate system that will generate new traffic and produce a greater overall yield to the hotel."[18]

Abbey also recommended basing pricing decisions on "solid market research and thorough understanding of the economics of price changes," rather than "intuitive judgments of what the market will bear."[19]

There is a third element. Common sense. If you're trying to lure customers with a discount, why not tell them about it?

In short, it's time to get rid of seat-of-the-pants pricing and a holier-than-thou attitude. The hotel industry should woo rate-sensitive travelers, before they learn that hotel rooms can be a "bargain for the insistent,"[20] and before they are lost completely. □

The Yield-Management Approach to

Hotel-Room Pricing

Yield management can dramatically increase revenues for a hotel operator. But it's not a substitute for poor marketing or poor sales. Here is how yield management can work for you

by Walter J. Relihan III

YIELD MANAGEMENT is a proven technique for maximizing revenues. It involves applying basic economic principles to pricing and controlling your rooms inventory for the purpose of maximizing revenues. It involves adjusting room rates in response to the level of rooms booked for future arrival dates.

The concept of yield management is not, in itself, new. Most hotel managers understand the idea of lowering prices to stimulate sales when demand is weak and raising prices in response to excess demand. What makes contemporary yield management so different

Walter J. Relihan III holds a master's degree in hotel administration from Cornell University and is a consultant with Aeronomics Incorporated, a consulting firm specializing in yield management.

from traditional pricing practices is the frequency and scope of the decision-making process. Advances in computer technology support immediate measurement of market forces and the practical application of economic theory. These techniques make it possible to update prices for all future arrival dates to match the market's demands each day.

This article focuses on the application of yield management to hotel-room pricing. This is by no means an exhaustive explanation of the techniques or applications for this emerging field. Length-of-stay and overbooking controls, for instance, are not fully explored here. But yield management will change our orientation to the entire sales process and particularly to the pricing of hotel rooms. It challenges such traditionally accepted notions as prices' correlating only to physical room type and season.

Traditional Pricing Practices

Room prices have been determined by considering just about everything except the customer's willingness to pay. Most of us are familiar with the rule of thumb that a hotel needs to charge one dollar for each thousand dollars' construction cost. Desired financial results, such as return on investment or break-even plus a profit percentage, have also been used to back into price and occupancy goals. Most often, however, hoteliers determine their prices in relation to the competition, as if the guy down the street somehow knew better!

Other industries. The use of technology to measure market forces is well accepted. As recently as July 1988, the *Harvard Business Review* proclaimed in one article's title: "Without a Total-Demand Forecast You're Operating in the Dark."[1] The recent financial successes of some airlines provide many lessons for our industry. Over recent years, the amount of discounting has increased, and, therefore, the average revenue per passenger-mile has steadily decreased, but many airlines are experiencing record profitability.[2] "Revenue improvements ranging from $200 million to $500 million have been attributed to sophisticated revenue control by managers of carriers with $1 billion to $5 billion in revenues."[3] Great similarities in the fundamental nature of the airline and hotel industries, such as the perishability of inventories and customer characteristics, indicate that the experience of the airlines would transfer to the hotel business. Just as the service levels of the two businesses differ, however, so must our approach in applying the aggressive strategies the airlines have pioneered.

The airlines embraced yield management after suffering major losses in the early '80s as a result of uncontrolled discounting. The airlines have learned from the demise of People Express and other discounters. Now they offer many fares and juggle their availability to maximize revenue. To achieve their revenue goals, the airlines need the sophisticated computers that have become an essential tool of their trade.[4]

Hotel sales. The sales process by which a hotel room is reserved influences the price of that room more directly than the type of room requested and certainly more

directly than the date of stay. Hotel guests pay different rates for staying in similar rooms. They accept this fact of life. Rooms for convention guests are reserved at rates established in advance through negotiation between the meeting planner and the hotel sales manager. Reservations made by a large local client can command a unique special corporate rate. The walk-in guest, by contrast, pays rack rate unless he or she produces a business card and demands a "corporate" rate. If hoteliers are to reap the gains of yield management demonstrated by the airlines, we must embrace the idea that availability of a rate should depend primarily on the specific market demand for that unique date.

A myth. Yield management is not a systematic approach to abusing customers. The practice only attempts to bring hotel room pricing into alignment with actual market forces. Think of it as a game in which all players can win. The harried business traveler finds a room on short notice for a peak busy night; the vacation traveler finds a time when deep discounts are available; and the hotel manager achieves both higher occupancy and higher average rate.

Picking Up Signals

Yield-management systems generate inventory-control pricing recommendations in much the same way that the financial industry's giant computer systems analyze global markets, albeit on a smaller and less centralized scale. "Technical analysis of financial markets starts with the assumption that markets follow trends determined by previous patterns of price behavior and that they rarely, if ever, move randomly. A computer trading system attempts to spot a trend from a combination of past price

[1]F. William Barnett, "Four Steps to Forecast Total Market Demand—Without a Total-Demand Forecast You're Operating in the Dark," *Harvard Business Review*, July-August 1988, pp. 28–38.

[2]"Fares Must Yield to the Market," *Airline Business*, January 1987, pp. 16–19.

[3]Beau Sheil, "Thinking About Artificial Intelligence," *Harvard Business Review*, July-August 1987, pp. 91–97.

[4]"American Airlines—A Shock to Their Systems," *The Economist*, 302, No. 7484 (February 7, 1987), pp. 40–44.

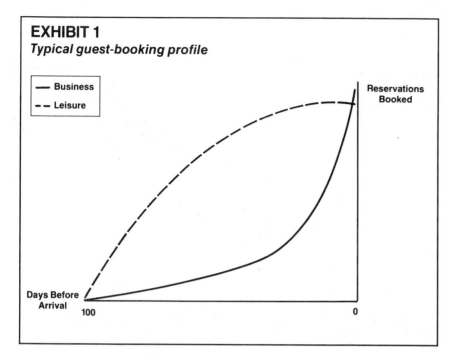

EXHIBIT 1
Typical guest-booking profile

Legend:
— Business
-- Leisure

Reservations Booked

Days Before Arrival   100   0

movements and other statistical data, and then throws up buy and sell signals whenever [it detects] significant shifts in the pattern."[5] Yield management in hotels starts with an understanding of customers' purchase behavior and a comparison of current demand with forecasts of future occupancy. By thus identifying sales opportunities, yield management strikes a balance between supply and demand through constant small adjustments in the economic variable that the hotel manager can most effectively control—to wit, price.

The price at which hotel rooms are offered affects the demand for those rooms. Nationwide or marketwide demand may be relatively price inelastic because it is finite, but on the local level in which any single hotel operates, even small differences in price can mean the difference between winning and losing business. Since hotels within a vicinity are closer substitutes for each other than those on the other

side of a metropolitan area, price differences between individual neighboring properties are likely to have more impact.[6] Segmenting the hotel market by the degree to which it is price elastic is important, because that process dictates what price will sell rooms. Equally important is the manager's knowledge of a market segment's time sensitivity, because time-related behavior determines when demand will occur.

Business and Leisure

Hotel guests are commonly grouped into roughly two segments, business and leisure, each sharing distinct price-elasticity and time-sensitivity characteristics. As the airlines have learned, "leisure traffic normally books early, as holidays are planned well ahead. (They may be time sensitive to some degree, but price is the overriding factor in the decision.) Business bookings, on the other hand, tend to be concentrated in the days im-

mediately before [a trip]."[7] This relationship is illustrated in Exhibit 1. As Carol Greenberg pointed out in an earlier *Quarterly* article, "an examination of room-rate structure also lends support to the hypothesis that business travelers as a group are willing to pay more than tourists for lodging."[8] Notice the coincidence of price-inelastic (high rate-paying) demand occurring just before arrival and price-elastic demand (bargain hunting) occurring well in advance.

In the practice of yield management, the late demand is anticipated, and an appropriate number of rooms are offered only at the higher rates these guests are willing to pay. If a hotel fills up days in advance, the difference between the high rate it could have charged and the lower rate at which the room was actually reserved would be "spilled." Continued high-rate spill would indicate the need for higher rates or more hotel rooms. As Eric Orkin pointed out in his article on yield management in the February 1988 *Quarterly*, "The displacement of future, high-rate transient reservations by groups that are paying lower rates must be a carefully considered decision. This decision takes on an added dimension when one considers that a portion of the displaced transients will be spending the night at a competitor's hotel."[9] When strong or late-booking demand is unlikely to occur, on the other hand, rooms should be offered at the discounts necessary to stimulate leisure travelers' interest, thereby preventing a waste of room-nights. Judging whether that late-booking, price-inelastic demand will materialize is

---

[5]"Computers Challenge the Stock Market Gurus," *The Economist*, 302, No. 7490 (March 21, 1987), pp. 82–83.

[6]Carol Greenberg, "Room Rates and Lodging Demand," *The Cornell Hotel and Restaurant Administration Quarterly*, 26, No. 3 (November 1985), pp. 10–11.

[7]"Innovations in Fare Competition," *The Avmark Aviation Economist*, June 1988, pp. 18–20.
[8]Greenberg, p. 11.
[9]Eric B. Orkin, "Boosting Your Bottom Line with Yield Management," *The Cornell Hotel and Restaurant Administration Quarterly*, 28, No. 4 (February 1988), pp. 52–56.

yield management's primary function. This concept is illustrated in the graph in Exhibit 2.

Forecasting Demand

Yield management depends on accurate demand forecasts. These can be created in several different ways. Some hotels' systems employ sophisticated statistical analyses of reservations history, as the airlines do. Other systems provide a format for hotel managers to "teach" a computer a set of rules that describe the typical demand pattern of the specific hotel. In the not-too-distant future, a new type of computer system will be able to teach itself the rules.

Statistical analysis. In airline research departments, squads of Ph.D.s generate forecast assumptions by statistical analysis of reservations databases. Regression analysis would typically be used to find a set of formulas, depicted as curves, that best represent the airline's entire reservations history. The representative data might also be deduced after fitting data to curves with cubic splines.[10] Systems will soon be able to regenerate new formulas as new bookings occur. Other statistical methods can even use non-numerical data, substituting logical operators to develop rules for expert systems, in a process called "rule induction."

Four Approaches

The most common approach to adjusting room rates starts with a comparison of actual demand with a forecasted or threshold value. The actual booking level for a day is compared to a desired or ideal pattern that is usually derived from statistical analysis of the hotel's booking history. Strong demand

[10]Ian E. Ashdown, "Curve Fitting with Cubic Splines," *Dr. Dobb's Journal of Software Tools*, 119 (September 1986), pp. 24–30.

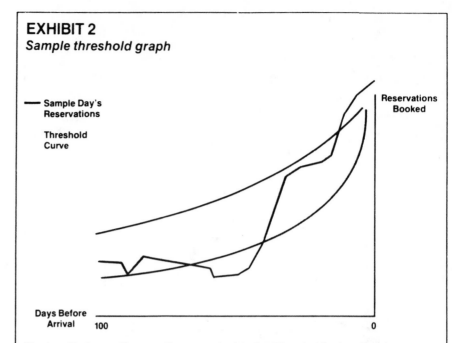

EXHIBIT 2
Sample threshold graph

— Sample Day's Reservations

Threshold Curve

Reservations Booked

Days Before Arrival   100   0

The band between the smooth curves depicts the "threshold values" or the expected demand pattern for this hotel in this market on this day. The actual booking level is represented by the line between occupancy points, one for each day. When actual bookings vary from the expected or ideal pattern, that date is flagged as having potential to generate more revenue by adjusting rates.

When the line representing actual bookings is outside the threshold band, prices should be adjusted. In the graph above, near-future bookings exceed threshold levels, indicating that discounts can be eliminated. Where actual bookings fall below the threshold, near the middle of the graph, management is advised to open discount rates to encourage more reservations.

may result in a day's booking level crossing the threshold. This flags an opportunity to offer rooms at higher rates. If the booking level falls off, the system identifies an opportunity to stimulate demand by offering discounts. In short, pricing can be adjusted to the vagaries of the market by measuring the swings in actual demand above or below a threshold value.

The threshold approach has many practical benefits. It is easy to install, it can monitor reservations progress and produce daily recommendations, its scope of outlook can be set far into the future (allowing plenty of opportunity to take action), and it prevents overreaction. Should the manager's actions produce an undesirable result, the comparison of that booking level to the current thresh-

old value will set off a new flag on subsequent days. It is best used as a guide for raising and lowering prices, however, and it does not develop an optimum solution. The threshold approach works best in competitive environments that experience excess demand, and daily pricing is the only control it addresses directly.

Expert systems. Forecast expectations are part of a knowledge base, or set of rules, that drive expert systems (artificial-intelligence systems).[11] The rules are created by a hotel manager. "Trigger points" fire the rules (making them operative). A "lead-time expectations form" would allow multiple lead

[11]For a discussion of expert systems, see: John T. Bowen and David N. Clinton, "Expert Systems: Advisor on a Disk," *The Cornell Hotel and Restaurant Administration Quarterly*, 29, No. 3 (November 1988), pp. 62–67.

EXHIBIT 3
Revenue-optimization curve

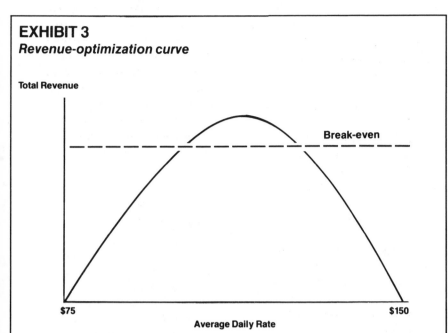

The potential benefit of an optimization approach can be illustrated by the relationship between average daily rate and total revenues represented by the curve above. One end slopes downward despite rates so low that occupancy soars. The other extreme also slopes downward because high rates have discouraged potential guests. The revenue curve arches upward in the middle because the offsetting factors of high rate and high occupancy are in better balance. Given the market's demand and price sensitivity, mathematical optimization routines can define the single value that is the apex of this curve for any particular property at any time. In the daily sales activity of a hotel, this process can be used to define the best price.

times and associated acceptable percentages (say, 10 percent of rooms booked 180 days before arrival, or 30 percent at 90 days, 45 percent at 60 days, and so on).[12] The lead-time values are analogous to the threshold values of statistical systems.

It is possible for true expert systems to address other room-inventory controls by creating the appropriate rule base. Expert systems, however, are at their best in static environments. Few would argue that the hotel environment is static.

Optimization. One of the most promising new techniques, optimization, goes beyond thresholds and expert systems. Instead of generating model or archetypal patterns, optimization seeks to derive the single, exact best solution from mathematical algorithms that consider the particular circumstances of time and place. This approach is heavily invested in demand forecasting, probability theory, and elasticity measurement.[13]

Optimization holds the promise of expanding the range of issues and the practicality with which yield management addresses these issues. It will be able to give specific recommendations based on current and projected demand. Optimization may provide anticipatory recommendations for the other variables of room-inventory control—namely, length of stay

and overbooking—as well as giving more specific answers to pricing questions. Even the best expert can do no better than attain the mathematical optimum. No model, however, can judge value for all business decisions, such as whether to accept a politically important group at a lower than optimum rate, or the long-term competitive advantage gained by positioning in the short term for market share. The ideal approach is interactive. An expert, a skilled hotel manager, working with an optimization model should produce better results than either can alone. The graph in Exhibit 3 illustrates the optimization approach.

Neural networks. New kinds of computers, called neural networks, hold great promise for solving such problems as those posed by yield management. Neural networks learn the same way human minds do, from experience. They are "truly intelligent computers—capable not only of dealing with unforeseen situations, but also of synthesizing knowledge from random data with little or no help."[14]

One approach possible with neural networks is a kind of grandiose trial-and-error method. An optimum solution can be closely approximated by rationally selecting trial criteria to produce better results until the margin of error in the variables is extremely small. At that point, neural networks may even be able to recommend changes in the original set of constraints or problem assumptions, so that the resulting solution is better than the original optimum solution that was based on an inferior set of constraints. The usefulness of these systems is limited, because their results generally lag behind

[12]Dave Berkus, "The Yield Management Revolution—An Ideal Use of Artificial Intelligence," *The Bottomline*, June-July 1988, pp. 13–15.

[13]See: Peter C. Yesawich, "A Market-Based Approach to Forecasting," *The Cornell Hotel and Restaurant Administration Quarterly*, 25, No. 3 (November 1984), pp. 47–53.

[14]"They're Here: Computers that 'Think,'" *Business Week*, January 26, 1987, pp. 94–98.

the acquisition of enough new examples or experience to remain current. Moreover, despite their attractive potential, the technology is still in the laboratory.

A Major Limitation

While each approach to yield management has its inherent limitations in terms of accuracy and practicality, the greatest limitation on maximizing revenue does not necessarily lie with yield management at all. The inventory controls and sales tools within property-management and central reservations systems cause far greater distortions. Most reservation systems are limited to just a few rate classes, for example. Management's ability to influence a hotel's demand (and potential for revenue gain) increases with finer discriminations in rate classes. The primitive use of length-of-stay controls is another example. Most systems use the length of stay only as a ceiling on high-capacity nights and are not otherwise capable of offering rates geared to extending the length of stay to increase profit.

Practical Application

Here is how a yield-management system should behave. It should match room prices to market demand. It should prevent you from filling your hotel before the last-minute, high-rate customers book rooms, and it should advise discounting when necessary to fill rooms.

These objectives are more easily achieved with the appropriate computer support for forecasting and measuring market demand, but the goals of yield management are really common-sense applications of economic supply-and-demand theory.

What You Can Do Now

While a sophisticated yield-management system may not be a part of your hotel's immediate future plans, there are a number of steps you can take today to lead your hotel toward yield management.

(1) *Analyze your pricing structure.* Price is the most easily controlled economic variable, and it has the greatest influence on market demand. Control is exercised by making one rate available and restricting another. For this procedure to be successful, rates must be offered that influence the market demand by small degrees without producing adverse customer reaction. Map out all your rates to form a coherent picture of their interrelationships. Identify and eliminate awkward jumps between rates that would compromise your degree of control.

(2) *Use reservation systems to the fullest.* Reservation systems are the instruments of room-inventory control, yet most managers have only a superficial understanding of their capabilities. Worse, many systems are muddled with "creative" inventory practices to accommodate a lack of adherence to stated policies, such as entering "ghost" blocks in anticipation of group additions after a cut-off date. Various minimum length-of-stay restrictions are a good example of frequently cited but poorly understood reservation-system features. Thorough understanding of your reservation system can often help make up for its limitations as a yield-management tool. For example, packages can often be used to make up for a lack in the number of rate classes.

(3) *Save your reservations history.* Customer information is a precious company asset. Only with a foundation of accurate information specific to a hotel can any yield-management system provide its full value. In addition, many marketing applications not yet conceived of are likely to be impossible without this knowledge. The cost of saving this information is comparatively small, and having it readily available may put you several months to years ahead of the competition in installing an effective yield-management system.

The Future of Yield Management

Yield-management applications for hotels are relatively new, and they will evolve rapidly. Graphics will enhance analysis and decision making, especially as yield-management systems migrate from the mainframe environment to PCs, where graphics are a more native capability. The obvious cost advantage of smaller computers will also increase the availability of yield-management systems. Methodology will continue to advance, broadening the scope of issues that yield management addresses. Models will be developed that define true optimum pricing, validate package plans in consideration of costs and probabilities of future demand, accept or reject group business, incorporate seasonality, and recommend specific rates depending on length of stay.

Eventually, yield-management functions must integrate with reservation and property-management systems. Ideally, an on-line system would quote a price for reservation calls as they are answered, and yield management would support such marketing applications as special-account recognition. □

Magic Numbers:
Psychological Aspects of Menu Pricing

Formula-based pricing strategies are more prevalent in the food-service literature than in restaurant operations, a study reveals. What are the magic numbers that stimulate sales—and why are restaurateurs more likely to employ "psychological" pricing techniques than formulas?

by Lee M. Kreul,
Purdue University

ECONOMIC THEORISTS generally depict demand curves as smooth and negatively sloped from left to right, as shown in Exhibit 1. However, popular restaurant pricing practices suggest that restaurateurs perceive the demand curve near the even-dollar point as jagged, as shown in Exhibit 2, and marked at other price points by other kinks and nonrandom variations.

The assumed relationship between price and demand depicted in Exhibit 2 is inferred from the findings of a recent study on restaurant pricing practices.[1] The survey was conducted to determine which prices were most used by restaurants. All of the restaurant prices published in newspaper advertisements in 21 U.S. metropolitan areas, representing most major food-service markets,

were recorded for one week.[2] Menu prices from 242 restaurants of all categories were analyzed. Some of the pricing practices identified by the study follow:

• The most popular (58%) *terminal digit* for meals priced *at or below $6.99* was 9, followed by 5 (35%), followed by 0 (6%);

• 1, 2, 3, 4, 6, and 7 were not used as terminal digits;

• For meals priced *from $7.00 to $10.99,* 5 became more popular as the ending digit (71%), followed by 0 (15%) and 9 (11%);

• Meals in the $6.00 to $6.99 price range were the most frequently advertised, with most ads for meals under $6.99; few meals priced above $9.99 were advertised.

These findings correspond both to pricing practices in other retail

industries and to the practices of manufacturers and wholesalers. Two earlier studies of the pricing practices of retail food stores, for example, indicated that prices ending in 9 are by far the most popular, followed by those ending in 5. In fact, these two digits accounted for more than 80 percent of prices studied.[3]

What does the popularity of 9 and 5 as ending digits signify? Restaurateurs apparently believe that consumers are more likely to buy at the 9 and 5 price points than at other prices. To put it another way—as shown in Exhibit 2—they apparently believe that boosting an item's price from $1.99 to $2.00 will lead to an observable and disproportionate drop in demand for the item.

This approach to pricing has variously been called "psychologi-

---

[1] Conducted by Lee M. Kreul and Anne M. Stock in 1981 and sponsored by Purdue, the project was entitled "A Study of Terminal Digit Pricing in the U.S. Food-Service Industry."

[2] Although one cannot generalize about restaurant prices on the basis of advertised prices, this study design allowed the researchers to obtain considerable data efficiently. Moreover, one might assume that restaurateurs choose to advertise those prices they consider most likely to stimulate purchase behavior; thus, studying advertised prices allowed the researchers to identify the "magic numbers" as perceived by restaurateurs.

[3] Dik W. Twedt, "Does the 9 Fixation in Retail Pricing Really Promote Sales?," *Journal of Marketing,* 29 (October 1965), pp. 55–65; and Lawrence Friedman, "Psychological Pricing in the Food Industry," in *Prices: Issues in Theory, Practice and Public Policy,* ed. Almarin Phillips and Oliver Williamson (Philadelphia: University of Pennsylvania Press, 1967), p. 187.

cal," "irrational,"[4] "intuitive," and "rule-of-thumb" pricing. Whatever term is used, the approach relies more on experience, pricing traditions, and judgments about consumer purchasing behavior at different price points—called "magic numbers"—than on a rigid set of mathematical formulas.

This article explores the use of the "irrational" pricing approach in the food-service industry, examines how it differs from "rational" approaches, and investigates its soundness, with a view toward gaining a few clues about restaurateurs' understanding of consumer price perceptions.

Rational Pricing Approaches

"Rational" pricing is often the first, and only, pricing approach discussed in textbooks and college-level food-service management classes. Price strategies based on mathematical formulas, competitive prices ("follow the leader"), general price levels in the geographic area, and menu product category all represent rational approaches.

Mathematical-formula pricing. The approaches based on mathematical formulas include the cost-plus, gross-profit, break-even, and marginal-cost approaches. The latter two are best used when coupled with estimates of demand.[5]

Miller[6] has catalogued at least seven cost-plus and gross-profit

[4]A. N. Zelomek, "Business Pricing," in *Prices: Issues in Theory, Practice and Public Policy*, ed. Almarin Phillips and Oliver Williamson (Philadelphia: University of Pennsylvania Press, 1967), pp. 200–213.
[5]Eric B. Orkin, "An Integrated Menu-Pricing System," *The Cornell Hotel and Restaurant Administration Quarterly*, 19, No. 2 (August 1978), p. 7.
[6]Jack Miller, *Menu Pricing* (Boston: CBI Publishing Co., 1976).

EXHIBIT 1
Conventional demand curve ($2.00 price range)

A demand curve is a graphical depiction of the effect of price on demand. It is widely believed that as a product's price drops, the demand for the product increases.

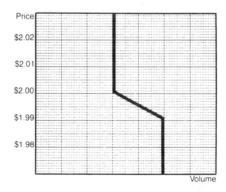

EXHIBIT 2
Restaurateurs' perception of the demand curve ($2.00 price range)

Restaurateurs' pricing practices suggest that the demand curve for restaurant products is marked by kinks and other nonrandom variations.

EXHIBIT 3
Factor pricing system

	Item A	Item B
Raw Food Cost	$2.17	$2.53
Desired Food Cost (% of Sales)	40%	40%
Price Factor	100/40 = 2.5	100/40 = 2.5
Price (Price Factor × Raw Food Cost)	$5.43	$6.33

approaches, including a wide array of single- and multi-factor methods. In the simplest (and most criticized) approach, the operator bases a menu item's price on the item's raw food cost and a target food cost (expressed as a percentage of sales). In other words, the cost of the raw ingredients is simply multiplied by a fixed number. Exhibit 3 depicts how prices for two menu items would be computed using this method.

The factor system and other cost-plus approaches are simple and easy to apply. They offer the restaurateur no incentive to improve operations, however, because they obscure costs that should be questioned; they also completely ignore demand. Whether a consumer would be more or less willing to buy at another price is not considered. Simply stated, a price set in this manner may be psychologically too high or too low.

Incorporating other cost, profit, and risk factors in the formula can compensate for some of the single-factor method's shortcomings. However, if pricing strategies based on quantitative formulas were as prevalent in restaurant operations as they are in the food-service management literature, prices would presumably be distributed more evenly over the ten digits than they were found to be in the study. If, indeed, these simple rational approaches are actually applied, they are apparently

Lee M. Kreul is an associate professor at Purdue, where he teaches lodging management, cost control, accounting, and consumer behavior. A certified hotel administrator, Kreul holds an M.B.A. from Michigan State.

used to derive only an *approximate* price. Formula-based pricing may very well be an archaic remnant of a more simple business environment in which competition between restaurants was not as pronounced as it is today.

The break-even and marginal-cost approaches to pricing also have weaknesses. Break-even analysis, as a pricing tool, suffers from several limitations. First, it assumes linearity in the cost structure, while in reality no cost reacts in perfect proportion to volume. Second, some costs cannot even be considered, as there is no analytical technique available to separate joint costs. Finally, using both the break-even and marginal-cost pricing approaches, a demand curve must be assumed and a price selected that maximizes profit. If demand is estimated incorrectly, profit will not be maximized.

Competitive pricing. There is no doubt that in today's environment the prices asked by local competitors (even supermarkets) also have some bearing on the pricing decision. The operator must consider the competitive positioning of the restaurant product. The practices of local price leaders, whether the product is new, and whether the operator aims to expand market share or enter a new market (such as breakfast) all affect the pricing decision. In today's highly competitive, imitative, multi-unit, corporate environment, competitive pricing approaches with short-term objectives are common. The pricing problem has become very complex, and many specialists— including the accountant and the marketing executive—are contributing to the pricing decision. Because the objective of pricing is to maximize profit, and because pricing is an aspect of the business that is totally controllable by management, pricing has become a collective decision in which a purely quantitative or competitive price gives way to the price that will prove most acceptable to the customer—an "irrational" price.

Irrational Pricing Approaches

Such approaches as intuitive, rule-of-thumb, and psychological pricing differ from rational approaches in that they are not based on tight mathematical formulations or long-standing economic theory. They are difficult to teach because they may incorporate a range of factors. The label "irrational" is rather unfortunate, however, for it implies that experience (knowledge gained from observation, success, failure) is seldom reliable, that psychology is not a science, and that the behavior, opinions, and perceptions of individual consumers cannot be quantified—implications we know are untrue.

Although business operators prefer to claim that some rationale or scientific basis underlies their pricing decisions, many prices that turn out to be profitable are set on the basis of intuition, experience, and the background of the individual doing the pricing. The individual often applies some vague rule of thumb that is applicable in a general, theoretical way.

Psychological Pricing

So-called psychological pricing principles are not without reason, logic, or rationality. They are, however, based on concepts of consumer behavior or pricing customs that are often obscure and sometimes conflicting. The pricing study confirmed what is obvious to consumer and restaurateur alike: that such psychological pricing practices do exist, have existed for a number of years, and are firmly entrenched. Whether unkinked demand curves would exist if prices were distributed more evenly over all the digits (as they would be if based on strict formula approaches) is immaterial. *The fact is that restaurateurs think they would not and price their menus accordingly.*[7] In attempting to maximize profits, restaurateurs merely exploit prices they believe to be psychologically stimulating to their customers. They view the pricing continuum as being marked by "magic numbers" (like 9 and 5) that can stimulate sales.

"Odd-cents" pricing, the rule of 9s and 5s, is one of the most interesting examples of psychology in pricing. Other common assumptions reflect a psychological approach:

• that the first figure in the price (far left) is dominant in the consumer's price decision;
• that the length of the price may affect elasticity;
• that consumers may mentally "round" a whole range of prices to one price;

---

[7]Eli Ginzberg, "Customary Prices," *American Economic Review*, 26, No. 2, p. 296. Ginzberg has reported on a trial conducted by a major mail-order house to determine whether odd-cents pricing stimulated sales of catalog items. Despite remarkable control of all variables and considerable analytical effort in interpreting the results, the researchers determined that the data were inconclusive. Other studies have offered conflicting evidence regarding the value of odd-cents pricing as a sales stimulant.

• that price increases may be better accepted if the psychology of how (or whether) the consumer will perceive the price is understood;
• that the difference between the lowest and the highest price on the menu may affect which item or items the customer will buy. Let us examine some of the logic behind these concepts and the ways in which they are used by the industry.

Odd-Cents Pricing: The Rule of 9s and 5s

"Odd-cents pricing" has three general meanings: the practice of ending prices in odd numbers (1, 3, 5, 7, 9); that of ending prices in a number other than zero; and that of pricing just below a zero (.49, .99, .98, 5.95, 9.95, etc.). The first and last approaches appear to be popular in the food-service industry, and deeply rooted in tradition. The apparent originator of this approach, the founder of what is now the retailing firm of

R. H. Macy Company,[8] is said to have used it to reduce employee dishonesty (odd-cents prices forced employees to give change to each customer, and thus to ring up each sale on a cash register). Because the advent of sales taxes and credit cards effectively eliminated the necessity for odd-cents pricing as a control, this history does not explain why the practice continues today.

It may be that, after the long-time use of such prices, consumers have come to expect them—and would not easily accept a change from the prices they are accustomed to seeing. Some writers have suggested that customers forced to wait for change might be induced to purchase other items; others, that customers simply like to receive change (the basis, perhaps, of the recent fast-food advertising offering "change back from your dollar"?).

The more logical explanation of odd-cents pricing is that it creates an illusion of a discount that reduces the buyer's resistance to purchase. It is not that $1.79 is perceived as such a dramatic departure from $1.80. But when consumers see a $1.79 price, their reaction may be that the restaurateur is giving them a one-cent discount from the true price of $1.80. On the other hand, a price of $1.81 is viewed negatively—as if the restaurateur were trying to make a penny off the consumer. Carrying this notion further, Harper notes that customers may actually buy *less* when price is lowered from a magic number like $1.99 to an even price like $1.96.[9] If so, the demand curve may take the form shown in Exhibit 4.

[8] P. C. Kelley and N. B. Briscoe, *Retailing: Basic Principles*, 3rd ed. (Englewood Cliffs, NJ: Prentice-Hall, 1957), pp. 27–28.
[9] D. V. Harper, *Price Policy and Procedure* (New York: Harcourt Brace and World, 1966), pp. 282–83.

EXHIBIT 4

Some writers suggest that customers may actually buy less of an item when a price is lowered, if it changes from a "magic number" (e.g., $1.99) to an even number (e.g., $1.96).

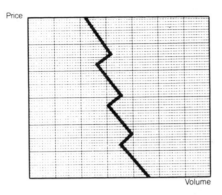

A change to 5 as the most popular terminal digit appears to occur around the $7.00 price range. There are several possible explanations for this change. First, a higher meal price may make a one-cent discount less appealing to the patron; it may take a larger discount (five cents) from the round price to create the discount illusion.

A second explanation: The purchaser of a meal in a higher-priced operation often has a different objective in eating out from the customer patronizing a less expensive operation—a difference that may be expressed as the desire to "dine" rather than to "eat." Seeking an opportunity to linger over and enjoy a meal (rather than a speedy alternative to an at-home meal), the patron of the higher-priced operation is less sensitive to price and more sensitive to other in-house merchandising techniques that will help make the meal a special occasion.

There is a third, somewhat related explanation—namely, that a price ending in 9 (suggesting discount, low-quality, hurried service) is associated with the price-sensitivity appropriate in an inexpensive operation but not in a higher-priced restaurant. Indeed, there is evidence that consumers may interpret high prices as signifying high quality and low prices the opposite.[10]

Unfortunately, because higher-priced operations do not often advertise their prices in newspapers, little objective evidence of pricing practices above $10.00 was available for the present study. Subjective observations suggest, however, that 0 is quite common as a terminal digit above $10.00. Operators of exclusive restaurants may very well achieve the discount illusion by pricing, for example, at $19.00, rather than at $20.00.

Other Magic Numbers

Both this study and interviews with food-service marketing people suggest there are other magic-number prices that stimulate sales.

The first figure. Restaurateurs recognize that consumers regard the first figure (the far-left digit) in the price as more significant than the other digits. For example, consumers perceive a greater distance between 69¢ and 71¢ than between 69¢ and 67¢—resulting, as stated earlier, in greater demand elasticity between 69¢ and 71¢ than between 67¢ and 69¢ or 62¢ and 67¢. As a result, restaurateurs are more reluctant to move a price from 69¢ to 71¢ than from 62¢ to 67¢.

The length of the price. Second, customers are also sensitive to the number of digits in the price—the length of the price "field." As a result, they view the distance between $9.99 and $10.25 as much greater than the distance between $9.55 and $9.99.

[10] O. Knauth, "Considerations in Setting of Retail Prices," *Journal of Marketing,* 14 (July 1949), pp. 1–12.

Many restaurateurs therefore strongly resist pushing menu prices beyond the $10.00 mark even when rising costs would seem to demand it—just as many fast-food operators strongly resist pricing some items over $1.00. A fast-food operator may hold prices below $1.00 for as long as possible, and then jump to $1.25 or higher, not so much to make up for lost time, but because there is less purchase resistance once the dollar barrier has been jumped.

Price rounding. A third tendency among consumers is that toward rounding, or viewing a whole range of prices in terms of one magic number. For example:

$0.86 to $1.39 rounds to "a dollar"

$1.40 to $1.79 rounds to "a dollar and a half"

$1.80 to $2.49 rounds to $2.00

$2.50 to $3.99 rounds to $3.00

$4.00 to $7.95 rounds to "the $5.00 range."[11]

Restaurateurs may deduce that a price increase that does not cross into a higher range will not be mentally rounded to a higher price and thus will be less noticeable and more acceptable to consumers than an increase to a higher range.

Frequency and Size of Price Increases

In times of rapid inflation, the restaurateur must strike a balance between the frequency and the size of price increases. Too rapid or too large a price rise may lead customers to reject the product. General rules of thumb suggest limiting the menu increases to two- to five-percent jumps;[12] keep-

---

[11]John Lyon, "Pricing Considerations in Menu Expansion and New Product Development" (speech to National Restaurant Association Market Research Group, New Orleans, September 24, 1981).

[12]Lyon, op. cit.

EXHIBIT 5
Adjusting the price spread

	Item A	Item B
Raw Food Cost	$2.00	$5.00
Desired Food Cost	35%	35%
Price Factor: 100/35	2.86	2.86
Price by Factor Method	$5.71	$14.29
Gross Margin, Factor Price	$3.71	+ $9.29 = $13.00
Adjusted Prices	$8.75	$11.25
Gross Margin, Adj. Prices	$6.75	+ $6.25 = $13.00

---

ing prices stable through four to six guest visits; and, in the fast-food segment, increasing menu prices no more than three times a year. An increase in menu prices is also more easily accepted if it occurs coincidentally with the rise of wholesale and supermarket food prices.

Finally, at least one restaurateur has begun to use the generally unpopular terminal digits— forcing customers to remember more digits if they wish to make comparisons between new prices and old.

Price Spreads between Menu Items

Restaurateurs also recognize that an excessive price spread between the lowest- and highest-priced items encourages the guest to order lower-priced items and thus lowers the overall gross margin. For example, imagine a restaurant with a two-item menu. The cost-conscious restaurateur aims for an overall food cost of 35 percent. Item A has a raw food cost of $2.00; item B, a raw food cost of $5.00. Using the factor method, prices of $5.71 for item A and $14.29 for item B would be in or-

der. However, it is very likely these prices would cause consumers to concentrate on item A and ignore item B. Why? First, the price spread would be viewed as unfair, especially by customers with some knowledge of the raw food cost of the two items. Second, customers would mentally round the $14.29 menu price to $15.00, the $5.71 to $5.00, further increasing the perceived price spread. Finally, item B would be priced above the $10.00 barrier. A savvy restaurateur would be less concerned with the food cost and more concerned about customer behavior, and would narrow the price range by raising the price of item A and lowering the price of item B. (Some restaurateurs suggest that the highest-priced item be no more than two times the price of the lowest.) Adjusting the price structure in this way, as shown in Exhibit 5, would improve the popularity of item B and allow the operator to achieve a greater overall contribution margin. Excessive price spreads may account for low profitability in many operations.

Conclusions

The evidence provided by the pricing study suggests that the use of psychological prices or magic numbers is quite common in the food-service industry and rooted in restaurateurs' assumptions about their customers' purchase behavior. While the validity of these assumptions should be studied, real-world research of the relationship between purchase and pricing is extremely expensive. The present study provides a first step by suggesting that rational pricing techniques, if used at all, may provide only approximate prices in practice; and that psychological pricing is not irrational. □

Whatever Lola Wants...? Lola Wants Service

Introduction by Bonnie Knutson

Service will be the buzzword of the 1990s. In "Pul-eeze! Will Somebody Help Me?", the author laments what appears to be the demise of good service -- or of any service -- in today's business culture. In light of increasingly-demanding consumers and a decreasing-quality labor pool, providing good service is a major challenge for the hospitality industry.

The best way to satisfy your customers is to exceed their expectations for service. By following the "Ten Laws of Customer Satisfaction", Bonnie Knutson believes you can create a large pool of satisfied customers who will keep coming back -- and will tell others about you too!

But before you can improve your service quality, you have to know which attributes of your hotel/restaurant are most likely to win compliments, which usually show up on complaint lists, and which don't seem to make a difference to your customers. Three articles -- by McCleary and Weaver, by William Martin and by Cadotte and Turgeon -- explain various ways you can learn how well your operation is meeting customers' service standards. Once you have established this benchmark, you can then train to improve your employees and evaluate along these important service quality attributes.

The hospitality industry is, of course, not the only industry concerned with improving service quality. Automotive. Banking. Health Care. Communication. All industries are taking a closer look at what their customers mean by "good service". Michael Haywood synthesizes what is happening in the area of service management in other service industries, looks at the relevance to hospitality management, then offers some important implications of service management for hospitality managers.

Pul-eeze! Will Somebody Help Me?

Frustrated American consumers wonder where the service went

 For Harry Hapless, it was a rough day in the service economy. His car, a Fiasco 400, started sputtering on the highway, so Harry pulled into a gas station for help. "Sorry, no mechanics, only gas!" shouted the attendant. "How can you call this a service station?" yelled Harry. He went to the bank to get some emergency cash for a tow truck, only to find the automatic teller machine out of order, again. "Real nice service!" he muttered. Then Harry decided to use a credit card to buy a tool kit at the Cheapo discount store, but he couldn't find anyone to wait on him. "Service! Anyone, please! Help me!" was his cry.

It had been a trying day indeed, Harry thought as he rode a bus home, but at least he could look forward to a trip to Florida the following week with his wife Harriet. That is, until Flyway Air called: "Sorry, Mr. Hapless. Due to our merger with Byway Air, your Florida flight has been canceled." Harry got so angry he was going to call the Federal Aviation Administration immediately. But just then his phone went dead—no doubt because the Bell System had been split up, he imagined. Well, that was the last straw. A few minutes later a wild-eyed Harry burst into the newsroom of his local newspaper. "I've got a story for you!" he cried. "There is no more service in America!"

More and more consumers are beginning to feel almost as frustrated as Harry Hapless. Personal service has become a maddeningly rare commodity in the American marketplace. Flight attendants, salesclerks and bank tellers all seem to have become too scarce and too busy to give consumers much attention. Many other service workers are underpaid, untrained and unmotivated for their jobs, to the chagrin of customers who look to them for help. The concept of personal service is a difficult quantity to measure precisely, to be sure; the U.S. Government keeps no Courtesy Index or Helpfulness Indicator among its economic statistics. But customers know service when they miss it, and now they want it back. Says Thomas Peters, a management consultant and co-author of *In Search of Excellence:* "In general, service in America stinks."

Economic upheaval is to blame. First came the great inflation of the 1970s, which forced businesses to slash service to keep prices from skyrocketing. Then came deregulation, which fostered more price wars and further cutbacks. Meanwhile, service workers became increasingly difficult to hire because of labor shortages in many areas. At the same time, managers found that they could cut costs by replacing human workers with computers and self-service schemes. It all makes perfect bookkeeping sense for businesses, but the trend has left consumers without enough human faces to turn to for guidance in spending their billions of dol-

Reprinted from *Time* with permission. © 1987.

lars on services. Americans tolerated, and even welcomed, self-service during an era of rising prices, but now a backlash is beginning. Result: some companies are scrambling to make amends, and "quality of service" is on its way to becoming the next business buzz phrase.

Ominously, the rising clamor suggests that something fundamental may be wrong in the vaunted U.S. service economy, in which the country has put so much hope for future prosperity. If service industries are beginning to dominate the economy, one might ask, why is there so little good service to be found? Is America in danger of becoming the no-can-do society? The question is becoming increasingly urgent. As manufacturing has declined in relative importance, the service sector has become the engine of U.S. economic growth. Of 12.6 million new jobs created since the end of the last recession, in 1982, almost 85% have been in service industries as opposed to goods-producing fields.

Sloppy service could become more than just a domestic annoyance. Economists have begun to warn that slipping standards could cost the U.S. its international competitive standing in services and thus worsen the country's trade problems. Japanese banks, for example, have already made inroads into the U.S. market. In the November-December issue of the *Harvard Business Review*, Professor James Quinn and Researcher Christopher Gagnon of Dartmouth's Amos Tuck School of Business contend that many U.S. service businesses have developed the same shortsighted habits and inattention to quality that American manufacturers have been guilty of—with disastrous results. "While there is still time," they write, "it is essential to take a hard look at how we think about services, how

we manage them, and how much they contribute to the nation's economic health."

The potential of service businesses losing touch is chilling because it was the U.S. that practically invented the concept of good service on a mass-market scale. The country's huge appetite for reliable service gave rise to such pioneers as AT&T, IBM, American Express, McDonald's and Federal Express. But many U.S. companies today are failing to achieve the right balance of high-tech expedience vs. personal attention. "The state of service is pretty bad," admits Kenneth Hamlet, president of the Holiday Inn Hotel Group.

Among consumers, swapping horror stories about their confrontations with poor service has become a cathartic exercise. Many have never obtained satisfaction for their gripes, despite exhausting efforts. Kevin Kinnear, a Chicago software engineer, became increasingly angry with each of four trips to his car dealer to get the cruise control repaired on his 1985 Buick Century. Finally, he gave up when the mechanics made it clear that they no longer wanted to deal with his problem. Jane Ullman, a Santa Monica, Calif., sculptor, thought her refrigerator problems were over when deliverymen installed a new deluxe model in her kitchen. But her woes were just beginning: the workmen broke the refrigerator's copper pipes, which took several visits from repairmen to fix. "People have learned to take shoddy service in stride," she says wearily. Even when they speak up and get their money back, consumers often come away with a feeling of being abused. Earlier this month, when a Los Angeles homemaker took back a foul-smelling piece of fish to a supermarket on

the city's west side, she got a refund only after answering brusque questions and signing papers. At no time did anybody apologize or give the slightest sign that they regretted spoiling her dinner.

Some of the longest, most tortured consumer stories involve home delivery. When Tony and Sandra Cantafio of Redondo Beach, Calif., bought a bed last October, they had to wait four weeks for it to arrive because of lost paperwork and other snafus. The result for Cantafio was an aching back from sleeping on the sofa. But there was another pain: to get the bed finally, Cantafio had to take an entire day off from his job as an aerospace executive because the deliverymen refused to predict what time they would arrive at his home.

In other cases, workers spoil an otherwise fine job with an almost creatively bad gesture. A Manhattan woman who bought carpet from a tony department store was pleased that the two installers were so friendly and efficient, but puzzled about why they left "like two robbers in a getaway car." Later she discovered the reason: they had used her bathroom as a Dumpster for a three-foot pile of carpet clippings and packing material.

Sometimes consumers encounter sales clerks who cannot find the "on" button on electronic equipment they are selling. A clerk handling vacuum cleaners in a department store confesses to a customer, "I don't know a damn thing about these." Over in the shoe department, clerks nowadays may simply dump boxes at customers' feet rather than helping them with the merchandise.

Consumer grief is even becoming part of the pop culture. Comedian Jay Leno says that when he chided a supermarket clerk for failing to say thank you, she snapped, "It's printed on your receipt!" The film *Back to the Future* cracked up its audiences with a scene in which Michael J. Fox's character, who has traveled back in time, walks past a 1950s-era filling station and is flabbergasted to see four cheery attendants in neatly pressed coveralls. Like a pit crew at the Indianapolis 500, they dash up to a car and proceed to fill the gas tank, check the oil, clean the windows and polish the chrome.

Current U.S. levels of service sometimes appear lax to Americans when they return home from trips to Japan and Western Europe. While no country boasts the highest standards in every field, other cultures are more demanding of some services than America is. Most European countries insist on timely and efficient service on their railroads and airlines, which receive state subsidies to assure that performance. Americans who visit London typically come away with fond memories of the city's excellent taxicabs and subway system. The shortage of personal attention comes just when U.S. consumers are enjoying a cornucopia of novel products and services. Thus the deterioration of basic, personal service is taking the fun out of the new offerings. Shoppers can now find ten kinds of mustard and a dozen varieties of vinegar in a supermarket, but where is a clerk who can give a guiding word about these products? Airlines offer a bonanza of cheap fares, but many travel agents no longer want to be bothered handling such unprofitable business. That leaves consumers on their own, so they have to grab brochures and do their homework if they hope to make a correct decision. To take advantage of consumer advances today requires a tougher and smarter buyer.

Yet a growing number of shoppers have no time to get smart. Two-income householders have become hooked on convenience. Their expectations of quick, personal service have risen at a time when they are less likely to find it. Result: growing friction between harried workers and hurried customers. Says Irma Reyes, a New York City bank teller: "We try to service customers within three minutes after they walk into the bank, but they expect you to work miracles for them. Some customers get annoyed simply because you ask for identification."

The widespread perception of poor service has reached most corners of the U.S. because some of the worst offenders are national chains. Yet big-city consumers more frequently encounter poor service because some businesses feel they have an abundant supply of customers and thus are not dependent on long-term relationships with the shopper. Says Paul Schervish, a sociology professor at Boston College: "The situation is adversarial in a peculiar way. The seller acts as though the customer's gain is his or her loss and not mutually beneficial." In small towns with a more limited pool of shoppers, by comparison, buyer and seller have a long-term expectation of encountering each other again.

The simple reason that service workers have so little attention to give is that businesses often overwork them to save labor costs and keep prices low. Flight attendants, for example, once had time to chat with their passengers, but now their work is so speeded up that they can barely make sure all seat backs and tray tables are in their upright positions. If today's jumbo jets were staffed at the levels of a decade ago, an airline-union official says, the planes would carry 20 flight attendants instead of twelve to 14.

Service workers who handle customers over the telephone have been speeded up most of all. Any consumer who regularly talks to rental-car reservations clerks or mail-order takers probably feels the rush. Reason: computers monitor the workers' calls to measure performance. If a phone operator spends too much time with one customer, it spoils his or her average and standing on the job. Operators have been known to fake a disconnection when customers ask questions that are too complicated. Observes Harley Shaiken, professor of work and technology at the University of California at San Diego: "These assembly-line methods increase profits by boosting productivity, but there is a long-term hidden cost—the decline in service."

Many businesses would hire more service workers if they could, but a post-baby-boom shortage of young workers has created a critical scarcity of labor to handle minimum-wage ($3.35-an-hour) positions in restaurants and stores. Moreover, many salesclerks, delivery-truck drivers and other service workers are unmotivated because of the low pay and lack of career path in their jobs. Says Journalist David Halberstam, whose recent best seller *The Reckoning* chronicled the decline of America's auto industry: "The main questions are: Does this job lead to anything? Does it have any dignity? No. We are dividing ourselves along class lines by education."

Too many service workers lack any pride or satisfaction in their jobs, especially in a society that, like America's, puts so much emphasis on speedy upward mobility. Says Thomas Kelly, an assistant professor at Cornell University's School of Hotel Administration: "In our culture, these jobs are not considered a worthwhile occupation. When workers view giving service as beneath them, it shows." The problem is notable among restaurant waiters, whose jobs were once regarded as legitimate careers. Now most waiters spend too little time in their jobs to become seasoned. "Sometimes I miss the graying at the temples among my staff," says Joseph Baum, co-owner of Manhattan's service-minded Aurora restaurant.

Businesses in general spend too little time training and motivating their front-line employees, whom they treat as the lowest workers on the ladder. The tendency has been to economize on the training process by designing service jobs to have the fewest possible skills. That keeps employee mistakes at a minimum, but it may hurt morale and make it difficult for workers to use their heads to solve unusual consumer problems when they arise. "Service people can become so robotized in their actions that they greet any customer request with a standardized response," write Karl Albrecht, a management consultant, and Ron Zemke in their 1985 book, *Service America! Doing Business in the New Economy*.

Too much of the training tends to dwell on handling the machinery of a job rather than the feelings of the customers. Cashiers must typically type a multidigit inventory code into a computer just to sell a 50¢ birthday card. That process reduces the number of accountants needed back at corporate headquarters but does nothing to help either the customer or the salesperson's sense of worth. Confesses an Avis car-rental clerk at a desk in a posh Los Angeles hotel: "The computer training was real good. I know how to do all this technical stuff, but nobody prepared me for dealing with all these different types of people."

Consumers want smiles more than ever because they have become strongly resentful of machines, even though computers have made services more efficient in many respects. Behind-the-scenes mainframes enable auto-rental firms, for example, to keep a customer's account information on file so that making a reservation takes only 30 seconds on the telephone. No one would want to give up such conveniences, yet the more that computers come into play in handling consumers, the more customers crave reassurance that humans will intervene when help is needed. Gripes Howard Mileaf, a New York City lawyer and Chemi-

cal Bank customer: "I used to have the illusion that a real person was looking after my account, but now I know better!"

Some computer-buff managers tend to impose technology almost compulsively, whether it is appreciated or not. When Virginia Boggs of Bellflower, Calif., went to a department store to buy a wedding gift, the clerk told her to go to a nearby computer and punch in the bride's name to learn her silver pattern. Boggs, who is computer-illiterate and proud of it, refused. "I don't even use the computer in my own business," she said. "Why should I run theirs?"

Disgruntlement with services runs almost counter to the prevailing attitude about products. Consumers show a reasonable level of satisfaction with the merchandise they buy, thanks largely to technological advances. But the harsh world of the service economy intrudes once again on their contentment when a modern product suffers a breakdown. In a sense, consumers are victims of high-tech

bounty. "The complexity of technology has increased much more rapidly than the ability of the consumer or the service personnel to keep track of it," says Stephen Brobeck, executive director of the Consumer Federation of America. Products have become so diverse and complex that friendly neighborhood repair shops can no longer provide service. In most cases, everything from videocassette recorders to food processors must be sent to regional repair centers. Autos have become such sophisticated machines by and large that only dealers with space-age diagnostic devices can fix them.

The heyday of personal service probably came early in the postwar era, when labor was relatively cheap and prices were fairly stable. Businesses could afford to lavish attention on customers, who in turn shopped for the most personable service. Music stores, for example, provided record players so that customers could give disks a spin before buying them, and drugstores offered free delivery. But during the decade of rampant inflation in the 1970s, when prices rose 87%, consumers became willing to give up service in return for the lowest possible price tag. They began buying in bulk, bagging their own groceries and shopping in warehouse-like mega-stores.

As discount chains like K mart and Wal-Mart flourished in the retail industry, rivals were forced to cut their payrolls to stay competitive. In that environment, in which shoppers began to think of brand-name products as commodities, businesses that still offered knowledgeable sales help were taken for a ride by consumers and competitors. Shoppers

Accountants to Zoologists

Who belongs to the swelling ranks of the U.S. service economy? Such workers are often depicted as a legion of hamburger flippers and computer programmers, but in fact they constitute a huge, diverse group whose members range from cashiers to lumberjacks. The vast majority of the U.S. labor force, more than 76 million workers, belong to the service sector; 25 million others are in goods-producing jobs, and 3 million are in agriculture. The Labor Department defines the goods-producing sector as manufacturing, mining and construction, but the rapidly growing service-producing sector tends to be much broader, encompassing many new types of jobs that do not seem to fit into any other category.

Simply put, the service economy is the sector that runs on trade and information. Of the nearly $2.3 trillion in private services generated in 1985, 27% came from finance, insurance and real estate. Retail business accounted for 16%, wholesale trade for 12%, transportation and utilities for 12%, and communications for 5%.

Service jobs come in every imaginable description, from powerful (President of the U.S.) to humble (janitors), noisy (auctioneers) to quiet (librarians), outdoorsy (hunters and trappers) to indoorsy (accountants and pharmacists). Among the largest job classifications are professionals (13.8 million), executives and managers (12.2 million), sales workers (12.7 million) and secretaries (4 million). In more specific categories, the Labor Department counts 131,000 dentists, 102,000 economists, 84,000 professional athletes, 124,000 messengers, 324,000 bartenders and 126,000 news vendors. The country employs eight times as many hairdressers and cosmetologists (707,000) as it does barbers (91,000).

While the service economy offers a far brighter employment picture than manufacturing, many of its jobs are relatively low paying. An estimated 556,000 new cashier jobs will open up between 1984 and 1995, but the average weekly earnings for such workers at the beginning of that period was only $195. Some 452,000 registered nurses will be hired in that span; their weekly earnings averaged just $415. The service sector also includes such highly paid groups as lawyers and psychiatrists, some of whom can easily generate as many complaints as a surly salesclerk.

quickly learned to visit a service-minded store for a free lesson about a particular product, then go down the street to a discount house to buy the item for 25% less. The headaches often come later, because discounters tend to offer very little follow-up service. Says Butch Weaver, a second-generation appliance repairman and president of a Maytag store in Gaithersburg, Md.: "A lot of this the public has done to themselves. If they're going to go for these cut-rate prices, something's got to give, so it's usually service."

Businessmen point out, of course, that self-service has spawned great conveniences, ranging from simpler telephone-connecting jacks to coin-operated car washes and even videocassette vending machines. Many storekeepers say that self-service often enables customers to meet their needs faster than would be possible if they relied on clerks. At Child World, a chain with 134 stores, the company last fall arranged toys in "learning centers," where customers can examine and play with the products. Says President Gilbert Wachsman: "The shoppers are out more quickly. It reduces our expenses, and we pass the saving on to the customers." Fayva, a discount shoe chain where consumers select their choices from the rack, has grown to 650 stores in 15 years.

A Kroger grocery store in Morrow, Ga., has taken the self-service concept to an extreme. Customers check out their own merchandise by scanning the price codes with electronic readers. Human clerks collect the payment, and computerized sensors monitor the flow of merchandise to check for any fraudulent item switching.

But while consumers will embrace self-service if they think they are getting a bargain, they usually demand attention if they believe it is included in the price tag. Shoppers generally put up with the scarcity of sales help in low-end stores but quickly grow impatient when the trouble arises at mid-price and prestige retailers. Says John D.C. Little, a professor at M.I.T.'s Sloan School of Management: "Stores will have problems if they pretend to be up-market but aren't." He chides pricey department stores like Bloomingdale's for sometimes providing less service than their upscale image leads customers to expect.

While inflation taught consumers to be more price conscious, it was deregulation that forced banks, airlines and other industries to streamline their services so they could survive the new competition. Many banks, locked in an expensive battle to offer the highest interest rates for savers, found they could no longer afford to provide cheap or free services to small-account holders. By raising service charges dramatically, some banks actively discourage small accounts, because the profits in serving them are slim or nonexistent. Most depositors must wait in line to see a banker, while big-account holders are whisked into private offices.

Yet just like retail stores, banks are offering a trade-off that they believe most customers will accept: more products in exchange for less personal service. Today's depositors with as little as $500 to invest will find that banks give them more possibilities than ever before. Banks now offer an array of money-management accounts and even discount stock-brokerage service. Banks have vastly improved upon old-time bankers' hours of 9 a.m. to 3 p.m. New York's Citibank boasts that 80% of its depositors use its 24-hour automatic-teller machines and that more than half of all customers say they no longer need to venture inside the bank.

Deregulation has prompted airlines to make daring experiments with service, sometimes to harrowing ends. People Express provided an example of just how far consumers can be pushed in a trade-off for low fares. Its aggressively no-frills service, featuring such hassles as on-board ticketing and extra fees for checked baggage, gave the airline a negative image among business flyers and probably hastened its demise. Its rival, Texas Air, which officially bought People Express last month, prevailed partly by making a point of offering low fares without reducing service below generally accepted levels. The airline-merger boom, too, has disrupted service in the airline industry, as huge airlines combine their schedules and crews. The Department of Transportation announced earlier this month that complaints about poor airline service, especially delays, increased 30% during 1986.

A prime indignity for airline customers is to be bumped, or denied a reserved seat, because the carrier has booked too many passengers on a flight. Overbooking is a product of fare wars; because airlines are collecting less per seat, they want to ensure a full load to make a profit. The practice of overbooking crops up in other businesses when managers want to make the most of a prime-time rush of custom-ers. At peak times popular hotels and restaurants sometimes bump customers who show up even modestly late for their reservations.

For many consumers the breakup of the Bell System in 1983 contributed to the decline of Western civilization. The split of old reliable Ma Bell into seven regional operating companies left many customers convinced that they were worse off, even though long-distance competition has brought better rates. Indeed, according to a scorecard published in November by *Communications Week*, local service and repair are now fairly inconsistent across the U.S. The trade publication gave the top grade of A-minus to Ameritech, which serves Illinois, Indiana, Ohio, Wisconsin and Michigan. The lowest grade of C-plus went to Southwestern Bell (Arkansas, Kansas, Missouri, Oklahoma and Texas) and NYNEX (New York and New England).

Consumers miss the personal touch in health care especially. Technology has brought great improvements in curative powers, but patients wish they could get more attention from their doctors rather than being seen mostly by nurses and technicians. Says Victoria Leonard, executive director of the National Women's Health Network: "We see doctors not answering questions, giving curt answers, not spending enough time with patients. Years ago a doctor was more of a family adviser. Now medicine tends to attract the person who enjoys the high-tech procedures. Almost by definition, that's not a people person."

Sensitive to the mounting criticism, the business world is starting to make amends. Says Alan Raedels, professor of business administration at Oregon's Portland State University: "If stores are competing with the same products at basically the same price, then the next major battlefield is going to be service." Claims Steve Shelton, who represents an association of Southern California gas-station operators: "The market is begging for attention today. Motorists seem tickled when someone is actually giving old-fashioned service and cares about the condition of their car." Quality-service gurus like John Tschohl of Bloomington, Minn., are now in heavy demand to give speeches to top managers. Says he: "We teach them the financial impact of good customer service. They're interested only in hard dollars and cents."

One company that seems to have come to this conclusion the hard way is Sears, the largest U.S. retailer. Sears managed to smudge its image in recent years by grouping its salesclerks around cash registers for fast check-out, which reduced the number of employees who were in the aisles to answer questions. Sears still helped customers in its custom-drapery departments, for example, but left buyers of prepackaged drapes to struggle for themselves. Now the company apparently believes it went too far. "We've been

looking at service in the past 18 months with heightened intensity," says Everett Buckardt, a Sears vice president. "We have put more people on the sales floor."

Other examples are multiplying. In Miami all 5,000 of the city's cab drivers are required to take a three-hour course in courtesy called Miami Nice, which has reduced the rate of customer complaints by 80%. To do better in the highly competitive health-care industry, California's Santa Monica Hospital Medical Center put its 1,500 employees through a two-day seminar on customer service. One result: the hospital changed its emergency-room admission procedure to one in which staffers "greet and comfort" patients before bothering them with the paperwork.

Nearly all the experts agree that the way to improve America's service industry is to understand the lot of the front-line worker. At this point, too few businesses recognize that many service workers are doing a relatively new, difficult kind of work that could be called emotional labor, a term coined by Arlie Russell Hochschild, a Berkeley sociology professor, in her 1983 book, *The Managed Heart: Commercialization of Human Feeling.* Just as factory workers can become estranged from the products they manufacture, says Hochschild, service workers can feel distanced from their put-on emotions. Flight attendants, for example, often feel that their smile belongs to the company. One solution Hochschild recommends is for businesses to give employees a chance to rest and recharge their smiles by temporarily rotating to less stressful jobs.

Cosmetic approaches will not do. K mart, for one, tried to cue its employees to be more personable by putting TYFSOK on their cash registers, which was supposed to remind them to thank customers for shopping K mart. But some harried clerks reportedly mocked the procedure by blurting "Tyfsok!" at puzzled customers. Other companies have tried to get across an impression of personal service with tired slogans to the effect that "people are our most important asset."

But American business had better deliver the real thing, because shoppers like Arlene Cantlon of Riverdale, Ill., are starting to make a scene. Cantlon lost her temper recently in a Venture Stores discount outlet because the chain was making a habit, in her opinion, of failing to have advertised goods in stock. "I asked to speak to the salesgirl in the shoe department, but nobody knew where she was. I waited 35 minutes while they looked for her. Nobody could find her, so I asked to see the store manager. At this point, I had a crowd of customers cheering me on. One woman told me, 'It won't do any good, but good for you!' " Cantlon finally got her audience with the manager, and got some of the merchandise she wanted as well. It was a notable victory, but it need not be all that rare. American consumers would be well advised to follow Arlene Cantlon's example and make noise if they really want their satisfaction guaranteed.   —*By Stephen Koepp. Reported by Jay Branegan/Washington, Lawrence Malkin/Boston and Edwin M. Reingold/Los Angeles*

A Homecoming Lament

When TIME *Correspondent Edwin M. Reingold moved to the magazine's Los Angeles bureau last September after an eight-year assignment as Tokyo bureau chief, he was stunned by what he perceived as a sharp decline in American service during his absence from the U.S. His reflections:*

To a returning American grown accustomed to the civility and efficiency of modern Japan, the U.S. seems to have become a quagmire of bureaucracy, ineptitude, mean spirit and lackadaisy. In Los Angeles, New York, Miami and other cities, the repatriate is appalled and depressed by the lack of efficiency and of simple courtesy and caring.

The deterioration of service is apparent almost immediately. When a new customer tries to open an account at the Wells Fargo Bank, an officer haughtily sniffs that it will not be possible until his signature has been verified and his banking history thoroughly checked. Then she simply turns away.

At what used to be called a service station, the attendant, who sits behind bulletproof glass, can do nothing to help a novice learn the new greasy, smelly routine of pumping his own gas. Memories flood back of the typical Tokyo station, where a horde of neat, well-mannered and expert attendants take charge of the car, fill it up, wash it and check the tires. Then they doff their hats, shout their thanks and stop traffic so the customer can drive away.

The sign in the lobby of the West Los Angeles city hall says the planning department opens at 8 a.m. On a recent morning a clerk finally shows up at 9, without apology. As the petitioner pays the application fee for home-improvement permits, the clerk says the process will take 75 to 120 days. It is 132 days and still counting.

The new homeowner receives a cordial letter inviting him to apply for a charge account at J.W. Robinson's, a department-store chain. But his application for credit is rejected with a form letter alleging an "insufficient credit file." It should have read, "We are too lazy to check further."

When a clerk at an appliance store does not know how to turn on the tape recorder he is trying to sell a customer, something seems terribly wrong. The mind flicks back to Tokyo again, to the electronics center called Akihabara, where every clerk is knowledgeable and unfailingly polite, eager to make a sale. In Japan some manufacturers even make house calls if a product breaks down.

Nowhere is the malaise of American service more obvious than in the airline business. Cabin attendants often stand by unconcerned, aloof and bored, while old folks and children struggle with their bags. Untended airplane toilets reek. Every flight seems to be late and/or overcrowded.

To an American old enough to remember American competence, work well done and pride in fine service swiftly rendered, it is jarring to realize how much Americans have forgotten, and how quickly.

Where the Customer Is Still King

A gallery of U.S. companies that prosper by aiming to please

Amid growing anger over the decline of American service, many U.S. companies defy the trend and flourish handsomely because of the care they lavish on customers. A sampling:

Nordstrom. In the low-margin, highly competitive world of department-store sales, Seattle-based Nordstrom has turned exacting standards of customer service into a billion-dollar annual business. The rapidly expanding chain, which has 45 stores in California, Washington, Oregon, Alaska, Montana and Utah, has drilled its staff incessantly with the venerable dogma that the customer is always right. Result: the chain's sales, 73% derived from women's retailing, passed the $1 billion mark for the first time in 1985 and reached an estimated $1.6 billion for 1986. Sales per square foot of space, a basic retail performance yardstick, is about double the average for the industry.

A major ingredient in Nordstrom's success is the quality of the salesclerks. They are paid about 20% better than those of competitors, and they are well trained and encouraged to do almost anything within reason to satisfy customers. In Seattle, a store salesclerk personally ironed a customer's newly bought shirt so that it would look fresher for an upcoming meeting. Thomas Skidmore, vice president of a Los Angeles–area real estate brokerage, tells of bringing back a squeaky pair of year-old shoes to a local Nordstrom outlet, hoping merely for repairs. Instead, he got a new pair of shoes free.

Throughout the chain, the sales help strictly follow a dictum laid down by the company's president, James Nordstrom, 46: replace anything on demand, no matter how expensive, no questions asked. Although the policy is sometimes abused by shoppers (who may, for example, order a $500 dress, wear it once to a party, and then return it), it works well for Nordstrom. Says Skidmore: "I couldn't believe how nice they were being. I bought another pair of shoes on the spot."

Nordstrom was founded in Seattle in 1901 as a retail shoe store by a Swedish prospector, John Nordstrom, who had struck it rich in the Klondike. Now a publicly traded concern, the firm is still closely controlled by members of the founder's family and propelled by their hands-on style. Says Edward Weller, a senior analyst in the San Francisco office of the Montgomery Securities investment firm: "Nordstrom's movitates people, not just by paying them well but by congratulating them and encouraging them."

Byerly's. In the 19 years since Don Byerly, now 47, opened his first store in the Minneapolis suburb of Golden Valley, he has almost never publicly advertised a product or price. "We spend the advertising money on service," he explains. The payoff has been impressive. There are seven Byerly's outlets in the Minneapolis area, and an eighth is under construction. Sales for the chain reached $135 million last year, and are expected to climb to $150 million in 1987. Byerly analyzes his success this way: "The only reason people will come back to our store is because of what happened to them the last time they were here."

At his carpeted, chandelier-bedizened supermarkets, Byerly offers 24-hour, seven-days-a-week grocery shopping, complete with full-service meat and fish departments. The outlets are attractive, but the difference is, as he puts it, "the way they're run." Each store is managed semi-independently by a single boss, who tailors the contents to neighborhood needs with little overseeing from top management. Company-wide, Byerly's has 2,100 employees, but only five work in what the proprietor jokingly calls "world headquarters" in the Minneapolis suburb of Edina.

Byerly's places special emphasis on helpfulness. Each store employs a full-time home economist, who can work with customers on everything from menu planning to getting bubble gum out of household carpets to figuring how much food to buy for a party of 300. The home-ec experts maintain "special-foods programs" of particular dietary products at each outlet. Says Byerly: "Let's say your doctor prescribed a low-sodium diet. The home economist will give you a blue folder listing everything that you can buy in the store that's low sodium. And each of the products is marked with blue tags on the shelves." The same system is used for low-cholesterol and low-calorie diets. As at many supermarkets, Byerly's employees will place customers' groceries in their autos, but on those rare occasions when the wrong bags are put in the trunk, the right goods are delivered directly to a shopper's door, along with a free cake or other goody by way of apology.

Byerly insists his prices are competitive with regular supermarkets' despite the many services. Says he: "We take the advertising savings and try to be price competitive. We're aimed at the average shopper." Whoever shops at Byerly's, the appeal is obviously spreading. Lea Plotke, a resident of neighboring St. Paul, claims that she always takes out-of-town guests for a look-see at her Byerly's. Why? Because, she says, "it's like a tourist attraction."

Mini Maid Services. In 1973 Homemaker Leone Ackerly, mother of three, wanted to buy a new auto. To earn the money, she hired herself out as a cleaning lady. She has since, as they say, cleaned up. Now 41, Ackerly drives a Jaguar XJ6 and oversees a maid-service empire, based in Marietta, Ga., with 900 employees at 96 franchises in 24 states. Annual revenues: more than $9 million. Mini Maid is about to launch franchises in Germany, Italy and Australia. The secret of Ackerly's success? Says she: "We do one thing one way for one price."

Inspired by the meticulous regimen of fast-food outlets like McDonald's, Ackerly's Mini Maid operation offers a menu of 22 basic daily cleaning chores that its four-member crews will perform in an average time of 55 minutes for a fee of $39.50 to $49.50. The duties of the blue-and-white-clad cleaning squads—primarily young mothers and homemakers—range from washing kitchen floors to scouring porcelain to bed making. Says Ackerly: "We arrive with a smile, we have knowledge, we deliver what is asked of us, and we call back new clients the next day to see what could be done better."

Following the McDonald's formula, Ackerly eventually distilled her knowledge of "team cleaning" into a 300-page manual of dos and don'ts. The book serves as the basis for training new Mini Maid personnel. Among its teachings: pick up statuary in the middle, rather than at the top and bottom, and clean animal-skin rugs with a whisk broom rather than a vacuum cleaner. Sums up Ackerly: "The homeowner does not have to feed us, pick us up, give directions. We don't give a song and dance about our car breaking down as a reason for not showing up. We are successful because we have learned the hard way."

Amica Mutual Insurance. Among the behemoths of the insurance business, Amica Mutual figures far down the list. The Providence-based company, which specializes in property and casualty coverage on such items as homes, autos and boats, earned $13 million last year on revenues of only $400 million. Nonetheless, the 80-year-old Amica has earned a top grade from the monthly *Consumer Reports* and an A-plus billing from the A.M. Best insurance-company rating service. With a modest crop of 400,000 customers and only 39 branch offices across the country, Amica has consciously avoided increasing its size to match its reputation. Says Amica Vice President Charles E. Horne: "We address a very small segment of the market, and we try to do it well. We simply seek not to be the biggest but to be the best."

Amica has not strayed into commercial lines of insurance, choosing to remain focused on individual-customer care. The firm never advertises and relies on referrals for most of its customers. It employs no independent agents and hires its own adjusters and underwriters. The company's unusually high ratio of 1 employee for each 140 clients allows it to meet high performance standards, like routinely answering all customer mail within a day of receipt. Amica tries to respond to claims in the same speedy manner. The company's adjusters have been known to take extraordinary pains to assist clients in duress. After Hurricane Gloria hit the New England coast in 1985, one Amica homeowner policyholder was unable to get any government agency to remove a ten-ton tree that had fallen onto her house. When she called Amica for help, an adjuster came out and made arrangements the same day for a construction company to cart the tree away.

L.L. Bean. Freeport, Me. (pop. 6,700), is an unlikely Mecca. Yet every year 2.5 million American worshipers of sensible, frugal and unpretentious products for the outdoors descend on the Yankee seaside town. Their aim: to visit the one and only L.L. Bean company store, which is open around the clock and features 6,000 items, ranging from moccasins to sleeping bags to camel-hair cardigans. However, many more Americans know the company through the 75 million L.L. Bean catalogs that are mailed out annually. Celebrating its 75th anniversary this year, the company, founded to market a superior hunting boot, has become a $362 million business that sells its merchandise 24 hours a day by telephone and employs 1,850 workers full time, with an additional 1,800 on duty during the peak fall-to-Christmas season.

Mail order forms the bulk of Bean's business: last year $308 million of the company's sales came from catalog orders. The firm's reputation for homey efficiency comes from its ability to deliver virtually any item almost anywhere in the U.S. and Canada within 72 hours. During peak season, more than 28,000 telephone orders a day flood the Bean switchboards. Computers help keep track of the models, colors and sizes that are in stock at any given moment, and orders are filled accurately 99.8% of the time. The company provides repairs as well as sales. Each year, for example, it resoles some 17,000 pairs of its famed Maine hunting boots for $24, about half the cost of a new pair.

Bean employees receive 40 hours of training before they deal with their first customer. Much of the instructional emphasis is on care and thoroughness in filling orders and on general courtesy and helpfulness. People around the U.S. call the company for advice on what accessories to provide for children on their way to camp, what to take on a first trip to Alaska and what to wear while cross-country skiing. If a Bean staffer cannot answer the question, the customer will be switched to someone who can.   —*By George Russell.* *Reported by Meg Grant/Seattle and William Szonski/Boston*

THE 10 LAWS OF CUSTOMER SATISFACTION

Bonnie J. Knutson
School of Hotel, Restaurant and Institutional Management
Michigan State University

In the PBS documentary on <u>In Search of Excellence,</u> Stu Leonard attributes the success of his Connecticut grocery store to his belief that only satisfied customers come back.[1] That's good to know but it doesn't answer the all important question owners and managers face every day: JUST <u>HOW</u> DO WE SATISFY OUR CUSTOMERS?

In looking for that elusive answer, I've talked with many successful managers, reviewed a myriad of books, articles and market studies and come to the conclusion that there's both bad news and good news. The bad news is, of course, that no single answer exists. There is no elexcer you can drink nor pixie dust you can sprinkle over yourself that will magically enable you to specifically answer the "HOW...." question. And since most of us would like to have a nice simple solution, even though the problem is complex, this is bad news.

The good news is, however, that there are several common threads which do run throughout all the conversations about and literature on customer satisfaction. When woven together, these threads form a picture of a <u>set</u> of answers to the "HOW...." question. This set I call the 10 LAWS OF CUSTOMER SATISFACTION.

In reading these laws, I'd like to you keep their two underlying principles in mind. First, <u>customer satisfaction is directly related to customer expectations</u>. While few may agree on the exact meaning of customer satisfaction, the concept is easy: it's basically the guest evaluating an experience in light of what he expected that experience to be.

Whenever a customer walks into a hotel or restaurant, he has certain expectations. These expectations are formed from past experiences -- experiences of the customer (including seeing and hearing all types of promotion) and experiences told to him by others (word-of mouth or radial advertising).

When these expectations are <u>met</u>, the guest is satisfied and will likely come back. When the experience of being in your property <u>exceeds</u> expectations, you not only have a satisfied guest who probably will return, but you have a positive "advertiser" as well. If, however, the expectations go <u>unmet</u> (i.e. experiences fall below expectations), the result is often lost future business -- from both the guest and from those whom he tells.

Another point must be made about the relationship between expectations and experiences; that is, the greater the difference between the expectation and the experience, the greater the guest's level of satisfaction (or dissatisfaction) and the greater the guest's likelihood of becoming an advertiser (positive or negative). This is the WOW factor. In other words, the better we are at performing -- of "wowing" our guests -- the better our chances of increasing future business.

This leads to the other underlying principle. <u>Marketing is operations; they are two sides of the same coin.</u> There can be no line dividing marketing from operations because they both directly impacts guests' satisfaction. Marketing's assignment is to make a promise to the guest about the kind of experience he will have when he "walks through the door." Operations' responsibility is to keep the promise made, to give the guests such a great experience that they want to come back.

If the world were a carnival, marketing's job would be that of the barker. "Step right up, ladies and gentlemen....Right here under the Big Top...a really big show for your entertainment and pleasure." Operations is everything that happens under the Big Top; it's the collection of grips, trainers, musicians, clowns and performers -- all led by a ringmaster -- who put on the show.

The most effective marketing strategy starts, then, by making sure that what happens in the restaurant or hotel (operations) really satisfies (meets or exceeds expectations) guests.

With these two principles as background, I'd like to share with you the 10 LAWS OF CUSTOMER SATISFACTION.

LAW OF RECOGNITION

THE TWO MOST BEAUTIFUL WORDS IN ANY LANGUAGE ARE YOUR NAME. When we walk into a business and are greeted by a "Hi Doris," or a "Mr. Sergeant, how are you doing today?" we feel special and we like that feeling.

It was easier for hoteliers and restaurateurs in "the olden days" before mega-hotels, the proliferation of multi-unit restaurants and the increase in brand-hopping by consumers. Employees knew customers and customers knew employees.

There are still pockets of neighborhood restaurants or small country inns which welcome the same guests time after time. For them, it's easier to greet their visitors by name. But for many managers, that intimate relationship between staff and guest is a luxury they think went out with "Ozzie and Harriet" and "Leave It To Beaver". They're wrong!

At the very time when there seems to be a rise in depersonalized service, people have an increasing need to be recognized and treated as special individuals. John Naisbitt coined a phrase for this phenomena: High Tech/High Touch.[2] In essence, he says that whenever new technology is introduced into society, there must be a counterbalancing human response -- i.e. high touch -- or the technology is rejected. The more high tech we get, the more high touch we need.

Think about it. A hotel guest can make reservations on a computer, check-in through an automated terminal, wake-up by a recorded message and check-out via the television in the room. These technological changes undoubtedly allow for more efficient services and cost reductions for the hotel, but, Naisbitt's theory says they must have a compensating human response or guests will not be comfortable (i.e. reject the technology) in the situation.

While it may be impractical to expect every employee to recognize each of your guests by name, a genuine (repeat, genuine) smile and a warm hello go a long way toward becoming as beautiful to your guest as his or her name.

LAW OF FIRST IMPRESSIONS

YOU DON'T HAVE A SECOND CHANCE TO MAKE A GOOD FIRST IMPRESSION. The first experience guests have with your business will be <u>indelibly</u> fixed in their minds. This is akin to the process animal biologists call "imprinting" -- a term used to describe the few seconds it takes to etch the identify of its parent into the mind of a new born animal.

In a similar fashion, a hotel or restaurant "imprints" on its guest's mind in those critical seconds of initial interaction. Is your parking lot well lit at night? Is the paint chipped or carpet worn in the entrance? Does the porter, front desk people, host, hostess and servers know and live by the First Law?

Walt Disney understood this law, so did Ray Kroc. They also recognized that sometimes it's the small details which imprint that first impression, too. Why else would these driving forces behind the two most successful family-oriented businesses in the world have such a penchant for consistently spotless facilities? They knew that clean imprints; that cleanliness is definitely next to godliness for their guest families.

Imprinting can also take place before a guest ever sets foot on your property. Look at your advertising. Does it make the impression you want it to make? A colleague recently showed me an ad for a major hotel which appeared in a national magazine. The text touted the spaciousness of the rooms, the comfort of the accommodations, the convenience for the business traveler. The accompanying picture (which took up half of the ad space) showed a businessman sitting on a bed with papers spread all around him. His coat was off, his tie was loose and his shirt sleeves were rolled up. He talking on the telephone. He was working. Does that ad imprint? Probably. Does that ad imprint spaciousness, comfort and convenience for the business traveler? Doubtful.

LAW OF EXPECTATIONS

GUESTS EXPECT A HASSLE FREE ENVIRONMENT. Customers don't read your operating manuals; they don't understand your company's policies and procedures. What's more, they don't care to. All they know is that they have a need which has to be met and they want it met without aggravation.

This is a tale of a coney dog: Having spent the morning giving a seminar on (ironically) these 10 LAWS OF CUSTOMER SATISFACTION, I was tired, hungry and on a tight time schedule before dashing off to a meeting. So I stopped at a nearby deli-type restaurant featuring "New York Dogs". When I saw both chili and hot dogs on the menu board, I knew exactly what I wanted -- no, what I needed -- for lunch: a nice, long, juicy chili and onion covered coney dog. I love coney dogs!

Stepping up too the counter, I was greeted by a very friendly order taker. The conversation went something like this:

"Hi. Can I help you?

"Yes," I replied, my stomach growling and my mouth watering.

"I'd like a coney dog and black coffee."

She looked perplexed. "We don't have coney dogs."

"I know they're not on the menu. Just put some chili and

onions on the hot dog and we'll call it a coney dog."

"But m'am, we don't <u>have</u> coney dogs."

I was determined. "You have hot dogs, don't you?"

"Yes."

"You have chili, don't you?"

"Yes."

"Then there's no problem," I beamed. "Please, just put some chili on the hot dog, some onions on the chili and I'll have my coney dog."

"But," she exasperatedly continued, "We do not have coney dogs."

You get the picture. This conversation went on for another three minutes before I learned that the reason she couldn't sell me a coney dog is that she didn't know what to charge me. It wasn't in the manual. And company policy didn't give anyone at the unit level the authority to "create" a menu item or change a price.

I didn't care. All I wanted was a coney dog.

LAW OF EFFORT

CUSTOMERS WANT TO EXPEND AS LITTLE EFFORT AS POSSIBLE. The effort must come from your side. Think about the last time you bought a present for someone in a department store. Did you really want to walk all the way back to "Customer Service" to get a gift box?

We are becoming a "Time Poor/Money Rich" society. Convenience is our byword. Anyone who doubts this just has to take a look at the phenomenal growth in restaurant drive-throughs, take-out and delivery services.

Again, its often the little things that can mean a lot to your guests. Take, for example, the case of a Mr. Steak franchise. They had a loyal customer base; a large segment of which was the "empty nester". For many years, the standard procedure for guests paying their bill was to have the waitress set the check on the table, then the guest would take it and pay at the cash register. Sometimes, when it was busy, guests had to wait in line to pay. Through market research, Mr. Steak learned that their customers didn't like waiting in line; they felt like they were wasting their time. So management began giving guests the option of either having the waitress take the money to the cash register or letting the guest continue to take it up. A funny thing happened on the way to increased guest satisfaction and increased frequency, guests completely stopped making the effort to take the money up themselves. They transferred that effort to the restaurant. And were happy to do so. The lesson is clear: Anything you do to make it easier and more convenient for your guests will be rewarded with repeat business.

LAW OF DECISION MAKING

BASICALLY, CUSTOMERS DON'T LIKE TO MAKE DECISIONS. In their minds, you are the expert; you help them make the decisions. That's why they've come to you. What a great opportunity for suggestive selling. (Notice, I didn't say up-selling!)

When most of us think of suggestive selling, we think of a waiter or waitress standing by the table explaining the specials of the day. But suggestive selling can also be successfully plied through other more subtle merchandising techniques. A folded linen napkin attractively placed in a pre-set wine glass forces the diner to notice the glass. It helps him "decide" to order wine. A flaming dessert or smoking (with dry ice) drink purposely carried, high on a tray, throughout the dining room to a table in the "far corner" is sure to attract attention. Offered to the unsuspecting guests with "the compliments of the house," this theatrical presentation is guaranteed to help at least eight other guests "decide" to have one too.

And helping guests make their decision is where the old advertising adage of "Repeat, Repeat, Repeat" comes into play. A case in point. A New York hotel was featuring a new summer time drink in their lounge: "La Bamba". A fancy, fruity, ice cream concoction, it provided a very high contribution margin. Naturally, they wanted to sell many. So the first thing guests saw when they entered the lobby was a life size cut out of a smiling young lady, festively dressed in a Caribbean costume, holding a "La Bamba". This same young lady was featured on a lapel button worn by the front desk clerk. Guests met her again on the wall insert when they were riding up in the elevator. And she smiled at them one more time from a three-dimensional table tent in their rooms.

By the time the guest came back down in the elevator, walked across the lobby and into the lounge, he had been <u>helped</u> at least six times in his decision. He was ordering a La Bamba!

LAW OF PERCEPTION

A CUSTOMER'S PERCEPTION IS THAT CUSTOMER'S REALITY. Your customers and potential customers don't necessarily see things the way you do. It doesn't matter if your prices are in line with your competition, or if you have knowledgeable employees. If your customer sees you as more expensive, then you are more expensive, no matter what the menu says. If your customer believes your employees don't know enough to solve their problem, then they don't know enough. And if your customer believes that your competition is "X", even though you <u>know</u> it is "Y", then, <u>in the customer's mind</u>, your competition is "X".

In their classic book on positioning, Ries and Trout point out that a business creates a position in the customer's mind -- one that reflects not only the company's own strengths and weaknesses but those of its competitors as well.[3] When a person is exposed to your advertising, product or sales claim, the person looks inside his mind and says, "That's right" or "That's wrong." The mind, the authors maintain, accepts only new information which matches what it currently believes. Therefore, it's very difficult -- if not impossible -- to change what people think you are. Truth is the perception that's inside the mind of the prospective customer. It may not be your truth, but it's the only truth with which you can work. This fact is one which you have to accept and deal with.

Here's an example of what can happen when management doesn't see what the customers see. An upscale, seafood restaurant company had seven units in the Detroit area. When I began working with management to develop a new three year marketing plan, one of my first questions was, naturally, "Who is your competition?"

Their reply came quickly and confidently. "Oh, that's easy. We're up against 'The River Crab,' 'The Golden Mushroom,' and places like that." "Are you sure?" I asked. "Oh yeah. Our competitors are all the fine dining seafood restaurants in town."

When we asked their customers (through market research studies), however, the answer to the competition question was quite different. To them, the competition was NOT " 'The River Crab,' 'The Golden Mushroom,' and places like that". It was Red Lobster!

Red Lobster? For years, this restaurant company had been planning, strategizing and marketing under a wrong premise. All the resources (financial, time, personnel) which they targeted against the competition were targeted against the wrong enemy; the "troops and artillery" were not aimed in the right direction. They weren't as effective as they should have been. And while the overall business was profitable, how much higher could the bottom line have been if decisions had been based on the reality of the customers' truth rather than illusion of management's perception.

LAW OF TIME WARP

THE MIND WARPS REAL TIME BY A 4:1 RATIO. This is a corollary to the Law of Perception. For every minute you keep a customer

224

waiting, it seems like four. Remember the last time you sat in a waiting room, were put on hold, or expected a critical shipment from one of your suppliers? How long did it seem to you? Perceived time is real time to your customer.

In a recent study on good service in fine dining restaurants, people said they were willing to wait two minutes for the host or hostess to greet them.[4] Given the 4:1 time expansion factor, what these diners were really saying is that they will wait about 30 seconds before becoming irritated.

Thirty real seconds is not a long time; it just seems long.   A telephone will ring about six times in thirty seconds. You can see two commercials on television. Doing an eight minute mile, a running back can catch the football in his own end zone and go 110 yards down the field to score a touchdown. But thirty seconds is a long time to a waiting customer; it is two minutes long. And perception is reality.

LAW OF MOTIVATION

PEOPLE ARE MOTIVATED TO RECREATE THE GOOD TIMES THEY REMEMBER. This maxim is the reason why a business can build customer loyalty. People like to feel smart, that they've made the right decision to eat at your restaurant or stay at your hotel. If your customers feel good about their experience with you, you can bet they'll be back. And, if they feel really good, they'll probably tell others about it too. -- an average of two or three others. That's word-of-mouth advertising -- the best that money can't buy.

In his book, Winning!, Pete Stevens tells the following story:

I was an attendee recently at a three-day conference, held at the Marriott Copley Place in Boston. I arrived in Boston late-morning, borrowed a friend's car to handle some other business, and headed for the hotel shortly after dark (in the rain).

I couldn't find the damn hotel. I'm circling the block -- and BANG! I hit a median curb; flattened the left-front tire.

I got out of the car in the rain, ran across traffic in the rain toward a covered building entranceway where I encountered a red, white and gold-uniformed doorman. I was at the Marriott.

Brad came toward me and asked if he could help. I explained my car trouble, told him I was checking in, and asked where I might find a phone to call for assistance.

Brad went with me to the car, held traffic while I made a U-turn, told me that he'd fix the tire, and directed me to the front desk. Later in my room I received a call from Brad, letting me know that the tire was fixed and the car was in the garage.

Three days later, when I was leaving for the airport, there again was Brad. He waved and said, 'Hope you enjoyed the conference, Dr. Stevens. Have a safe trip back to Michigan.'[5]

Pete Stevens wants to feel that good again. So I guarantee the next time he goes to Boston, he'll stay at the Marriott Copley Place; the next time I'm in Boston, I probably will too.

In no other industry is this law as important as it is in the hospitality-service industry. Good times and memories of good times are all we really sell. We sell intangibles; we don't sell tangibles. When customers leave an automobile dealership they drive away in their shiny new car. When they walk out of a grocery store, the bag of apples, sugar, milk and meat go with them. But when they walk out of a restaurant or a hotel all they take with them are the memories of their experiences. It's the good memories that keep customers coming back.

LAW OF MEMORY

PEOPLE REMEMBER BAD EXPERIENCES LONGER AND IN BETTER DETAIL THAN POSITIVE EXPERIENCES. And they also tell more people about them -- an average of seven people more than if they are motivated to relate a Brad-type story.

Do you remember playing the game "Telephone" when you were a child? The child who was "it" would whisper something to the child sitting next to him. Then that child would turn and relay the message on to a third child and so on until it was told, in turn, to everyone in the circle. When the last child heard the message, he would repeat it aloud. Needless to say, the final version was never even close to the original story.

It is the same when customers relate their horror stories about what happened to them in "that" restaurant or "that" hotel. Not only do disgruntled guests remember every unhappy detail longer, but they also tend to embellish the events with each telling. And do you recall the Law of First Impression and Law of Perception?

LAW OF WHO OWES WHOM

AFTER THE SALE IS MADE, YOUR CUSTOMERS MUST FEEL THAT THEY "OWE" YOU, NOT THAT YOU "OWE" THEM. This final commandment should be incorporated into every mission statement of every hotel and restaurant. After marketing has made the promise and after operations has kept the promise, your goal is to have your guests walk out of your property feeling that the price-value teeter-totter is tipped all the way in their direction. You want them to feel as if they got so much value for the price they paid (in terms of their time, their effort as well as their dollars) that they "owe" you another visit.

Customers get angry at us (hotels and restaurants) not so much for wasting their money but for wasting the opportunity to enjoy themselves. In an editorial on the unforgiving customer, Peter Berlinski summed it up well by relating the following customer comment: "If my wife and I had known you were going to give us such a poor experience, then we would have simply driven through your parking lot, thrown the money out the window, and continued on to another establishment. Then, at least, we would not have wasted out evening."[6]   In that scenario, who owed whom?

A final point about customer satisfction should be added. Aside from the altruistic motive of satisfying your guests, there's an underlying cost motive to the premise that only satisfied customers come back. Simply stated, it costs more to get a customer than to keep one. The ratio is about 10:1. For every ten dollars you spend on advertising, public relations, price incentives and other promotions to get a new customer in your door, it costs you only one dollar to get a present customer into coming back. And word-of-mouth advertising is free! Your bottom line will thank you.

ENDNOTES

1.The Public Broadcast System's (PBS) presentation was based on In Search of Excellence by Thomas J. Peters and Robert H. Waterman, Jr. Harper and Row, New York, 1982.

2.Naisbitt, John. Megatrends, Warner Books, New York, 1982.

3.Ries, Al and Jack Trout. Positioning: The Battle for Your Mind. McGraw-Hill, New York, 1986.

4.Anderson, Michael, Darly Lengel and Yin Jian Zhou. "Survey of Good Service in Fine Dining Restaurants." Working Paper. Graduate School of Business Administration, Michigan State University. May 1988.

5.Stevens, Dr. Pete, Winning. Hospitality Publications, Okemos, Michigan, 1987.

6.Berlinski, Peter R. "The Unforgiving Customer," Restaurant Business. April 10, 1986, p. 22.

Improving Employee Service Levels Through Identifying Sources of Customer Satisfaction

Ken W. McCleary and Pamela A. Weaver

A major source of satisfaction for customers of hospitality operations is the service employees provide. In order for employees to be trained to perform activities which provide customer satisfaction, it is necessary for the hospitality manager to determine what service actions bring about satisfaction. The major thrust of this article is to describe an objective approach for designing an instrument that may be used to identify components of customer satisfaction. The identification of these specific measurable behaviours will be a great asset to hospitality managers in training and evaluating their employees, ultimately leading to a higher level of customer satisfaction.

Key words: Hospitality   employee   behaviour   customer   satisfaction   measurement

Introduction

One of the greatest problems facing the hospitality industry is how to train employees so that they exhibit desired behaviour and then how to measure the extent to which that behaviour is exhibited. The behaviour that most industry people would like to see displayed by employees is that behaviour which provides customer satisfaction. Customer satisfaction is brought about by such things as a good employee attitude and customer orientation. Because customer satisfaction and a good attitude are very difficult to define, there is a tendency for hospitality managers to talk in generalities and use unmeasurable and sometimes meaningless terms.

It is not surprising that hospitality managers use general instead of specific terms to describe employee behaviour, because most hospitality educators also speak in generalities. Educators stress the need to develop good attitudes and to rate employees on their performance without telling students how to define a good attitude for employees or how to measure an employee's level of competency in a given area. What is needed is a way to design jobs and encourage behaviour that provides customer satisfaction. Since customer satisfaction is a nebulous term, it is necessary to first define it. It is simply not enough to tell

employees to have a good attitude if they do not know what constitutes this.

In any service operation it is difficult to measure how pleased or displeased a customer is, but unless managers are aware of what pleases their customers it is very difficult to ensure that employees will do those things that bring about satisfaction. For example, most customers like to be greeted by a friendly waitress. But what is friendly? Friendly is a subjective term with different meanings for different people, so to tell a waitress to be friendly is not a very effective description of desired behaviour. However, for most people, a smile is a component of friendly service. A smile is something that is measurable and can be demonstrated and thus understood by employees.

Efforts to develop employee behaviour which leads to customer satisfaction can be condensed into a three-stage process:

(1) Identifying components of a customer satisfaction.
(2) Developing a vehicle for evaluating the amount or level of satisfaction provided by an employee.
(3) Providing feedback to employees through the evaluation process.

Reprinted by permission from INTERNATIONAL JOURNAL OF HOSPITALITY MANAGEMENT, Vol. 1, No. 2, 1982, pp. 85-89. © 1982 Pergamon Press Ltd.

Identifying components of customer satisfaction

Customer satisfaction is ultimately exhibited through continued patronage. Thus, a hotel or restaurant that is profitable, with a reasonable amount of repeat business, can be fairly certain that whatever it is that employees are doing is providing satisfaction. However, unless satisfaction-producing behaviour is identified so that new employees can be indoctrinated, the repeat business picture can change as managers and employees leave and new personnel change the training and behaviour expectations.

The customer is the primary information source for identifying components of satisfaction. Many hotels and restaurants make attempts at determining components of customer satisfaction through a variety of methods, most of which are informal, or at best, statistically unreliable. One of the most popular methods is to place a questionnaire in the guest room or on the patron's table in the restaurant. Designed properly, questionnaires can provide valuable information, (McCleary and Wilson, 1981). Unfortunately, most questionnaires used in service operations broach only the questions of whether guests were satisfied or not, and ignore attempts to determine sources of satisfaction. For example, a questionnaire picked up recently at a Days Inn asked, 'How would you describe the *attitude* of the Days Inn employees toward you?' Response possibilities include good, fair, and poor, with a place for a checkmark by each response. A response to any of the possible answers is almost meaningless from a personnel development standpoint. While completed questionnaires which consistently indicate a response of poor provide management with a warning signal, they give no indication as to what is wrong with employee attitudes.

Another way managers gather information regarding customer satisfaction is to wander through the establishment and talk informally with guests. This method of obtaining feedback at least provides two-way communication, but there is also a tendency to get less than truthful responses from many people, because they are reluctant to criticize specific employees for fear of 'getting them into trouble'. Or if guests are particularly pleased, it is difficult for a manager not trained in interviewing techniques to ask questions which identify specific actions which provide the pleasure.

A perceptive manager can gain insight by simply observing employees in action. By watching guest response during interactions with employees, a manager can get a feel for what individuals do to make guests happy. Indeed, many managers have excellent records of hiring good employees based on a 'gut feeling' developed through years of experience. However, unless the manager does all the hiring and training, much of the responsibility for personnel will be delegated. Thus, people responsible for training must be made aware of actions which provide satisfaction so that this information can be passed on to employees.

The task facing a hospitality manager, then, is to gather information in a systematic manner that accurately identifies sources of satisfaction which can be translated to employee training and effectiveness. To accomplish this task, managers have available to them the same tools that have been used for years by companies like Proctor and Gamble and General Motors to conduct consumer research. The first step toward generating sound information is to develop a sound data gathering instrument.

Designing an instrument for developing customer-satisfying behaviour

In constructing a valid and reliable instrument for information gathering, it is important to note that technically the reliability or validity of a particular instrument refers to only one specific set of respondents at one particular point in time. Therefore, any calculated reliability coefficient varies over time and respondent group. This caution is presented to point out that an instrument constructed for use in a fast-food restaurant which is reliable and valid for that restaurant's customers and employees will not contain the same degree of reliability and validity for a hotel or fine dining restaurant. In fact, an instrument constructed for a hotel in Chicago will not provide the same degree of accuracy for another hotel in the chain which is located in San Francisco, although it is likely that one instrument could be used chainwide with only minor modifications if there is a great deal of similarity between the two properties.

The first step necessary to construct the data-gathering instrument is to generate a large pool of experimental items. These items should be generated to reflect opinions of managers, employees and clientele of the property so that comparisons can be made among the group regarding perceptions of the importance of items which constitute satisfaction. The inclusion of the three groups becomes important in helping to point out misconceptions on the part of employees and management as to what customers consider to be a good service and accentuates differences which can be focused on in training. Information for item generation can be gathered through focus group and/or personal interviews conducted separately for each of the three categories of respondents (Green and Tull, 1978). The interviews might centre around the theme of comparing the best and worst service encountered in an establishment of the type in question. The interviewees' responses should be coded so that they can be content analysed by the respondent group, question by question.

The second step in constructing a measuring device consists of evaluating the items generated in step one. Here again it would be highly beneficial, although not essential, to include representative samples from employees and management as well as from clientele, for the reasons mentioned previously. Evaluation is conducted by directing the respondent to reply to a standard series of questions for each evaluative item. These questions, while having the same content, are worded somewhat differently for the employee and management groups than for the clientele group. For example, the management and employee groups may be asked to respond to the following series of questions for each proposed evaluation item:

(1) Does this item present information which could be used to improve your service? (Yes/No)
(2) If you were to construct an evaluation instrument would you include this item? (Yes/No)
(3) Would you need additional information to interpret the response to this item? (Yes/No)
(4) Do you believe clientele can accurately evaluate you on this item? (Yes/No)

The clientele group will respond to a parallel set of questions for each trial item. The questions, however, might be phrased as follows:

(1) Do you believe this item is relevant for appraising the described service? (Yes/No)
(2) If you were to construct a questionnaire for

gathering information about service, would you include this item? (Yes/No)
(3) Would you want to qualify your response to this item? (Yes/No)
(4) Do you believe you have enough information and/or are competent to evaluate those aspects of service referred to by this item? (Yes/No)

As the clientele group is responding to the questions which evaluate each item, they may also be asked to respond to the evaluative item itself with regard to their satisfaction with the service at the property sponsoring the instrument development. Although the completed instrument will probably not contain all of the items being evaluated in step two, it will not contain any additional items. Having clientele respond to each item relating to service, in addition to evaluating the items, will allow management to do a comparison study of perceived service level both before and after a training and evaluation program, centred on the instrument, has been instituted.

Finally, clientele will also be asked to respond to a global item designed to assess overall satisfaction with employees' service delivery. This global item might be formulated as the following question:

Would you please rate your overall satisfaction with the service provided by the employees of .... hotel?

(1) Very satisfied
(2) Satisfied
(3) Neither satisfied nor dissatisfied (neutral)
(4) Dissatisfied
(5) Very dissatisfied

The reasons for including the global question are twofold. The first reason revolves around the validity issue. The instrument would demonstrate concurrent validity if the clientele were responding to both the individual items and the global item in a similar fashion. An example of a hypothetical situations follows: it has been determined that it is important that a desk clerk refer to guests by their full name. An instrument would have concurrent validity if in fact the desk clerk did refer to guests using their full name and also the guests responded positively to the global question. Obviously, concurrent validity refers to the evaluation of the global item in conjunction with all of the evaluative items, not just one of them.

The second reason for using a global question is

consistent with the reasoning used for having sample members respond to individual evaluative questions. The responses provide a comparison of the overall service level before and after incorporating the use of the service rating instrument in the company's training program.

The third and final step in constructing an evaluation instrument involves analysing the data gathered in step two and selecting items to be included in the final instrument. Selected items must be examined to determine if they need to be qualified in any way in order to be understandable and to be sure that items can be used for meaningful evaluation. Even if clients feel that items are important, the items should not be included unless they are in a measurable state which will contribute to the management decision process.

An evaluation instrument can then be developed from the information generated in the three-step process presented above. If a computer service is available, the items that were considered appropriate for inclusion in the final instrument may be manipulated with a factor analytic technique. Factor analysis clusters items according to common groupings. This would make the evaluation process more manageable by allowing the evaluator to consider certain related behaviours, such as service components at check-in, as a group. The instrument, at this point, may even be reduced if certain behaviours appear redundant in nature.

The final instrument should be pretested on a group of managers for readability, clarity and comprehensiveness. It is also necessary to determine if the changes that were made have enhanced the final instrument. The results from this final pretest may be incorporated in the finished instrument.

Measuring employee performance

After management has developed a valid and reliable instrument and has used this instrument to identify specific employee behaviours desired by guests, the gathered information can be used for assessing individual employee performance. To reiterate, in order for objective assessment to take place, each component of customer satisfaction must be measurable. As mentioned earlier, attitude is not measurable, but components of a good attitude can be. Each item generated from the data-gathering instrument will be measurable, and together these items will measure components of attitude and customer orientation.

To clarify what a typical evaluation instrument may contain, Fig. 1 presents an example of some measurable items which might be generated for front desk performance during check-in.

I. Guest was greeted with a smile	Yes _____ No _____
II. Guest's reservation was located within thirty seconds	Yes _____ No _____ Actual time _____
III. Guest's name was repeated three times during check-in	Yes _____ No _____ Actual number _____
IV. Guest was given directions to the elevators	Yes _____ No _____ Comment _____
V. Guest was given directions to guest's room	Yes _____ No _____ Comment _____
VI. Desk clerk was able to answer guest's questions regarding hotel	Yes _____ No _____ Comment _____
VII. Total check-in time was under three minutes	Yes _____ No _____ Comment _____
VIII. Guest was dismissed with a smile	Yes _____ No _____
IX. Guest was wished an enjoyable stay	Yes _____ No _____

Fig. 1.

The items in Fig. 1 are all measurable simply by observing what a clerk does while checking in a guest and noting the level of performance on an employee rating form. In the example, some items are measured nominally with a simple yes and no as to whether the behaviour was present or not. Other items allow for not only an assessment of whether a standard was met, but also allow raters to develop standard deviations from an ideal point such as with total check-in time. A highly sophisticated rating system might set up tolerable deviations depending upon the level of customer traffic at a given time of day.

Measurable items like those in Fig. 1 can be set up for all areas of the hotel and restaurant and for each phase of service where employees interact with customers. While it is recognised that different customers will desire somewhat different behaviours, the process of gathering information on a mean desired level of behaviour at least provides management with a base for measuring performance. This process, of course, will not and should not take away the individual employee's ability to insert his/her own personality into the employee/guest interaction. The attempt here is to lend an element of objectivity and measurability to an otherwise totally subjective process of measuring employee performance.

The assumption behind measuring employee performance is that there is a correlation between high behavioural performance ratings and consumer satisfaction. Thus, the level of customer satisfaction should also be monitored to determine if in fact satisfaction has been improved. This can be accomplished by using the original items generated to determine satisfaction for developing a questionnaire administered to a sample of guests from time to time.

Improving employee performance

The ability of employees to exhibit customer-satisfying behaviour depends not only on their own motivation but also on the property's ability to manage and a commitment to developing an atmosphere conducive to providing customer service. For example, because some of the items in Fig. 1 are not totally within the control of the employee, managers must understand the importance of designing work situations which make it possible for employees to perform activities which provide satisfaction. In a situation where there are not enough desk clerks on duty or there are too few terminals, employees will not be able to meet the ideal point for check-in time through no fault

of their own. Unless management responds by providing necessary resources, designing customer-oriented jobs, and then rewarding employees based on the performance of behaviour which provides customer satisfaction, the whole process of evaluation becomes frustrating and non-productive. It is counter-productive to tell a waiter that he must spend extra time selling wine to a table and then evaluate him on how many customers are served in a given time period.

The basis for how successful the property will be in providing satisfaction lies in the training and evaluation of employees. Once it has been determined what actions provide satisfaction, employees must be told of the desired actions and trained in their performance. This is much easier when specific behaviours can be communicated and demonstrated than when phrases like 'develop a good attitude' are used. In addition, employee rating forms can be used periodically in an appraisal interview to point out specific reasons, (such as a failure to repeat the guest's name) for the rating received by the employee. The use of video tape can be a valuable aid in demonstrating performances such as how to check-in people efficiently, and also in capturing more subjective behaviour in handling guests. This can be accomplished by taping outstanding employees in specific situations to use as a model.

Conclusion

If we expect our guests to be satisfied with our service and we expect our employees to do those things that guests find satisfying, we must be able to identify what customers expect from employees. The advantages of a good system to assess customer needs will accrue to management so it is up to the manager to be able to develop assessment systems. The identification of specific, measureable behaviours simplifies training, makes employee ratings more defensible, and leads to consistently good service. Managers who are able to use available techniques to measure satisfaction and performance will be better able to cope with the demands of customers and the need for continually developing efficient service delivery.

References

Green, P. E. and Tull, D. S. (1978) *Research for Marketing Decisions*, 4th edn. Prentice-Hall, Englewood Cliff, N.J.
McCleary, K. W. and Wilson, T. C. (1981) The in-room questionnaire as a marketing information tool. *J. Hospit. Educ.* Winter, 45–59.

Measuring and Improving Your Service Quality

Before you can improve your restaurant's service level, you need to assess how well the operation meets your service standards. This article, the conclusion of a two-part series, shows you how to discover and build upon your service strengths and remedy your deficiencies

by William B. Martin

IF YOU are the owner or manager of a food-service operation, you have some sense of your current service quality and of your operation's weak and strong areas. The techniques discussed in this article will help you transform this general conception into a list of specific service problems, ranked by how serious they are. The better you focus on identifying your specific service problems, the more successful you will be in solving them.

In my previous article, I discussed how to develop specific indicators of quality service for your operation.[1] In this article, I will show you how to use these indicators to design and conduct a service audit, and how to use a "customer-service assessment scale" (CSAS). The service audit and CSAS will help you paint a complete and accurate picture of your service level. I will also suggest strategies for implementing necessary changes.

[1] William B. Martin, "Defining What Quality Service Is for You," *The Cornell Hotel and Restaurant Administration Quarterly*, 26, No. 4 (February 1986), pp. 32–38.

The Service Audit

The service audit is a form of "management by wandering around" (MBWA), which Peters and Waterman found was one technique used by successful managers.[2] During your service audit, you

[2] Thomas J. Peters and Robert Waterman, Jr., *In Search of Excellence* (New York: Harper and Row, 1982).

will examine the service part of your enterprise, and you will get a feel for how the operation is functioning. But the service audit goes beyond simple MBWA, because it gives a structured format for the walking around. It gives you a sense of direction and identifies those areas that require your attention.

Indicators. The first step in conducting your service audit is to construct a service-audit form. Portions of a sample service-audit form are shown in Exhibit 1. You will notice that the form is simply a series of measurable quality-service indicators. Since these indicators must be specific to a particular operation's needs, service-audit forms

*A restaurant-industry consultant, **William B. Martin**, Ph.D., is an associate professor of hotel, restaurant, and travel management at California State Polytechnic University in Pomona. He is the author of* Quality Service: The Restaurant Manager's Bible, *published by* The Quarterly *(see page 104). This article is adapted from that book.*

EXHIBIT 1

Excerpts from a service-audit form for food servers

Scoring: C = Consistent
       I = Inconsistent
       N = Nonexistent

Organized Flow

____ Each table in a section is in a different stage of the service cycle

____ The crew is working at a steady but comfortable pace

Timeliness

____ Customers are greeted within one minute of sitting down

____ Beverages arrive at the table within four minutes after they are ordered

Customer Feedback

____ Customers are asked how their meals are within two minutes of being served

Anticipation

____ Customers are asked about refilling cocktails and beverages when glasses are one-quarter full

____ An adequate amount of supplies and equipment is on hand

Communication

____ Order tickets are filled out neatly, cleanly, and with proper abbreviations

____ Servers are clearly understood when they talk

System Accommodation

____ Menu items are adjustable to meet customer desires

Supervision

____ A manager is visible on the floor of the dining area

____ Customer problems and complaints are handled by the manager

Effective Selling Skills

____ The customers' awareness of items available is expanded by servers' telling about menu items

Attentiveness

____ Each party is approached according to its needs. This includes:

    ____ Meeting special needs of senior citizens

    ____ Recognizing special occasions and celebrations

Friendly Tone of Voice

____ Spirit and enthusiasm are maintained in the voices of service personnel:

    ____ At the beginning of the shift

    ____ During the middle of the shift

    ____ At the end of the shift

Use of Customers' Names

____ Repeat and regular customers are greeted by name

____ If a name is recorded on a reservation or waiting list, that name is used to address the party

Helpful Suggestions

____ Servers suggest personal favorites when customers are indecisive

____ Servers demonstrate complete product knowledge of the menu (including preparation methods)

Positive Attitude

____ On a ten-point scale, servers rate a 10 on pleasantness and cooperativeness

____ On a ten-point scale, servers rate a score of 10 on enthusiasm and high energy

Tactful Words

____ Proper etiquette is exhibited by all service personnel

____ Correct language and grammar are heard in the dining room

Gracious Problem-Solving

____ Complaining customers leave happy

____ Managers make contact with all complaining customers

---

will differ from restaurant to restaurant. The indicators will also vary among different job functions. The audit form should have a rating scale on which to record the frequency of each observed behavior.

The sample audit form shown uses a three-point scale (C, I, N) to rate the frequency of each behavior. Instead of the three points given in the example, your form could use five, seven, or ten points. But to use the service-audit form effectively, you *must* record some frequency for each indicator.

The process of auditing your service requires careful scrutiny of each service step and function. Performing a service audit helps food-service managers look at the right things and talk about the right things, as well as reinforcing and rewarding the behavior that generates quality service.

Flexibility. The service audit can be used for observing an entire service operation, specific work group (i.e., lunch food servers), or a single individual. Regardless of the group or number of persons you are observing, the audit form should be used as the basis for discussion and analysis. Throughout the audit, observers should maintain an analytical frame of reference, rather than one of blame. To limit emotional reactions, several managers could fill out the audit form and compare their results. You can then tally the management team's results and develop a list of major strengths and weaknesses. Credit, recognition, and reward should be given for appropriate service behavior, for when it comes to improving behavior in service personnel, a "pat on the back" is far more effective than a "kick in the butt."

A dangerous misuse of the service audit is to go out on the floor merely to criticize. This approach to the service audit will soon turn any effort to improve service into a disaster. It is far more effective to

EXHIBIT 2

Sample items from the Customer-Service Assessment Scale

Name _____

With this group or individual in mind, answer the following questions according to *how often the behavior occurs.*	Usually, if not always	Fairly often	Occa-sionally	Rarely or never
• Does service occur in a timely manner consistent with customer needs?	3	2	1	0
• Is communication with customers conducted in a timely, accurate, and thorough manner?	3	2	1	0
• Is enthusiasm displayed toward the job?	3	2	1	0
• Is feedback from customers used to improve quality of products and service?	3	2	1	0
• Are customers made to feel neglected in the rush of other activities?	0	1	2	3
• Is service tailored to the specific needs of customers?	3	2	1	0
• Are supervisors closely involved in the training of group members?	3	2	1	0
• Are complaints handled graciously and to the customer's satisfaction?	3	2	1	0
• Are suggestive-selling skills emphasized in training?	3	2	1	0

catch service employees doing something right than to harp on what they are doing wrong. The service audit is designed to help managers become more aware of strong service areas, as well as weak ones. Use the service audit to reinforce the behavior you want. Be positive and encouraging.

If you do use the service audit as a means of finding fault and casting blame, you will establish a climate of distrust and cut off communication. Without a climate of trust and support, your efforts to change your service staff's behavior will probably fail.

When you notice that some desirable indicators occur only infrequently, flag them for the moment, but act only after strategies for improvement have been formulated.

The service-audit form is designed specifically for your use as you observe your operation. The observations you make during your "wandering" audit, however, are just part of the information you should gather before determining how to improve your service. The remaining information will come from the observations of your staff and supervisors (and yourself) on the "Customer-Service Assessment Scale," which I will explain next.

CSAS

The Customer-Service Assessment Scale (CSAS) is useful for determining how adequately your restaurant is meeting your customers' needs. The scale is a needs-analysis and problem-identification instrument that consists of 40 items describing certain characteristics of a customer-service operation. Half the items are procedural (mechanics) and the other half relate to service's convivial dimension (warmth). Using a four-point rating scale, you measure how frequently your employees (or a specific target group or individual) exhibit each desirable service behavior. Sample items from the CSAS are shown in Exhibit 2.

Four Service Arenas

Four basic patterns emerge from plotting the CSAS responses on a graph. These four arenas of service quality, shown in Exhibit 3, are (1) the "freezer," (2) the "factory," (3) the "friendly zoo," and (4) the "full balance." I will describe each of these in turn.

Chilly reception. The *freezer* is a limited-service arena of poor procedure and meager conviviality. The small size of this arena shows there is a great deal of room for improvement. Freezer operations provide inadequate procedural service that is hardly convivial. Because service is slow, inconsistent, and disorganized, customers at these restaurants experience a great deal of inconvenience and frustration. Worse, the service staff is generally insensitive to the customers' feelings, conveying an attitude that is impersonal and aloof. Servers communicate no sense of interest to the customer and broadcast this silent message: "We don't really care about you."

Head 'em up and move 'em out. The service at *factory* operations is skewed strongly toward procedural efficiency. These restaurants are doing at least some things right. I say they are procedurally skewed because their service is timely and efficient, but their employees are cold. This configuration leaves room for improvement in the convivial dimension. Service may be fast and efficient, but it's also unfriendly and insensitive to customers' personal needs. This type of service conveys the following message to the customer: "You are a number. We are here to process you as efficiently as we can."

A comedy of errors. The *friendly zoo* is skewed toward convivial warmth, the other extreme of the

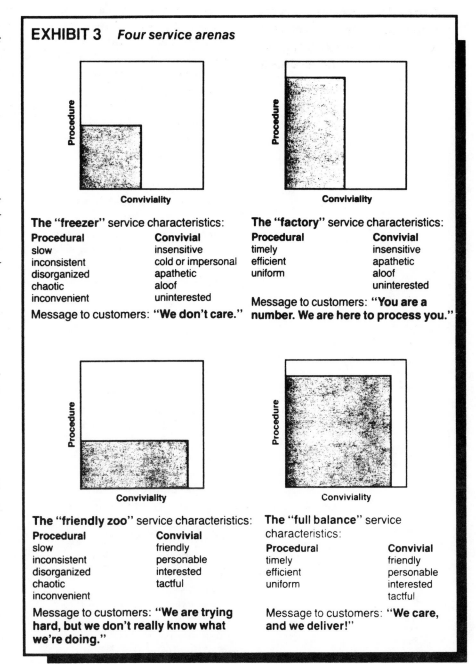

EXHIBIT 3   *Four service arenas*

The "freezer" service characteristics:

Procedural	Convivial
slow	insensitive
inconsistent	cold or impersonal
disorganized	apathetic
chaotic	aloof
inconvenient	uninterested

Message to customers: **"We don't care."**

The "factory" service characteristics:

Procedural	Convivial
timely	insensitive
efficient	apathetic
uniform	aloof
	uninterested

Message to customers: **"You are a number. We are here to process you."**

The "friendly zoo" service characteristics:

Procedural	Convivial
slow	friendly
inconsistent	personable
disorganized	interested
chaotic	tactful
inconvenient	

Message to customers: **"We are trying hard, but we don't really know what we're doing."**

The "full balance" service characteristics:

Procedural	Convivial
timely	friendly
efficient	personable
uniform	interested
	tactful

Message to customers: **"We care, and we deliver!"**

237

Improving customer service should become a part of your restaurant's regular procedures.

factory. While service is friendly, personal, and warm, it is also slow, inconsistent, and disorganized. Service people may show friendly interest in their customers and be tactful and polite, but the inconvenience of procedural problems often overshadows all the "warm fuzzies" the staff provides. We often see this kind of service in newly opened restaurants run by inexperienced operators. The message to the customer from this kind of service is, "We are trying hard, but we don't really know what we're doing."

Satisfying experience. Of course, what we should be striving for in our food-service operations is a service configuration as close as possible to the *full balance*, in which both dimensions are well-matched. Even though I call this a full-service arena, the graph still reflects some possibility for improvement, since perfection is rare. On the whole, however, the procedural and convivial dimensions are well-handled in this operation. With regard to procedure, service is timely, efficient, and uniform—consistently good. The service is also convivial, friendly, and personal. The service personnel show a real interest in customers as individuals. To the customer, the message is, "We care about you, and we deliver."

Using the CSAS

The application of the CSAS is flexible. It can be used to rate an individual or a group. It can be used for self-evaluation or for rating others. It can be used by an individual to obtain input from others regarding his or her individual service abilities. Managers can use it to receive feedback about themselves or to give feedback to their service personnel—and service personnel can use it to obtain feedback or give it to their managers. Regardless of its application, the CSAS's

usefulness lies in its ability to expose service strengths and weaknesses.

Self-assessment. Service supervisors and personnel alike can gain insight into their own customer-service behavior by completing the CSAS for themselves. Their responses to the 40 items will generate a personal service configuration and show areas needing improvement. In addition, their responses on each of the individual items will help pinpoint their personal service assets and liabilities. Individual items receiving a low rating (0 or 1) should be given attention. The employee can list these problem areas in order of importance so that he or she can focus on improving the highest-priority items first.

Assessment by others. Self-evaluation serves as a useful tool for an individual's own professional development, but it is often biased by the difficulties of self-perception. Our self-perception is usually filtered by our experiences and ego. We see the world—and ourselves—through our own individual set of lenses. That is why our self-evaluation is usually different from someone else's evaluation of us. Asking others to rate us on the CSAS provides valuable information, because it tells us how we are coming across to others. This helps us see ourselves as others see us. All in all, this process provides worthwhile insight into our service skills.

Managers' assessment. Restaurant managers can ask their service employees to complete a CSAS self-evaluation, while the manager fills out one for each employee. Then the manager can compare responses with each employee. This process works best in an atmosphere of openness, trust, and respect. Similarities and differences in responses can be discussed. From this session, the boss and employee can develop a third scale that represents a mutual agreement regarding the employee's service behavior.

Supervisors' self-assessment. Supervisors can also evaluate their own service strengths and weaknesses by using the CSAS. After they do that, they should ask their employees to rate them on the same scale. To ensure objective responses, employee assessments should be kept anonymous. A supervisor will get more honest responses from employees when they don't have to worry about recriminations over their feedback to the boss.

After receiving the responses from the service crew, managers can tally the results to create a "composite service configuration." They can compare this configuration with the one based on their own evaluations. This comparison will provide valuable feedback to the managers on how they are being perceived by their service personnel. Using these data, managers can make a list of their major service problems—the areas that consistently received low scores on the CSAS. Problem areas should be listed in order of priority and solved one at a time.

Group analysis. When using the CSAS for group analysis and problem-solving, respondents should be asked to rate the group as a whole. Individual respondents may be indirectly rating themselves as a member of the group in question, but it is the entire group, not the individual, that must be considered. This means that respondents should mentally *average* the ratings of individuals within the group or

derive a "total group" service rating for each of the 40 items on the scale.

Group analysis for managers. The supervisory group can apply this technique to themselves, responding to the scale for themselves *as a group*. Their ratings of the group can then be tallied and compared with others'. Again, a complete configuration can be drawn for these combined responses. When this process is combined with friendly discussion and analysis, it can serve as a useful tool for exposing service-skill deficiencies among the members of the management team. And when this rating is compared to the service employees' ratings of management, a relatively complete view can be constructed of the team's service-skill assets and liabilities. This is a crucial step in the process of improving customer service.

Group analysis for servers. When analyzing the behavior of various service groups (e.g., food servers, cocktail servers, buspersons, bartenders), everyone in the group should be asked to fill out the CSAS for his or her particular group. Buspersons respond for buspersons, food servers for food servers, and so on. Furthermore, responding employees must be asked to rate only the group working their shift. The lunch crew and the dinner crew, for example, will need separate analytical sessions if the individual members of these groups don't work with each other. Because respondents must be familiar enough with other group members to respond accurately, the group should also have worked together for some time.

One of the most constructive ways to analyze the group's results

is for the group members themselves to discuss their individual responses and generate a list of what they consider to be their top five or six major service deficiencies.

This procedure works best in groups of five to seven persons. When groups are larger than this, divide them into subgroups. Smaller groups facilitate discussion and give all group members a chance to make suggestions and give their point of view. Once the specific groups are defined, the name or description of each group should appear on the top of each completed scale coming from that group. The names of individual group members are usually not necessary. In fact, responses will be more candid when individual names are left off the form.

Work to be done. The result should be a definitive list of service deficiencies for a given service group, generated by the group itself. This process usually works well, because the people actually performing the service are given the opportunity to analyze their own service behavior. They become active participants in their own professional improvement. They have the chance to take an objective view of the service they are providing and to discover how the others in their group see things. Participants are usually less defensive and resistant to subsequent changes in service procedures as a result of participating in the CSAS evaluation. In fact, the group's commitment to improving the operation's customer service is usually enhanced through this self-assessment process.

Moreover, the CSAS helps crew members see what they are doing *right*. As a result, their confidence should increase, and they should be more aware of the behavior that translates directly into quality service.

Developing Solutions

Once you have identified your customer-service problems and placed them in order of priority, you should develop a strategy or a group of strategies to solve the problems. As you analyze each problem, you will discover certain factors that are preventing you from reaching your quality-service goal and other factors that are working in your favor. By listing the positive and negative factors in a "force-field analysis," you can determine why your service quality stands at its current level. In designing strategies to improve your service, you should work at eliminating or reducing negative forces. Merely reinforcing or building up positive factors in an attempt to "overpower" the negative forces rarely generates significant progress toward goal achievement, and may cause substantial organizational turmoil. Reducing or converting negative forces, on the other hand, will certainly move you closer toward your goal.

Generating Solution Strategies

Solution strategies should be chosen with care. The first idea that comes to mind for solving a particular problem is not always the best one. But when an array of solution alternatives is available, the chances of finding a successful strategy are increased. Comparing and contrasting alternatives helps uncover the solution that will best fit your operation.

Better solutions grow out of an investigation of the options available to you. There are two excellent ways of bringing your options to light. One is brainstorming, and the other is keeping abreast of what's going on within the food-service industry.

Brainstorming. The brainstorming process is a group activity based on the adage "two heads are better than one." One group member's ideas stimulate ideas in others. To start, assign one person the job of recording all ideas generated, and then ask the group to suggest ideas for possible solutions. The goal is to come up with as many ideas as possible, so participants' imaginations should be given free rein. In brainstorming, any idea is acceptable. Don't stop to analyze or criticize a particular suggestion during the session, or you may shut off creativity and discourage innovative suggestions.

The time to begin analyzing the ideas is *after* the group can come up with no additional ideas or suggestions. The ideas with the greatest promise can then be discussed further. Ultimately, one or more of those suggestions may hold the answer to your service problems.

Industry trends. Next to group brainstorming, the best way to gain exposure to a wide variety of alternatives for improving your customer service is to find out what others are doing. Acquaint yourself with periodicals, articles, and books on the subject of service; be active in your state association and the National Restaurant Association; attend conferences and workshops. Discover what the competition is doing—and know your options. Remember, the objective at this stage is not necessarily to make a decision but to accumulate a wealth of alternative strategy solutions. Once you are satisfied that you have identified all your alternatives, you can begin the process of choosing your solutions.

Making the Choice

Choose your solution strategies carefully. Pick solutions that fit you, your operation, and your people. Choose a strategy that you can afford and that you can "try on for size" before committing yourself completely. The following solution criteria should help you to make your final selections.

(1) Your solution strategy should be *sound in principle*. Choose techniques that are based on sound management and organizational principles, and not on fads or "quick-fix" remedies.

(2) Your solution strategy should have a *positive effect* on performance and productivity. Avoid making the mistake of gaining a few short-term successes that lead to long-term losses.

(3) Your solution strategy should be *cost-effective*. If you are not going to get your money's worth from an idea, discard it.

(4) Your solution strategy should be *compatible* with your existing operation. Shy away from solutions that require major operational changes.

(5) Your solution strategy should be *divisible*. You should be able to divide the strategy into smaller "pieces," either functionally or geographically.

(6) Your solution strategy should be *flexible*. The more flexible your solution is, the happier you will be with your choice.

(7) Your solution strategy should be *easily understood*. If the solution is simple to explain, it will be easier to implement.

(8) Your solution strategy should have realistic *time requirements*. You and others in your organization should have the time required to implement the solution fully and completely, without cutting corners or sacrificing quality.

(9) Your solution strategy should fit your *space requirements*. The strategy should fit your physical plant.

(10) Your solution strategy should take into account the amount of *training* that will be needed. Effective training is the key to customer service. Don't proceed with any solution without considering training requirements.

Lasting Change

Once you have determined the best strategies for improving the quality of service in your restaurant, you must turn your attention to the implementation of these strategies. Don't make the mistake of grabbing hold of a strategy without considering the best way to make the changes that the strategy will require. I say this because changes almost always engender resistance—resistance from individuals and resistance arising from organizational characteristics.

Just because *you* want to make a change in the service behavior of your supervisors and servers, don't assume that *they* want to make a change. In fact, your staff may be quite content with the way things are right now. Certain "roots of resistance," inherent in the psychological makeup of most people, will stand in your way. These roots of resistance result from the following factors:

- differing perceptions,
- existing habits,
- personal weaknesses,
- existing group norms and expectations, and
- vested interests (i.e., money, power, status).

In implementing your strategies for improvement, you must build on the following four foundations of change management to offset the roots of resistance.

1: Sharing information. To begin with, give your crew all the information you can about what you want to do and why. Hold information-sharing meetings, and make as many personal contacts as you can.

Emphasize the ways in which your proposals fit with the organization's existing values and the ways in which employees will benefit from the new procedures.

2: Employee involvement. Bring your managers and servers into the implementation process as much as possible so they feel they are "in" on things. When your people have a hand in molding and constructing service-improvement strategies, they will perceive proposed ideas for changing service behavior as their own. They may also make suggestions for further improvements.

3: Incremental implementation. A common trap for many advocates of change is biting off more than the organization can comfortably digest at any one time. You're not going to alter anyone's service behavior by calling a mass meeting and reading your staff the riot act. Spend your energy constructively by working first with *one* major problem in *one* group. Build on that initial success by tackling more widespread problems.

4: Flexibility. Your chances of succeeding will be enhanced by adapting and readapting solution strategies throughout the implementation process. Even when you have done a careful job of selecting and adjusting your service-improvement strategies to your operation, you may find that still more adaptation is necessary. Be prepared to make concessions to meet the legitimate objections of managers or employees.

Power. Sometimes—unfortunately—collaboration doesn't work. When you have exhausted all efforts to build on the four foundations of change mentioned above, you may have to implement the changes from your rightful position of authority. Refrain from taking this approach unless and until you absolutely have to.

Making It Stick

Once you have started implementing your quality-improvement program, you must not consider your job at an end. Instead, you must make sure that your staff is rewarded for meeting the upgraded service standards. Without reinforcement, your strategies may produce only short-term results.

There are many different ways to provide reinforcement and feedback to your staff. Give regular and specific verbal commendations. Conduct more-formal job appraisals periodically so that you can point out to your employees where they are succeeding and where they need to improve. Record sales performance to give servers a target and a standard of comparison. Encourage your customers to say what they think of the service. Offer incentives. Give rewards.

If you use the methods outlined in these two articles (and explained in greater detail in the book *Quality Service: The Restaurant Manager's Bible*), you will build a food-service operation that shines in the customer's estimation—one that builds a positive reputation and repeat business. Once you have upgraded your standards for quality service, you should continue monitoring how well your staff performs. This information will provide you with the basis for further refinement and redefinition of your quality standards. And as a result, improving customer service becomes a part of your restaurant's regular procedures—just as it should be.

Key Factors in
Guest Satisfaction

Some attributes of a hotel or restaurant are most likely to win compliments, while others usually show up on customers' complaint lists. Still others don't seem to make a difference at all. Knowing which factors are most likely to earn compliments or complaints can help a manager improve guest satisfaction

by Ernest R. Cadotte
and Normand Turgeon

CUSTOMER COMPLIMENTS and complaints have long been a source of feedback on a hotel or restaurant's market performance. Executives often use customer feedback as an exception-reporting mechanism to identify weaknesses to be corrected or strengths to be promoted. Although they are not likely to be representative of the customer's complete experience with a hotel or restaurant, complaints and compliments do highlight the dimensions of a product or service about which customers really care. The fact that customers take the time to voice their dissatisfaction or satisfaction suggests the attributes are salient in their evaluation of a hotel or restaurant experience.

In 1978, an effort was undertaken to determine the frequency of complaints and compliments in the hospitality industry. Members of the National Restaurant Association and American Hotel & Motel Association participated in surveys about the frequency and types of complaints and compliments they received. In most respects, the survey findings were straightforward, but we were interested in a pattern to the compliments and complaints. In this article, we will explain that pattern, and discuss how our findings can help hoteliers and restaurateurs improve guest satisfaction.

The data from the surveys suggest that some attributes have a greater potential to cause dissatisfaction (as indicated by complaints), while other attributes are more likely to be involved when a customer is highly satisfied (as indicated by compliments). Some aspects of restaurant and hotel service cause dissatisfaction when they are not right, but not high satisfaction when they are done well. That is, customers complain when an unspoken performance standard is not met, but exceeding that standard does not necessarily provoke compliments. By the same token, some kinds of service can lead to high satisfaction and garner compliments, while the absence or poor performance of that service does not necessarily cause complaints.

***Ernest R. Cadotte**, Ph.D., is professor of marketing at the University of Tennessee, Knoxville. **Normand Turgeon**, Ph.D., is a professor at l'Ecole des H.E.C. in Montreal. The authors acknowledge the assistance of Larry M. Robinson, Ph.D., in collecting the survey data discussed in this article.*

EXHIBIT 2

Comparative rankings of food-service attribute compliments and complaints

Attribute	Complaint Rank	Compliment Rank
Availability of parking	1	19
Traffic congestion in establishment	2	26
Noise level	5	24
Spaciousness of establishment	8	18
Hours of operation	9	20
Cleanliness of establishment	14	4
Neatness of establishment	11	5
Size of portions	12	5
Employee appearance	17	7
Responsiveness to complaints	20	9
Quality of service	3	1
Food quality	7	2
Helpful attitude of employees	6	3
Quantity of service	10	8
Prices of drinks, meals, and service	4	10
Management's knowledge of service	23	11
Availability of food on menu	16	12
Beverage quality	24	13
Variety of service	21	14
Uniformity of establishment appearance	26	15
Quality of advertising	25	16
Convenience of location	15	17
Quietness of surroundings	18	21
Accuracy of bill	19	22
Litter outside restaurant	22	23
Reservation system	13	25

We infer from these observations that the triggering mechanism for complaints and compliments may be bounded in one direction or the other for certain attributes. First, we will examine where different attributes of restaurants fit into this theory, and then we will discuss hotel attributes. Finally, we will offer some recommendations for how to deal with typical customer reactions to various attributes.

NRA Survey

In the 1978 survey of NRA food-service executives, responses were received from 432 firms representing 22,000 food-service units. Nearly all survey responses came from management. Over 97 percent of the respondents were general managers, vice presidents, presidents, or owner-operators. Most respondents were reporting for a single unit (i.e., 78 percent of the responses represented the guest-satisfaction experience of an individual restaurant). Over 30 percent of the respondents operated a unit that was affiliated with either a corporation or a franchise chain. The other 22 percent of the repondents were corporate officers of a chain or franchise organization.

The respondents represented several types of restaurants. The largest group (44 percent) operated either a limited-menu or fast-food unit. The remaining managers were mostly running full-menu restaurants (39 percent). The respondents reported average dinner checks of $4.90 (in 1978 dollars); 19 percent reported an average check under $3.00, and just three percent reported an average check of $15.00 or more.

In summary, although the respondents covered a good cross-section of the food-service industry, they do not constitute a statistically representative sample of all commercial restaurants.

Compliments and Complaints

Respondents were asked to rate the frequency of complaints and compliments for 26 service categories on a scale of 1 (seldom) to 5 (often). (The ratings were undertaken separately for complaints and compliments.) The ten most frequent complaints and the most frequent compliments are listed in the tables in Exhibit 1.

Complaints. The restaurateurs reported that availability of parking was the complaint they received most frequently. Traffic congestion in the establishment (e.g., lobby, parking lot, dining room) and the quality of service also rated high on the complaint list. Next in frequency were complaints about the price of drinks, meals, and other services, noise levels in the restaurant, helpfulness of employees, and the quality and method of food preparation. Occurring less frequently but still in the top ten were complaints about the spaciousness of the establishment, hours of operation, and quantity of service.

Compliments. With surprising consistency, respondents said their top compliment was on quality of service. They also reported many compliments on quality and method of food preparation, the helpful attitude of employees, cleanliness and neatness of the restaurant, and the size of portions. Farther down the list were compliments on the appearance of employees, quantity of service, responsiveness to complaints, and the price of drinks, meals, and other services.

Complimentary Diners

The executives reported receiving far more compliments than complaints. Each of the ten most frequent compliments were reportedly received more often than the number-one complaint. The executives also said they received two complimentary letters for every complaint letter. When asked what percentage of all comments made by their guests were favorable and what percentage unfavorable, they consistently indicated that over 76 percent were favorable, 15 percent were mixed or neutral, and only nine percent were unfavorable.

It should not be surprising that the executives reported more compliments than complaints. If the opposite were the case, the restaurants would not be in business for very long. Furthermore, the executives were probably more receptive to compliments than complaints, resulting in the possibility of a certain amount of selective perception.

Patterns

Although guests are apparently more likely to give compliments than complaints, we can still make certain observations regarding the relative frequency of different complaints and compliments. Let us assume the average frequency rankings in the tables in Exhibit 2 are simply indicators of the relative frequency of the complaints and compliments. The items with comparatively high rankings are probably the service areas that receive the most complaints or compliments. The items with comparatively low rankings are probably service areas that receive few comments of any kind.

The rankings suggest that some restaurant attributes are more likely to earn guest complaints than compliments. Availability of parking, hours of operation, traffic congestion, noise level, and spaciousness of the establishment all appear in the top-ten complaint list. Yet few operators reported compliments concerning these attributes. It would appear that customer satisfaction in these areas will not enhance the guest's perception of the restaurant, but failure to meet standards would certainly detract from a guest's experience.

In contrast, guests express appreciation for high performance in some areas, but rarely complain when performance is only so-so. The survey results suggest that guests react favorably to a clean, neat restaurant, neat employees, ample portions, and responsiveness to complaints.

The quality and quantity of service, food quality, helpfulness of employees, and the prices of drinks, meals, and other services appear in both the list of most frequent complaints and the list of the most frequent compliments. On these attributes, guests are more likely to voice their opinions, good or bad. It's also possible that restaurant operators have difficulty maintaining consistent levels of performance in these areas. The same restaurant can be very good or very poor depending on the day and the employee.

Finally, there are several areas that don't involve a significant number of either complaints or compliments. The relatively low incidence of commentary suggests either that they are not salient or that customers are easily satisfied on these scores.

Lodging Survey

The 1978 survey of AH&MA members also gathered data on the relative frequency of 26 categories of complaints and compliments. Survey responses were received from 260 lodging executives representing 280,000 rooms. Most responses again came from management, including general managers, regional managers, vice presidents, presidents, and owners. The experience of an individual property was represented in 88 percent of the responses, and the other 12

EXHIBIT 3
Frequent complaints and compliments in hotels

Complaints	Compliments
1. Price of rooms, meals, and other services	1. Helpful attitude of employees
2. Speed of service	2. Cleanliness of establishment
3. Quality of service	3. Neatness of establishment
4. Availability of parking	4. Quality of service
5. Employee knowledge and service	5. Employee knowledge and service
6. Quietness of surroundings	6. Convenience of location
7. Availability of accommodations requested	7. Management's knowledge of service
8. Checkout time	8. Quantity of service
9. Cleanliness of establishment	9. Spaciousness of establishment
10. Adequacy of credit	10. Quietness of surroundings

EXHIBIT 4
Comparative rankings of hotel attribute compliments and complaints

Attribute	Complaint Rank	Compliment Rank
Price of rooms, meals, services	1	15
Speed of service	2	11
Availability of parking	4	17
Availability of accommodations	7	18
Checkout time	8	23
Adequacy of credit	10	21
Accuracy of bill	11	25
Helpful attitude of employees	12	1
Neatness of establishment	15	3
Convenience of location	23	6
Management's knowledge of service	21	7
Quantity of service	13	8
Spaciousness of establishment	20	9
Cleanliness of establishment	9	2
Quality of service	3	4
Employee knowledge of service	5	5
Quietness of surroundings	6	10
Responsiveness to complaints	16	12
Variety of service	17	13
Uniformity of establishment appearance	25	14
Employee appearance	22	16
Hours of operation	19	19
Quality of advertising	24	20
Overbooking	18	22
Traffic congestion in establishment	14	24

EXHIBIT 5
Typology of potential for compliments and complaints

		Potential for compliments	
		Low	High
Potential for complaints	High	Dissatisfiers	Criticals
	Low	Neutrals	Satisfiers

percent came from corporate chain or franchise executives.

The respondents represented properties of all sizes, and occupancies and room rates roughly corresponded to industry averages of the time. The sample provided a fair cross-section of the innkeeping field, but the small size of the sample means that the results are not statistically representative of the lodging industry. As in the NRA survey, the data provide insight into sensitive areas of consumer evaluation.

Complaints and Compliments

The lodging executives rated the 26 service categories in terms of how often they received compliments and complaints on each. The ten most frequent complaints and compliments are shown in Exhibit 3. The three most frequent areas of complaint were the price of a guest room, meals or other services, and the speed and quality of service. Following those were complaints about parking availability, employee knowledge and service, quietness of surroundings, and availability of accommodations. Rounding out the top ten complaints were checkout time, cleanliness of the property, and credit policies.

The hotel executives reported receiving the most frequent compliments about the helpful attitudes of employees, followed closely by the cleanliness and neatness of the property, and the quality of service provided to guests. The rest of the top-ten compliments involved employee knowledge and service, quantity of guest service, spaciousness of the property, and quietness of surroundings.

Relative Frequency

Like the restaurant executives, responding hoteliers reported receiving two complimentary letters for every complaint letter. When asked what portion of all guest comments were favorable, the hotel executives held that more than 70 percent were favorable and only 12 percent unfavorable. (Other comments were either mixed, neutral, or indifferent.) And like restaurateurs, the hoteliers' ratings regarding the individual service attributes clearly indicated a preponderance of compliments relative to complaints.

Patterns

Compared to compliments, guests were more likely to complain about such service areas as the price of rooms, speed of service, availability of parking and accommodations, checkout times, and adequacy of credit. It would seem that high performance in these areas will not enhance the hotel or motel's image in the guest's eyes, but weak performance will seriously detract from the guest's evaluation of the hotel.

The attributes that drew many compliments compared to complaints were the helpful attitude of employees, neatness and spaciousness of the property, convenience of location, management's knowledge of service, and quantity of service (see Exhibit 4).

The areas with mixed results, in which it appears innkeepers might have difficulty maintaining high levels of performance, are cleanliness of the property, quality of service, employee knowledge and service, quietness of surroundings, and speed of service.

A number of attributes didn't make the top ten for either complaints or compliments. We conclude they are not salient or else guests are easily satisfied with these factors.

Typology

The results of this ten-year-old survey are still valuable today. The data seem to fall into a four-fold typology that compares how likely an attribute is to garner compliments versus the frequency of complaints. Some attributes have the capacity mostly to cause dissatisfaction and not satisfaction. Others have the capacity to generate great satisfaction, but rarely cause dissatisfaction. Still others are critical; they can cause either pleasure or pain, depending on how well they are handled. And some are neutral— apparently eliciting no response whatsoever (see Exhibit 5).

Dissatisfiers

Dissatisfiers are more likely to earn a complaint for low performance or absence of the desired feature than anything else. But an operation that exceeds the threshold performance standard apparently will not receive compliments on the attribute. Parking at a restaurant is a good example of a dissatisfier. If guests are always able to find a parking place, they think nothing of it. But if they cannot find parking places or have to walk a block, they are quick to complain about it. Similarly, a guest hardly cares about whether a hotel accepts two or 20 credit cards, as long as one of those cards is the one the guest intends to use. The availability of credit is a nonissue until a customer is left with no way to pay the bill.

In theoretical terms, dissatisfiers are likely to have a performance rating skewed toward the lower end (see Exhibit 6). The typical level of performance for these factors is probably well defined in the form of generally accepted industry practice. The zone of indifference on these factors is likely to be broad, encompassing all but the very top end of the distribution of performance levels.[1]

[1] Robert B. Woodruff, Ernest R. Cadotte, and Roger L. Jenkins, "Modeling Consumer-Satisfaction Processes Using Experience-Based Norms," *Journal of Marketing Research,* 20 (August 1983), pp. 296–304.

The key to guest satisfaction is to concentrate resources on the factors that matter most to guests, such as quality of food and service.

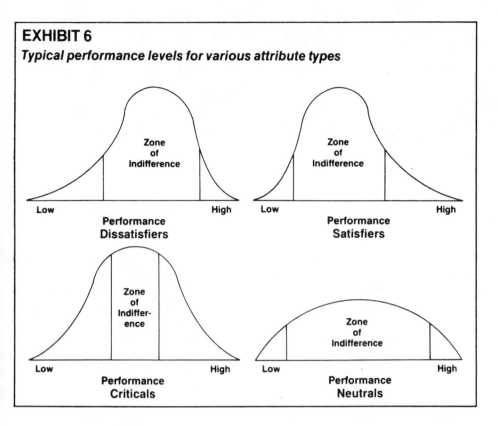

EXHIBIT 6
Typical performance levels for various attribute types

Zone of Indifference

Low — Performance — High
Dissatisfiers

Zone of Indifference

Low — Performance — High
Satisfiers

Zone of Indifference

Low — Performance — High
Criticals

Zone of Indifference

Low — Performance — High
Neutrals

From management's point of view, dissatisfiers represent the necessary or basic (but not sufficient) conditions of service performance. Minimum performance must be maintained in these areas, but efforts to achieve high performance will probably not be noticed or rewarded by customers.

Satisfiers

Satisfiers are those variables where unusual performance apparently elicits compliments, but average performance or even the absence of the feature will probably not cause dissatisfaction or complaints. Hyatt Regency atrium lobbies are good examples of satisfiers. Most hotel and motel lobbies do not merit much comment. Generally of modest size, they are usually decorated in earth tones with unremarkable furniture. In contrast, the atrium lobbies are large, open spaces, with trees, hanging plants, and glass-encased elevators. The absence of these large, open lobbies will generally not cause dissatisfaction, but when they are present, the guest receives a pleasant surprise.

Large portions are an example of a restaurant satisfier. Most restaurants feature standard-size portions for their entrees and side dishes, and garnishes of parsley, lettuce, or tomatoes are typically used to create an impression of a full plate. Normal portions do not generate much discussion or dissatisfaction. In contrast, a heaping full plate often delights the restaurant guest.

From a theoretical viewpoint, satisfiers are probably skewed toward the upper end of the performance curve. Most offerings are probably distributed in a narrow band around an industry norm or standard. Customers have probably become accustomed to this standard, which now falls into their zone of indifference.

From a management viewpoint, satisfiers represent an opportunity to move ahead of the pack. Custom-

ers appear receptive to higher levels of performance on these attributes by virtue of their willingness to go out of their way to compliment the establishment. Efforts to improve performance in these areas may yield favorable returns.

"Criticals"

Critical variables are capable of eliciting both positive and negative feelings, depending on the situation. Quality of service, for instance, ranks high in both industries in eliciting both complaints and compliments, probably because it is intangible and difficult to control. Service is highly dependent upon an establishment's personnel, and its consistency probably reflects the natural variability of human endeavor.

Critical factors in restaurants involve the heart of the food-service business: helpful attitude of employees, food quality, and quantity of service. Critical factors are also the key to hotel and motel operations: cleanliness, quality of service, employee knowledge and service, and quietness of surroundings.

From a theoretical viewpoint, we suspect there is a great variation in the distribution of performance of critical variables. Customers may also be more sensitive to what is acceptable, since these attributes appear to be the heart of the hospitality industry. The zone of customer indifference may be quite narrow, for this reason.

From a management viewpoint, critical factors represent both a threat and an opportunity. At the very least, management must control the delivery mechanism and provide a minimally acceptable performance. Hotel rooms must be quiet, for instance, and restaurant food must taste good. Once minimum standards are met, management can shift its resources to providing higher levels of performance on a consistent basis.

Neutrals

The several factors that received neither a great number of compliments nor many complaints are probably either not salient to guests or easily brought up to guests' standards.

In Transition

The classifications of these factors constantly change. Some satisfier-type attributes were probably critical at one time. Higher industry standards, though, may have improved performance to the extent that most hotels are able to meet guests' requirements on these factors. (Few lobbies are downright dingy, for instance.) Similarly, some neutral values may have been dissatisfiers, but the incidence of poor performance has either been reduced, or the attribute now appears industry-wide. Extended hours in restaurants, once a rarity, are now common enough to be expected by many customers. Short hours of operation, once neutral, now could be a dissatisfier.

We believe it may be possible to shift some neutral variables into the satisfier category. Burger King's "have it your way" campaign effectively caused some consumers to place more importance on being able to make the hamburger to order rather than to accept it as is. The ability to get a custom burger easily would then be a pleasant surprise.

Improving Guest Satisfaction

The restaurant and lodging surveys highlight the service areas that are important to guests. With so many executives reporting similar experiences, it seems likely that the top complaint and compliment categories are customer motivators. If so, these items deserve special attention. If customers are regularly willing to go out of their way to speak out about a certain attribute,

they are certainly willing to take the performance on that attribute into account when making a decision about whether to return to a hotel or restaurant. In setting priorities, therefore, you should keep a watchful eye on the service areas at the top of each list.

Dissatisfiers particularly require management control to prevent poor performance. Minimum standards should be established, and the focus should be on maintaining these standards. The industry norm is probably an acceptable standard for a dissatisfier, since an exceptional performance probably won't be noticed. Be as good as your competition, but do not waste resources trying to be better.

Satisfiers, on the other hand, represent an opportunity to shine, to move ahead of the pack, and to stand out from the crowd. Your objective is to achieve a customer reaction of "Hey, that's great!," "What a clever idea!," or "What a nice place to come to!" The emphasis is on pleasantly surprising the guest.

Industry norms are again helpful in establishing performance goals for satisfiers. Unlike dissatisfiers, however, hitting the norm is not good enough. You must be *noticeably* better than your competition to penetrate the guest's consciousness. Study successful competitors, and look for better ways to do the job or fill the need. Innovation, not imitation, is the key.

Critical factors deserve special attention, because of their potential for both hurting and helping a business. Like dissatisfiers, minimum standards must be set to avoid negative responses to your service. A policy of maintaining minimum standards fails to take advantage of the opportunity to please guests on these factors.

It is not enough, for example, to require that floors be cleaned twice a day or to require that all customers be greeted with a smile. These tasks can become very mechanical and may miss the objective. Guests are pleased to find your facility clean and your staff friendly, but make sure that the guests are all treated as if they were special. For the critical attributes, the objective is to raise performance beyond the norm. The guests will respond positively.

These recommendations involve determining competitive norms and performing at or above industry standards. This is because guest satisfaction is determined on both an absolute and a relative basis. Basic needs of hunger, shelter, comfort, and safety must be met, of course, but this is usually not an issue in today's market. Most restaurants and hotels can satisfy basic needs.

The question is, how do the customers judge performance after the basics are satisfied? They compare your service to what they have experienced elsewhere. If they are accustomed to better treatment than what you accord them, they will probably be dissatisfied. But if your waitress is friendlier, your hamburger tastier, and your room cleaner than most, customers will be motivated to return and to recommend your business to others.

The use of industry norms as benchmarks for comparison will always be a challenge, because they represent moving targets. Good ideas are quickly copied. What was a differential advantage last year may become a requirement next year. Consequently, your eye must always be on the competition. Be at least as good as the competition on dissatisfiers, and far better on satisfiers and critical factors, and your guests will be giving you compliments and more business.

Service Management Concepts:
Implications for Hospitality Management

by
K. Michael Haywood
Associate Professor
School of Hotel and Food Administration
University of Guelph, Ontario, Canada

The study and application of hospitality management has progressed on its own for many years; however, managers are not immune to the knowledge gained from study of other service industries. The author synthesizes what is happening in the area of service management, looks at its relevance to hospitality management, and identifies a few important implications of service management for hospitality managers.

With the burgeoning of service industries and the need to adopt distinctive service orientations, there has been an accompanying demand for more appropriate management concepts, approaches, and techniques. While much of what we already know about effective management applies to service industries, some of the traditional concepts of management are inadequate in solving the problems faced by service businesses.

If a body of knowledge to be known as "service management" already exists, or is being developed, where does it fit relative to hospitality management? One way to answer the question is shown in Figure 1. The highest level of abstraction, theories of general management, constitutes a body of knowledge with general applicability wherever there is a business. Unfortunately, at that level of abstraction the transition from concept or theory to managerial application is often arduous. As the level of abstraction reduces, the range of application narrows, but the transition to use is easier. Thus at the lowest level we expect the techniques and concepts that have been developed in the area of hospitality management to have direct and immediate application to the industry but little capacity for generalization.

Until recently, management concepts and techniques at the first level of abstraction only existed and were generalizable for a vast array of manufacturing industries. Service industries, including hospitality businesses, borrowed from this body of knowledge, but the resulting "fit" has often been judged to be poor. With the growing importance of service industries, a need for a new body of knowledge is beginning to fill the void for a first level of abstraction for service industries, and as an important part of the service sector, hospitality businesses are bound to benefit.

Figure 1
A Context for Service Management

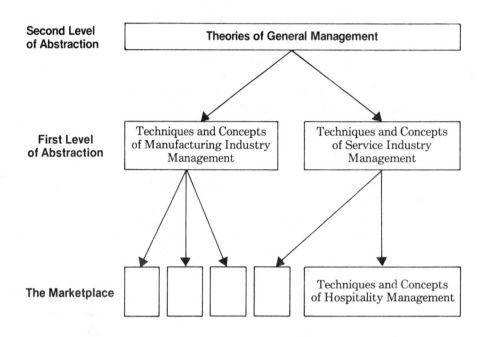

Second Level of Abstraction: Theories of General Management

First Level of Abstraction: Techniques and Concepts of Manufacturing Industry Management — Techniques and Concepts of Service Industry Management

The Marketplace: Techniques and Concepts of Hospitality Management

Source: Adapted from John Bateson, et. al., *Testing a Conceptual Framework for Consumer Service Marketing.*

There are four criteria used to judge service management:

- the perceived body of common problems at the management level
- the real structural difference between services and goods
- the conceptualization of the management decision process
- the link between the common problems, structural differences and decision processes[1]

Common Problems Exist at Management Level

Service businesses are said to suffer from low productivity or output of service workers. This often results in a faster rate of price increases in comparison to goods. However, introduction of a "production line" approach, increased computerization, and use of new technological advances is serving to mitigate this problem. In a classic study of four service industries in France-distribution, banking, hotel and transportation-a more specific set of common problems has been identified:

Problems for the organization

- lack of inventories to balance supply and demand (services can't be stored)

- no patent protection

- complex employee/client interface

- physical setting and environment effect quality of service but are difficult to control

- growth of firm requires development of its own distribution network

- innovation is difficult because it implies the need for client education to change behavior

Problems for the client

- client must have considerable confidence in the firm and its ability to deliver the service

- a "mental image" of the service is difficult to formulate

- reduction of perceived risk in buying the service necessitates word of mouth or personal influence

- there is a tendency to become emotionally involved with a service firm when consuming the service[2]

These and other concerns such as the difficulty in setting prices or the difficulty in centralizing production have prompted many questions. Can service businesses become less people-intensive (more industrialized) while maintaining "personalization" and/or improving service quality? Can positive word-of-mouth be stimulated? How should customers be managed in order to even out demand? What are the best methods for communicating a clear image of the service? Clearly hospitality businesses share many of these problems with other service businesses.

Structural Differences Can Be Found

Most of the previously-noted problems can be traced back to the differences that exist between services and goods. A review of the literature on the unique characteristics of services suggests that the key structural difference hinges on the intangibility of services.[3] That is, services can't be touched or easily understood; they are acts or performances. Service is an outcome between a physical environment and/or facilitating goods, the service personnel, and the customer. Therefore, there is more or less a simultaneous production/consumption of the service. This results in an inability to inventory, the necessity to deal with or sell directly to the customer, the need for multi-site locations close to the customer, and so on. It is this shared characteristic of intangibility that provides hospitality businesses with an identifiable link to other service businesses.

It should be noted, however, that there are significant differences among services businesses with regard to the intensity or importance of intangibility. Hospitality business have important tangible attributes; in fact, food goes through a manufacturing process.

Lovelock suggests, therefore, that service businesses be distinguished from one another.[4] His categorization is based on marketing characteristics consisting of five attributes:

- the nature of the service encountered

- the degree of customization and judgment on the part of the service provider

- the nature of demand and supply for the service

- the manner in which the service is delivered

Models Are Developed for the Management Decision Process

Over the past few years a variety of system models have been developed to explain the service process, that is, how the service is designed, produced, delivered, and consumed. Development of these models has grown out of different approaches to the question: "What is service management?" At the Harvard Business School, for example, Sasser, Olsen, and Wyckoff attacked the problem from the point-of-view of manufacturing strategy,[5] while Eiglier and Langeard at the Universite de Droit approached it from the perspective of marketing.[6] More recent conceptualizations have been oriented toward an operations research focus,[7] or a strategic, organizational, and management leadership focus.[8] Each of these models is depicted in Appendices A-E. There is sufficient similarity among them that allows us to identify and characterize their basic decision elements: the customer/client, the service concept, the service delivery system, service levels, and the service provider.

The customer/client: In asking the question: "How shall we approach the management of service?," Albrecht and Zemke note the central importance of the customer: "This service triangle, as we call it (see Appendix D), represents the three elements of service strategy, people, and systems as more or less revolving around the customer in a creative interplay."[9] The centrality of the customer is common to each of the models. The customer is identified as the key to defining the nature of the service and to determining how it is delivered. As such it is crucial for service management to

- identify the particular types of customer for which the service system is designed

- have a clear understanding of customers' expectations and perceptions so that the service concept can be well defined, communicated, and produced

- understand and know how to deal with the customer as a part of and/or participant (physically, intellectually, or emotionally) in the service delivery system

The service concept: The intangible nature of services and the presence of the consumer in the process requires development of a total service experience. For this reason services are often identified as packages consisting of four attributes:

- the physical items or facilitating goods, e.g., food, utensils

- the supporting facility, e.g., the hotel, a dining room

- the sensual benefits or explicit services, e.g., taste, aroma, social and structural atmospheres

- the psychological benefits or implicit services, e.g., comfort, status, reassurance

In other words, it is recognized that each service requires the use or presence of equipment, physical facilities, or hardware. The intangible services can be realized through interaction with contact personnel, the supporting mechanisms, and even other clientele.

Richard Normann differentiates between core services, the big benefits the customer is looking for, and peripheral services, the little things, or added bonuses that go along with the big benefits.[10] Similarly, Albrecht and Zemke differentiate between the primary service package and the secondary service package:

- **Primary service package:** The center piece of your service offering. It is your basic reason for being in business....It needs to reflect the overriding logic of your service strategy and needs to offer a natural, compatible set of goods, services, and experiences that go together in the customer's mind to form an impression of high value.

- **Secondary service package:** To support, complement, and add value to your primary service package. The secondary package should not be a hodge podge of 'extras' thrown in with no forethought. All of these secondary service features should provide 'leverage,' that is, help build up the value of the total package in the customer's eyes.[11]

In a highly competitive situation, there is a synergistic relationship between the primary and secondary service packages that can lead to creative and effective approaches to the design of the service.

Service delivery system: Sasser, et. al., describe the service delivery system as a process that creates the service and delivers it simultaneously to the customer, i.e., the customer is actively involved in the process.[12] Design of the delivery system, however, is contingent upon the definition of the service package. Examples of approaches to service system design are depicted in Figures 2 and 3 and range from personalized service to self-service. It has been noted that the pressures for control and lower costs tend to force many service businesses to decrease the degree of interaction and customization, thereby creating a service factory.[13]

The service factory frequently results in a movement away from personalized service toward self service. Paradoxically, this translates in-

Figure 2
Approaches to Design of Delivery Systems

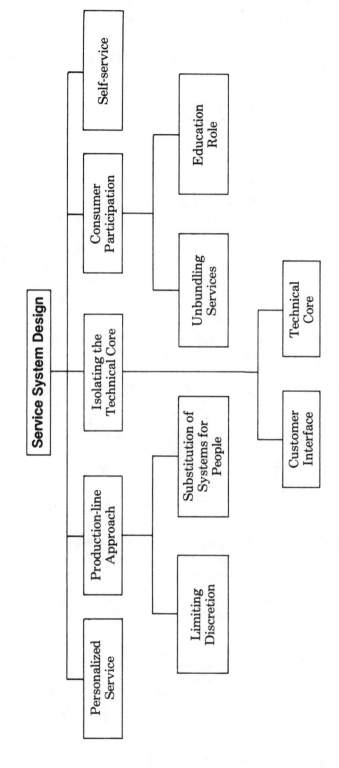

Source: James A. Fitzsimmons and Robert S. Sullivan, *Service Operations Management*, p. 149.

Figure 3
Fitzsimmons and Sullivan's Service System

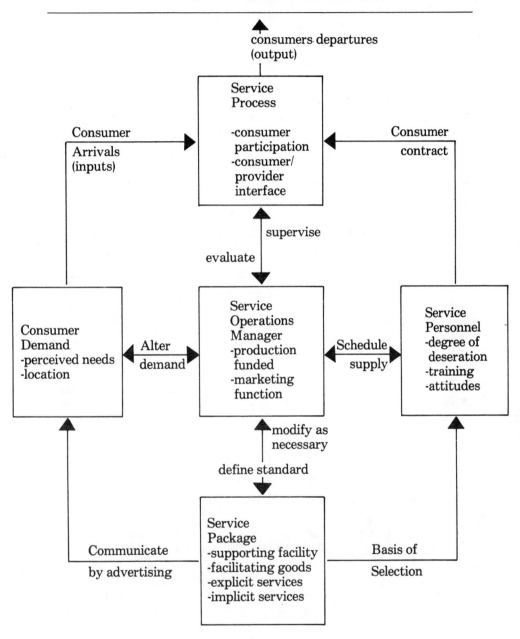

Source: James A. Fitzsimmons and Robert S. Sullivan, *Service Operations Management*, p. 27.

to managing customers. Costs are cut and profits boosted by turning customers into more efficient "employees." However, unless customers are willing to perform as expected and understand what they are expected to do and where they must go to do it, frustration, stress, and dissatisfaction will result. Consequently, service delivery systems must be designed with the customer in mind and customers may have to be educated if they are to learn how to do their "jobs."

Service levels: Sasser, et al., refer to service level as "the consumer's perception of the quality of service."[14] Since customers explicitly and implicitly rank different attributes of the service package (e.g., waiting time, cleanliness, staff attitude, etc.) on the basis of service level and price, management must determine the appropriate mix and balance of service attributes and how they can best be designed into the service delivery system. Of course, other key concerns revolve around the correct communication of the service concept with emphasis on the appropriate attributes, managing the service levels through training and quality assurance programs, and maintaining corporate focus on the critical success factors.

Service provider: The unique characteristic of service is the interaction or interplay of employees with every other aspect of the service system. Since each and every service encounter gives rise to dozens of what have been called "moments of truth," individuals in the organization must know their role and responsibility in producing and delivering the service attributes important to the customer. Well-trained, helpful, and courteous staff create memorable moments. Unfriendly, uncooperative, or uninterested staff create dull and disastrous moments. Clearly the survival of organizations is contingent upon ensuring a highly motivated and committed staff.

As Normann emphasizes, service businesses are "personality intensive" in that they enjoy a high degree of discretion to influence specific situations.[15] Therefore, Albrecht and Zemke's warning, "If you're not serving the customer, you'd better be serving someone who is," is a constant reminder of what management must do to ensure the outcome of each moment of truth.[16]

Since the ultimate success of service businesses is dependent upon the quality of service provided, special attention must be paid to the service encounter. In particular, attention must be given to contact employees who provide what may be termed "emotional labor."[17] Therefore, employee needs and problems in service encounters need to be balanced against the needs and expectations of customers. Service encounters should not be left to chance; they must be properly managed.[18]

Links Must Be Made Between Problems and Decisions

Each of the service management models has a slightly different perspective when it comes to linking the essential service elements. Since service is a social process, the most important part of management consists of identifying the critical factors which make the particular service system function and of designing powerful ways of controlling and maintaining these attributes in a concrete manner. Therefore, we differentiate between an overall service strategy and an operational strategy.

Service strategy: First and foremost in a service strategy is the need to position the service organization in the marketplace. A service strategy is a distinctive formula for delivery of a service; such a strategy is keyed to a well-chosen benefit premise that is valuable to the customer and that establishes an effective competitive position.[19] This chosen strategy must be based on a thorough assessment of customer expectations, analysis of competitive strengths and weaknesses, and the alignment of customer expectations with service capabilities. Strategy should serve as an organizing principle that allows contact personnel to channel their efforts toward benefit-oriented services that make a significant different in the eye of the customer; it should also help describe the value to be offered.

To this end Heskett shows how Porter's three generic competitive strategies–overall cost leadership, differentiation, and focus–can be matched to the level of service delivered (as perceived by customers) and cost of service delivery.[20] However, a service concept cannot be all things to all people. It must also be reviewed in the context of innovation segmentation.

Service strategy also takes into account corporate philosophy. Choice and commitment to a service strategy relies largely on a prevailing corporate culture and normative philosophy. Normann feels that the following ingredients epitomize a solid service organization:[21]

- orientation toward quality and excellence

- development of a long-term relationship with clients

- investment in people and high social technology orientation

- rigorous control systems with regard to factors vital to success in the client relationship

- strong focus on delivering client value for the money and tailoring services to particular market segments.

Implementation of these attributes requires strong leadership. Therefore, leaders must be visible, set and communicate standards, evaluate and reward people, make their organization credible, and create an image that reinforces the strategic vision. There are, therefore, a number of dimensions to operating strategy--the design of services, quality and productivity, marketing of services, and operations research.

Operating strategy/design of services: Every service system requires procedures to ensure that the service package is properly designed. Upon implementation, systems must then be put in place to ensure that the "right" things are done right.

Shostak suggests that service organizations should subject service development to more rigorous analysis and control.[22] By identifying the processes that constitute the service, by noting the fail points, and by establishing a time frame and analyzing profitability, a service blueprint can be created. She indicates that such a tool is useful in helping to highlight tangible evidence, plan service encounters, modify a service, focus on quality and productivity improvements, and determine where automation may fit and where personalized human contact should be maintained.

Operating strategy/quality and productivity: Virtually all the models of service systems note that successful services are those that are predictable, uniform, and dependable. Hence the importance of setting and monitoring standards for quality and productivity. However, service quality is not merely a mechanistic procedure. First of all, quality must be viewed as a philosophy pervading a whole organization: It refers to an attitude of excellence. Secondly, service quality must be seen in relative terms--relative to expectations, competitive situation, and employee capabilities--as well as in absolute terms.

Service quality invariably focuses on customer/personnel interactions. To positively influence this interaction Normann suggests that service firms have to

- get employees to empathize with client needs and to find ways to adapt accordingly

- use systems and tools to reinforce the position of the service provider, creating and enriching the interaction with the client

- create opportunities for interaction so that the employee can receive positive feedback

- shape the expectations of the client and prepare him to enter the interaction in such a way as to contribute to the social dynamic that engenders his own quality experience

- ensure that a positive, open, and service-minded climate pervades the organization[23]

However, both Normann and Hothschild question how far managers can go in improving the quality of interpersonal encounters.[24] For example, it is possible to offend the more general goals of human dignity, divert attention from more genuine attitudes of care and helpfulness, and damage the internal climate of trust and control.

Since the service concept and the appropriate market segmentation are the first factors to consider in any discussion of quality, service managers must make sure that the right people are in the job in the first place. Quality must also be built into the purchases of all other ingredients in the service package. For example, quality in the service delivery system must be assured. That means that such things as appropriate waiting and service times must be determined and standards set and enforced.

Questions relating to the productivity of services can't be divorced from issues of quality. It is not enough to restructure jobs, substitute mechanical devices or computers for service personnel, or encourage greater customer participation. Productivity can only be enhanced positively when firms concentrate on developing customer trust, understanding customers' habits, pre-testing new procedures or equipment, understanding customers' motivations and behavior, and teaching customers how to use service innovations in a non-threatening way.

Operational strategy/marketing of services: Marketing practitioners and academics are actively exploring, applying, and extending marketing ideas and practices in a wide range of service situations. Service marketing books by Rathmell,[25] Lovelock,[26] Cowell,[27] the service marketing conference proceedings of the American Marketing Association,[28] and recent working papers on service marketing by the Marketing Science Institute[29] have created a wealth of new marketing knowledge. Not only is the concept of "product" being rethought, but marketing mix ingredients have been expanded. Marketing strategy is being developed to encourage word of mouth communication; customers are being given more tangible clues with which to judge and evaluate services; and differentiation between advertising and internal marketing activities is being advised.

Operations/strategy/operations research: Methods and techniques for establishing and controlling service levels, designing jobs, planning and managing capacity, forecasting demand, determining facility locations, etc. are part of the new thrust into operations research applied to service firms.[30] As in the case of service marketing, the distinctive characteristics of service operations suggest new insights into the problems of managing service capacity and points to the need to integrate the functions of marketing and operations in services. For example, if service is derived from the interaction of customers with the service facilities and with customers contact personnel, then the different functional departments--operations, marketing and personnel--are forced to be interdependent (See Figure 3).

Figure 3
The Service Management Triangle

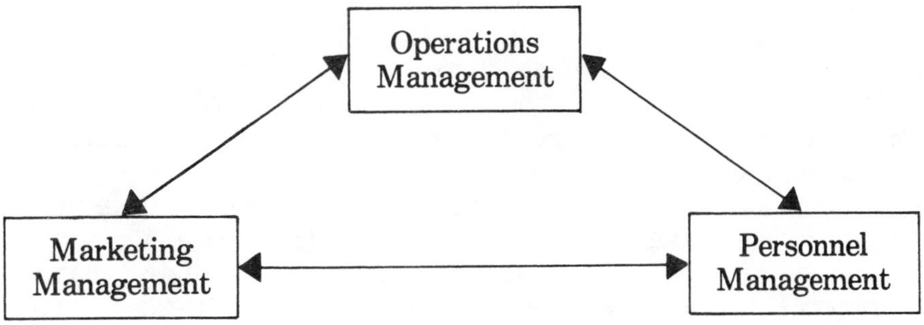

In many service businesses, however, interdependence is hard to achieve. Independence tends to be the operative word with operations guiding the way because of its predominant position. As a result, there is often a lack of balance between different orientations (cost versus revenue), different time horizons (short versus long), different motivations for change (technology driven versus customer-driven), and different approaches to change (traditional versus innovative).

Service management is becoming a recognized and accepted subset of general management. Given the continued growth of the service sector, and the almost universal belief by managers and academics that service management is in certain key respects different from goods or manufacturing based management, the rapid growth of service management literature in recent years is not surprising. A further acceleration of this interest and research activity in the years ahead is not only expected but is necessary as far more questions than answers exist at this time.

Implications Exist for Hospitality Management

For hospitality managers and educators numerous intriguing implications arise from a study of the field of service management. Knowledge of service management concepts introduces opportunities to more thoroughly understand and improve hospitality management. Possible courses of action that lead from our understanding of service management are numerous.

First and foremost is the necessity for managers to become thoroughly conversant with the service management literature. In this way new service management concepts and linkages can be explained and introduced into existing management systems. For this to occur all students, whether they be part of corporate training programs or enrolled in a college or university program, should be given the opportunity to work on a wide range of service management problems in a variety of service industry settings. By understanding that airline or advertising companies share similar concerns, future hospitality managers will be able to capitalize on the service concepts used or found in other service settings. Furthermore, hospitality firms should research or help fund research to expand the application of service management concepts in a hospitality industry context.

A high quality service orientation is such a powerful competitive weapon that it is now recognized as an essential part of business strategy, not a frill. Hospitality businesses that cannot demonstrate a significant commitment to the needs of their guests will be left further and further behind. In every successful service business quality of service has become top management's most important issue.

Unfortunately, service is taken so much for granted by hospitality managers that the nuances and the subtleties of the service encountered are frequently ignored. By noting how other service businesses handle the practical difficulties involved in designing and managing encounters from a blend of views--guest perceptions, provider characteristics, and production realities--hospitality managers can develop exciting insights into the psychology of employee/guest interactions as well as the field of environmental psychology or the guest/setting interactions.

The design of service delivery systems often gets short shrift in hospitality businesses. Not only is the simultaneous production and consumption of service often ignored, but the whole design process is often left in the hands of misinformed architects and interior designers whose focus is primarily aesthetic. Continuous emphasis on lowering labor costs, improving guest and employees satisfaction, and reducing real and perceived levels of risk will require hospitality managers to become more diligent.

By studying the three basic approaches to the design of service delivery systems utilized by other service businesses, the technocratic production line approach, the consumer participation approach, and the consumer high-low contact approach,[31] new opportunities for simultaneously improving productivity and quality may be discovered.

Opinions may differ on the impact of service management concepts, but probably the most important message is the radical departure from the standard organizational charts as depictions of how a business works. By viewing businesses as processes rather than merely as structures, it becomes easier to see the customer as the center of focus, shaping and shaped by the integration of the service strategy, the operating systems, and the service providers. In this constant interplay, management's responsibility is to service the needs of the people who are serving the customers. Hospitality managers may want to seriously deliberate on this point and assess their role in providing honest-to-goodness service and hospitality within their own firms.

Service management places particular emphasis on a strategic outlook. Hospitality firms would be wise to carefully examine how they are perceived in the marketplace vis-a-vis their service concept, position, competitive situation, and management's leadership abilities. As many service businesses are beginning to discover continually rising customer expectations, competing service concepts, difficulties in building a loyal and dedicated staff, and quickly evolving technology provide the right conditions for obsolescence. Learning from the experiences of other service firms can help keep a company on track, that is, providing needed and valued services.

Appendix A
Sasser, Olsen and Wyckoff's Service System

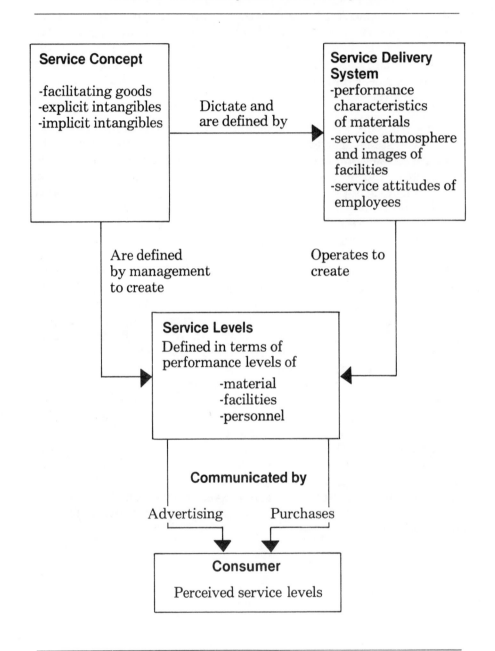

Source: W. Earl Sasser, R. Dave Olsen and D. Daryl Wyckoff
Management of Service Operations: Text, Cases and Readings, p. 21.

Appendix B
Eiglier and Langeard's Service System

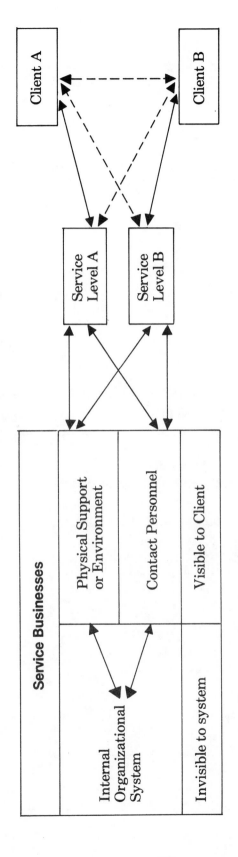

Source: Pierre Eiglier and Eric Langeard, "Principles de Politique Marketing pour les Enterprises de Services," Working Paper, L'Institut d'Administration des Entreprises, Universite de Droit d'Economie et des Science's d'Aix Marseille, December 1976.

Appendix C
Normann's Service System

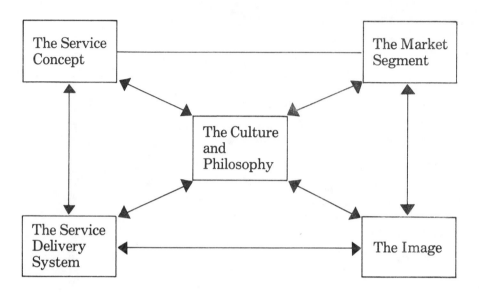

Source: Richard Normann, *Service Management: Strategy and Leadership in Service Businesses,* p. 20.

Appendix D
Albrecht and Zemke's Service System

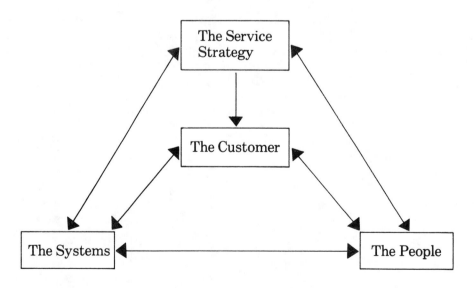

Source: Karl Albrecht and Ron Zemke, *Service America: Doing Business in the New Economy,* p. 42.

Appendix E
Heskett's Service System

Target Market Segments

Positioning

Service Concept

Value Cost Leveraging

Operating Strategy

Service System Integration

Service Delivery System

☐ Basic Element

⌐⌐ Integrative Element

Source: *Source:* James L. Heskett, *Managing in the Service Economy,* p. 30.

References

[1]John Bateson, et al., *Testing a Conceptual Framework for Consumer Service Marketing*, (Cambridge, Mass.: Marketing Science Institute, 1978), pp. 8-9.

[2]*Ibid.*, p. 10

[3]*Ibid.*, p. 11, and John Bateson. "Why We Need Consumer Marketing," in O.C. Farrell, et al., *Conceptual and Theoretical Development in Marketing*, (Chicago, Ill.: American Marketing Association, 1978), pp. 131-146.

[4]Christopher H. Lovelock, "Classifying Services to Gain Strategic Marketing Insights," *Journal of Marketing*, (Summer 1983), pp. 9-20.

[5]W. Earl Sasser, R. Paul Olsen and D. Daryl Wyckoff, *Management of Service Operations: Text, Cases and Readings*, (Boston, Mass.: Allyn and Bacon, 1978), p. IX.

[6]Pierre Eiglier and E. Langeard, "Une Approache Nouvelle du Marketing des Services," *Revue Francaise de Gestron*, (March-April, 1975), p. 1.

[7]James A. Fitzsimmons and Robert J. Sullivan, *Service Operations Management*, (New York: McGraw-Hill, 1982), p. 2.

[8]Richard Normann, *Service Management: Study and Leadership in Service Businesses*, (New York: John Wiley & Sons, 1984), p. xi; Karl Albrecht and Ron Zamke, *Service America: Doing Business in the New Economy*, (Homewood, Ill.: Dow Jones-Irwin, 1984), p. vi; James L. Heskett, *Managing in the Service Economy*, (Boston, Mass.: Harvard Business School Press, 1986), p. 1.

[9]Albrecht and Zemke, *op. cit.*, p. 40.

[10]Normann, *op. cit.*, p. 23.

[11]Albrecht and Zemke, *op. cit.*, p. 81.

[12]Sasser, et al., *op. cit.*, pp. 14-15.

[13]Roger W. Schmenner, "How Can Service Businesses Survive and Prosper?" *Sloan Management Review*, (Spring 1986), pp. 21-32.

[14]Sasser, et al., *op. cit.*, 18-19.

[15]Norman, *op. cit.*, pp. 9-10.

[16]Albrecht and Zemke, *op. cit.*, p. 40.

[17]Arlie Russell Hochschild, *The Managed Heart: Commercialization of Human Feeling*, (Berkeley, Calif.: University of California Press, 1983), p. 7.

[18]John A. Czepiel, et al., *The Service Encounter: Managing Employee/Customer Interaction in Service Businesses*, (Lexington Mass: Lexington Books, 1985), p. IX. "Each of the articles in this book deals with key issues in managing service encounters, for example, the psychology of waiting lines, risk perceptions, environmental psychology, and non-verbal communication."

[19]Albrecht and Zemke, *op. cit.*, p. 64.

[20]Heckett, *op. cit.*, pp. 46-47.

[21]Normann, *op. cit.*, pp. 130-132.

[22]G. Lynn Shostack, "Designing Services That Deliver," *Harvard Business Review*, (January-February 1984), pp. 33-39.

[23]Normann, *op. cit.*, pp. 44-50; and Hochschild, *op. cit.*, pp. 89-136.

[24]Normann, *op. cit.*, pp. 108-110.

[25]John M. Rathmell, *Marketing in the Service Sector*, (Cambridge, Mass.: Wintrop Publications, 1974).

[26]Christopher H. Lovelock, *Service Marketing*, (Englewood Cliffs, N.J.: Prentice-Hall, 1984).

[27]David Cowell, *The Marketing of Services*, (London: Heinemann, 1984).

[28]James H. Donnelly and William R. George, *Marketing of Services*, (Chicago, Ill.: American Marketing Association, 1981).

[29]John A. Czepiel, *Managing Customer Satisfaction in Consumer Service Businesses*, (Cambridge, Mass.: Marketing Science Institute, 1980).

[30]Sasser, et al., *op. cit.*, pp. 177-301; Fitzsimmons and Sullivan, p. 11. "Each of these authors provides an operations research focus, though their individual approach to the topic is different."

[31]Fitzsimmons and Sullivan, *op. cit.*, pp. 148-154.

A bigger picture: some context

Introduction by Ken McCleary

We in the United States do not operate in a microcosm. U.S. firms are impacted on by foreign competition and *vice versa*. The list of American firm operating abroad is long and includes, for example, Marriott, Holiday Inns, Westin, Hilton, Hyatt, to name just a few. A walk down the *Champs-Elysees* from the *Arc de Triomphe* will land you in a Burger King or McDonald's, and Kentucky Fried Chicken is available from Tokyo to Grand Caymen Island.

With takeover mania affecting the hospitality industry as dramatically as other industries, it's difficult to keep up with who owns whom. Ramada, Burger King and Stouffer's are now owned by corporations from Hong Kong, Great Britain and Switzerland, respectively. A result: people of various nationalities traveling around the world to jointly-manage hospitality operations. And, of course, it is the hospitality industry that services many of the needs of all international travelers. As Edward Pritchard, president of Compri Hotel Systems in Phoenix, Arizona has said, "This is the decade for globalization, and to be successful a company must create a marketing network worldwide." This is the bigger picture.

A Framework for International Marketing provides a very large view of marketing, for it deals with marketing an entire country. But the principles laid out in the article can be used for individual products. Marketing is at the same time different and alike as applied in a worldwide context.

A framework for national tourism marketing

Ken W. McCleary

Department of Marketing and Hospitality Services Administration, Central Michigan University, Mount Pleasant, MI 48859, U.S.A.

Marketing an entire country is a difficult task. As products, countries are complex entities with many dimensions. However, in order to do an effective job of attracting tourists, it is important for a nation to use marketing tools to develop an image and communicate with its target markets. This paper provides a general framework.

Key words: tourism   marketing   planning   pricing   promotion   distribution

Many individual states in the United States of America have found success in aggressive marketing programs. Perhaps the most well known program was developed by the State of New York and centers around the slogan 'I love New York' (Maas, 1980). The success of the New York program has led other states to also take a serious look at the potential of developing coordinated, comprehensive tourism marketing plans. For example, the State of Michigan raised the budget of its Michigan Travel Bureau from $3.6 million in 1981–82 to $8.5 million in 1982–83 when its 'Say Yes To Michigan!' promotional campaign was launched. Of the total budget, $4.7 million was earmarked for the Say Yes! program. The campaign was so successful that an additional $1.35 million was added to the budget in 1985–86 when the campaign was renewed under the shortened slogan of 'YesM!ch!gan' (Morris, 1986).

Other states such as Florida, Texas and Illinois as well as Canadian provinces like Quebec and Ontario have also discovered the usefulness of well constructed marketing plans and have instituted sound programs. It is difficult to market entire states and provinces with all their diversity. It is equally, and in many cases more, difficult to market an entire country. The difficulty grows with the size and diversity of the nation. But a comprehensive tourism plan, aimed at building a coherent image in potential visitors' minds is an efficient and effective way of maximizing a country's benefits from tourism, particularly when compared to a fragmented and uncoordinated effort.

There are countries which have already implemented sound marketing plans for their tourism sector. As a result, tourism has become an effective means of earning foreign exchange and benefiting the country's population. The Cayman Islands devised a marketing plan in 1977 which has had great success in guiding superstructure growth and attracting new, appealing market segments (Duea and Guernsey, 1984). Jamaica has had some success in remarketing the country by using marketing communication to alter its image of being unsafe for tourists (Duea and Guernsey, 1984).

While smaller countries may have an easier time of developing a clear image and controlling marketing variables, larger countries can also use coordinated marketing programs to improve their tourism pictures. This is particularly true for countries with a poor image or no image at all. However, it takes more than just the use of the marketing variable, promotion, to accomplish the task of developing a comprehensive strategy. The United States has only recently recognized the potential which marketing has for aiding the country in attracting foreign tourists. Through extensive marketing research, the U.S. Travel and Tourism Association has been able to identify basic consumer reasons for traveling to the United States. These identified motivators are now being used to develop an overall theme for a campaign to promote the country as a whole and develop a clearer and more favorable image. The campaign theme, 'America — Catch the Spirit' has already been tested in Germany (Palmer, 1986).

A successful marketing program must reflect the objectives of the company, organization or political entity initiating the program. In the case of tourism marketing for an entire nation, the objectives set must also realistically reflect what the country has to offer relative to the needs of its target markets. For example, a country may have abundant natural resources in the way of sun, sand and water but have a relatively short, uneventful history. Objectives for the country's tourism planning will likely include preservation of its natural resource products and a communications plan which promotes to a sun-loving target market.

The discussion which follows provides a marketing framework for any country, regardless of its size, its objectives or its target market. The focus of a marketing plan is the same for any organization: identify differential competitive advantages, develop a product which exploits advantages and at the same time meets the needs of a target market, select a price compatible with the target market and then make it as easy as possible for consumers to acquire and use the product (in the case of tourism the product is a visit to the country). While the terms used to describe a plan for marketing a country's tourism product may be different than for most products, the principles are much the same. The Appendix entitled 'Checklist for Marketing a Country's Tourism Step by Step', found at the end of this article, provides a summary of how a marketing program might be developed. This 'Checklist' will be referred to throughout the text of the article.

The marketing plan

The first step in devising any plan is to determine what it is that the plan should accomplish. Is the goal of tourism development to increase employment, attract investment dollars or simply to encourage a larger proportion of one target market to spend money in the country? As is indicated in step 1 of the 'Checklist', potential goals should be researched and the specific goal selected should be realistic given what the country has to offer.

Ideally, a marketing oriented organization will first determine the needs of some target market and then produce to meet those needs. From a pragmatic point of view, this is not always possible for a country to do. Certainly it is true that tourism personnel can be trained, the population educated to the values of tourism and infrastructure built. But a country is basically stuck with a certain climate, topography and culture. Thus, research efforts will be constrained by the realism of what is already available. However, some creative approaches to traditional marketing can be helpful in turning disadvantages into marketable characteristics. The key is to select target market segments carefully and to research them thoroughly.

Product elucidation

'The product area (of marketing) is concerned with developing the right "product" for the target market. This product offering may involve a physical good and/or service. The important thing to remember in the product area is that your good — and/or service — should satisfy some customer needs' (McCarthy and Perrault, 1984). The product sought by the tourist is an experience consisting of a combination of goods and services.

A country faces a great deal of difficulty in presenting a clear picture of what kind of experience a tourist is likely to encounter. Once again, the more diverse the country, the more unclear will be the product offering. Thus, a country needs a focus on product elucidation rather than compiling a long list of tourist attractions. A statement such as 'experience life in the home of an Irish farm family' is much more poignant than 'see farmhouses, scenery, castles and pubs in the Irish countryside'.

Often, a tourism offering needs explanation to be sure that confusion over what kind of experience might be expected is eliminated. A simple definition of a country's tourism product is not sufficient. Tourism planners, very familiar with their own country, often have difficulty describing their own product in lucid terms. To say that their country offers rest and relaxation may bring a clear image of quiet beaches and sunshine to nationals, but to foreign tourists unfamiliar with the country, rest and relaxation may conjure up very different images. While the definition of a cow as 'a domestic bovine animal' may elicit similar images among a variety of adults, to a child who has never seen a cow, the definition means little. Similarly, simply listing the components of a cow will also bring about an unclear image. What is needed for the child to understand a cow is elucidation. Tourists unfamiliar with a country need the same kind of careful guidance.

The first task in developing the tourism product is to conduct a tourism inventory (step 2-A in the 'Checklist'). A comprehensive inventory involves the examination of every area in a country in terms of what it has to offer to the foreign tourist. Restaurants, lodging, historical sites, natural resources such as lakes, rivers and mountains, transportation modes, major industries and cultural events are some of the specific items that would be included. In other words, anything potentially of interest or service to tourists should be listed. To facilitate the compilation of an inventory, a comprehensive list of possible items should be given to researchers to use as a guide. There is a tendency for people who live in an area to overlook items of importance because they have become commonplace to the local environment. Items essential for tourism development but which are not present should be noted for future product improvement.

After an inventory compilation comes the difficult task of deciding how to package a product that presents a clear image of the country. A close look at potential target market segments is helpful in providing direction for combining inventory items and deciding what should be stressed and what should be ignored.,

Larger companies have several product lines; so may countries. Individual regions may be noted for special experiences while individual cities may be noted for certain events. The key, and the most difficult communications task, is to blend the various regions together in a way that presents a general country image which is both desirable and lucid without being overly restrictive. Companies such as General Motors, Nestlé and IBM have been able to produce a good overall image but at the same time are still able to market individual product lines. Thus, a country like Belgium might build a general image of being the friendliest in Europe but still build regional images for commerce, cuisine or history. A danger lies in allowing a regional image to supersede a national image. For example, to many Europeans and Asians, the image of the United States is the Wild West of cowboys and cactus, an image gleaned mostly from American western movies. This image reduces the chances of attracting tourists who might be more inclined to enjoy the gentle charm of the South or the history of the East. The truth is that the cowboy image actually fits very little of the U.S. population. Indeed, many New Yorkers don't even own an automobile, let alone a horse.

It might be argued that it is impossible to take a diverse and complex product like a country and develop a clear image. This argument is not only unfounded, but is dangerous to tourism. If national tourist offices don't overtly select and promote an image, individuals will form their own impression, correct or incorrect. Even worse, travelers will have no image at all and not even consider a country in their evoked set of possible travel experiences (Woodside and Sherrill, 1977). This is not to say that an image must be unidimensional or that it is impossible to target several markets. What is necessary is that something specific and favorable comes to mind when the consumer hears a country's name.

Pricing the tourism experience

The selection of a correct pricing strategy is critical to a firm's profitability, which is the main measure of its success. Profit is usually defined by the equation: total revenue minus total cost equals profit. A country's profit from tourism includes revenue producing results such as higher employment, foreign exchange earnings and product indigenization, and also includes 'profits' in a more general sense such as an increased cultural exchange. Thus, both economic and noneconomic goals must be considered in devising a national pricing stretegy for tourism. Once general goals are set, specific pricing tactics, as shown in step 3 of the 'Checklist', can be selected as part of the overall strategy.

Pricing strategy will be dictated by the target markets selected. Most governments will have more flexibility in influencing pricing than individual firms because of their abilities to levy customs duties, institute airport taxes and award subsidies. However, world tourism is a highly competitive business which means that countries can price themselves out of the market. In addition, pricing can influence the overall image of the country not only in terms of being cheap or expensive, but as being high or low class.

As indicated in step 3-C of the 'Checklist', a country is able to raise the price of the tourism experience by increasing duties and entry taxes. If the goal is to attract upper income tourists, coupling higher prices with controlled building of luxury accommodations is a way of matching the product offering with the target market. On the other hand, some countries expand the range of potential tourists by lowering prices through direct subsidies to national transportation agencies.

Next to the inability to control competitors' prices, the impact of monetary exchange rates is perhaps the most difficult pricing variable to deal with. However, countries which have a philosophy of heavy government involvement in tourism can partially offset exchange rate swings by adjusting taxes on typical tourist expenditures such as lodging and airport departures. In Great Britain, for example, many retail stores make it easy for tourists from outside of the European Economic Community to obtain refunds of the value added tax (VAT) on purchases over a certain amount. In the face of a stronger U.S. dollar, these refunds provide American tourists with a lower price perception of the country.

An important point to remember is that pricing policy has an impact on product image as well as revenue generation. For example, Switzerland is seen by many Americans as having a high priced image which discourages some tourists from spending time there. If a country does not cover a large geographical area, an overt decision to price high in order to maximize revenue from a limited number of upper income tourists may be a wise one, assuming that superstructure and the total tourism experience is compatible with the market. In contrast, a country with a large physical area and strong culture which wishes to encourage cultural exchange, might price lower through encouraging bed and breakfast or youth hostel development and subsidizing rail and bus passes for foreign visitors.

Product distribution

Distribution of the tourism product requires some very specific considerations, as is outlined in step 4 of the 'Checklist'. Traditional methods of delivery used for physical products must be rethought when designing distribution systems for a country's tourism product. The same principles of making the product as accessible as possible at minimum cost are still distribution goals, but the application is different. In many ways, the process for distributing a country's tourism product is the reverse of the process used for tangible products. That is, instead of transporting the product to the consumer, the consumer must be transported to the product. Because the essence of the tourism product is intangibility, the product is incapable of being stored (Lovelock, 1984). Thus, the task of the tourism marketer is to seek a continual flow of product users in the same proportion as product availability. With most tangible products, supply can be expanded by increasing production capacity and warehousing. Much of the tourism product is finite; there are only so many beaches, mountains, etc., and there is a point where cultural carrying capacity is incapable of being expanded (Kaiser and Helber, 1987).

How then, does the tourism marketer improve distribution? Once again, a tourism inventory is necessary. As with any marketing entity starting at a point in time, it is essential to know what products are available and in what quantities. Inventory used in a tourism sense means not only listing physical goods available for consumption by tourists (food, souvenirs, shopping articles, etc.), but also the capacity to meet non-tangible needs (lodging, entertainment, history, etc.). Goods and capacity can both be expanded over the long run, up to the area's carrying capacity. But over the short run, the distribution specialist will seek to match the number of tourists with the current capabilities.

A major distribution trade-off is between cost and the size of shipments. Movers of physical goods seek to keep costs down by shipping in carload, truckload or full container lots. Charter airlines have worked under the same principles to keep fares low. Another trade-off is between speed and cost. The Concorde versus other commercial airplanes is an example of how that trade-off is made in tourist transport. The point is that efficient distribution will match transportation modes and cost trade-offs with the needs of the target market.

Facilitating the flow of tourists from one country to another should be a major goal of tourism distribution. Difficulty in clearing customs is an often voiced complaint of international travelers (Shane, 1986). To facilitate movement, countries could simplify regulations and increase the number of customs officers.

To carry the comparison of the distribution of tourists to the distribution of physical goods to the extreme, another distribution goal should be considered. That goal is to minimize damage in transit and has become a major concern for the tourist carrier in terms of air travel and, with the Achille Lauro incident, boat transport as well. Shippers, like tourists, are aware of what transportation means are the safest and most reliable. Broken goods provide no revenue; neither do tourists blown up in an airplane or shot down at a loading gate.

Without market access a product cannot be successful. Access is provided by channels of distribution, referred to in step 4-D of the 'Checklist'. Countries have available a well developed system in a variety of world markets through established tour wholesalers, travel agents and major packagers. The basic decision becomes which channel arrangements are the best given the target market? Possibilities range from going direct to the consumer by marketing through a government tourism office to using an uncontrolled, loosely arranged system of several intermediaries. The latter type of channel is the most prevalent in international tourism, although state run agencies and wholesalers are common in countries with centralized governments. But even the iron curtain countries recognize the need to distribute through travel agencies in market countries. Perhaps the major role of government should be to encourage the opening of new markets and to ensure that travel intermediaries are regulated to discourage disreputable firms from operating in the country.

To summarize, the distribution process for tourism should:
(1) inventory tourist products and need satisfaction capability;
(2) 'assemble' inventory to match the needs of the target market;
(3) select channels of distribution compatible with the target market;
(4) provide transportation means compatible with the target market;
(5) facilitate movement into the country with efficient customs and within the country with good roads, clear directions and traveler aids.

Promotion

Tourism marketers must rely heavily on promotion. Because most of the tourism product cannot be transported to other countries, it is necessary to rely on verbal and visual depictions of the potential tourism experience. There are ways, however, of providing samples of the product with much the same effect as providing samples of a new product at a supermarket. The idea behind sampling is to provide a taste of the product large enough to let the consumer know what the product is like but small enough to leave him wanting more. Methods which a country might use to provide samples are listed in step 5-A of the 'Checklist' and include mediums such as cultural exhibits, travel trade shows, world fairs and regional expositions. One of the most unique vehicles for introducing international tourism products to a large number of potentially prime target customers is through the World Showcase at Disney World's EPCOT Center near Orlando, Florida. To a lesser degree, sampling takes place through traveling performing arts troupes and the distribution of films describing certain aspects of a country.

Most countries market their tourism product to large numbers of people and the best way to reach a mass market is through media advertising. While most advertising by countries is still through popular travel magazines and newspapers geared toward the ultimate consumer, and through trade publications and direct mail to reach intermediate suppliers, certain countries have turned to limited television and radio spots to augment traditional vehicles.

The rules for selecting promotional techniques for marketing a country, outlined in step 5-B of the 'Checklist', are essentially the same as for any product. The selection of general promotional tools (advertising, personal selling, sales promotion and publicity) will depend upon both the target market and the method of distribution used. If advertising is to be a part of the communications mix even specific media selection will depend on the size, concentration and personal characteristics of the target market.

The point to remember in designing a promotional strategy is to have a clear objective for each expenditure. Objectives should include both the development of a country image and specific demand stimulation. The exhibit of the People's Republic of China at EPCOT is a good example of developing a general image for a country. Visitors who previously had no image of China emerge from the exhibit with the distinct impression that China is a country of diverse natural beauty. The China exhibit does a good job of what Kotler (Kotler, 1980) calls conversional marketing. Conversional marketing is necessary when major target segments actively avoid the product. For many, previous information about China was limited to pictures of

huge armies and images of masses of people packed together in communes. The 360 degree film which surrounds the viewer at EPCOT, changes the image from warriors and crowding to one of a gentle people living in a spacious land of unspoiled beauty.

Once the desired image is communicated, more specific messages can be offered to develop and stimulate more precise market segments. Targeted promotion is more efficient than shotgun promotion for well defined segments. For example, the French might concentrate promotional effort for the Bordeaux and Burgundy wine growing regions by advertising in wine magazines or by putting promotional packages together that travel agents and tour operators can aim at wine societies or individual connoisseurs. Italy and Ireland might use radio as a medium to attract root-seeking travelers from such areas as New York or Philadelphia where there are high concentrations of people of Irish and Italian descent.

While that amalgam of printed brochures and catalogues, known as collateral in the travel trade, is still the mainstay of the industry, other promotional techniques such as personal selling and media advertising should be considered as well. The Italian wine industry was immensely successful during the 1970s in selling specific brands of wine in the United States by first building an image of Italy as a wine country through sales promotion and personal selling. After the image was accepted by suppliers and consumers, the promotion to specific market segments was considerably easier. The successful strategies used for marketing goods internationally can be adapted to market tourism.

Choosing marketing strategies

Like the pieces of a jigsaw puzzle which yield a clear picture when put together properly, marketing activities can be combined to form a clear, precise strategy. Step 6 in the 'Checklist' presents guidelines for strategy development. How marketing tools are used is dictated by the task to be performed. A developing country may have to emphasize product development to build infrastructure and superstructure to stimulate latent demand. Italy, which has a good physical tourism product already but faces problems with crime and terrorism, may emphasize promotion to communicate its efforts to ensure safety and then offer short term price incentives to revitalize demand.

A company devises its marketing strategy based on the characteristics of its products, needs of its target markets and the current environment in which it is operating. Marketing a country for tourism requires the same flexibility and customized marketing strategy to meet its tourism goals.

Selecting specific techniques and tools

The tools and techniques presented in the 'Checklist' are, for the most part, universal and can be used by any country to market its tourism. However, which specific techniques should be used by a specific country is situational and depends on the country's goals, tourism budget and what is available in the target country. Thus, selecting precise strategies, communication media, and channels of distribution is a difficult task which will vary from country to country.

To help ensure success, marketers seek to match their product with the needs of the customer. To do this with an internationally marketed product requires a knowledge of the target country's local environment. Some countries, such as the United States, have large amounts of data gathered on travel patterns and motivations. For example, information as precise as what magazines are read and what television programs are watched by people who have traveled internationally in the last year is published each year in the *Simmons Study of Media and Markets*. This and other reports are valuable aids in selecting specific marketing tactics.

Unfortunately, many countries do not have comprehensive travel data available to help foreign travel marketers. Nevertheless, there is no excuse for not knowing the market before developing a tourism marketing program. It is usually ineffective, costly and can do permanent damage to a country's image if inappropriate marketing is used. At the very least a tourism expert from the target country should be retained as a consultant. As techniques are tentatively selected, they should be exposed to travel experts in the target country for feedback. Also, local travel organizers who are familiar with consumer behavior in the target market should be consulted.

Marketing any product internationally is a challenge. International tourism is at least a product that already holds favorable connotations for most people. By following the framework presented in this article and researching target markets for local nuances, national travel marketers can develop strategies and select specific tools which will be successful in attracting international tourists.

Conclusion

As with a corporation, in order for a country to be successful in marketing its products, it must have a strong marketing department with direct input to tourism product planning decisions. A successful company is well organized and attuned to the market place. A country, to be a successful tourism marketer, must have a strong tourism organization which allows the marketing function to be coordinated and directed by marketing experts who understand the consumer.

Granted, it is difficult to convince members of a country's tourism industry to support a marketing plan that does not include each and every segment in promotional literature. The job of a department store marketer is to bring customers in the door, after which each department manager has a chance at sales. This is done by creating an image of the store and featuring only a few items at a time. To market a country also means creating an image which gets the tourist 'in the door'. It is then, and only then, that the individual members of the tourist industry can sell their tourism products.

References

Duea, Karen P. and Guernsey, Cindy (1984) Highlights of the 15th Annual TTRA Conference. *Journal of Travel Research*, Summer pp. 27–35.

Guernsey, Cindy and Hayden, Gin (1985) Highlights of the 16th Annual TTRA Conference, Palm Springs, California, June 9–13, 1985. *Journal of Travel Research*, Summer **XXIV**, 34–43.

Kaiser, Charles Jr and Helber, Larry E. (1978) *Tourism Planning and Development*. CBI Publishing Company, Boston, MA.

Kotler, Philip (1984) *Marketing Management*, 5th Edn. Prentice-Hall, Englewood Cliffs, NJ.

Lovelock, Christopher H. (1984) *Services Marketing*. Prentice-Hall, Englewood Cliffs, NJ.

Maas, Jane (1980) Better brochures for the money, *The Cornell Hotel and Restaurant Administration Quarterly* **20**, 21–34.

Mayo, Edward J. and Jarvis, Lance P. (1981) *The Psychology of Leisure Travel*, CBI Publishing Company, Boston, MA.

McCarthy, E. Jerome and Perreault, William D. Jr. (1984) *Basic Marketing*, 8th Edn. Richard D. Irwin, Homewood, IL.

Morris, David (1986) Chief of Research and Evaluation, Michigan Travel Commission. Telephone Interview, January.

Palmer, Michelle (1986) Research plays big role: Tuttle Eyes aggressive approach for increasing foreign tourism. *Hotel and Motel Management* **201**, 1, 30.

Shane, Sheldon (1986) What price to pay to enter the U.S.A. *Travel/Holiday*, January.

Appendix

Checklist for marketing a country's tourism step by step

Step 1 — gather information and set goals for tourism.
A. Examine what is available in terms of natural resources, infrastructure and superstructure.
B. Assess carrying capacity of cultural and physical assets.
C. Determine expected return in terms of foreign exchange earnings, attracting investment, world image, cultural exchange, product indigenization and profits to the tourism sector.

Step 2 — define the product and select target markets.
A. Conduct a tourism inventory and consider your tourism assets relative to the characteristics of the people who would be attracted to them.
B. Consider who you want to visit your country.

C. Adjust product offerings to meet the needs of your selected target or develop new tourism products with the target market in mind.

Step 3 — Develop a pricing strategy compatible with your target market and both economic and noneconomic goals.
A. Set price levels which are congruent with the product you have to offer and the market you wish to attract. (1) Do you wish to attract a limited number of high income tourists? (2) Will a lower price strategy attract a larger number of tourists?
B. Consider world economic factors and the position your currency holds relative to target markets. Use exchange rate changes as a variable in your pricing strategy.
C. Use subsidies to lower prices, use taxes and duties to raise prices.
D. Adjust prices to adjust tourist flow for different seasons and to reflect yearly supply and demand changes.

Step 4 — Develop easy tourist access (product distribution).
A. Assess levels of tourism inventory and adjust to meet demand.
B. Remove barriers to travel. (1) Provide fast and efficient customs. (2) Make obtaining passports and visas easy and quick. (3) Provide convenient currency exchange facilities.
C. Develop rapid and efficient physical movement. (1) Develop good roads, easy car rental, modern airports, easily understood signs, efficient rail, bus and taxi services. (2) Provide appropriate numbers and sizes of airplanes and trains to provide comfort and maintain profitable load factors. (3) Provide safe and clean airports and train stations with multilingual personnel.

D. Use appropriate channels for distributing the product. (1) Aid tour wholesalers and airlines in packaging the product. (2) Provide travel agencies with a means to have questions answered and obtain information. Make it easy for intermediaries to sell your country's tourism product.

Step 5 — Select promotion techniques which reflect your goals and target markets.
A. Use general promotion to build an image, e.g. trade shows, travel films, good publicity program, world fairs and expositions, general image advertising, public relations with suppliers and intermediaries.
B. Select specific techniques and media to sell specific products to specific markets. (1) Use personal selling to wholesalers and at travel shows. (2) Use direct mail of travel collateral to travel agents and for response to requests for information from consumers. (3) Advertise in travel magazines and newspaper travel sections. (4) Use radio and television where markets are concentrated or for building a general image.

Step 6 — Develop marketing strategies.
A. Make the satisfaction of consumer needs and wants the focus of all strategies.
B. Produce a clear national image.
C. Develop regional images.
D. Use specific marketing tools to stimulate demand for specific cities, regions, sectors and activities.
E. Consult members of the tourism sector in strategy planning and then communicate the strategy to those affected.

About the Author

Dr Ken McCleary is a Professor in the Department of Marketing and Hospitality Services Administration at Central Michigan University. His teaching specialties are in marketing and tourism. He also owns and operates (along with his wife, Dr Pamela Weaver) the Wightman House which is a bed and breakfast inn, in Mount Pleasant, Michigan.

Where to find more stuff: a guide to library and other sources of marketing information.

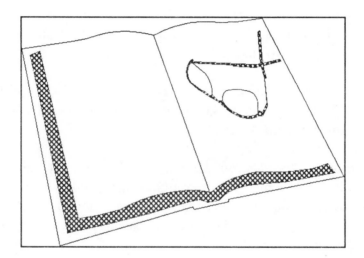

Information provided *vis-a-vis* where to find sources in libraries is the editors' "generic best guess", so, we think, a good place to start. Not all libraries, however, will put stuff where we think they should.

General Information

Daniells, Lorna M. *Business Information Sources*, Rev. ed., 1985. (Ref. Desk, Business Area) Chapter 18, pp. 429-481, "Marketing"-- Listing of sources for use in the field of marketing.

Graham, Irvin. *Encyclopedia of Advertising*, 2nd ed. 1969 (Ref.HF 5803 .G68 l969) Encyclopedic dictionary of terms relating to advertising, marketing, publishing, public relations, publicity, and the graphic arts. Because of its age, does not include some of the newer terms.

Shapiro, Irving. *Dictionary of Marketing Terms*, 4th ed. 1981 (Ref. HF 5412 .S52 1981) Provides concise and up-to-date definitions for over 5,000 terms of interest to marketers.

Urdang, Lawrence, ed. *Dictionary of Advertising Terms.* 1977. (Ref. HF 5803 .T37 1977) Includes over 4,000 entries of terms and words used by North American marketers.

Standard Industrial Classification Manual (Ref. Desk, Business Area) A classification scheme for manufacturing and non-manufacturing industries covering all areas of economic activity. These SIC numbers are used in many other books and indexes to group information about like industries.

Statistical Information

Statistical Abstract of the United States (Doc. C 3.134). Statistical compilation serving as a prime source for U.S. industrial, social, and economic statistics--includes national and regional studies. The source note at the foot of each chart indicates where information was obtained and where more current data could be requested.

County and City Data Book (Ref. Desk, Business Area) A supplement to *Statistical Abstract* (above) that provides extensive information on states, counties, cities of 25,000 or more, and places of 2500 or more. Includes such information as population makeup, number of households and families, housing, educational levels, income, wholesale and retail travel, and labor force.

Market Area, Company, and Industry Information

Editor and Publisher Market Guide (Ref. Desk, Business Area). Provides market data for over 1800 U.S. and Canadian cities covering facts on population, households, banks, principal industries, climate, retail outlets, per capita income, number of retail stores, disposable income, and estimates by 9 retail store groups.

Survey of Buying Power (Ref. Desk, Business Area). Put out by the periodical *Sales and Marketing Management* as extra issues four times a year. Provides extensive demographic and economic data, retail sales information and projections and summaries for television markets.

Survey of Current Business (Doc. C59.11:). Monthly Publication of the U.S. Department of Commerce regarded as the most important single source of current business statistics covering general business indicators, commodity prices, labor, earnings, finance, foreign trade, and industries.

U.S. Industrial Outlook (Ref. Desk, Business Area and Doc. C61.34:). Annual publication providing five-year projections for 200 industries based on current data for previous year and year-end estimates. Each chapter reports on the description and key elements for an industry -- size, employment, shipments, competitive trade-- and then projects growth and development.

Moody's Investors Service. Moody's Manuals (annual with semi- weekly supplements). Indexed in *Moody's Complete Corporate Index* (Ref. Desk, Business Area).

> *Moody's Bank and Finance Manual*
> *Moody's Industrial Manual*
> *Moody's International Manual*
> *Moody's Municipal & Government Manual*
> *Moody's OTC Industrial Manual*
> *Moody's Public Utilities Manual*
> *Moody's Transportation Manual*

These important manuals cover U.S., Canadian and other foreign companies listed on U.S. exchanges. The information about each company usually includes a brief corporate history; a list of subsidiaries, principal plants and properties; business and products; officers and directors; comparative income statements, balance sheet statistics, selected financial ratios; and a description of outstanding securities. The center blue sections in each manual provide useful statistics, including a "Ten-year Price Range of Stocks and Bonds," Moody's averages, and lists of largest companies.

Standard & Poor's Corporation. Industry Surveys. (Ref. Desk, Business Area) This is a valuable source for basic data on important industries, with financial comparisons of the leading companies in each industry. The "Basic Analysis" for each is a pamphlet of about 40 pages, revised annually. A short "Current Analysis" of about 8 pages is revised quarterly for each industry. Received with this is a 4-page monthly on "Trends and Projections," which includes tables of economic and industry indicators.

Thomas Register of American Manufacturers (Ref. Desk, Business Area). Multi-volume set providing lists of products and services; alphabetical lists of companies, their addresses, branches, subsidiaries, products, approximate capitalization, etc.; an index to product classifications, trade names, and commercial organizations; and catalogs of companies.

Harris Michigan Marketer's Industrial Directory (Ref. Desk, Business Area) provides information on companies in Michigan. Lists manufacturers, representatives, distributors, industrial service organizations, and importers located here by geographical location, SIC code, and alphabetically. Also provides statistical information. Similar directories for many other states are available in those states.

Standard and Poor's Register of Corporations, Directors, and Executives (Ref. Desk, Business Area). Vol. 1 lists information on about 40,000 companies, giving basically the same sort of information as *Moody's*. Vol. 2 is a listing of executives and directors, with brief biographical data. Vol. 3 contains indexes by SIC code, geographic location, and corporate family.

Million Dollar Directory (Ref. Desk, Business Area). Multi-volume set containing information on 115,000 U.S. businesses with an indicated worth of over $500,000. The information included is similar to the *Moody's* and *Standard and Poor's* publications mentioned above.

Advertising Information

Standard Rate and Data Service (Latest issues Ref. Desk, Business Area; older issues Ref. HF 5905) is issued in the following volumes:

Business Publication Rates and Data. Issued monthly. Lists over 3,000 U.S. business publications. Data furnished include how often published, advertising rates, mechanical requirements, circulation and distribution.

Consumer Magazine and Publication Farm Rates and Data. Issued monthly. Covers some 580 U.S. magazines and over 250 U.S. farm publications. Data include publisher, frequency of publication, representatives, rates, mechanical requirements, issuance and closing dates, and circulation.

Network Rates and Data. Issued monthly. Gives all national radio and television network rates and data. Each network is listed with its affiliates, costs, locations, and facilities. Special promotion days, weeks, and months are shown separately.

Newspaper Circulation Analysis. Published annually. Gives detailed data on newspapers by area. Includes metropolitan and county data as well as ranking in size and specific area penetration.

Newspaper Rates and Data. Issued monthly. Lists 1,600 United States newspapers, plus comics, magazine supplements, papers appealing to special groups, and foreign language newspapers. Information includes time of publication, representatives, advertising rates, mechanical requirements, and circulation.

Spot Radio Rates and Data. Issued monthly. Lists over 3,800 AM stations, 1,000 FM stations, and 100 regional networks. Data included give station power, facilities, program rates, personnel, representatives, and general announcements.

Spot Television Rates and Data. Published monthly. Lists all U. S. television stations with their power, facilities advertising information and rates, special features, film programs, personnel, and representatives.

Standard Rate and Data Service (continued):

> *Transit Advertising Rates and Data.* Published quarterly. Lists some 500 transportation facilities. Facts include national representatives; ownership; population of area served; mechanical requirements; advertising rates for full service, half service, and quarter service; circulation; and traveling display rates.

> *Weekly Newspaper Rates and Data.* Published twice a year -- March 5 and September 15. Gives pertinent data on publication days, when established, advertising rates, mechanical requirements, key personnel, and circulation of United States and Canadian weekly, bi-weekly, and tri-weekly newspapers.

Standard Directory of Advertising Agencies (Ref. Desk, Business Area). For each of 17,000 U.S. and Canadian agencies listed, gives specialization, officers, account executives, approximate annual billing, percent of media, and names of accounts. A ranked list of the 25 largest firms is included.

Standard Directory of Advertisers (Ref. Desk, Business Area). Provides information on the largest U.S. advertisers. Includes name, advertising appropriations, media used, etc.

Broadcasting/Cablecasting Yearbook (Ref. Desk, Business Area). Includes data on U.S. and Canadian television and radio stations, ad agencies, networks and programming, and other valuable information. Provides ranked list of television markets, television and radio billing sales.

Simmons Market Research Surveys or *Mediamark Research Surveys* (Ref. Desk, Business Area). National sample of consumers, projected to reflect total U.S. media habits, product and brand consumption, and demographic and life-style characteristics. Numerous volumes cover different product types.

Periodical and Newspaper Indexes

F & S Index of Corporations & Industries. Predicasts, Inc. (weekly, cumulated monthly and annually.) (Index Table 12.) This is the best periodical index to use when searching for current information on companies or industries in a wide selection of business, industrial, and financial publications, and also, in a few brokerage house reports. The yellow pages in the weeklies and the green pages in cumulated issues list articles (or data in articles) on SIC industries; the white pages list articles on companies. Since many of the entries refer to very brief citations, it is important to note that major articles are designated by a black dot, which precedes the abbreviated title of the journal.

Business Periodical Index. Monthly. (Index Table 12) The best known index for its overall subject coverage of selected periodicals in all fields of business.

InfoTrac. (On compact disc. Ref. Desk.) Indexes large number of popular periodicals plus a substantial number of business publications. Also indexes most recent few months of the *Wall Street Journal* and the *New York Times.*

Some Additional Books

Into The Future

Ken Dychtwald and Joe Flower. *Age Wave: The Challenges and Opportunities of an Aging America.* Los Angeles: J.P. Tarcher, 1989.

Marvin Cetron and Thomas O'Toole. *Encounters with the Future: A Forecast of Life into the 21st Century.* New York: McGraw Hill, 1982.

Landon Y. Jones. *Great Expectations: America and the Baby Boom Generation.* New York: Coward, McCann & Geoghegan, 1980.

John Naisbitt. *Megatrends.* New York: Warner Books, 1982.

Without These, You're Nothing

Michael LeBoeuf, Ph.D. *How to Win Customers and Keep Them for Life*. New York: G.P. Putnam's Sons, 1987.

Theodore Levitt. *The Marketing Imagination*. New York: Free Press, 1983.

Michael E. Porter. *Competitive Advantage*. New York: Free Press, 1985.

Al Ries and Jack Trout. *Bottom-Up Marketing*. McGraw-Hill, New York. 1989.

Al Ries and Jack Trout. *Positioning: The Battle for Your Mind*. New York: McGraw-Hill, 1986.

Information Is Power

Donna Woolfolk Cross. *Media-Speak: How Television Makes Up Your Mind*. New York: New American Library, 1983.

William Lazer. *Handbook of Demographics for Marketing and Advertising*. Lexington, Massachusetts: Lexington Books, 1987.

Arnold Mitchell. *The Nine American Lifestyles*. New York: Warner Books, 1983.

Al Ries and Jack Trout. *Marketing Warfare*. New York: McGraw-Hill, 1986.

Art Weinstein. *Market Segmentation*. Chicago: Probus Publishing, 1987.

What's On The Menu

Dr. Pete Stevens. **WINNING!!!** <u>*THE*</u> *name-of-the-game GUIDE to winning in the restaurant business: Getting customers, keeping customers, and making money*, second edition. East Lansing, Michigan: Hospitality Resources Ink, 1989.

Whatever Lola Wants...? Lola Wants Service.

William B. Martin. *Quality Service: The Restaurant Manager's Bible*. Ithaca, New York: School of Hotel Administration, Cornell University, 1986.

Thomas J. Peters and Robert H. Waterman, Jr. *In Search of Excellence*. New York: Harper and Row, 1982.

Tom Peters and Nancy Austin. *A Passion for Excellence*. New York: Random House, 1985.

Donald I. Smith. *Service: Managing the Guest Experience*. New York: Lebhar-Friedman Books, 1988.

Comprehensive Hospitality Marketing Texts.

Robert C. Lewis, Ph.D. and Richard E. Chambers, M.B.A. *Marketing Leadership in Hospitality: Foundations and Policies*. New York: Van Nostrand Reinhold, 1989.

Robert Reid. *Hospitality Marketing Management*, second edition. New York: Van Nostrand Reinhold, 1989.